SLIPPERY PASTIMES

READING THE POPULAR
IN CANADIAN CULTURE

Cultural Studies Series

Cultural Studies is the multi- and interdisciplinary study of culture, defined anthropologically as a "way of life," performatively as symbolic practice and ideologically as the collective product of media and cultural industries, i.e., pop culture. Although Cultural Studies is a relative new-comer to the humanities and social sciences, in less than half a century it has taken interdisciplinary scholarship to a new level of sophistica-tion, reinvigorating the liberal arts curriculum with new theories, new topics and new forms of intellectual partnership.

The Cultural Studies series includes topics such as construction of identities; regionalism/nationalism; cultural citizenship; migration; popular culture; consumer cultures; media and film; the body; post-colonial criticism; cultural policy; sexualities; cultural theory; youth culture; class relations; and gender.

The new Cultural Studies series from Wilfrid Laurier University Press invites submission of manuscripts concerned with critical discussions on power relations concerning gender, class, sexual preference, ethni-city and other macro and micro sites of political struggle.

For further information, please contact the Series Editor:
Jodey Castricano
Department of English
Wilfrid Laurier University Press
75 University Avenue West
Waterloo, Ontario, Canada, N2L 3C5

SLIPPERY PASTIMES

READING THE POPULAR IN CANADIAN CULTURE

Edited by
Joan Nicks and Jeannette Sloniowski

Cultural Studies Series

Wilfrid Laurier University Press
[WLU]

We acknowledge the financial support of the Government of Canada through the Book Publishing Industry Development Program for our publishing activities.

National Library of Canada Cataloguing in Publication Data

Main entry under title:
  Slippery pastimes : reading the popular in Canadian culture

(Cultural studies series)
Includes bibliographical references.
ISBN 0-88920-388-1

1. Popular culture—Canada.   I. Nicks, Joan, 1937–
II. Sloniowski, Jeannette Marie, 1946–   III. Cultural studies series.

FC95.4.S55 2002   306'.0971   C2002-900012-2
F1021.2.S55 2002

© 2002 Wilfrid Laurier University Press
Waterloo, Ontario, Canada   N2L 3C5
www.wlupress.wlu.ca

Cover design by Leslie Macredie,
using an illustration entitled "The Hikers."
Illustration © Doug Martin / www.i2iart.com

The following previously published articles have been revised for this volume:

Karen Dubinsky, "'The Pleasure Is Exquisite but Violent': The Imaginary Geography of Niagara Falls in the Nineteenth Century," *Journal of Canadian Studies* 29.2 (Summer 1994): 64-88.

Neil Earle, "Hockey as Canadian Popular Culture: Team Canada 1972, Television, and the Canadian Identity," *Journal of Canadian Studies* 30.2 (Summer 1995): 107-23.

Valda Blundell, "Riding the Polar Bear Express: And Other Encounters between Tourists and First Peoples in Canada, *Journal of Canadian Studies* 30.4 (Winter 1995): 28-51.

The author and publisher have made every reasonable effort to obtain permission to reproduce the secondary material in this book. Any corrections or omissions brought to the attention of the Press will be incorporated in subsequent printings.

Printed in Canada

for Joe
and
for Ben, Suzanne and Kenji

TABLE OF CONTENTS

INTRODUCTION

Cultural activity belonged to leisure time, to the amateur. It existed on Mount Olympus far away from the masses, from commerce, from the music, folk dances, and plays of New-Canadian cultural groups, and from the American forms of popular culture upon which ordinary Canadians, according to Bernard K. Sandwell, had become "absolutely dependent" by 1913.

—Maria Tippett, *Making Culture*

WHY *SLIPPERY* PASTIMES?

This collection of essays on the Canadian "popular" brings together varied research representing several fields of cultural and media studies. As co-editors we have endeavoured to elicit strong, accessible writing that is analytical and engaging for both academic and culturally interested readers. All but three of the essays (and these three have been revised) are original pieces for this publication. The book's overall focus is largely, though not exclusively, on English-Canadian topics, addressing historical, theoretical, and ideological issues, and effectively attempting a cultural reading of the Canadian popular. The purpose is serious, though not necessarily dry or antiseptic, exploration. The collection is analytical and reflective, avoiding mere celebration of, indifference towards, or disavowal of the Canadian popular.

We have given priority to examinations of popular culture that address primary artifacts and their contexts in order to enlarge interest in and understanding of, for better or for worse, something beyond what is deemed to be current or, on the other hand, passé, as media ploys would have us believe. Some of the artifacts analyzed by the authors are no longer in production or even widely circulated in the culture, which does not negate their popular-use factor, past or present, given the many personal resources (video-and audio tapes and other retrieval and storage modes) employed by readers, viewers, and listeners of all ages. We have taken the view that readers are interested in something more than reading about immediate moments of popularity (what's "in" or "on" today), assuming that critique can both enrich and question how we perceive the popular in a period or a place. This may not be as urgent a project for Canadian society as it has been historically for cultures where the first level of annihilation (Pol Pot's Cambodia) or of revolutionary action (Castro's Cuba) was the power of the popular. But our experiences with students and non-academic communities indicate that citizens increasingly want to discuss how the popular works as culture, not only as mixed pleasure, and why the Canadian popular should invite debate.

John Storey in his book *Cultural Studies and the Study of Popular Culture* refers to popular culture as "production in use" (8), observing that this does not necessarily mean "a degraded culture" (6). In devising *Slippery Pastimes* as the title for this collection, we have in mind the *ambiguities* and *processes* enveloping popular culture. The term "pastimes" evokes the pleasures associated with the popular, not only leisure time but everyday experience. Popular culture crosses our daily activities, making us participants in its products and processes whether or not we are conscious of the visual, auditory, and textual operations at play. To define pastimes as "slippery" suggests sleights of hand: popular culture as unstable or elusive, sometimes serious but also shallow, merely clever or cunning. But the term "slippery" can also describe subtleties that can't always be accounted for in the production, promotion, or reception of the artifacts that make up popular pastimes. Within Canadian culture, there have been numerous government reports and public discussions on the *slippages* in Canadian/U.S. border matters. Canadian media and cultural concerns about the gatekeeping of international television/cable boundaries provoked wide debate. The freighted issues of how to "prove" the existence of the Canadian popular ("there is no such thing as Canadian popular culture") continue, as do the ardent efforts to "fool-proof" Canadian culture ("Canadian culture is distinct and must be protected from external, especially American, interventions").

The dynamics of popular culture are variously "slippery," and especially so within a Canadian context, and this collection is an attempt to chart the complexities of how and why this is so. The concept of "slippery pastimes" offers potential for analyses and methodologies that both historicize and question slippages between cultural and personal "ownership" of popular pastimes, between media appropriation of popular pleasures and our negotiations as spectators, between generic forms of popular culture and embedded inflections of, or interventions into, "Canadianness." In the end it is impossible to study the popular without recourse to the methodologies of Popular Culture, but also of other disciplines like Cultural and Women's Studies, Sociology, and Communications Studies. Indeed, the reader will find our authors slipping in and out of various disciplines as they pursue their interdisciplinary analyses of the popular.

Popular culture becomes *slippery* when media productions use the conventions of genre forms but also "let slip" what they are supposed to be as popular products. Whether or not we like the products, or perceive them as deceptions or distractions, slippage can indicate adroitness with the conventions of a genre or a form. Adroitness within media forms can help us as audiences to decipher popular productions as constructions outside our control, but within our culture, and also used, and sometimes cleverly "misused," by us as spectators, listeners, and readers. As cultural and individual users of popular artifacts, our own reception can become slippery because reception cannot be entirely contained or predicted. The reception of popular artifacts can shift from recognition, to reflection, to refutation, to negotiation—or the conjunction of at least some of these responses. If we accept the plural notion of audiences (and we do), rather than the singular concept of audience associated with mass consumption, then popular artifacts can be said to "slip" from their originating media moorings, and they can continue to "slip" within and among the diverse user-constituencies within a culture. Such processes are not "Canadian" alone, but this collection examines them within, and from, this cultural location.

THE ARTICLES AND ISSUES

Traditional scholarship on popular culture ranges from a kind of ironically amused dilettantism, or downright rejection, to a recognition of

the power and importance of mass-mediated images—however cor-
rupting some commentators deem those images to be. In most discussions of the popular, "American" and "popular" are conflated, with
America cast as the villainous imperial power colonizing the world
through the glamour of Hollywood, consumable celebrity, and mass-
marketed forms, and the ubiquity of a multi-billion dollar television
industry. But where in this often heated debate does the Canadian popular fit? More crucially, how does the Canadian popular struggle to pro-
claim itself amid the noisy, glittering barrage aimed at Canada, not only
by Americans, but also by Canadian media driven to protect Canadian
culture or to exploit it for the profits that inevitably seem to follow in
the wake of *Baywatch* and the like? It seems to us that this question, not
new by any means, persists for students of popular culture, but also for
those Canadians still interested in the nature of "the nation."

Some of the authors included here are convinced of a subversive or
boldly executed potential within the popular in general. Others argue
that the homogenizing, conservative tendencies of global mass-produced culture block potentially progressive content. Some find regional
tendencies in popular forms, like music, that can speak to issues of
race, localities, and the imagination, both within Canadian boundaries
and without in a North American sense of the popular. These contradictions allow a productive place from which to study the popular in a
country that seems to produce less popular culture by the day. The
debates over the "common ground" focus attention on exactly what
common ground we have—or have not. Indeed, in several essays the
idea of the popular and the mythical are explored in such a way as to
make the Canadian popular one of the central underpinnings of our
sense of nation.

The authors in this book engage with these questions in their own
individual ways. While this volume is dedicated to the study of popular culture, many of the essays are informed by the aims and methodologies of Cultural Studies. More explicitly and formally political than
Popular Culture Studies, Cultural Studies seeks to draw the wider
social and ideological issues from culture in its broadest sense. Many,
but not all, of our authors see the popular as a site of negotiation and
contestation, and the processes of reception as political in a very
pointed sense. Drawing on many disciplines influenced by Cultural
Studies (Sociology, Women's Studies, Anthropology, Political

Science), our authors tend to see popular culture as "an arena of consent and resistance," after Stuart Hall in his groundbreaking work on culture (239-77).

Karen Dubinsky, author of the hilariously entitled book *The Second Biggest Disappointment: Honeymooning and Tourism at Niagara Falls*, opens the Heritage section with an article in which she invokes the idea of "imaginary geography" to analyze Niagara Falls, the honeymoon capital of the world. Niagara Falls holds a unique place within the Canadian popular because it is at once a natural wonder of the world and the carnivalesque, sleazy centre of the Canadian tourist industry. Home of the ribald honeymoon joke, Planet Hollywood, and Ripley's Believe It or Not! Museum, Niagara Falls, according to Dubinsky, has been since the early 1800s an imaginary site of fear and forbidden sexual pleasures. Noting the false virgin-sacrifice tale of the Maid of the Mist, Dubinsky analyzes the attraction felt by Victorian couples for the sexualized natural wonder, deepening her analysis with an examination of the often contradictory popular literature of the time, both pornographic and touristic.

While Dubinsky is concerned with the imaginary geography of the popular, Valda Blundell, also interested in tourism, invokes the idea of "cultural tourism" to analyze the ways in which the Canadian government uses Canada's indigenous peoples to offer tourists "cultural or heritage experiences." In a wide-ranging essay that looks at a variety of sites where First Nations People represent themselves, or are represented by the dominant culture, Blundell asks several key questions about how indigenous people are portrayed to tourists. Do "official" sites rely upon dated stereotypes to give tourists a kind of comforting, nostalgic representation that confirms their own unexamined "Eurocentric" view of "Indians"? Are issues of racism and colonialism ignored, and native peoples relegated to the Canadian past—but deleted from the Canadian present—at these sites? And crucially, do sites created by First Nations People themselves fall back on the same dated stereotypes in order to give the tourists what they want, while neglecting current, and often contentious, cultural issues that trouble the relationship between indigenous peoples and mainstream Canadian culture? Or, on the other hand, do these sites offer meaningful opportunities for real contact between natives and tourists: do they offer tourists insights into Native culture both past and present?

In both articles the terms "cultural tourism" and "imaginary geography" provide suggestive metaphors for understanding popular culture. Drawing on Cultural Studies paradigms, both authors clearly delineate the ideological aspects of the popular to make clear for the reader that seemingly simple, pleasurable activities like tourism have far deeper and more important implications for tourists, students of popular culture, and First Nations People. "Recreational" activities can symbolize crucial interactions between, on the one hand, tourists and a natural wonder, and, on the other, indigenous peoples where "first contact" happens again and again but in a far different and highly charged context than historical first-contact meetings.

Both Christine Boyko-Head and Loretta Czernis write about how specific cultural icons can be used and manipulated over time to serve the cultural needs of different eras. Boyko-Head takes on that historical Canadian heroine, cultural icon, and "symbol of Loyalist womanhood," Laura Secord, when she looks at the Secord figure as it has been used by novelists, playwrights, poets, and, in the end, quite differently by advertisers. She traces the evolution of the Secord myth through its early appearances in drama, to its best-known incarnation in the Laura Secord candy ads, arguing that the changes indicate a shift in mainstream representations of women, but also prompt the female spectator to question the process of gendered representations. The very figure of Secord herself may be open to progressive/disruptive readings because of the "heroic" and perhaps non-traditional nature of the historical figure herself.

In the ads, however, chosen from different periods in the chocolate company's history, Boyko-Head argues that the historical figure has been used to mark conservative social and ideological changes in the mainstream conception of women. These changes include Secord as symbol of an imperialist/colonialist ideal, and, later, as simultaneous "dutiful woman" and exotic fantasy image associated with the oral gratification of the consumption of chocolate. These images span a nascent Canadian nationalism confounded with both subservience to English Canada's British heritage and later to a continentalism that marks Canada's new place within the North American sphere. Far from the disruptive potential of other Secord incarnations, the ads work to contain the potential transgressiveness of the historical figure by depoliticizing her, making her a consumable, quasi-erotic object.

Loretta Czernis is concerned with the adaptation of a famous Canadian painting, Ozias Leduc's *Le petit liseur*, for a Canadian postage stamp. Czernis argues that Canada Post adapted, and appropriated, Leduc's original painting to suit an ideologically driven, governmental version of Canadian culture. "Institutionally commodified," the painting as stamp is a decontextualized, stripped-down version of a highly characteristic piece of Québécois art by a now image-conscious federal government bureaucracy seeking a more homogeneous Canada than many Quebec nationalists would like. Adapting ideas from Benjamin, Berger, and Wernick, Czernis sees the postage stamp as part of "promotional culture," where local and regional art forms are made to speak for a national culture that is quite alien to them. The "aura" of the work of art has been adapted and used to foster a federal nationalism that is the antithesis of the painting's regional origins. One of a series of great Canadian works of art adapted for postage stamps, Leduc's work loses the charming ambiguity of the original, but gains a visibility for the painting it had never enjoyed before. What the painting loses in regional cultural context and ambiguity, it gains in "consumability" and notoriety. Just as Laura Secord becomes literally consumable, so the Leduc painting becomes reproducible and valuable as a commodity rather than as a complex depiction of a Quebec culture held in little esteem by a federal government bent upon smoothing out the "rough" edges of a unique society.

Will Straw's article concludes the Heritage section with an overview of the traditional scholarly arguments on the plight of Canadian culture. For Straw, Canadian scholars and students have adopted a series of positions, of varying usefulness, from which to "manage" their own, frequently uncomfortable feelings about Canadian film, television, and popular music. All of the positions, *to some degree*, express a nationalist anxiety whereby Canadians not only see their culture as threatened by the policies of their own government, but also by powerful global forces from the outside—primarily the United States, but also Britain in the case of music. This anxiety is reinforced by a guilt many Canadians are said to feel over their apparent lack of interest in the products of Canadian culture. Straw argues that Canadians regard much of their own popular culture as medicinal—good for the body politic, but in the end somewhat unpalatable.

Ignoring the traditional divide between elite and popular culture, Straw introduces ideas of taste and connoiseurship in popular culture. He grapples with the problematic of a society which knows that it has generally been peripheral to most significant moments in world art and media culture, but still tries to preserve a sense of its own worth and "place" within the world through its popular arts. Every position Straw examines is tied to the idea that cultural production of all kinds is crucial to the development of a sense of citizenship in a country that is not only extremely heterogeneous ethnically, but geographically dispersed as well.

In the end, he argues that perhaps Canadian popular culture is "compensatory." That is, it sets out to fill the gaps in what comes from outside by creating "idiosyncratic variations of dominant cultural forms" that are of interest to some Canadians and also marketable outside Canada. He argues that the downside of this position is that the Canadian popular renders itself marginal by abandoning the attempt to make "massively popular" films or television. Straw again addresses the common question about why Canadian popular culture is not popular: because the compensatory view of the role of the popular marginalizes cultural production so that this "popular culture" is only the culture of a small, prosperous cultural elite. Straw's question about popularity should raise other questions about how much more difficult it is to measure the reception of popular culture over the consumption and demographics associated with mass-produced entertainment products.

Jim Leach's article on *E.N.G.* opens the Television section with the premise that an analytical understanding of how television texts work is important to the cultural issues and contexts reproduced in the series' narrative situations around news-gathering and -making. Independently produced by Alliance Entertainment, *E.N.G.* did not have the state mandate of public television, yet its narratives implicitly called into question the cultural protectionism of the CBC's mandate. Leach's point is that television reception is a telling cultural and individual variable, and that viewership can and does subvert the ideology of popular texts.

Leach uses John Fiske's theory of democratized TV reception to make his case for the intertextual play of TV forms, narrative formulas, and audience reception. Fiske's major work on television, *Television Culture*, proposes that the audience is an active participant in the creation of meaning when watching television—in other words, the imposition of meaning upon the audience is neither complete nor even entirely possible. For Fiske, the conservative and ideologically driven content of much television is offset by the polysemous and dialogic nature of much popular culture, which allows for subversive and alternative readings of what might be deemed as the very conservative messages of mainstream popular culture.

Leach's aim is not to discover *the* meaning of a television text, which the casual and distracted quality of TV viewing tends to disallow, but rather to read *E.N.G.* as an example of a television construction that makes links between viewers and their cultural contexts. He reads a particular episode of *E.N.G.* that incorporates an actual, major news event, China's Tiananmen Square incident, into a narrative formula based on a variety of characters and loosely connected, dove-tailing plots. The formula sets up the narrative structure and also organizes the audience's expectations. Leach sees a balance between formula and what Cultural Studies theorist Raymond Williams terms "flow," whereby the interplay of the fictional narrative episode, commercials, TV programming, as well as audiences' viewing patterns, result in the exposure of contradictions and the questioning of popular meanings. Leach concludes that the globalization of television should not find Canadians just "going with the flow," finding only our own, individual meanings in popular texts. Canadians need to find cultural and social meanings in viewing popular texts, which, he argues, *E.N.G.* facilitated.

Sheila Petty's article on *A nous deux!* is concerned with how the Québécois *téléroman* (soap) localizes timely social issues within its soap-opera format. *A nous deux!* (Face to Face) is a low-budget, state-financed (Radio-Canada) production, unlike *E.N.G.*'s production in the private industry. Petty locates this television serial's singularity in its co-authored writing and deviation from the soap's formula of emotional devices, to construct a critique of certain traditions (e.g., the Catholic Church) within Quebec culture and the province's francophone nationalist agenda. In the episode Petty analyzes, Quebec culture is reconstructed as a pluralist society that, in this instance, recognizes black minority and community struggle. Notions of nation are made more inclusive within the serial's Quebec setting. As with Leach's analysis of *E.N.G.*, Petty emphasizes *A nous deux!*'s narrative treatment of social injustices with a historical sense of topical issues. This strategy gives viewers room to read the complex structure of the serial's current-affairs focus, and Petty herself reads an explicitly ideological operation in its focus on Quebec issues.

Petty argues that *A nous deux!* creates debate and critique inside its narrative structure, and potentially enables viewers' reception of issues, over emotional reaction. This link between the social and the popular— in this episode, contemporary race relations in Montreal and a case of harassment—de-emphasizes the personal relations that drive the American soap-opera form. Petty's focus on minority issues in *A nous deux!* is similar to the case that Jim Leach makes for the English-Canadian *E.N.G.*'s Tiananmen Square episode. The Quebec serial's open structure of multiple viewpoints, perspectives, and ideologies, as well as the tendency to use neutral camera angles and to avoid closure or comforting narrative resolutions, allows spectators to sample diverse ideas. Petty concludes that the indigenously produced *téléroman* in Quebec television has a tradition of playing to the popular but with a social capacity that expands generic formula.

Joan Nicks, in her article on the teen television series *Straight Up*, argues that Canadian popular culture has the potential to "decolonize" the mind through aesthetic experiment, narrative play, and generic modification. Her analysis fits into Straw's category of the compensatory function of the Canadian popular by arguing the differences to be found between this series and the typical teen television show, both Canadian and American. That is, certain television series alter the norms established for the medium, and yet deliver productions that both entertain and question culture. Nicks analyzes episodes of *Straight Up* to demonstrate the means by which the series "uninvents" the popular as it sets itself against the banal global consumer culture of its background settings—fast food, TV, pop music. The series' non-stereotypical teen characters test their individuality and cultural responses at the margins of the adult world. Flying in the face of melodramatic, mainstream fare for teens, *Straight Up*'s committed production standards (strong scripts, collaborative rehearsal processes, and stylish direction) and postmodern images tend to liberate the imaginations of youths within the distinct episodes, rather than satisfy youth-genre conventions and formulas. With a knowing edginess, the series' youths do not serve the nation so much as contest their place in a dispassionate culture. Stylistic excess at the visual, structural, and narrative levels of this late CBC-TV series performs the function of pulling viewers away from those forms of the popular that seek to contain them or make them merely consumers of glamorous images of youth.

In her article on *The Valour and the Horror*, Jeannette Sloniowski takes a different view than Leach, Petty, and Nicks, who concentrate on the negotiating potential of television series that permit spectators to engage with social issues by at once working against genre and into Canadian positions. Sloniowski argues that TV documentary is fraught with problems endemic to how the medium of television typically works and how "the popular" is constructed. The strategies of journalism versus documentary, of so-called reality TV, tabloid TV, TV movies of the week, and docudrama forms, all have pertinence in her examination of the CBC's miniseries and the particular problems of making and programming history as television fare.

Sloniowski argues that the conventions of popular historiography created problems for the McKenna brothers in their controversial retelling of Canadian military history in *The Valour and the Horror*. The McKennas, who have extensive journalist backgrounds in CBC-Television (*The National, The Journal*), simplified complex historical issues around the Second World War in their attempt to make a popular history of Canadian military men's and women's personal experiences during the war.

The sheer volume and variety of the images and sounds, underlined by the dramatic use of a thematic music score, was organized by the McKennas into a biased, closed dramatization. Sloniowski observes that this miniseries' authority comes from television's almost fetishistic convention of going to the scene of a crime (or history), as if validity and factuality are proven by the producers' presence on, in this case, historical Second World War sites. The rhetorical strategies, devised by the McKennas, in retrospect, close to the fiftieth anniversary of the Second World War, condition television audiences to respond emotionally as believers. *The Valour and the Horror*'s therapeutic discourse of televisual confessionals, namely, the memory of war veterans, is neither complete nor problematized by the McKennas, but is an exercise in mythmaking. Sloniowski critiques the McKennas for papering over their own ideological biases in their dramatized depiction of the Second World War as television fare—a major CBC-TV special—which can rarely escape the traps of the medium.

The Music section opens with Bart Testa and Jim Shedden's expansive article on English-Canadian rock music, in which they make a case for rock 'n' roll's instability. Historically, rock's hybridity and contradictions operated by processes of decay over the decades and through stylistic genre changes across North America. The "half-life" of different styles in different periods, in different localities, makes rock unstable, they argue, hard to pin down by genre and culture alone. "Canadian rock" is an even more complicated and contradictory concept.

In analyzing The Band, for example, Testa and Shedden observe that it was a group whose music and lyrics could be claimed and interpreted regionally on both sides of the Canada-U.S. border. Their core discussion of Bachman-Turner Overdrive's and Rush's "hard rock" in the 1970s focuses on the "hybridized style" in each case, however Canadian these two bands' origins. Testa and Shedden chart their discussion of regionalisms and localisms through a framework of rock's formative and evolving "moments." Their concentration on socio-economic factors, regional and local inflections, and industrial and media constructions (radio as "rock's premier delivery system") distinguishes between aesthetic and national interpretations of rock music and lyrics. It puts in motion a reading of the evolution of rock styles within the contexts of the popular music industry (the "business" of rock), changing technologies, and, notably for Canadian rock bands, the CRTC's policies affecting Cancon radio play in the 1970s.

Nick Baxter-Moore explores Celtic folk music and pop/rock blends in his article to argue that strong regional practices in Canada's east coast evolved into a form of national popular music. The Canadian Maritimes have been a preserve of the Gaelic language and Celtic music because historically these provinces to some degree lived "in isolation from originating cultures" (Ireland, Scotland, Britain).

To set up his discussion on the east coast sound, Baxter-Moore takes up part of Barry Grant's discussion (1986) of popular music, specifically, the genre bending and inflection at work in Canadian popular music, with certain cultural differences from American genres. In effect, what develops in the book's section on music is a debate between Baxter-Moore's emphasis and the Testa/Shedden argument against making "nationalist" arguments for Canadian popular music. Baxter-Moore is in accord with the argument that Canada has lacked indigenous rock music traditions, largely because the Canadian music industry has been a "branch plant operation" of the U.S.; in other words, industrial factors have overridden aesthetic ones. But he reads syncretism at work in the development and output of the east coast sound: a merger between Celtic and rock affected by local fiddle styles and house parties, and familiarity with "roots" dancing by regional audiences within a "specific geo-cultural region," the Canadian Maritimes. He applies this argument in an analysis of the east coast band Rawlins Cross. And, in an empirical reading of the fusion forms found in an Ashley MacIsaac concert at an Ontario university, he observes that the non-Maritimes audience both recognized and responded to the fiddler's east coast sound and his pop bending of that sound into an "alternative" performance.

William Echard situates his analysis of Stompin' Tom Connors in the singer's circulation as a popular icon within Canadian cultural land-scapes that include urban Toronto neighbourhoods as well as Connors's east coast origins. Connors's folkloric populism has made him what Echard terms "a hobo citizen of the entire country." Echard traces Stompin' Tom's humble origins as an orphan, his rise, his persona, and his withdrawal from and return to stage performance, and demonstrates how the singer's combined populism and "national agenda" have been both lived and marketed by him.

As a musicologist, Echard links his cultural reading of Stompin' Tom to an analysis of the music and how it connects in performance to the singer's loyal, participatory audiences. Echard provides a kind of listener's guide to how Connors's music and audiences stimulate each other, and thus how "nuance" emerges. Echard reads "nuance" (not mere simplicity) in the dynamic between what he terms the "force" of Connors's performance and persona, and the singer's oscillation from the serious to the absurd in his songs and singing style. Formally, it is Stompin' Tom's plain-speaking and -singing rhetoric, his humorous resistance to country music forms, and the communal drive of his per-formances that circumvent clichés and maintain the seriousness of the Canadian agenda in his music.

In his article, Rinaldo Walcott takes the position that unquestioned attention to the discourse of experience (e.g., feminism, gay and black experience) that arose in the 1960s is a limited approach to reading the popular idioms of contemporary black rap music in the 1990s. He traces a history of how the discourse of experience came to be, then argues that an anthropological approach does not suffice or serve the psychological and imaginative aspects embedded in rap music and the historical and contemporary contexts that frame it.

The discourse of experience, often aimed at institutions that excluded blacks, became "sacred," fuelling what Walcott calls the "foundational claims" for a "singular collective narrative." The problem Walcott perceives is that personal testimony does not, and cannot, stand in for a collective black experience. His goal is to open up this problem, theoretically and in application to black rap music affected by a black diasporic sense that cuts across North America and opens the boundaries of the music's imaginative and psychic impulses through media-borrowing references.

Walcott pushes his case for including psychic and imaginary realms as expressive of black musics and cultures. The black youth inventors of hip-hop and rap in North American music were affected by their "subaltern status." But seeing only "protest" and "realism" in rap does not do justice to the psychic and imaginary areas that Walcott perceives to be crucial for the "different socio-cultural reading" he wants to pursue. Within this argument, "desire" and "fantasy play key roles in rap," as have black rappers' reclaiming of "vinyl" when records were discarded for the technologically favoured CD.

Within a Canadian culture where blackness has "no place of imagining blackness within," Walcott discusses the Dream Warriors and Maestro Fresh-Wes, as well as the *Africville Suite* CD where jazz pianist and composer Joe Sealy recalls a black section (long gone) of Halifax, but without treating the music as history. Sealy's imaginative "takes" on Halifax's dismantled Africville community in the 1960s evoke the heart of its past without being the experience or suggesting that its history and mythologies speak to all black experience in Canada. For Walcott, playing into and out of fantasy or interior qualities enlarges the means of listening to and analyzing such black musics.

In analyzing Ian Tyson's music through the singer/songwriter's *Cowboyography*, Terrance Cox closely examines Tyson's lyrics for how they draw their cowboy sensibility from the "northern range." Cox argues that Tyson redefines the "cowboy artist" by rendering this figure sometimes in documentary terms, sometimes in metaphor. Cox reads Tyson's songwriting and performance as at once modern, associated with living a cowboy's life of breaking horses, and mythic, harnessing the characters and characteristics of cowboy life into poetic odes with simple musical lines.

Cox traces the folk and urban roots inflected in Tyson's construction of cowboy places through the very "unhip" persona of a working cowboy "trying to write songs" that link his art to life on the land that nourishes the singer. Tyson the cowboy artist is unpretentious, populist, and bardic, and, in Cox's argument, also postmodernist in a reflective tribute to American songwriter Irving Berlin. Cox links the sentiments of the music to Tyson's taking up of a cowboy's life in Alberta, a life, which, even in regional-Western terms, is marginal. By playing out the popular through lyrics that are both direct (what Cox calls Tyson's insistence on "the present-tense reality of cowboy life") and "aesthetic analogues" of a Western past, Tyson eschews nostalgia.

Set against the background of a globalizing culture of "Microsoft, Benetton and karaoke," Andrew Wernick's article anchors the Sports section with a close analysis of a Ray-Ban advertisement in *Maclean's* magazine made to appeal to Canadians at the time of the Atlanta summer Olympic games. Wernick's essay, in harmony with his groundbreaking work on promotional culture (*Promotional Culture: Advertising, Ideology, and Symbolic Expression*), takes one thread of what has been said in this book to its logical conclusion. A good deal of the Canadian popular is concerned with selling a homogenized, globalized, transnational version of Canada to Canadians, and in the end prompts the reader to wonder what this really has to do with Canada at all.

Or, indeed, is nationalism a dated concept rapidly being replaced by the global, popular culture lifestyle depicted in many ads? Wernick notes that nationalism "has been reconfigured as a market category." The famous athletes depicted in most ads could be replaced instantly by any other celebrity athlete regardless of national origin. Indeed, Wernick notes the peculiarity of this homogenization in the Olympic movement itself. While philosophically committed to ideas like world youth and pan-nationalism, the movement itself fosters intense national rivalries that seem to undermine much of what the Olympic movement officially stands for. The same might be said of the ad in question. It appeals to an apparent Canadian nationalism. At the same time, it problematizes that very nationalism by depicting an athlete as part of a slick, sexualized global form of celebrity that has little to do with his origins in Canada.

In this context, one can easily question whether Canada can survive as a distinct culture given the homogenizing drive of multinational capitalism. Advertising is only one aspect of this movement toward a global culture. Straw, Blundell, Boyko-Head, and Wernick note that these forces are present throughout Canadian popular culture, from the tourist art produced by aboriginal peoples to the glossy lifestyle advertising in *Maclean's*.

What would a book on Canadian popular culture be without an essay on hockey? As Neil Earle notes, hockey seems central to the Canadian popular and even to Canadian "manhood." Indeed, he calls it an "imaginative knit" that at well-defined moments helps hold Canadians together—for reasons that no one has really managed to define. Earle engages with the mythical nature of the game, noting how it symbolizes heroism and survival in a cold, dark place. He argues that the boyhood myths which surround the game even manage to cover over its sexism and violence, leaving us with a "northern pastoral myth"—the very symbol of the "true north strong and free" with its connotations of good sportsmanship, hard work, and team spirit.

Employing metaphors of Greek drama and ritual performance (sport as holy text), Earle tries to situate the game within the Canadian psyche. Following John Fiske, he also argues a possible difference between mass and popular culture on the level of heroism; while many hockey artifacts are mass-produced, they are also attached to sports heroes, and thus take on a more personal aura. The symbolic investment made by fans moves hockey consumables from merely mass-produced commodities to a more popular and meaningful status. Furthermore, the aesthetics of television help to promote the intimate familial aspects of spectators' engagement with the game.

It is not much of a stretch to see Earle's view of hockey as crucial to our national sensibility and in some ways related to Straw's idea of the Canadian popular as compensatory. This perhaps helps to explain the frenzy around the 1972 Team Canada victory. This is a place where a Canadian popular form excels upon the world stage. Here the popular, argues Earle, becomes something primal, something so powerful that images of it are rooted in the minds of players and fans; indeed, Earle notes that many players said that they were never the same after the series. As with the first-contact experiences of tourists, popular moments can become indelible moments of epiphany, and, as Earle notes, the popular can become "the celebration of a collective myth as enhanced by electronic technology."

WORKS CITED

Dubinsky, Karen. *The Second Biggest Disappointment: Honeymooning and Tourism at Niagara Falls*. Toronto: Between the Lines Press, 1999.

Fiske, John. *Television Culture*. New York: Routledge, 1987.

Hall, Stuart. "Notes on Deconstructing the Popular." *People's History and Socialist Theory*. Ed. R. Samuel. London: Routledge, 1981.

Storey, John. *Cultural Studies and the Study of Popular Culture*. Athens, GA: U of Georgia P, 1996.

Tippett, Maria. *Making Culture: English-Canadian Institutions and the Arts before the Massey Commission*. Toronto: U of Toronto P, 1990.

Wernick, Andrew. *Promotional Culture: Advertising, Ideology, and Symbolic Expression*. London: Sage, 1991.

ACKNOWLEDGEMENTS

Early on in this project, it became apparent that seeking strong essays in the field of Popular Culture Studies would not be as expeditious as we had assumed, and it has, in fact, proved to be a very lengthy task. We are grateful to our authors for their fine essays and for their patience and co-operation throughout the extensive editorial processes. We hope that publication of the collection nourishes wider interactions between academic and cultural communities in the interests of continuing a lively public and scholarly discussion on the Canadian popular.

We are grateful to Wilfrid Laurier University Press for the collective work and support of Catharine Bonas-Taylor, Penny Grows, Brian Henderson, Kathy Joslin, Carroll Klein, Leslie Macredie and Sandra Woolfrey, to the outside readers and Jodey Castricano for their astute suggestions on the manuscript, and to copy-editor Charles Anthony Stuart for his sharp eye for textual details. We thank the numerous individuals who graciously helped us in the course of our work as co-editors: Nick Baxter-Moore, Lesley Bell, Bridget Cahill, Barry Grant, Derek Knight, Jack Miller, Mary Pisiak and Will Straw. We thank Brock University for the Research Seed Fund award that helped us launch the initial stages of this project, the Department of Communications, Popular Culture and Film, and the institutions specifically cited in the essays for granting copyright permission.

Joan Nicks and Jeannette Sloniowski
St. Catharines, Ontario

HERITAGE

"THE PLEASURE IS EXQUISITE BUT VIOLENT": THE IMAGINARY GEOGRAPHY OF NIAGARA FALLS IN THE NINETEENTH CENTURY[1]

Karen Dubinsky

Historians, sociologists, geographers and anthropologists have begun to subject tourism to scholarly scrutiny. As one of the most popular tourist destinations for the past two centuries, it's not surprising that Niagara Falls has been the subject of several historical and cultural studies, which have charted its broader social meanings for tourists, artists and industrialists.

Elizabeth McKinsey's visual history of artistic depictions of Niagara illustrates that a host of different identities have been assigned to the Falls over time: religious, natural and scientific, patriotic, sentimental and, of course, commercial. Historian Patricia Jasen has demonstrated how the quest for "wild things" brought scores of pallid, urban-dwelling middle-class travellers to the shores of Niagara to bask in the recuperative powers of water and forest. Others have asked why certain sites become designated as culturally desirable to "do" (such as Niagara Falls, Peggy's Cove or the West Edmonton Mall) while others (there are plenty of waterfalls, fishing villages and shopping malls in the world) do not. As sociologist John Urry suggests, tourist attractions

Notes on page 34.

21

are never natural; even the most spectacular phenomenon acquires meaning through a number of possible signs (McKay; Wilson).

I have chosen one popular Niagara identity—sexuality—and analyzed the sexual meaning of Niagara Falls. Understanding the long-time association of Niagara Falls with the honeymoon is part of this project. There is, I have discovered, no definite conclusion about the origins of this phenomenon, but I will raise several questions about this curious waterfall/honeymoon juxtaposition. Of all the possible "gazes" that could have been applied to the Falls, why did the area develop as a site for honeymooners in particular? How was the town of Niagara Falls packaged to promote itself as the "Honeymoon Capital of the World," and how has this image been sustained and reinvented?

The modern honeymoon evolved from the nineteenth-century upper- and middle-class custom of the bridal, or wedding, tour, during which the bride and groom, often accompanied by relatives, visited other relatives who could not attend their wedding. By mid-century, wedding trips had become "the standard sequel to a middle-class wedding," but it was not until the 1870s that the notion of the honeymoon as a time of exclusive, romantic seclusion of the couple superseded "the need for affirming community ties" by visiting others (Rothman 175).

Sexual rituals did not figure prominently in the Victorian honeymoon, but this had not always been the case. Lawrence Stone finds the origin of the honeymoon in the "bridal night" of sixteenth- and seventeenth-century England, an institution that contained several explicit sexual references. In upper- and middle-class families, he explains, "the pair were brought to the bedroom in state by relatives and friends, often accompanied with horseplay and ribald jests, and were only left alone...once the curtains of the four-poster bed closed" (Stone 223). Such public sexual rituals ebbed at the end of the eighteenth century, when upper-class English couples began to regard them as vulgar and unnecessary.

Some would have preferred to see the end of the honeymoon altogether. Religious newspapers and clergymen especially spoke out strongly against the ritual, arguing that it was a needless expense that created artificial happiness. Some marital experts were also unenthusiastic. A popular 1900 sex manual lamented that newly married couples consider the ritual a "necessary introduction" to "connubial joy." "There is nothing in the custom to recommend it. After the excitement

and overwork before and accompanying the wedding, the period immediately following should be one of rest" (Jeffreys and Nichols 200).

The way most people in the nineteenth century dealt with the growing
gulf between the honeymoon's overtly sexual legacy and public prescriptions for sexual modesty was to submerge the erotic features of the
ritual. Sexual advice manuals of this era illustrate the desexing of the
honeymoon. Wedding-night dangers were thought to arise from an unfortunate convergence of three problems: exhausted wives, oversexed husbands, and the rigours of travel. Wedding planning and organization fell
squarely on the bride's shoulders, and this had disastrous consequences.
The result was "brides with pallid cheeks and colourless lips, whom the
white wreath and the long veil made appear more like the bride of death
than the woman who was about to assume the sacred duties of wife and
mother." Of course, feminine frailty—for white, middle-class women—
was a truism of Victorian culture. But this frenzy of female activity was
particularly unfortunate, for "if there is any time in the life of a young
woman when she needs the largest store of physical endurance and glowing health," it was on her wedding night (Stall 228-29).

The alter ego of the timid, fragile Victorian woman was the sexually
rapacious Victorian male. Sex experts were frighteningly candid in their
depictions of the newlywed husband. Some claimed that new husbands
treated their wives as "beasts of burden," and thus the first months of
marriage were "a season of prostitution" (An Old Physician 122).
"Rape" or "legalized rape" were the terms used by many to describe the
actions of brutish husbands upon their exhausted, innocent wives.
Jeffreys and Nichols argued that "many a young husband often lays the
foundation of many diseases of the womb and of the nervous system in
gratifying his unchecked passions," and urged men to "prove your manhood, not by yielding to unbridled lust and cruelty, but by the exhibition
of true power in self control and patience with the helpless being con-
fided to your care!" (Jeffreys and Nichols 202).

It would, of course, be simplistic and wrong to conclude, based on
this evidence, that nineteenth-century honeymoons were unhappy
endurance tests for both bride and groom. Neither is it possible to contrast these public discussions of "what ought to be" with the "what
was" of sexual practice, for personal testimonials about the wedding
night from this era are rare. One such memoir, published in 1897, is
frustratingly discreet. Jean Brassey, a middle-class New Yorker, took

his new bride to Niagara Falls, stopping also at different points in New York State along the way. Like many of his contemporaries, however, he too submerged the erotic aspects of the ritual. It is possible to read his account of his first evening with his bride in terms of sexual codes and metaphors: he is nervous, he, like many honeymooners, displaces his anxieties into travel problems and forgets to purchase his train tickets to Niagara until the last minute. His wedding night is recounted as a battle against nature: "it rained in torrents during the night and I had to get up and close the window, and to do so it was necessary to pull the awning down, which was too much of a struggle; but in a little while I succeeded in getting it down. By this time, the lower part of the pyjamas had fairly left my body" (Brassey 5). Perhaps this stands as sexual metaphor or, to paraphrase Freud, perhaps sometimes a rainstorm is just a rainstorm. In any event, Mr. Brassey was one of the few of his generation who saw fit to record his honeymoon story.

Yet, judging from another source of honeymoon wisdom, nineteenth-century pornography, Victorians were not completely successful in their attempts to put a new, sexually cleansed public face on the ritual. Pornography, of course, is where the repressed and forbidden tends to lurk. Nineteenth-century honeymoon-themed pornographic writings subverted the dominant narrative in fascinating ways. In titles such as *Honeymoon Confidences by the Bride Herself* (1909), *A Dialogue between a Married Lady and a Maid* (1900) and *Letters From Laura and Eveline* (1883), readers are treated to robust wedding-night accounts, in which bride and groom alike display voracious sexual appetites. Written, as their titles imply, as first-person narratives from the bride to a female friend (though the sex of the author remains unknown), these stories are usually written as instructional manuals for women. The lesson is simple: sex—described in explicit detail, in infinite variations—is fun and orgasmic, and the wedding night is extremely pleasurable. While the men in these stories are the leaders and initiators (indeed, in these tales women are thankful for sexually experienced men, because they make better husbands), their wives prove willing and eager students. The only moment of unhappiness occurs occasionally when husbands (following the advice of sex experts) tenderly bid their wives good night the first evening without sex, causing their brides crashing disappointment.

Pornography overturned virtually every wedding-night convention that Victorian culture was trying to establish. Honeymoon-themed pornography from this era also extended sexual awakening beyond heterosexuality. Newly sexualized Minnie muses about her other friend, Kate, "the gayest and loveliest girl in the crowd," and declares "how I would like to be the man who sleeps with her the first night of her wedded life" (*First Three Nights* 23). The most subversive of the genre, *Letters from Laura and Eveline*, is a remarkable story of a homosexual man's mock wedding, complete with homoerotic decor ("splendid silver-gilt candlesticks, each one of which represented the emblem of our worshipping: a huge priapus"), two cross-dressing "brides" ("no one would have known us from lovely girls of seventeen or eighteen") and a sexual-initiation scene that brilliantly parodies heterosexuality: a tangle of the bride's "splendid clitoris," "arse," "cunt" and the groom's "foot long, muscular cock" (57). This is about as far away from the apparently chaste, modest ritual encouraged by the advice dispensers as it is possible to get. Yet they are products of the same culture, and both illustrate that the nineteenth-century transition to the passionless private honeymoon was a contested process.

Another problem with post-wedding travel, according to conventional wisdom, was that it exposed the couple to the "staring gaze" of crowds, and the bride, especially, was likely to suffer when made "the object of public attention and remark" (Stall 202). So, despite its problems, the private honeymoon had one important advantage over the more public wedding tour: it allowed the couple to escape the prying eyes of friends and relatives. As one young woman complained, she "did not want to be stared at or commented on by strangers" on her bridal tour. "Let us go to some quiet spot in the mountains or by the sea, and let us live with each other and with nature," she suggested as an alternative (Wood-Allen 270). "Nature" was a great honeymoon destination. Rigidly separated from "culture" in this era, nature was inherently private. The fact that some humans—native people, for example—lived there scarcely counted. The country acted as a purifying tonic for many of the ills of the city. Just as nature might cure delinquent youth, wayward women, criminals and sick people, so too might it work its magic on heterosexual romance. As one doctor put it, "studying and admiring nature together...is the great cementer of hearts" (Fowler 530).

American novelist William Howells's fictional characters, Basil and Isabel March, illustrate well this attempt to combine public modesty with private romance. Howells's 1871 novel, *Their Wedding Journey*, follows Basil and Isabel on their tour from Boston through Niagara Falls and points east. The couple take their journey several weeks after their wedding ceremony, for which Isabel, especially, is extremely grateful. "How much better," she declares, "than to have started off upon a wretched wedding-breakfast, all tears and trousseau, and had people wanting to see you aboard the cars. Now there will not be a suspicion of honey-moonshine about us" (2).

Even during the Victorian period, everyone—as Isabel March feared—knew what a honeymooning couple stood for. In a culture that considered sexual relations permissible only within the institution of marriage, the wedding provided heterosexual couples with a social licence to become sexual beings. In earlier times, this was acknowledged and celebrated as part of the post-wedding ritual. To young Victorian middle- and upper-class couples, however, the private honeymoon provided a means of reconciling the embarrassment of this passage into adult sexual citizenship with nineteenth-century prescriptions for public sexual modesty. Even so, as Isabel March fretted about, and many others experienced, newlyweds were visible, marked creatures, and the private honeymoon was contradictory and illusory. The first North American hotel to feature a honeymoon suite, for example, was New York's Irving Hotel in 1847. The *New York Tribune* gushed at the elegance of what it called the "fairy boudoir," decorated with lace and white satin (White 141). But of course the "privacy" of a honeymoon suite designated for the exclusive use of newlyweds was, like the honeymoon itself, a contradiction, as many would have learned when they were spotted and mocked in hotel lobbies or on board trains to their destination. As the porter at Niagara's Cataract House hotel recalled, "a bride and groom didn't want anybody to suspect that they'd just been married. Seemed as if they'd almost rather be caught stealing!" (*American Magazine* 92).

Theorist Michel Foucault has termed the honeymoon a "privileged or sacred or forbidden" place, set aside for those who are "in relation to society and to the human environment in which they live, in a state of crisis." So, like the menstruating woman, the pregnant woman or the adolescent, the honeymooning couple exists "nowhere," passing through this moment of crisis outside conventional geographical markers (Foucault 24-25). Nineteenth-century honeymooners certainly had a peculiar relationship to their culture; they were, for a moment at least, decided oddities and outsiders. Social conservatives voiced their firm disapproval for the ritual, doctors and sex experts thought they should be filled with dire warnings and then, for a period, banished, and pornographic writers delighted in mocking social convention by exposing the main premise of the institution: entry into heterosexual culture. Yet it is not completely true that honeymooning couples existed outside conventional geographic markers, for Niagara Falls has been privileged as a site for the enactment of this ritual for the past two centuries.

The association of Niagara Falls with the honeymooning couple is almost as old as the "discovery" of the Falls itself for tourism, dating from the early nineteenth century. Niagara was famous as a honeymoon resort through the nineteenth century, but ironically, the first obvious hard sell of the region to honeymooners did not occur until almost one hundred years after the first "honeymoon craze" of the 1830s. The first short-lived local honeymoon promotional scheme occurred in 1910. Businessmen and civic boosters who were organizing the first "Niagara International Carnival" had to call off their plans for a "Public Wedding," which, they hoped, would act as an advertisement to honeymooners, owing to "adverse criticisms of the churches and a large number of the citizens" (*Niagara Falls Daily Record* May 27, 1910). One had to tread carefully where public representations of sexuality—even sanctioned, wedded heterosexuality—were concerned, and this is likely why there was so little honeymoon advertising in the early part of this century. Of course, another reason was that the honeymoon, like travel itself, was not an affordable object of mass consumption, and thus it was not massively promoted. The 1920s saw the first stirrings of the widespread commodification of the Niagara Falls honeymoon, but the real selling of Niagara as a honeymoon haven—including the creation of honeymoon certificates, honeymoon specials in restaurants, honeymoon hotels and other promotional devices—began during and immediately after World War II. How do we understand, then, why huge numbers of honeymooning couples "voted with their feet" and visited the Falls in the nineteenth century, without being directly encouraged by anyone?

This raises the question of how certain sites become designated as popular places to visit, as well as how places become invested with certain qualities. Places are more than simply locations; the spatial is also socially constructed. Social divisions are often spatialized, and places become labelled, much like "deviant" individuals. This combination of social divisions and spatial metaphors (the "wrong side of the tracks") become incorporated into what geographer Rob Shields calls "imaginary geographies," so much so that certain sites become associated with "particular values, historical events and feelings" (Shields 11, 29). Tourist promoters can take these associations of places with values, events and feelings, and create successful enterprises from them. But this has limits. For Niagara Falls to become a popular honeymoon spot—especially in the absence of massive promotion until the twentieth century—there must have been something there to begin with. The answer to this puzzle—honeymoon popularity a century or so before honeymoon promotion—lies in the way romance, sex and danger were incorporated in the imaginary geographies of nineteenth-century Niagara Falls visitors. Niagara Falls began as an elite vacation spot, hosting forty thousand visitors annually by the 1840s. It was especially popular with the Southern U.S. aristocracy, who escaped the summer heat on the plantation on the breezy verandahs of Niagara's grand hotels. The waterfall was, of course, the main attraction, but there have always been plenty of sidelines: battlefields, General Brock's monument and other famous war sites. Two of the most popular attractions were the American Cave of the Winds and the Canadian Table Rock tours, both begun in the 1830s, in which people can walk through the Falls, buffeted by wind and water, and end up viewing them from "inside." Another attraction, the *Maid of the Mist* steamer (named after a European-invented "Indian legend" of virgin sacrifice), began its journeys to the base of the waterfall in 1840.

But the main part of the itinerary of visitors was quiet contemplation of the waterfall. To really "do" Niagara, one stayed for a long period of time, and contemplated the Falls from different vantage points. We know a lot about what the nineteenth-century traveller felt and thought about Niagara, because a good many of them wrote it down. To many, Niagara evoked both pleasure and terror. From the first written description in 1683 by Father Louis Hennepin, who called it "the most Beautiful, and at the same time most Frightful Cascade in the World," such ambivalence has characterized much writing about Niagara. "The pleasure is exquisite but violent," wrote one visitor in 1821. Yet, the lure of Niagara was as potent as its danger. As another early-nineteenth-century traveller commented, he could "hardly consent to leave this seemingly dangerous, and enchanting spot" (McKinsey 11, 39). What had transfixed this visitor, and many others, were the parallels between the beauty and danger of the waterfall and nineteenth-century views about sexuality and gender. One literary device used by many writers was to attribute human feelings and emotions to the rushing waters. Some simply compared the waters to humans. "When one has looked at the waters for a certain time one feels certain that the mass is alive," declared one typical visitor in 1873 (Grant 60). Isabella Bird described the American rapids "rolling and struggling down, chafing the sunny islets, as if jealous of their beauty," and then "flung [themselves] upwards, as if infuriated against the sky." "There is something very exciting in this view," she concluded, "one cannot help investing Niagara with feelings of human agony and apprehension" (224). Novelist Henry James saw the Horseshoe Falls as an exhausted swimmer, "shrieking, sobbing, clasping hands, tossing hair" (Conrad 16). Niagara Falls, declared the Niagara Parks Commission in a 1920s guidebook, gave tourists the opportunity to see the "awe inspiring spectacle of nature in one of her turbulent moods."

This last passage indicates another common descriptive device: the waters were not simply humanized, they were gendered. And, overwhelmingly, they were gendered female. To almost all writers who gendered their descriptions, Niagara was female: the "Queen of the Cataracts," the "Water Bride of Time," the "Daughter of History" and the "Mother of all Cascades." Niagara Falls has always been gazed upon as a specifically female icon.

When gender enters the imaginary geography of landscape, what happens to the thoughts and feelings of spectators? Incorporating female imagery into their descriptions of Niagara, many writers also projected suitably gendered physical and emotional responses. Sometimes this took the form of simple flattery, particularly of the "costume" of the waterfall. Niagara "wears a garb that wins from man…wonder, awe and praise"; at "her" base, she "wrap[s] herself saucily in the rainbow robe of mist" (Menzies 19; Dow 259). During the reign of "King Winter," Niagara dons a "coat of crystal," and sparkles like "a gem in the diadem of nature." One particularly poetic writer saw, in Niagara's winter scene, "trees...bowed down to the earth with their snowy vestments, like so many white nuns doing saintly homage to the genius of the place" (Allen 46). Others saw Niagara's mist as a veil; sometimes bridal, at other times ghostlike.

To many, Niagara was *like* a woman; others were more literal. William Russell claimed that "I never looked at it [the waterfall] without fancying I could trace in the outlines the indistinct shape of a woman, with flowing hair and drooping arms, veiled in drapery" (Dow 318). The invented tale of the Indian "maid of the mist," who went over Niagara, was fuel for many such fantasies. Promoters of Canada Steamship Lines tours to the Falls in 1915 invited tourists to imagine that "instinctively we see the Indian maid in her flower-bedecked canoe approach the apex of the Falls, her body erect, her demeanour courageous" (Canada Steamship Lines 2). Images of naked native women going over the waterfall adorned postcards and promotional brochures, as well as "high" Niagara Falls art, through the nineteenth and twentieth centuries.

The positioning of the waterfall as female and the viewer as male enhanced the spectatorial pleasure of "doing" Niagara. It is not surprising, then, that sexual imagery abounds in descriptions of the Falls. The spray from the mist was often described as a "kiss," the sound of the water rushing was a "moan," islands rest on the "bosom" of the waterfall, and the "soft shales" of the cliff "gradually yield before the attack" of rushing water. The "clinging curves" of water "embrace" the islands, and water "writhes," "gyrates" and "caresses the shore"; the whirlpool is "passionate." Some recoil from the "mad desire" of the waters; for others, "no where else is Nature more tender, constrained, and softly clad." Niagara—"nature unclothed"—was "seductively restless," and "tries to win your heart with her beauty" (Dow 257, 263, 339, 345; Ferree 23; Howells, *Niagara Book* 130; Bell 32).

This imagery helped construct sexualized responses to Niagara Falls. "Like a beautiful and true, an excellent and admirable mistress," wrote George Holley in 1872, "the faithful lover may return to it with ever new delight, ever growing affection" (Holley 1). Poets spoke of the "smooth, lustrous, awful, lovely curve of peril...cruel as love, and wild as love's first kiss!" Another evoked the image of Sappho, "that immortal maid—enchantress sweet." One poem, published in a collection in 1901, illustrates well the "exquisite pleasures" of Niagara:

Nymph of Niagara! Sprite of the mist!
With a wild magic my brow thou hast kissed;
I am thy slave, and my mistress art thou,
For thy wild kiss of magic is still on my brow

I feel it as first when I knelt before thee
With thy emerald robe flowing brightly and free
Fringed with the spray-pearls and floating in mist
That was my brow with wild magic you kissed.

The narrator continues, describing how the waterfall has "bound" him:

...thy chain but a foam-wreath, yet stronger by far
Than the manacle, steel-wrought for captive of war
...While the foam-wreath will bind me forever to thee,
I love the enslavement and would not be free. (Pritchard 67)

Fictional treatments of visits to Niagara also reveal the magnetic
sexual lure of the waterfall. Agnes Machar depicts Niagara as the first
stop in her story of a holiday journey of several young Canadians. The
protagonist, May, is joined at Niagara by her cousin Kate, and Kate's
cousin Hugh, whom May has not met previously. Young May is initially shy around Hugh, but after their first look at the waterfall together
(a "curving, quivering sheet of thundering surge...dazzlingly pure in its
virgin beauty"), May looks at Hugh in a new light. She feels "much less
shy" around him, and notices him physically for the first time; she is
mesmerized by his "heightened colour," and the "absorbed expression
of dark blue eyes." Hugh, it turns out, is also transformed by his view
of the Falls. "I never felt," he tells May, "as if I had got so near the state
of self-annihilation, the 'Nirvana' we read about." May has "much of
the same feelings herself," though she is "too reserved to say it out." As
the party continue their journey, across Lake Ontario and down the St.
Lawrence River, the romantic tension between May and Hugh height-
ens, and by the end, Hugh proposes marriage, asking May to "travel
down the river of life together" (Machar 12-15, 263).

The waterfall could also—befitting a moody female—turn ugly.
The fatal lure of the waters was commented on by many horrified but
fascinated visitors. "As you gaze upon the rush you feel a horrid
yearning in your heart to plunge in and join the mad whirl and see the
mystery out," declared one (Dow 271). Some suggested "scientific"

explanations for this, positing that the sight of such a "frightful emi-
nence" caused a rush of blood to the brain, which in turn produced a
"partial derangement" (Johnson 37).[2] Yet most other descriptions
relied less on science than common discourses of feminine sexuality,
depicting the waterfall as an alluring and enchanting female, bewitch-
ing and entrapping legions of male suitors. "With all this fear," wrote
one promoter in 1856, "there is something so imposing in our situation as to render it pleasing....We are in the presence of the
enchanter" (Burke 62). "The beautiful stream permits itself to be
toyed with," wrote another visitor, "its smiling accessibility is most
alluring, but is most dangerous. Every rock and ledge has its story of
the fatal attraction of the waters" (Dow 331). Like a designing
woman, Niagara Falls often tricked the unsuspecting. "One of the
chief charms of the Falls of Niagara is the familiarity with which they
can be approached," warned one guidebook, "but beware of their
relentless power" (*Chisholm's* 14).

As these passages reveal, the relationship between self and other,
which is fundamental to travel, and travel writing, is often more revealing about self. At Niagara, gendered, sexualized descriptive imagery,
the perceived "fatal attraction" of rushing waters, tales of death and
destruction, as well as invented stories of romance and tragedy, were all
of a piece, and helped create a highly romantic, sexual and frightening
image of Niagara Falls. Such imagery helped, in the nineteenth century,
to fix an image of the Falls in the minds of North Americans as a place
of forbidden pleasures.

And it wasn't just "in their heads." Two of the most popular Niagara
Falls excursions, the Table Rock and Cave of the Winds tours, reveal
dramatically how a visit to the Falls might *actually*, not just imaginatively, heighten one's sensations of pleasure and danger. The tours
behind the Falls, through the tunnels at Table Rock, and inside the
American Cave of the Winds, were quite elaborate. At the entrance to
each, women and men entered separate change rooms, and completely
disrobed ("down to the skin," as one traveller marvelled, "with
no thought of retaining even your underclothes") (Howells, *Niagara
Book* 32). They donned a suit of flannel blouses and trousers, covered
by an oilskin coat, and then followed a guide through the maze of rock
and thundering spray. At their final destination, hearty travellers celebrated their accomplishment by frolicking in the waters. Upon their

return, they were awarded with certificates that they had successfully completed this most dangerous tour.

The costume itself was enough to startle many visitors. One called it "the scantiest set of garments in which I have ever appeared in public" (Dow 311). Women and men wore the same dress, which also caused some consternation to nineteenth-century visitors, so accustomed to rigidly gendered styles of clothing. Like many, Isabella Bird balked at the idea of disrobing completely, and when she emerged from the dressing room her "appearance was so comic as to excite the laughter of my grave friends" (Bird 232).

The most pleasurable description of the tour itself comes from Frederic Almy, in 1896. He spoke of the water "foaming and rushing about your knees, and lugging at you with an invitation that is irresistible. I have seen grave men frolic in the water, their trousers and sleeves swelled almost to bursting with imprisoned air....To play so with Niagara brings an exhilaration that is indescribable (Howells, *Niagara Book* 37). Even a most scholarly and upright Victorian gentleman, Professor John Tyndall, writing for a scientific journal in the 1870s, was enthusiastic about the "sanative effect" of the Cave of the Winds: "Quickened by the emotions there aroused, the blood sped healthily through the arteries, abolishing introspection, clearing the heart of all bitterness, and enabling one to think with tolerance, if not with tenderness, of the most relentless and unreasonable foe. Apart from its scientific value, and purely as a moral agent, the play, I submit, is worth the candle" (28). Most agreed that it was a "terrible ordeal, which no one should miss undergoing" (Roper 418).

The tradition of the Niagara Falls honeymoon was popularized and commodified in the twentieth century, but it was not invented then. Many people have speculated about why Niagara Falls became associated with the honeymoon. The question has provoked an endless series of jokes, witticisms and bon mots, but the answer is complicated. It doesn't lie in mimicry alone; it did not happen because famous people honeymooned there in the early nineteenth century. Nor does another popular answer—falling water creates negative ions, which cheer people up and make them think about sex—get us very far. Niagara Falls did, as I have argued, make people think about sex, but the creation of the place as a honeymoon mecca was a complex process that brought together several strands: its pre-existing status as an elite tourist resort;

changing mores about the honeymoon itself in nineteenth-century social and family life; cultural depictions of Niagara as an icon of beauty, which were always expressed in terms of gender and hetero-sexual attraction; and the forbidden pleasures of sexuality, romance and danger, which countless travellers experienced while viewing, or play-ing with, the waterfall.

NOTES

1 This is a revised version of an article that originally appeared in the *Journal of Canadian Studies* 29.2 (Summer 1994) and also appears in a somewhat different form in *The Second Greatest Disappointment: Honeymooning and Tourism at Niagara Falls* (Toronto: Between the Lines Press, 1999).

2 Visitors in the mid- and late nineteenth century were consumed by the notion that the Falls made people want to kill themselves, but earlier vis-itors believed quite the reverse. Travellers in the 1830s were of the opin-ion that "the agitation of the surrounding air produced by the tremendous Falls, combines with the elevation and dryness of the soil" to produce "the most healthful [place] on the continent of North America." As proof of this, many noted that the "magic neighbourhoods" surrounding the Falls had remained untouched by the cholera epidemics of the 1830s, e.g., William Barham, *Descriptions of Niagara* (self-published, 1850); *Burke's Illustrated Guide* (1856); Menzies (1846). The association of water with curative powers continued through the nineteenth century in other places in Canada; a children's hospital was built on Toronto Island in the 1880s for precisely these reasons. See Sally Gibson *More than an Island* (1984) p. 93.

WORKS CITED

Allen, H. T. *Tunis Illustrated Guide to Niagara Falls.* Niagara Falls, NY: Gazette Printing, 1877.

American Magazine 102 (July 1926): 92.

Bell, R. R. *Diary of a Canadian Tour.* Coatbridge: Alex Pettigrew, 1927.

Bird, Isabella Lucy. *The Englishwoman in America.* London: 1856, reprinted Toronto: U of Toronto P, 1966.

Brassey, Jean. *My Honeymoon Trip.* New York: F. Berkeley, 1897.

Burke's Illustrated Guide. Privately published, 1856.

Canada Steamship Lines. *Niagara to the Sea.* 1915.

Chisholm's Complete Guide to the Grand Cataract. Portland: Chisholm Brothers, 1892.

Conrad, Peter. *Imagining America.* New York: Oxford UP, 1980.

Dow, Charles Mason. *Anthology and Bibliography of Niagara Falls.* Albany: J. B. Lyon, 1921.

Ferree, A. M. *The Falls of Niagara and Scenes Around Them*. New York: Privately published, 1876.

First Three Nights of Married Life. Paris: Vie de Boheme, 1900.

Foucault, Michel. "Of Other Spaces." *Diacritics: A Review of Contemporary Criticism* 16 (Spring 1986): 24-25.

Fowler, O. S. *Creative and Sexual Science*. Privately published, 1875.

Grant, A. R. C. and Caroline Combe. *Lord Rosebery's North American Journal, 1873*. London: Sedgewick and Jackson, 1967.

Holley, George. *Niagara: Its History, Geology, Incidents and Poetry*. Toronto: Hunter Rose, 1872.

Howells, William Dean. *Their Wedding Journey*. Boston: Houghton Mifflin, 1871.

_____. *The Niagara Book: A Complete Souvenir of Niagara Falls*. Buffalo: Underhill and Sons, 1893.

Jasen, Patricia. *Wild Things: Nature, Culture and Tourism in Ontario, 1790-1914*. Toronto: U of Toronto P, 1995.

Jeffreys, B. G. and J. L. Nichols. *Searchlights on Health*. Toronto: J. L. Nichols, 1900.

Johnson, F. H. *Every Man His Own Guide at Niagara Falls*. Rochester: Dewey, 1852.

Letters from Laura and Eveline. London: Privately published, 1883.

Machar, Agnes. *Down the River to the Sea*. New York: Home Book Company, 1894.

McKay, Ian. *The Quest of the Folk: Antimodernism and Cultural Selection in Twentieth Century Nova Scotia*. Kingston: McGill-Queen's UP, 1990.

McKinsey, Elizabeth. *Niagara: Icon of the American Sublime*. Cambridge: Cambridge UP, 1985.

Menzies, George. *Album of the Table Rock*. Privately published, 1846.

An Old Physician. *The Physiology of Marriage*. Boston: John Jewett, 1856.

Pritchard, Myron, ed. *Poetry of Niagara*. Boston: Lothrop, 1901.

Roper, Edward. *By Track and Train Through Canada*. London: Allen, 1891.

Rothman, Ellen. *Hands and Hearts: A History of Courtship in America*. New York: Basic, 1984.

Shields, Rob. *Places on the Margin*. London: Routledge, 1991.

Stall, Sylvanus. *What a Young Man Ought to Know*. Philadelphia: Vir, 1897.

Stone, Lawrence. *The Family, Sex and Marriage in England, 1500-1800*. Harmondsworth: Penguin, 1977.

Tyndall, John. "Niagara Falls." *Eclectic Magazine of Foreign Literature, Science and Art* 18.1 (July 1873).

Urry, John. *The Tourist Gaze: Leisure and Travel in Contemporary Societies*. London: Sage, 1990.

White, Arthur. *Palaces of the People: A Social History of Commercial Hospitality*. New York: Taplinger, 1970.

Wilson, Alexander. *The Culture of Nature: North American Landscape from Disney to the Exxon Valdez*. Toronto: Between the Lines, 1991.

Wood-Allen, Mary. *What a Young Woman Ought to Know*. Philadelphia: Vir, 1928.

ABORIGINAL CULTURAL TOURISM IN CANADA[1]

Valda Blundell

"This is not a contrived tourist experience," announced our guide over the train's intercom. With some two hundred other tourists, I was riding the Polar Bear Express, an Ontario Northland train that runs from southern Ontario to Moosonee and the Indian community of Moose Factory in the Arctic tidewater area of James Bay. My fellow travellers included Canadian and American tourists, many of whom had seen advertisements for this trip that depict the Cree Indians of the area and promise opportunities to experience the "reality" of their Native way of life. The Polar Bear Express is but one of a growing number of attractions promoted as opportunities for tourists to encounter the cultures of Canada's First Peoples, a trend that has been strongly supported since the mid-1980s by state tourism officials in their efforts to increase the country's tourism revenues.

I took the Polar Bear Express during the summer of 1991 as part of a research project on First Peoples and tourism in Canada. Given the widespread promotion of aboriginal forms for tourism, I wanted to determine what kinds of attractions are in place for tourists in Canada, what kinds of ideas about First Peoples these attractions convey, and how First Peoples are themselves involved in tourism. The present paper is a condensed and updated version of a report originally published in 1995-96 (Blundell). To understand the political and economic

Notes on pages 56-58.

contexts in which Canada's First Peoples have come to be linked more closely with tourism, I begin with a review of the tourism policies of state agencies over the past decade and a half.

THE TOURISM POLICIES OF STATE AGENCIES

Since the mid-1980s the promotion of aboriginal cultures for tourism has been part of a broader strategy by government agencies aimed at increasing tourism in Canada by highlighting the nation's distinctive cultural forms. By the mid-1980s, for example, federal tourism policy was calling for the increased promotion of a wide range of Canadian cultural forms to pleasure travellers, a form of tourism that is now widely referred to as "cultural tourism." While various definitions of "cultural tourism" have been offered, the term is generally used to refer to forms of international mass pleasure travel that provide tourists with opportunities to experience the cultural attractions and the cultural distinctiveness of the area they visit.[2] References are commonly made to a country's (or region's) art, craft, and heritage forms; its museums, art galleries, and historic sites; its culturally different populations; as well as to the different "sense of place" that tourists can experience.[3] In one definition widely quoted in Canada, Robert Kelly defines cultural tourism as "the consumption of cultural experiences (and objects) by individuals who are away from their normal place of habitation" (57). State officials have come to stress this view of cultural tourism as the "consumption of cultural experiences" while repeatedly arguing that such experiences can be commoditized for tourists. For state officials, the promotion of cultural tourism can generate benefits for the Canadian tourism industry and at the same time provide a means of economic development for marginal areas and disadvantaged groups who market themselves for tourism.

However, officials argue that cultural experiences promoted for tourism must be authentic ones, and this raises questions regarding what constitutes a contrived versus an authentic experience. In his analysis of federal tourism policy from the mid-1980s to the early 1990s, John Harp shows that tourism texts from this period represent regions and communities in less developed areas of Canada "within a rhetoric of 'heritage' whereby some idyllic past is presented as the authentic life and as something the urban dweller has lost" (196). In these texts, so-called "authentic" cultures are assumed to persist among "traditional" indigenous peoples, and also among some "peasant," "ethnic," and rural groups, so that travel becomes a way for tourists from urbanized, industrialized areas to reclaim this (lost) authenticity. Although these ideas have long recurred in the West, they are persistently challenged by critical scholars who worry that tourist attractions promoted as the loci of "authentic" experiences will provoke nostalgia rather than critical thought by romanticizing the past and hiding from visitors current social inequities and their real historical source (Overton; MacCannell; Hewison). Critics also worry that aboriginal, ethnic or rural peoples are being recruited to act as traditional peoples for others and to produce quaint, exotic-looking forms that conform to such romantic stereotypes of their cultures. They are concerned that individuals who don't behave in this way will be accused of having lost their own cultural identity, or, as James Clifford has put it, that what is considered different about their cultures will be "tied to traditional pasts" while their "inherited structures" will be seen to "resist or yield to the new" but not to produce it (*Predicament* 5). Finally, critics are concerned that cultural forms commoditized for tourist markets are replacing those that express a group's own lived experiences.

Despite the concerns of critics, cultural tourism is now considered a significant growth area in the global economy and a means to increase the flow of foreign revenues into Canada.[4] However, officials note that other countries are better known as destinations with impressive cultural attractions, and therefore Canada must compete with them for its share of "world tourism receipts." In particular, while Canada can offer neither the spectacular historic sites of Europe, nor the "peasant" peoples of Third World countries, state officials repeatedly remark that Canada does have a rich multicultural heritage and the presence of Native peoples, which can be promoted for cultural tourism. In tourism texts of the mid-1980s, for example, multiculturalism as a formula for national unity through cultural retention and sharing became muted in favour of multiculturalism as good for the tourist business.[5]

By the mid-1980s, market research undertaken by the then relevant federal agency, Tourism Canada, was being widely cited to reinforce the belief that cultural tourism would expand rapidly in the future.[6] In the case of Americans, who constitute the largest source of international pleasure travellers in Canada, the highly influential "U.S.

Pleasure Travel Market" study (USPTMS), conducted in the mid-1980s, concluded that Americans could be attracted to Canada not so much for its spectacular outdoor scenery (which they consider superior in their own country), but because it was a "foreign" country that could provide them with a culturally different experience.[7] Citing this study, officials recommended the intense promotion of "Canada's unique cultural heritage," including its "rich native and multicultural heritage,"[8] in order to "capitalize on its strength in this market" (21). Studies in Europe and Asia also pointed to the specificity of Canadian "culture," including the presence in Canada of Native cultures, as important "drawers" of tourism dollars.[9]

Between the mid-1980s and the early 1990s, the federal government moved toward a new mode of state intervention in the tourism industry that was designed to increase tourism revenues in Canada, but with reduced levels of government spending. As Harp shows, with the election of the federal Conservatives in the mid-1980s, Tourism Canada moved away from involvement in the direct funding of tourism projects to the provision of market research for Canada's tourism industry along with the sponsorship of advertising designed to cater to tourists' perceived tastes (196). Tourism Canada commissioned magazine and television ads in the United States and mounted promotional campaigns overseas that emphasized Canada's cultural attractions, including its aboriginal cultures. The federal government also mobilized support for its policies among the private sector, other levels of government, and various cultural and heritage organizations, which also increasingly adapted their programming for so-called "cultural tourists" and produced their own advertising materials. In 1995, the federal government replaced Tourism Canada with the Canadian Tourism Commission (CTC), a partnership between industry and government that provides information and advertising for the Canadian tourism industry. As of 2000, the CTC continued to advocate the expansion of cultural tourism, including aboriginal attractions, as a way to increase tourism revenues in Canada.[10]

TOURISM AND ABORIGINAL CULTURAL POLITICS

Since the mid-1980s, then, efforts aimed at linking Canada's aboriginal cultures more closely with tourism have been affected by the economic agendas of state agencies. However, these efforts have also occurred within a political context dominated by a volatile national debate on aboriginal rights as First Peoples have struggled to sustain their own cultures and transform their relations with(in) the Canadian state. Thus, while state agencies have been promoting aboriginal forms for so-called "cultural tourism," First Peoples have been demanding more control over the ways that their cultures are marketed to tourists. In the early 1990s, for example, the Canadian National Aboriginal Tourism Association (CNATA) was formed with the goal of promoting "aboriginal tourism" in ways that are consistent with First Peoples' values and aspirations, and in 1995, CNATA held a national tourism convention and trade exhibit where First Peoples from across the country discussed common goals and concerns.[11]

A range of practices have come under fire, including insensitive behaviours on the part of some visitors to aboriginal communities and the commoditization of aboriginal forms by non-aboriginal entrepreneurs, which many First Peoples say constitute acts of "cultural appropriation" with "non-aboriginal entrepreneurs benefiting at their expense" (Ames; Blundell, "Aboriginal Empowerment"). Also contentious is the fact that many of the public museums visited by tourists contain aboriginal objects that First Peoples want repatriated to their own local communities. As well, First Peoples have repeatedly challenged stereotypic representations of them and their cultures in travel ads and at tourist attractions, including exhibits in public museums. Too often such representations depict their cultures solely in terms of their arts, crafts, attire, and cuisine, without any reference to the economic and political forms of First Peoples, which may differ from both those of their past cultures and those of the dominant culture of Canada. Furthermore, some representations locate First Peoples in the past, and in nature, as part of Canada's "heritage," but exclude them from Canada's ongoing history. Finally, there are concerns about the ideological consequences of practices that inscribe as "authentic" only those so-called "traditional" or "heritage" forms thought to survive from the past.

Individual tourist attractions have also become sites of aboriginal cultural politics, as was the case for "The Spirit Sings," an exhibit of historic aboriginal artifacts that was mounted at Calgary's Glenbow Museum as the cultural event of the 1988 Winter Olympics. First

Peoples called for a boycott of this exhibit because it had received corporate sponsorship from the very oil company that was drilling on land claimed by Alberta's Lubicon Cree, and they also considered it hypocritical to celebrate historical aboriginal artifacts given inequities between First Peoples and other citizens of the Canadian state (Ames; Myers).

But while First Peoples have raised concerns regarding tourism, over the past two decades they have also increasingly looked to tourism as a means of economic development as well as a way to present their cultures to tourists in ways that avoid the (stereotypic) practices that they contest. To be sure, many aboriginal groups across Canada have a long history of involvement with tourism, particularly through their production of arts and crafts. However, a growing number are either expanding current offerings or developing new ones, and some groups have chosen to enter into co-operative ventures with various levels of government. For example, in Ontario, the Curve Lake First Nation and the provincial government now operate Petroglyphs Provincial Park co-operatively (Parry). In Alberta, Blackfoot First Nations have collaborated with the provincial government to establish the world heritage site of Head-Smashed-In Buffalo Jump, which I will consider in more detail below.

TYPES OF TOURIST ATTRACTIONS THAT REPRESENT FIRST NATIONS CULTURES

By the early 1990s, a range of attractions depicting First Peoples and their cultures were being visited by domestic and international tourists in Canada. Four general categories of attractions can be identified.[12]

I. FIXED SITES

A first category consists of more than five hundred attractions at specific locales that are generally open throughout the year. As well as national, provincial, and local public museums, there are cultural, heritage, and education centres, many of which are operated by First Peoples in their own communities and, like public museums, are dependent on various forms of government funding. Some public art galleries in Canada exhibit contemporary art produced by First Peoples, although human history museums generally hold such works.

As well as specific attractions, certain towns and villages are promoted as destinations where aboriginal cultures can be experienced. Such contemporary sites include Indian and Inuit communities advertised as places where tourists can see "authentic" Native cultures or purchase aboriginal arts and crafts. Historic and prehistoric sites, many of which are federal or provincial historic sites (or parks), also depict First Peoples. At such sites there may be an interpretive centre in place, as well as refreshment stands and arts and craft outlets, and some sites include the actual grounds where (archaeological) remains of past activities have been found. Across Canada there are also specific memorials, monuments, and works of public art, which were made by, or make reference to, First Peoples. As a final type of fixed site, there are a few commercial theme parks, such as Capilano Suspension Bridge Park north of Vancouver, to which I will return below.

II. COMMERCIAL ARTS AND CRAFTS OUTLETS

A second category consists of commercial arts, crafts, and souvenir outlets. Many of these are small shops owned or operated by aboriginal peoples, as is invariably the case for outlets located on First Nations reserves or as components of aboriginal-run museums or cultural centres.[13] Some aboriginal-run outlets also serve as workshops for artists and craftspeople and as galleries where their works, and the works of other First Peoples, are on display. Such settings provide opportunities for tourists to have face-to-face interactions with aboriginal people. However, many other commercial outlets that sell works by or about First Peoples are not aboriginal-owned or operated, and many, in fact, sell inexpensive mass-produced souvenirs that are not made by First Peoples but which replicate aboriginal forms.

III. EVENTS

As well as attractions at specific locales, which tourists can visit throughout the year, there are events that occur on specific dates. For example, across Canada each summer First Nations welcome tourists to powwows in their communities; indeed, the past two decades have seen a phenomenal growth in the number of aboriginal communities that put on annual powwows (Blundell, "Echos")[14] Other festivals, fairs, and stampedes include performances by First Peoples, sometimes on their own, and sometimes as a part of "multicultural" celebrations. Some provinces and local tourism agencies distribute brochures that list the festivals and powwows that occur during the summer tourist season.

IV: TOURS AND LIVE-IN EXPERIENCES

A final category consists of various tours and live-in experiences, including self-guiding tours taken by private automobile, bus tours, and a range of other offerings provided by aboriginal and non-aboriginal operators.[15] Such offerings are particularly appealing to aboriginal operators when they can establish them in their own locales, and they are of interest to tourists who want a more in-depth travel experience. Across Canada there are also some lodges and wilderness camps that are operated by First Peoples, and these also provide tourists with opportunities for more sustained interactions with First Peoples.

THE NATURE OF ABORIGINAL INVOLVEMENT AT TOURIST ATTRACTIONS

This brief overview indicates the kinds of attractions about First Peoples that tourists can visit and also some of the ways in which First Peoples are involved in their operations. Festivals invariably include aboriginal performers, and powwows are produced entirely by First Peoples. However, there is less involvement by First Peoples at fixed sites, many of which are located in the more populated areas of Canada, which are most likely to be visited by domestic and international pleasure travellers. In the early 1990s, for example, only about a third of the fixed sites across Canada were being operated by, or collaboratively with, First Peoples. Moreover, while arts and crafts outlets operated by First Peoples are an important source of income for them, many are operated in aboriginal communities that receive fewer visitors than the more populated parts of the country. It is therefore more likely that tourists will purchase items by, or about, First Peoples at a non-aboriginal-operated gift shop or souvenir stand at an urban airport or shopping complex.

In the case of fixed sites, aboriginal involvement is greatest for communities that have been promoted as tourist destinations, because most of these are reserves or other First Nations communities advertised as places to see aboriginal culture, purchase aboriginal arts and crafts, or see famous works of art such as totem poles. However, it is not clear whether aboriginal people are always consulted when government agencies promote their communities or works of public art in travel brochures. Nor is it clear whether tourists are entirely welcome in these communities. For example, during the summer of 1992 I visited several of the First Nations communities in the Hazelton area of British Columbia that were advertised as old pole sites in B.C.'s "Heritage and Native Sites" brochure and were also stops on several self-guiding tours. When I arrived at one of these communities, I stopped at the Band Office to request information about the local totem poles and was given a brochure regarding the totem poles prepared by this community. When other tourists saw me with this brochure, they asked where I had obtained it, as it was not advertised at the entrance to the community. In fact, the major concern in this village was not with its visiting tourists, but with the construction of a badly needed sewer system.

In contrast to this attraction, I also visited a Huron community near Quebec City where tourists were actively sought. Here, at Huron-Wendat, a well-marked Information Centre greets visitors as they enter the community. As one of the local attractions, a Huron entrepreneur has built a reproduction of a historic Huron village. Local Huron guides give tours through this attraction, and they include in their remarks details of Huron history as well as comments on the Huron's current political goals. Huron craftsmen make snowshoes on the premises, which are on sale at a craft shop also located at this attraction. Staff at the attraction told me that each day during the summer numerous tour buses stop here, thus bringing thousands of dollars into the local economy.

As these two examples suggest, aboriginal communities link with tourism in a range of ways. In some cases, there is little in place for tourists, while in other cases facilities have been specifically developed to attract them. As at Huron-Wendat, some attractions are private businesses owned by aboriginal entrepreneurs who employ other First Peoples in their operation. Other ventures are band initiatives, undertaken for the collective benefit of the community. This is the case, for example, at Six Nations near Brantford, Ontario, where tours are available to visitors and where local festivals and powwows annually bring many thousands of visitors to the community. Other aboriginal communities are involved in various "co-operative" ventures with non-aboriginal entrepreneurs or with various levels of government.

WHAT IS PROMISED, WHAT IS DELIVERED?

Tourists become aware of attractions that depict aboriginal peoples through promotional materials that they consult before they leave home, and these materials also play a significant role in determining the kinds of experiences that tourists come to anticipate as they tour. Indeed, the role of promotional materials has become increasingly significant with the growth of the Internet and its multiplicity of Web sites that now advertise tourist attractions, including those that depict indigenous cultures in Canada as well as in other post-colonial states.[16] As John Urry argues, contemporary tourism is "literally constructed in our imagination through advertising and the media" (13).[17] Urry's observation thus raises the question of how depictions of attractions in travel ads compare with what is actually in place at them for tourists (that is, it raises the question of the attraction as it is represented in ads versus the attraction itself as a site of representation).

To pursue one such comparison, I want to return to the Polar Bear Express and consider how the ads I saw for this attraction compared with what I experienced when I took this trip in the early 1990s. At this time, a widely distributed ad for this attraction promised "a trip through time and tradition" in Canada's James Bay frontier, as well as the opportunity to ride in a "real freighter canoe" and "taste authentic fresh-baked bannock in a teepee."[18] The ad's text also juxtaposed references to the area's (English) history, its natural environment, and its local aboriginal peoples. As in many travel ads, First Peoples were depicted pursuing activities widely thought of as "traditional" ones that persist from the past, like making bannock in a teepee or piloting freighter canoes, and it was these sorts of activities that were inscribed as "authentic," or "real." In this way the ad's written text worked to locate First Peoples primarily in Canada's past, as part of its heritage, and also as part of the natural world encountered by European settlers, thus echoing romantic nations of indigenous peoples as "Noble Savages." Furthermore, the ad's visual image reinforced this unproblematic view that aboriginal people were pursuing their authentic practices in the north and were eager to share them with patrons on the Polar Bear Express. In the ad, for example, a smiling female tourist was depicted in an Indian teepee tasting bannock prepared by a Cree woman who appeared content to serve her.

What I and other passengers on the Polar Bear Express experienced was considerably more complex, if not entirely at odds with this ad's happy scene. After a five-hour ride through Canada's boreal forest, we arrived in the small northern town of Moosonee where we could visit the local church, an educational centre, a museum, a reconstructed Hudson's Bay post, and various commercial shops. Many of us were met at the train by local tours that took us by bus to these attractions and then to a boat that crossed the river to the aboriginal reserve of Moose Factory. Here another tour bus took us not to the residential area of the reserve, but to a "park" with reconstructed historic build-ings and the "ancient church" that was marked in the ad.[19] Our next stop was a hall on the edge of the residential section of the reserve where refreshments were for sale and where we could visit the prom-ised teepee, in which Indian women were cooking bannock. The teepee was clearly there for tourists, while the permanent houses of Moose Factory were in view just beyond this stop. After visiting Moose Factory, I was one of a dozen or so tourists who spent the night in one of the two local motels in Moosonee so that we could explore on our own. The others boarded the train in the late afternoon for the long ride back south. Many had purchased Native crafts, in some cases directly from First Peoples, although other shops that tourists visited were non-aboriginal enterprises.

Not only was this particular tour of Moosonee and Moose Factory a short one for most visitors, but its primary focus was the area's past, which was being represented for the most part in a Eurocentric and romantic way. To be sure, there were some attractions where messages about the current lives of First Peoples were directed towards tourists. For example, in the reconstructed historic park adjacent to Moose Factory there was an exhibit organized by a local Cree woman on the contemporary significance of powwows, and inside the hall adjacent to the bannock tent, Cree were distributing pamphlets about their protest of a local hydroelectric project. And, importantly, for those of us who stayed overnight, there were opportunities for a closer look at the area and more sustained interactions with both aboriginal and non-aboriginal local residents.

Tourist Attractions as Sites/Sights of Representation

I do not mean to suggest that tourists be given greater access to the residential areas of aboriginal communities such as Moose Factory. No doubt limiting organized tours to the outskirts of a community's residential area can minimize the obtrusive effects that tourists too often have on local people. Rather, I want to distinguish such issues regarding access from those regarding representation in order to focus on the kinds of meanings that are signified through tourism.

As Jonathan Culler observes, tourists are the "accomplices of semiotics," because as they travel they read the meanings of "cities, landscapes and cultures as sign systems" (128). But such meanings do not simply arise at the moment of encounter between tourists and tourism sites. Instead, tourists leave home with ideas that are deeply entrenched in their own cultures as well as perspectives that derive from their class and gender locations and their personal biographies. Not only do tourists draw upon this *bricolage* of culturally constructed beliefs to make sense of their encounters, but in marketing objects and experiences for tourism, operators tap into these same widely held ideas in order to make their products appealing. For Western tourists, such widely held ideas about First Peoples and about travel include the very ones that have come to inform the arguments of state tourism officials, including the presumption that aboriginal peoples preserve an "authentic" past through their "traditional" or "heritage" forms, and the presumption that through their encounters with such forms tourists can access this past. Like the producers of travel ads, operators employ written and visual representational conventions specific to tourism in order to evoke these ideas (Blundell, "Take Home").[20] They encourage tourists to translate one system of meaning into another, so that the marketed product—for example, an encounter with a "traditional" aboriginal form such as a bannock teepee—comes to stand for a tourist's values, desires, and other feelings—for example, the desire to experience the past.

However, such a focus on the "traditional" in cultural tourism can have implications for the ways that tourists interpret (other) contemporary forms. The bannock teepee at Moose Factory exemplifies my concern here, given the way it is privileged as a site of authentic Cree culture, both in travel ads for the Polar Bear Express and as a tourist destination. My point here is not to question the authenticity of the ban-nock teepee; as Kenneth Little points out, "Denigrating tourist produc-tions as inferior and inauthentic originals seems not to be a very useful thing to do" (160). What is more useful is a questioning of "how authenticity as a category is produced." In the case of Moose Factory's bannock teepee, I want to suggest that when it is privileged as a site/sight of authentic Cree culture, tourists may be discouraged from interpreting (other) contemporary Cree forms as (equally) authentic, and interpret them instead as signs of assimilation or cultural loss (for example, the permanent houses that they see just beyond the bannock teepee). Therefore, while directing tourists towards "traditional" forms like the bannock teepee may be an acceptable trade-off for local people who wish to keep tourists at bay, such a strategy may run the risk of reinforcing tendentious meanings about First Peoples.

MIXED MESSAGES

Not all tourists accept tendentious views of First Peoples; some bring to bear more informed views as well as an attentiveness to alternative mes-sages about First Peoples that may also be directed towards them as they tour (Urry 11-12). Consider, for example, the "mixed messages" that American tourists may get when they visit Vancouver. One of Vancouver's most popular attractions is the Museum of Anthropology at the University of British Columbia. Here visitors see West Coast Indian objects displayed in ways that emphasize their aesthetic qualities (Clifford). This museum is also famous for its open storage cases, where objects generally hidden away in other museums can be seen. Visitors are encouraged to reach their own understandings of these items by con-sulting documents made available to them. On the museum grounds there are aboriginal architectural forms, including big houses, along with totem poles, accompanied by panels that explain their roles in West Coast aboriginal life. When I visited this museum during the summer of 1992, an aboriginal dance troupe was performing in one of the big houses, thus providing opportunities for insights into their systems of belief. First Peoples were also selling refreshments at the entrance to the museum, where tourists could talk with them in a friendly setting.

But for the many tourists that summer who travelled just a few miles north of Vancouver to Capilano Canyon and the Capilano Suspension

Bridge Park, very different meanings about First Peoples could be read. Attracting thousands of visitors each summer, the park features a suspension bridge across the canyon and a "theme park" with brightly painted totem poles and life-sized carved figures of Indians, most of which wear (stereo)typical Plains Indian attire. The totem poles have been purchased from local aboriginal people by a succession of the non-aboriginal owners of this park over the past sixty years, and a few aboriginal people have been hired to restore the poles and also to make souvenirs in a carving shed at the site. A booklet sold at the park indicates that local First Peoples occasionally perform totem-pole-raising ceremonies for tourists, but during my visit opportunities to learn about local cultures were limited. Most patrons were not on guided tours, and there were no informational panels about local aboriginal cultures. I was among the few to take a tour with a non-aboriginal university student who provided ethnographic context for the site, but also revealed that one of the park's most popular poles had been made by "Chinese artisans," and that the park's "wooden Indians" were carved during the 1930s Depression by two stranded Danish travellers in exchange for food and lodging.[21] Many visitors had their pictures taken alongside these figures; indeed the park seems designed to provide tourists with exotic photo opportunities.

REPRESENTING THE PAST AT CANADIAN MUSEUMS

Capilano Park's portrayal of First Peoples stands in stark contrast to practices at UBC's Museum of Anthropology. Museums are important sites to consider not only because so many of them have exhibits about First Peoples that tourists encounter, but also because museums have been identified in state policy texts as attractions that can be more intensively promoted for cultural tourism.[22] Indeed, financial cutbacks to public institutions over the past decade have led many public museums to frame their goals and their programming in terms of their potential to attract more cultural tourists.[23] Furthermore, in the wake of the controversy surrounding "The Spirit Sings," many of Canada's urban museums have become more sensitive to the ways in which they depict aboriginal cultures, with the result that the past decade has brought more involvement by First Peoples in programming activities and some highly innovative exhibits (Blundell, *Changing Perspectives* 95-99).

Nor is it only the large urban museums that are promoted for cultural tourism. Aboriginal cultures are also depicted at the many small public museums in towns and villages across Canada. Along with other heritage and historic sites, these institutions have become a focus for state tourism policy because of an unexpected finding from the USPTMS that Canada's greatest strength in the American market is the "touring trip," and not, as had been supposed, the "outdoor" or "adventure" trip. Defined by federal tourism officials as "the basic sightseeing experience involving travel to and through areas of scenic beauty, cultural, or historical interest," (Industry 16) the "touring trip" is generally taken by automobile, lasts approximately eight days, and as a trip type it accounts for nearly half of all international pleasure travel in Canada (USPTMS 14-15). By the early 1990s, officials had decided to target the market for the "touring trip" because studies also indicated that this is a market that is particularly interested in cultural attractions, with Americans surveyed by the USPTMS listing "visiting museums and galleries" in their top twenty, sought-after activities (USPTMS Highlights 18, Main Report 45, 47). Market studies also found that "touring trip" tourists plan their trips well in advance and tap into a variety of information sources including travel agents, travel magazines, newspapers, and TV, so they could be reached through marketing activities (USPTMS Highlights 15).

In 1991, en route from Ottawa to the Ontario town of Cochrane to board the Polar Bear Express, I visited several community museums. At the Champlain Trail Museum in Pembroke, Ontario, aboriginal artifacts were on display in cabinets in the central area of a large room. Objects from different time periods were displayed together, along with natural history specimens, recalling the "Cabinets of Curiosities" that became popular in Europe in the sixteenth century and influenced the exhibitionary practices of early nineteenth century human history museums (Ames; Blundell, "Aboriginal Empowerment"). At this museum, the labels for objects were quite cryptic, and there was little information about the cultures of origin of these objects. Along the sides of this large room, other exhibits constructed a Eurocentric view of Canada's history as beginning with "the natural world" of prehistory via an exhibit about whales in the ancient Champlain Sea that once covered this area. The next exhibit portrayed First Peoples at the moment of their "contact" with Europeans, while subsequent exhibits turned to the fur trade, the lumber industry, and finally to the community and domestic life of the area's European settlers (with the first appearance of women via a mannequin holding a feather duster in a simulated general store). After their brief appearance at the start of these displays, First Peoples disappear from the historical sequence, left in the past, with the whales!

Continuing up the road from Pembroke, I arrived at the Mattawa and District Museum, in Mattawa, Ontario. Here, First Peoples were represented as real human beings who were playing a part in the ongoing history of the local Ontario community. A personalized and contextualized view of First Peoples was accomplished through an exhibit about a local Indian man. Thus the caption for a canoe and a painting of an individual identified as Bernard Bastien reads, in part:

> Okimawabipine, Chief White Partridge: One of Mattawa's best known Native people was Bernard Bastien, whose Indian name (Chief White Partridge) was Okimawabipine. He worked most of his life but became a master craftsman....Some of his leather tools, moccasins, gloves and jackets are on display in the museum as part of the current Native exhibit. Bernard was also a master woodworker who made snowshoes, sleds and canoes. A sled and snowshoes can be seen in the museum.

At this museum the specificity of the local was being privileged, rather than being accommodated to a national (universalizing) narrative. This was in contrast to the Champlain Museum, where the Eurocentric exhibits had been designed to show how the local was but one instance of a broader historical sequence.

After viewing these exhibits in Mattawa, I visited the Museum of Northern History at the Sir Harry Oakes Chateau in Kirkland Lake, Ontario. Here, in a small room on the second floor of what was originally the private mansion of a local capitalist, I encountered exhibits about Ontario's Native peoples. Here I saw stone spear points and arrowheads, decoratively arranged in a large picture frame, along with a panel that remarked on the nature of the aboriginal cultures that were first encountered by Europeans. In contrast to the text at Mattawa, with its celebratory tone toward Mr. Bastien, the text here described First Peoples in terms of what they are presumed to lack. Note the Hobbesian tone to a caption on a wall panel regarding the Algonquian Indians of this area that reads, in part:

These people did not cultivate agriculture. They are described as being timid, quiet and harmless. They possessed an intense inherited fear of the Iroquois Indians to the south....The Indians lived in close threat of starvation. They did not cultivate foods but some gathered wild rice berries and nuts.

ALTERNATIVE EXHIBITS PRODUCED BY FIRST PEOPLES

As well as visiting non-aboriginal-run community museums, "touring trip" tourists also visit the growing number of aboriginal communities that operate local museums and cultural centres where their own representations of their cultures can be seen. Consider, for example, the permanent exhibits at the Museum of the Woodland Cultural Centre at Six Nations near Brantford, Ontario. Here the exhibits do not leave First Peoples in the past, but instead represent them within an ongoing and multifaceted historical process. Exhibits make reference to the role of the Mohawk as tall-building steelworkers in the twentieth century and to the importance of a pan-Indian movement in the mid-twentieth century. A mural in one of the museum's exhibit halls, painted by Bill Powless and entitled *A Prehistoric Village*, depicts local aboriginal people as they first encountered Europeans. In the same hall a mannequin wearing a black robe stands in for early Catholic priests in the New World; while this "Black Robe" conveys a foreboding feeling, the large mural in the hall is back-lit, creating a brighter, more hopeful mood. The caption for this mural, which contrasts sharply with the Hobbesian view at the Sir Harry Oakes Museum in Kirkland Lake, in part reads:

> Contact: History begins. The Algonkian and Iroquoian nations neither feared nor felt inferior to the arriving Europeans in the New World. The Algonkian enabled the early French explorers to survive and succeed. The New World and its inhabitants revolutionized the European's worldview by becoming a symbol of hope for Europe, which was now emerging from centuries of overcrowding, poverty and religious persecution. Our earliest evidence of contact in this area was the visit of a Franciscan Friar Father Daillon and his companions in 1626, although Étienne Brûlé most likely wandered through the area in 1615 on a mission for Samuel de Champlain to the Susquehanna. Here Daillon arrives into a village of neutral Iroquoian while [the Indian leader] Souharissen steps out to greet these unusual visitors.

Alternative representations are also in place at Head-Smashed-In Buffalo Jump, a world heritage site in southern Alberta. An interpretive centre has been built at this archaeological site, where aboriginal people drove bison over a cliff. The project was developed by the Alberta government in co-operation with local Blackfoot, who collaborated in the design of the centre's exhibits, work as interpreters at the site, and operate an arts and crafts shop and a restaurant at the centre.[24] Tourists are encouraged to begin their visit to the interpretive centre by taking an elevator to the top of the building, where a door provides access to an outdoor walkway along the top of the cliff. Here visitors take in the view and look down upon the base of the cliff, where the bison remains were found. They then re-enter the building and work their way down through a series of exhibit halls, one stacked above the other. The uppermost halls are named "Napi's World" and "Napi's People"; lower halls depict the buffalo drive and contact with Europeans; and the lowermost hall incorporates part of the actual archaeological excavations at this site. In the upper halls, the written versions of aboriginal myths are beamed down via hidden overhead projectors onto boulders placed throughout the exhibit space. These projected "messages" are held on the boulders for only a few seconds, a technique that captures the attention of visitors. If they fail to read the entire text during this brief showing, they must wait a few seconds for another chance. There are also panels in the halls that provide information regarding the area written in an academic style, such as knowledge about local aboriginal cultures and the archaeological dig itself. Such a representational strategy juxtaposes knowledge derived from Western science and knowledge encoded in local aboriginal oral traditions, without privileging one form of understanding over the other or inscribing aboriginal belief systems within an evolutionary narrative that relegates them solely to the past.

CONCLUSIONS

This example from Head-Smashed-In indicates one way in which First Peoples participate in tourism in order to gain economic benefits as well as control over how their cultures are understood. As we begin a new millennium, tourists in Canada have a growing number of opportunities to visit attractions designed by First Peoples. However, many tourists in Canada continue to experience aboriginal cultures primarily at attractions where there is little, if any, involvement by First Peoples, and often such attractions reconstruct some aspect of the past, where the real "subject" may not be First Peoples at all, but the actions of "discovering" Europeans.

What is at issue here is not that tourist attractions depict the past, but that many do so in ways that reproduce tendentious ideas about First Peoples. As Urry notes, what is at issue is "what is meant by heritage, particularly in relationship to notions of history and authenticity" (109). Too often tourism forms emphasize the so-called "traditional" or "heritage" forms of First Peoples in ways that disconnect them from their former and their contemporary lived contexts. Too often aboriginal forms are employed as mere props in a universal(izing) narrative of Canadian History that obscures the colonial and post-colonial relations that form part of the context within which tourism practices take place. Inscribed within a problematic discourse of authenticity, such representations rehearse tendentious ideas about First Peoples that freeze them in time and offer tourists "heritage fantasies" rather than critical understandings of the past (Urry 109).

As well as this focus on the past, there is also an emphasis in contemporary tourism on seeing, on what Urry calls "the tourist gaze," and this can also constrain the ways that tourists experience aboriginal cultures (Urry; Schulte-Tenckhoff). Therefore, while travel ads promise tourists the chance to experience "authentic" aboriginal cultures, often these promised experiences translate into opportunities to see something, either aboriginal-produced or, as in the case of most souvenirs, as a replica of an aboriginal form. Such experiences occur at specific locales or at performances that are included in individual travel routes or as stops on more structured group tours as tourists move from place to place over relatively short periods of time.[25] And at many attractions, tourists are positioned as passive observers with few opportunities to interact with the materials they confront.

But while many tourists in Canada still encounter First Peoples primarily through the representations of non-aboriginal operators, the past two decades have brought increased involvement by First Peoples in the tourism industry along with calls for more control by them over the way their cultures are promoted for tourism. In recent years, various levels of government have expressed a greater willingness to work more closely with First Peoples, although questions persist regarding how to balance economic goals with those aimed at sustaining the integrity of aboriginal cultural forms. For many aboriginal operators, tourism brings economic benefits and at the same time allows them to depict their cultures in innovative and non-stereotypic ways. In fact, the data at hand indicate that when First Peoples participate in tourism, they are far less likely to represent themselves to tourists as exotic "others" without histories or concerns about their current relations with(in) the Canadian state.

To be sure, there is enormous variability in how First Peoples are participating in tourism, and the ways in which they do so is always mediated by their own local situation, for example, the existence of more urgent needs in some communities, a lack of capital for development and advertising, ambivalent previous experience with tourists, and the complex relations that exist between First Peoples and non-aboriginal organizations such as public museums or between First Peoples and various levels of government.

In conclusion, "aboriginal cultural tourism" in Canada remains both contested terrain and a perceived site of opportunity for First Peoples. There are too many ways in which the policies and practices associated with tourism continue to reproduce inequities between First Peoples and other Canadians. But as First Peoples gain a real say in how their cultures are to be linked with tourism, these relations can be transformed. Clearly, for this potential to be more fully realized, public policies must empower First Peoples to determine how their cultures are directed towards tourists.

NOTES

1 I am grateful to Carleton University and the Social Sciences and Humanities Research Council for support of my research on cultural tourism.
2 For early discussions of cultural tourism see Smith.
3 For example, see discussion of cultural tourism in *A New Tourism for Canada: Can We Meet the Challenge*, prepared in 1988 by the Heritage Canada Foundation for the "Making Connections" Conference referred to below in note 5.
4 For statistics regarding international and Canadian tourism revenues see Blundell, "Riding the Polar Bear Express."
5 See *Making Connections*. Attended by representatives of government agencies, non-governmental organizations, and the tourism industry, this

conference was held as a result of the signing, in 1985, of a Memorandum of Understanding by the three federal agencies of Tourism Canada, Secretary of State (Multiculturalism), and the Department of Communications, in which they agreed "to develop effective and productive liaison between tourism and culture [and] take advantage of Canada's cultural diversity and assets through increased tourism activity" (8). See also John Harp.

6　For example, in 1989 Tourism Canada sent a representative to Miami to attend the first International Cultural Tourism conference where the potential of cultural tourism was heralded. See "Tourism Official Cites Growing Appeal of Culture-Related Travel," *Travel Weekly*, 18 May 1989, p. 16.

7　See also Taylor.

8　*The Challenges of Tourism Product Development: A Discussion Paper*, prepared by Tourism Canada for a Minister's Symposium with the Tourism Industry at the Federal/Provincial/Territorial Conference of Tourism Ministers, Calgary, Alberta, March 1988.

9　See Tourism Canada's *Overseas Advertising Plans*.

10　The Government of Canada contributes $65 million annually to the CTC, while private sector partners are reported to regularly match or exceed this amount; see <http://www.canadatourism.com/en/ctc/partner_centre/about/1.html>.

11　The convention was held in Calgary. The objectives of CNATA are set out by Parker in "Aboriginal Tourism." Aboriginal tourism was discussed in several other presentations at this conference, which was sponsored by the Travel and Tourism Research Association—Canada held in Regina in 1992 (see Reid).

12　Attractions were identified between the late 1980s and early 1990s in travel ads and other promotional materials produced by various levels of government, aboriginal communities, and the private sector.

13　By the early 1990s there were more than six hundred aboriginal-operated arts and crafts outlets across Canada as well as many hundreds (and probably thousands) of non-aboriginal-operated commercial outlets that sell items by, or about, First Peoples.

14　By the early 1990s, there were 351 events being advertised for tourism in Canada, of which 141 were powwows.

15　Two hundred and forty-nine such attractions were being advertised by the early 1990s.

16　As one of many examples that could be provided, see the Web site for Nunavut, which provides information on a range of attractions that depict aboriginal history and cultures: <http://www.nunavut.worldweb.com/index.html>.

17　As have other theorists of tourism, Urry also comments on the importance that photography has come to have in contemporary tourism: "Involved in much of tourism is a kind of hermeneutic circle. What is sought for in a holiday is a set of photographic images, as seen in tour company brochures or on TV programmes. While the tourist is away, this then moves on to a tracking down and capturing of those images for oneself. And it ends up with travelers demonstrating that they really have been there by showing their version of the images that they had seen originally before they set off" (140).

18 For example, this ad appeared in the June 1992 issue of the auto club magazine *Leisureways* (35); it is reproduced in Blundell, "Riding." See also the Web site for this attraction at <http://www.puc.net/pbx.htm>.

19 Tourists can also cross the river to Moose Factory in small aluminum boats on hire from local residents (the "freighter canoes" promised in the ad).

20 There is now an extensive body of work that identifies the conventions that work such ideological meanings in textual forms. For example, regarding conventions that link ethnicity and travel in tourism forms see Albers and James. See also Hall.

21 Historical details regarding this attraction were also provided in a booklet entitled *Capilano Suspension Bridge and Park: A Photo History* sold at the park's gift shop.

22 See, for example, discussion in *Challenges in Tourism Product Development* 24.

23 See, for example, Kelly 61, and MacDonald. See also Grant.

24 For the history of this project, see Brink, "Blackfoot and Buffalo Jumps," and Ed Sponholz, "Head-Smashed-In Buffalo Jump." See also the following Web page, which includes a diagram of the layout of the site <http://www.head-smashed-in.com/frmcentre.htm>.

25 In *U.S. Spring/Summer Advertising Plan* 1992/1993 1, Tourism Canada estimates that in 1991 U.S. travellers to Canada "stayed an average of 4.1 nights and spent approximately $303 per visit." Sixty-five percent of domestic travellers in Canada in 1988 made trips of four nights or less, according to Statistics Canada, Overlay 8.

WORKS CITED

Albers, Patricia C., and William R. James. "Travel Photography: A Methodological Approach." *Annals of Tourism Research*, 15 (1988): 123-58.

Ames, Michael. *Cannibal Tours and Glass Cases*. Vancouver: U of British Columbia P, 1992.

Blundell, Valda. "Aboriginal Empowerment and Souvenir Trade in Canada." *Annals of Tourism Research* 20 (1993): 64-87.

_____. *Changing Perspectives in the Anthropology of Art*. Ottawa: Golden Dog, 2000.

_____. "Echos of a Proud Nation: Reading Kahanawke Powwow as Post-Oka Text." *Canadian Journal of Communications* 18.3 (1993): 333-50.

_____. "Riding the Polar Bear Express and Other Encounters Between Tourists and First Peoples in Canada." *Journal Of Canadian Studies* 30.4 (Winter 1995-96): 28-51.

_____. "Take Home Canada: Representations of Aboriginal Peoples as Tourist Souvenirs." *The Socialness of Things: Essays on the Semiotics of Objects*. Ed. Stephen Riggins. Berlin: Mouton de Gruyter, 1994. 251-84.

Brink, Jack. "Blackfoot and Buffalo Jumps: Native People and the Head-Smashed-In Project." *Alberta* 3.1 (1992): 19-43.

Clifford, James. "Four Northwest Coast Museums: Reflections." *Exhibiting Cultures*. Ed. Ivan Karp and Steven Lavine. Washington, DC: Smithsonian, 1991. 212-54.

_____. *The Predicament of Culture: Twentieth Century Ethnography, Literature and Art*. Cambridge: Harvard UP, 1988.

Culler, Jonathan. "Semiotics of Tourism." *American Journal of Semiotics* 1.1-2 (1981): 127-40.

Grant, Laurence. *Federal Museum Policy, Working Paper 1*. Centre for Research on Culture and Society: Carleton U, 1991.

Hall, Stuart. *Representation: Cultural Representations and Signifying Practices*. London: Sage, 1997.

Harp, John. "Culture, the State, and Tourism: State Policy Initiatives in Canada, 1984-1992." *Culture and Policy: Post-Colonial Formations*. Ed. Tony Bennett, Graeme Turner and Michael Volkerling. Institute for Cultural Policy Studies: Griffith University, Queensland, Australia, 6.1 (1994): 183-211.

Hewison, Robert. *The Heritage Industry: Britain in a Climate of Decline*. London: Methuen, 1987.

Kelly, Robert. "Cultural Tourism: A Contradiction in Terms." *Interpretation and Tourism Ottawa 1988: Proceedings on National Heritage Interpretation*. Ottawa, 1988: 57-61.

Little, Kenneth. "On Safari: The Visual Politics of a Tourist Representation." *The Varieties of Sensory Experience*. Ed. David Howes. Toronto: U of Toronto P, 1991. 148-63.

MacCannell, Dean. "Reconstructed Ethnicity: Tourism and Cultural Identity in Third World Communities." *Annals of Tourism Research* 22 (1984): 375-91.

_____. *The Tourist: A New Theory of the Leisure Class*. 2nd ed. New York: Schocken, 1989.

MacDonald, George, and Stephen Alsford. "Museums as Bridges to the Global Village." *A Different Drummer: Anthropology from a Canadian Perspective*. Ed. B. Cox, J. Chevalier, V. Blundell. Ottawa: Carleton UP, 1992. 41-48.

Myers, Marybelle. "The Glenbow Affair." *Inuit Art Quarterly* 3.1 (1988): 12-16.

Overton, James. "Promoting the Real Newfoundland: Culture as Tourist Commodity." *Studies in Political Economy* 4 (1980): 115-37

Parker, Gary. "Aboriginal Tourism: From Perception to Reality." Reid 14-20.

Parry, Gwyneth. *Indigenous Cultural Tourism: an Examination of Process and Representation in Canada*. MA Thesis, Carleton U, 2000.

Reid, Laurel, ed. *Community and Cultural Tourism Conference Proceedings*. Brock U: Travel and Tourism Research Association, 1992. 14-20.

Schulte-Tenckhoff, Isabelle. "Potlatch and Totem: The Attraction of America's Northwest Coast." *Tourism: Manufacturing the Exotic*. Copenhagen: IWGIA Document 6, 1988.

Smith, Valene, ed. *Hosts and Guests: The Anthropology of Tourism*. Philadelphia: U of Pennsylvania P, 1977.

Spoonholtz, Ed. "Head-Smashed-In Buffalo Jump: A Centre for Cultural Preservation." *Alberta* 3.1 (1992): 45-59.

Taylor, Gordon. "The United States Pleasure Travel Market." *Journal of Business Research* 18.1 (1989): 1-79.
"Traveller's Tales." *Globe and Mail* June 11, 1992: A18.
Urry, John. *The Tourist Gaze.* London: Sage, 1990.

GOVERNMENT DOCUMENTS

Government of Canada. *Making Connections: A Report of a National Conference on Tourism, Culture and Multiculturalism.* 1988.
Harp, John. "Culture, the State and Tourism: State Policy Initiatives in Canada, 1984-1992." *Culture and Policy.* 6.1 (1994): 183-211.
Heritage Canada Foundation. *A New Tourism for Canada: Can We Meet the Challenge?* A discussion paper commissioned by the Department of Communications for the National Conference on Tourism, Culture and Multiculturalism—Making Connections. Montreal, April 1988. Prepared by Jim Mountain, program director, Regional Heritage Tourism. 1988.
Industry, Science and Technology Canada. *Tourism on the Threshold.* Minister of Supply and Services Canada. 1990.
Industry, Science and Technology Canada in conjunction with Tourism Canada. *U.S. Spring/Summer Advertising Plan.* 1992/93.
Kelly, Robert. "Cultural Tourism: A Contradiction in Terms." *Proceedings of Interpretation and Tourism Ottawa/88. A National Conference on Heritage Interpretation.* 1988: 57-61.
Longwoods Research Group Ltd. and the Minister of Regional Industrial Expansion. "U.S. Pleasure Travel Market: Canadian Potential: Main Report and Highlights Report." (USPTMS) 1986.
Tourism Canada. *The Challenges of Tourism Product Development: A Discussion Paper.* 1988.
_____. *Overseas Advertising Plans.* 1989.

WEB SITES

<http://www.puc.net/pbx.htm>.
<http://www.nunavut.worldweb.com/index.html>.
<http://www.canadatourism.com/en/ctc/partnercentre/about/1.html>.
<http://www.head-smashed-in.com/frmcentre.html>.

LAURA SECORD MEETS THE CANDYMAN: THE IMAGE OF LAURA SECORD IN POPULAR CULTURE

Christine Boyko-Head

I n June of 1813, Laura Secord walked twenty miles through the woods from her home in Queenston to Beaverdams, Ontario, in an area now commonly called the Niagara region. Her purpose was to warn the British-Canadian troops stationed there of an impending surprise attack by the Americans. Despite this display of courage and loyalty, Secord's action was merely a footnote to the War of 1812.

Today, the name "Laura Secord" is a living part of Canada's heritage. Like Henry Hudson, Sam Steele and Louis Riel, Secord has joined a select group of historical figures energized by popular culture. Generations of dramatists, poets, biographers, novelists and journalists have perpetuated the Secord legend and kept it alive in the imaginations of diverse Canadian communities.[1] Viewed collectively, the various artistic and popular representations transform Second's historical action into a national myth. As such, "Laura Secord" is a monument within Canadian mythology. Her icon is also part of a cultural process whereby ritual playfulness engages various communities and their subgroups, at different levels and different periods. Through an examina-

Notes on pages 77-78.

tion of three Laura Secord Candy Company advertisements—"War Savings Certificate," "The Story of Laura Secord" and "The Three Cameos"—I argue that Laura Secord's longevity in Canadian iconography can be attributed to ritual play whereby her image, imagery and legend transgress geography and social position. As a result, "Laura Secord" functions as an indicator of social, cultural and political environments with the capability of erasing ideological boundaries.

Each advertisement by the Laura Secord Candy Company promotes a revised, artistic performance or enactment of the Secord legend. These diverse, fictitious framings of the same social drama reveal that, being a homogeneous event, the socio-historical moment is a rich interplay of contradictions. The contradictions inherent to the social moment, likewise, are contained within the subsequent socio-historical emergences of the cultural symbol. Laura Secord's image becomes the location for a convergence of the "actual" event with a virtual representation. This blending of the actual rite of passage with a creative depiction of the rite—in itself a rite of passage for the spectator—contains the transgressive potential of ritual's excess and privilege. While the advertisements legitimate the power of their respective dominant cultures, the imagery invites a voluntary exploration of alternative readings that can take the reader beyond the regulatory functions of social organization. Within this invitation lies the transgressiveness where, as Turner argues, "something new may be generated. The performance transforms itself...the rules may 'frame' the performance, but the 'flow' of action and interaction within that frame may conduce to hitherto unprecedented insights and even generate new symbols and meanings, which may be incorporated into subsequent performances" (*Anthropology* 79).

Furthermore, popular culture's privileged position outside (so-called) high art's authoritative structure empowers those afflicted by Culture. Popular culture's transgressive potential, here demonstrated by the Secord icon and imagery, is synergized by ritual play's sacred and secular nature, which is capable of temporally crossing, ideologically erasing and psychically restructuring borders and boundaries.

Briefly, Laura Secord's transformation from a historical figure to a cultural symbol began almost seventy-five years after her woodland trek and illustrates the artists' desire to capture the story. In 1887, the request for a monument in memory of Secord coincided with Sarah

Anne Curzon's closet drama, *Laura Secord: The Heroine of 1812*. Prior to this, mention of Secord's journey appeared in the occasional history text as a discussion of the war. In fact, the first embellishment of the event—the cow—appeared in W. F. Coffin's *The War of 1812 and Its Moral* (1864). The story's anecdotal quality still overshadows its historical significance in educational textbooks. Curzon's drama, then, was the first attempt at a rounded portrayal of the woman and her experiences. Dismissed by current critics as a drama of poor quality and overzealous sentimentalism, it nevertheless ignited the popular imagination of its time.[2] The image suffered a temporary setback in the 1930s beginning with Merrill Denison's radio play, *Laura Secord* (1931). It is a double-edged drama combining historical seriousness with parodic undertones. Denison's Secord is a heroine by accident and is clearly demarcated in a domestic world.[3] The audience—because of Denison's portrayal—may tend to agree. The challenge to the Secord image's authenticity continues with *The Story of Laura Secord: A Study in Historical Evidence* (Wallace) and reaches its comedic climax in 1936 when a moustache "appears" on the upper lip of the portrait of Laura Secord hanging in the Ontario Legislature. The shadow was from the portrait underneath the Secord image. Not until the 1940s does the Secord image regain and hold its stature as a symbol of Loyalist womanhood. More recently, the Heritage Moment commercial on Secord depicts the physical hardship she endured in carrying the message to Colonel Fitzgibbon. However, its closing statement and image highlights the Mohawk tribe's role in the war over that of Laura's personal courage and sacrifice.

The longevity of the Secord image and its fluctuating popularity shows how symbols reflect cultural alterations within and between changing historical communities. Since cultural symbols are adorned with a community's values, systems of meaning and significance, changes to the latter ultimately affect the symbolic representation of the former.

"Laura Secord" has tremendous legendary power since references to her historical action can be interpreted as a metaphorical rite of passage where the actual woman is misidentified with other temporary roles her image is creatively made to perform. Her mythological journey as an icon takes on ritual significance as the cultural symbol moves geographically as well as psychologically from a private/domestic realm to a public/political one. Through a similar misidentification, various communities can manipulate the symbol to reflect, invert, subvert and even challenge current cultural trends. This interchange between communities and symbol also allots the symbol the power to manipulate the values and beliefs of community groups.

The belief that a ritual action can re-evaluate and restructure society differs from the traditional view of rituals that labels them as conservative and resistant to change. Ronald Grimes observes that "ritual had been portrayed as the most backward-looking, foot-dragging of cultural forms. It was hardly capable of acting on society; rather it was a 'repository' or 'reflection' of it. Always it was passive, inert" (Grimes 144). According to Grimes, the link between social drama and performance shows ritual to be a "cultural 'agent', energetic, subversive, creative, socially critical" (144). Ritual's transgressive dynamism—mirrored in the creative tension between signifier and signified, and reader and text—is responsible for popular culture's shifting energy. Within this performative frame, the image of Laura Secord becomes polysemous, either challenging or upholding cultural values by playing with and against accepted systems of meaning.

Generally, advertising upholds cultural beliefs and practices, yet it can also play with the symbols, even though advertising targets groups and also motivates new, untapped markets. The misidentifying playfulness of cultural symbols allows them the flexibility necessary to engage different readers at different levels of signification. According to Turner, ritual playfulness "although 'spinning loose' as it were…reveals to us…the possibility of changing our goals and, therefore, the restructuring of what our culture states to be reality" (Turner, *Anthropology* 168). Viewed as a cultural symbol, Laura Secord is capable of (re)establishing codes of social conduct, (re)interpreting Canadian cultural and political life, and (re)structuring the way Canadians envision themselves and their place in society.

All Secord representations promote an anglicized, national self-awareness that contradicts the myth that Canadians are patriotically passive. They do not, however, promote uniform gendered messages in relation to nation. For instance, Curzon's closet drama featuring Secord writes women into history while furthering the writer's feminist agenda; Denison's dramatic piece illustrates a backlash against such politics. The Laura Secord Candy Company's advertisements examined here are subtler in their use of gender politics. As I will specify later, the advertisements' popular, commercial framework restricts the icon's transgressive playfulness and speaks to a preferred reader who subscribes to the traditional image of women, regardless of the different periods (1917, 1951, 1993) represented by the three ads analyzed here. But the element of play is never univocal. The popular promotional frame also allows discriminating or resisting readers of the three ads—especially those readers engaged in feminist politics—to interpret the cameos as either memorials to women's past oppression or their continued manipulation in popular media.

An analysis of any cultural symbol cannot ignore the influence of economics and cultural politics on a popular text. Since an advertisement's purpose is to stimulate and manipulate consumer spending, such patterns are inexplicably associated with lifestyle behaviour. Yet, according to Ioan Davies, British and American popular theorists overlook economic factors by reading the popular "in relation to a conception of culture which [is] independent of economics and, to some extent, politics" (121). Victor Turner's concepts of ritual play merge with these ideas by arguing that mythic symbols are formed by, and are formative of, their respective cultural and economic communities. The three candy company advertisements demonstrate how the frolicking of ritual play with consumer values can be held accountable for the national, commercial success of a regional, historical figure.

In the candy company's eighty-nine-year history, the Secord icon has been changed twice from the original, in 1950 and 1993. Each of the icons displays a different, fictitious cameo of Secord, and together they demonstrate the symbol's subversive potential. Initially, by merging the company's image with imperialist ideals, the "War Savings Certificate" (circa 1917) (fig. 2) displays the economic advantages of Canada's then colonial position. The second advertisement (fig. 3) was created in the 1950s as a promotional flyer distributed to schools and explicitly links the stereotype of the dutiful woman with a new Canadian nationalism based on the concept of continentalism. This concept signalled the nation's separation from British colonialism and its easy absorption into a "continental," but subordinate, relationship with the United States. The candy company's advertisements embed the product in what Leiss calls "a symbolic context that imparts meaning to the product beyond its constituent elements or benefits" (244). In both cases, political trends of the respective periods are associated with the candy company in order to establish a relationship between the product, abstract social values and the consumer. Furthermore, Canada's political position as a colonial Other is used to expand the ad's denotation, thus enlarging the reader's interpretation of the product's qualities, which are then misidentified by the consumer as cultural information.

The most controversial of the three advertisements is the company's 1993 campaign in which the three cameo icons are juxtaposed in a single ad (fig. 1). This ad ran in various Canadian magazines.[4] Placing the two previously adopted cameos beside the new (1990s) icon splits the Secord image from public politics and immerses it in gender politics with woman as a divided self or Other. Both the historical and the legendary Secord are effaced. By linking the contemporary obsession with eternal youth and beauty with chocolate's oral gratification, the ad equates woman with fantasy image and pleasure with indulgence. This equation, then, reflects the common cultural values of a male-centred society that denies women full selfhood and instead defines them as commodities whose function is to fulfil male desire.

The 1993 ad's narrative technique reinforces an internalized male-oriented message by alluding to candy's role as a luxury item that signifies a link between political status and sexual power. The main text under the cameos reads: "It could be the hazelnuts from Rome. It might be the ripe cherries. Some would say the toasted coconut. Or maybe it's simply that Laura Secord chocolate is always fresh." The food imagery appeals to the reader's desire for oral gratification, thereby exoticizing the candy while eroticizing the Secord image. The metaphorical connection between Rome and romance, coconut and the foreign or exotic, and ripe cherries and virginity, suggests, as Rosalind Coward has argued, that "the desire for sexual relations is like the desire for food" (87). By creating this "delicious" feminine imagery, the ad presents woman as a consumable object of desire—thus commodifying the Laura Secord myth—and perpetuates the cultural belief that most women are insignificant and invisible in the public realm.

The advertisement's erotic connotations and Laura's deviance from the norm are introduced in the bold type at the top. "There must be something in the chocolate" suggests a secret ingredient that differentiates not only Laura the war veteran but also Laura Secord candy and its mood-altering attributes from other confectionery brands. The three icons in the 1993 Secord candy ad are framed and posed in a manner that differs little from pornographic representations of women that fragment women's bodies in order to fetishize them. First, their limbs are hidden or "bound" by the antique frames as well as by the marketing frame, presenting them as sexual fantasies. Second, their gaze presupposes a male voyeur. While only the 1950s icon looks seductively at the viewer, the 1993 icon is seductive in her vulnerability. Her seeming unawareness and the exposure of her youthful neck and upper chest suggest an invitation for the male predator to "taste" her "sweetness." The cloistered, maternal appearance of the 1913 cameo does not arouse, consciously, the same sexual temptations, yet this icon's averted gaze implies the vulnerability of all women to the male gaze, hence, male ownership. Third, one has only to open or "unclothe" the 1913 or 1993 box to possess the bite-size, fragmented pieces of female "goodness."

Fig. 1. Three cameos advertising campaign, 1993.

While the 1993 icon is directed primarily at a preferred male reader, the campaign cleverly uses psychical "lack" and desire to appeal to female readers. The line "What makes ours the best chocolate you can give or get?" invites women to participate in this male fantasy but only by internalizing subordinate images of women. The ad titillates both genders by claiming it can satisfy their desires. The sexual appeal aimed at male readers becomes a physiological illicitness for female readers searching for the elixir that will bring them the gift of eternal youth. By juxtaposing women's fear of aging and mortality with men's desire for female youth and beauty, the ad suggests both sexes want different yet similar objects. These objects are codified in the list of ingredients and posit a relationship between food, sexual gratification and women. Women's selfhood is reduced by this equation: their desire exists to fulfil male desire. But these images are possibilities only. The slogan "Whatever it is, it's working. Look what it's done for Laura" highlights advertising's reliance on "floating signifiers" that speak to diverse consumers. In the end, however, the ad encourages the same gender stereotyping exploited in pornography (as well as mainstream artefacts). According to Coward, pornography and food imagery "are creating and indulging 'pleasures' which conform or trap men and women in their respective positions of power and subordination" (102). The advertisement, then, upholds patriarchal values and traps women in subordinate conditions by disguising sexual fantasy in Laura Secord's altered historical image (itself still only a reference to the real woman).

The candy company's commodification of the historical Secord reflects a cultural process that perpetuates patriarchal ideology by reinforcing the polarization between subject/object or male/female. Even the earlier advertisements controlled and subordinated the Secord myth by associating it with contemporaneous political contexts that reflect a male code of significance. The Secord myth's challenge to patriarchal values is negated by the discourses of all three advertisements. By transforming Laura into a representative of specific social interactions—the dutiful woman or the fantasy woman—she is written out of the historical narrative.

In selecting the name of Laura Secord for his company, Frank P. O'Connor ignored Laura's resemblance to the "devouring mother" archetype. The Secord myth clearly states that Laura offered the sanctuary of her home to the enemy only to betray his trust. Artistically, she is portrayed as a maternal figure who transgresses the domestic realm through masquerade. By ritually "playing" at the feminine, she successfully invades the male's public sphere rather than satisfying his desire. If the Secord advertisements—especially the 1993 three-cameo ad—suggest an association between gender, transgression and the product, it is unintentional. In fact, great lengths have been taken to hide the woman's subversive behaviour: Secord is ignored historically, then maternalized artistically, and finally eroticized culturally.

The three separate advertisements disclose that cultural images must reflect changes in the contemporaneous public if they are to remain popular and competitive. But these images, all alterations, are contained within a playful ritual—the self-consciously fabricated print ad—that invites the consumer to read with or against the grain of imagery to challenge the prevailing literal message. This playfulness allows readers to actualize systems of meaning by engaging with the Other. Simultaneously, the imaginary, often naturalized world of the advertisement maintains its constructed status; any offensive message can be excused by its fiction.

The depth to which society has internalized patriarchal values and misogynist iconography is evident in the public's outcry against the 1993 campaign. According to Barbara Flewwelling, communications manager at Laura Secord, customers' calls and letters criticized the ad for its inability to accept a woman's aging process.[5] Customers did not want to see "their" Laura portrayed as a Kate Moss or a *Baywatch* girl. The public's negative response, then, was not over the text's illicit male fantasy, perpetuating female subordination; rather, the public apparently were disturbed by the juxtaposition of the three cameos with their uncomfortable reference to the aging process.

The cameos are supposed to represent the same woman at different periods in her life. However, these are not actual photographs taken from a family album, but illustrations, revealing the premise that popular culture is, as Ioan Davies discusses, "the study of our past articulations" (120). Thus, the cameos say more about the social ideology of the times (the 1990s) than about the actual product. According to Davies, problems arise as readers of popular culture *misidentify* themselves as being in this alternative, and usually more exciting, state. However, what Davies views as a problematic escape into cultural fantasy corresponds with the Secord myth's—and ritual's—transgressive potential, where "to read" the Other is to overpower society's restrictions on the self, because it is from within the locus of the Other that women can subvert its marginalizing tendencies. This "reading against the grain" is possible even for the sexist 1993 advertisement.

Misidentification with the product's image is how Barbara Flewwelling explained customer objections to the 1993 ad: "The public has claimed Laura as their own and any changes to the image made by the company can be taken personally by some customers." This personal reading may be problematic for ad agencies. Nevertheless, it is encouraged by advertising discourse, for example, in the frequent use of first- and second-person pronouns, and a gossipy conversational tone. The fact that the Laura Secord Candy Company now advertises exclusively in print media—they briefly experimented with radio and television advertising in the late 1980s—enhances the interchange between reader and image, since newspaper copy is singularly received but discussed collectively. Though the candy company won an award for the 1993 ad, according to Flewwelling, it is not proud of the campaign, indicating that public reaction and the subsequent buying power of consumers outweigh peer review. Also, while individuals may be aware privately of their personal insignificance and fragmentation in the flow of history and time, they do not want an advertising agency to expose their misidentification with a commercialized Other.

Undoubtedly, the candy company popularized the Secord myth and made it accessible to those who would not have read the early poems or dramatic texts featuring this historical woman. But the company's embarrassment over the 1993 campaign reveals that the drive motivating its appropriation and popularization of the myth differs from that of past poets and playwrights. While artists may be retrieving, rewriting and reforming cultural ideas, commercial icons or imagery initially reflect conservative consumer practices. O'Connor apparently felt that the company name had "better be that of a woman…because womanhood suggests homecooking, cleanliness, and good taste" (Chalmers 24). The company controlled the Secord symbol's potential by selecting and reorganizing previous artistic embellishments to the myth that best served its marketing strategy, a strategy reinforcing Laura's role as homemaker. Generally, a company's success is based on maintaining a uniform image and keeping a rein on ritual play. Within the corporate world, symbolic heterogeneity can be a playful way around restrictive ideals, examples being Benetton and Calvin Klein commercials. But it can also be disastrous for the company's image if the consumer "plays" the image beyond the company's promotional focus. While manipulating society's modern obsession with youthfulness, the 1993 advertisement expresses a deconstructive message that challenges the consumer's stable and finite world. It does this by suggesting that physical beauty is mere packaging that hides the actual "product." Likewise, the subordination of woman as Other by patriarchal codes is mere packaging, demonstrated in Laura Secord's gender transgression. An expansion of the ad's symbolic interpretation is possible, then, when the reader is aware of the Secord myth and its variants. By recognizing the role narrative techniques play in codifying images, the reader becomes more discriminating, less susceptible to manipulation and more playful with the floating signifiers.

"The 1913 War Savings Certificate" (fig. 2) reveals a less inhibiting marketing approach by highlighting myth's playful potential. This artefact unites the Secord myth's past imperial association with the new Canadian self-awareness discovered during the war years. The advertisement—a 5" x 3" folded pamphlet with red, white and blue strips forming the flag(s)—appropriates the images of Buckingham Palace, the Union Jack, and a smiling soldier, to encourage Canadians to support the war effort. "Laura Secord" is positioned only as the pamphlet's sponsor.

Fig. 2. The 1913 War Savings Certificate.

The visual images of the palace, flag and soldier are strong signals inviting immediate reactions. According to Marc Choko, in that period, "propaganda techniques were not highly developed, the messages not well controlled, and the imagery often naive" (15). This ad, unlike the (1993) three-cameo campaign, is explicit in its message by grouping these individual images and their independent significations, but all within an imperialist equation. The pamphlet's distribution in Canada during World War I further defines this relationship by signifying Canada's role in maintaining imperial power.[6] Since the palace and the flag are distant ideals encouraged in a colonial society, the soldier's smile assists in personalizing these allusive ritual symbols. But even the soldier needs familiarizing since he is represented anonymously, for anonymity is essential if the image is to convey a universal appeal. This appeal, however, is obviously directed at an anglophone readership since the soldier is delineated by his Caucasian-European facial characteristics, which are further defined by his appearance in an imperialist pamphlet sponsored by a company named after a famous Loyalist.

But the advertisement also works as an anglicizing tool for those labelled as Other culturally and politically: that is, new immigrants and Canadians of various backgrounds. There is no denying that Canada was and is a multicultural mosaic, but the meaning of a mosaic culture is controversial, since the traditions of Great Britain dominated the Canadian cultural landscape then. Within the last few decades the idea of subcultures or hyphenated Canadians has been identified as a valid form of wider collectivity. Yet, the legitimization of hyphenated Canadians does not protect them from the racial attitudes and misconceptions of the country's "founding" cultures. According to Kwame Appiah, "Cultural difference undergirds loyalties" (39). During wartime, cultural differences are transformed into issues of national security. Like other Canadian wartime communications, the "War Savings Certificate" visually and narratively negates cultural diversities by asking the multi-ethnic Other to integrate with the dominant Anglo group to end World War I. The flag exercise, then, becomes a means of indoctrinating the Other, or non-Anglo cultures, while emphasizing its marginalization from mainstream culture.

Despite Canada's pluralistic heritage, loyalty to the Empire in the early twentieth century was analogous to Laura's loyalty during the War of 1812. This allegiance was based on British-Canadian national feelings and a conservative desire to preserve the principles of Empire. Furthermore, the soldier utters the slogan "You *too* can serve," which connects both him and the reader with the full mythic significance of Laura Secord. The font style and its positioning at the front of the pamphlet link him to the scripted "Laura Secord" at the back of the sheet. This connection recalls the sentiments of the Loyalist revival in the late 1880s where, according to Carl Berger, "the loyalist tradition gave to Canadian imperialism a domestic and native tone, a feeling that the movement grew out of Canada's own past and was part and parcel of Canadian history" (108). The ad also attaches a foreign war to Canada by linking the conflict of World War I to the homegrown War of 1812 and its heroine.

The slogan highlights the imperialism and nativism by appealing to both British imperialists and Canadian nationalists. The slogan's emphasis ("You *too* can serve") and its proximity to the Anglo-Saxon "everyman" image of the soldier connect him to a Canadian nationalism based not on plurality and national autonomy but on imperial unity and fidelity to the crown. Since the soldier is a free-floating signifier divorced from a specific referential background through his placement on an advertisement, he represents these oppositional ideologies. According to Choko, fundraising through the purchase of government bonds was directed at all members of Canadian society in order to hasten the end of the war. The poem reveals that the pamphlet does not promote one political discourse over another; likewise, the visibility of "Laura Secord" does not exclude women from understanding the message. The propagandist pamphlet attempts to integrate an imperialist tradition with a new Canadian nationalism that is not, pertaining to this issue, gender specific.

Despite the 1913 ad's enforcement of wartime ideology, its hands-on quality leaves room for the subversive potential of play. The ad sends an imperialist message that naturalizes the individual's relationship to the country, making patriotism *every* Canadian's duty. The image of the smiling soldier is as constructed as the mythic, commercialized image of Laura Secord. Both are alienated from their pasts and their histories in order to fulfil an economic and ideological function. The pamphlet, however, discloses this constructed quality by an interactive gimmick whereby the Union Jack is composed of folding coloured strips. The consumer must follow the instructions to form the flag; the citizen must follow imperialist culture to belong to the Empire. The ad exploits the consumer's desire to experience an imaginary completeness. As the strips form one flag and then another, the idea of manipulation is extended to the concept of nationhood. The interaction between the pamphlet and the reader devours the imperialist-nationalist message by revealing its discursive strategy, whereby the soldier, Laura Secord, Buckingham Palace and the flag(s) are given over to play.

The "War Savings Certificate" is the most telling example of the early commodification of the Secord myth's popular potential for national propaganda. Arguably, the pamphlet transforms the Secord myth's gender play into an overt appeal for participation in the masculine construct of war, although ritually through the reader's interaction with the advertisement. This marketing ploy reveals that the responsibility for nation building, patriotic sentiments and national fervour lies with the individual—whatever their ethnic or gender positions—who must agree to participate in these social and political processes, at least symbolically. While this analysis is apparent today, a consumer of the period would have been prevented from deconstructing the entire communication system he or she helped to create through the symbolic action of folding the flag's strips. The imperialist, masculine agenda can be uncovered only if the reader chooses to acknowledge complicity within a system that asked its members to voluntarily sacrifice their young during World War I in order to preserve an imaginary allegiance to a foreign dynasty.

The Secord advertisement of the 1950s (fig. 3) also demonstrates how limited play within popular culture can both conserve and subvert authoritative ideals. The advertisement's use of the term "continental" to explain the actions of Major Ingersoll (Laura's father) during the Revolutionary War assists in downplaying the demarcation between American republicanism and Canadian allegiance to the Empire. For the sake of selling chocolates, the ad constructs a continental uniformity, amalgamating two diverse nations into one North American state. The ad takes the form of a historical document—it is folded into a booklet complete with eye-catching cover—with the text written by a Canadian historian, Bernard K. Sandwell. Considering the candy company's frequent distribution of promotional material to educational institutions,[7] this format legitimizes its continental version of history. Sandwell's text states that "no changes in the territory on either side" were made, thus eliminating the projection of past grievances into the present. He furthers this unifying dream, stating that "since 1814 the boundary between the two nations of North America had remained undefended." Positioned as a marketing tool with educational value, this "history" is not only "a tribute to the good relations existing between the two countries" but a commentary on the development of the Cold War in the 1950s and the company's attempt to depoliticize our past, within the context of a commercially designed history tool. Akin to the subject's denial of the object's selfhood, Canada is presented as the superpower's Other. Rather than being the source of strength through subversion, Canadians have internalized this subordinate relationship. But to accept the ad as a history text is also to recognize the fabricated aspect of all historical and propagandist narratives.

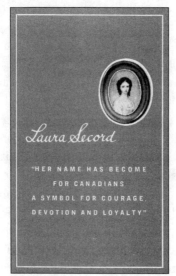

Fig. 3. Ad as historical document in the 1950s.

Furthermore, the reader must make an associative leap from North American history to the Laura Secord Company history, where the word "continental" becomes a political ideal with economic overtones. Here, the chocolates are made from the "finest food obtainable," prepared by "experts in the art of home cooking," making candies "famous for flavour and freshness everywhere." These culinary descriptions—unlike the three-cameo (1993) ad's exoticized descriptions—lack a definite sense of place, with place being a significant aspect of the Canadian struggle over identity. Where are the ingredients and the cooks from? Even the cooks' gender is enigmatic. The ad's "everywhere" becomes a political "nowhere" and a psychical "anywhere," a marked contrast with the British-inflected Canadian identity signified in the "War Savings Certificate." While the imperialist, patriotic appeal of the earlier, wartime advertisement is missing here, the myth's gender politics is present still in the 1950 ad. Submerged within a coherent, monoglot version of history is the reinscription of gender stereotypes. The fact that this recasting of history, and women, was endorsed by the education system's distribution of such material reveals that there was little or no public concern about the effacement of Canadian geography or mythology.[8]

By introducing the concept of "tradition," the advertisement dehistoricizes and depoliticizes Laura's initial transgression of gender roles, naturalizing the ritual symbol's commodification. In the 1990s, this commodification extends to the role of woman through the introduction of the new, younger cameo, feminized further by the portrait's pastel colour. Rejuvenating the previous cameo's brown tones, the new cameo emphasizes a sexually alluring Laura, and undoubtedly reflects our culture's changing values. Possibly viewed as a femme fatale by late-twentieth-century consumers, Laura Secord is no longer the domesticated image that associates the giving of chocolates with wholesome activities. Deeply embedded in our culture is the sense of obligation inherent in the receiving of a gift, and it is this sense that drives the male fantasy. Neither does the image endorse a self-empowered woman who transcends the boundaries of the feminine for higher ideals. Instead, the new Laura whispers of chocolate's mood-altering potential. The slogan "There must be something in the chocolate" short-circuits the symbol's playful excess by trapping women in a sexual-symbolic role as restrictive as the homemaking one of the 1950s. If the image of Laura Secord can indeed be viewed as an indicator of alterations in a culture's social and political life, the candy company's new cameo, when not placed alongside her other representations, signals a regressive view of not only the historical and mythic Laura Secord but of women in general. Yet (and there is almost always qualification in reading such imagery), the slogan and the new cameo can be the site of subversion; the female subject, by submitting to male desires, remains oblivious of the extent to which the symbol has shaped and continues to shape her.

The Laura Secord Candy Company was, and still is, a successful business. Its economic achievement bolstered the image of Frank P. O'Connor, who wrote himself into historical and cultural narratives by appropriating a historical figure for his commercial venture. Undeniably, the company's accomplishments also popularized the Secord legend and its permutations. The dynamic ritual process underlying the artistic representations of the Secord myth and their communal significance were fundamental to O'Connor's economic appropriation. As the Secord image gradually became part of Canadian popular culture, its original universal message, which illustrates the capabilities of individual desire to transgress socially imposed inhibitions and fears, became rooted not in the past of 1812 but in advertising's historic moments. According to William Leiss, advertising "communicates more about the social context in which products are used than about the products themselves...it is a cultural system, a social discourse whose unifying theme is the meaning of consumption" (352).

Advertising discloses culture as its "primary field of content." Within this cultural field also lies the psychical plane where transgressions abound. Popular culture presents potentially polysemous symbols, which, formative of cultural, economic and political environments, can cross, multiply or erase ideological frameworks. Depending on the reader and his or her historical moment, cultural symbols are potential tools of empowerment or codes of power. The longevity of Laura Secord's transgressive image and imagery in Canadian iconography suggests they can be both.

NOTES

1 The frequency of pieces devoted to the Laura Secord story—beginning in 1887 and continuing into the 1930s—indicates an audience eager for information concerning the heroine. See Further Readings.

2 Merrill Denison's representation is markedly different from that of Curzon, who portrays Laura Secord as transgressing gender boundaries only to find herself at the end of the play in a liminal space between her transgressive activity and her expected return to passive inactivity.

3 According to Lacan, "Masquerade...is precisely to play not at the imaginary, but at the symbolic, level." See Lacan, *The Four Fundamental Concepts of Psycho-Analysis* (New York: Norton, 1981) 193.

4. The company advertised nationally as well as regionally in publications such as *Bridal Magazine, Marriage and Mirage* (French Edition) and other wedding publications; ads were also printed in newspapers such as the *Globe and Mail*, the *Toronto Star* and the *Toronto Sun*.

5 Personal interview with The Laura Secord Candy Company's communications manager, Barbara Flewwelling, June 27, 1994.

6 Distribution information on this pamphlet and the 1951 flyer is difficult to obtain. Changes in corporate ownership have complicated archival collection and preservation. While the company can boast of an extensive collection of material, most documents lacked attribution and documentation outlining marketing strategies and the results of those strategies.

7 Promotional material was distributed to educational institutions via their school boards. Laura Secord was not unusual in distributing material in this way. Educational items sponsored by various companies included bookmarks, book jackets, maps, colouring books, etc.

8 The material's content was de-emphasized in comparison to its function in protecting, in the case of book jackets, the school board's investment in textbooks. Teachers accepted, allowed and even encouraged the deface-ment of a Canadian heroine by budding Emily Carrs.

WORKS CITED

Appiah, Kwame Anthony. "Identity–Political not Cultural." *Field Work: Sites in Literary and Cultural Studies*. Ed. Marjorie Garber, Paul B. Franklin, and Rebecca L. Walkowitz. New York: Routledge, 1996. 34-40.

Berger, Carl. *The Power of Sense*. Toronto: U of Toronto P, 1970.

Butler, Judith. "Performative Acts and Gender Construction: An Essay in Phenomenology and Feminist Theory." *Performing Feminisms: Feminist Critical Theory*. Ed. Sue-Ellen Case. Baltimore: Johns Hopkins UP, 1990. 270-82.

Chalmers, Floyd. "Frank P. O'Connor is the Man Behind the Laura Secord Chain." *The Financial*. November 1924.

Choko, Marc. *Canadian War Posters: 1914-1918, 1939-1945*. Ottawa: Meridien, 1994.

Coward, Rosalind. *Female Desires: How They Are Sought, Bought and Packaged*. New York: Grove Weidenfeld, 1984.

Davies, Ioan. *Cultural Studies and Beyond: Fragments of Empire*. London: Routledge, 1995.

Grimes, Ronald. "Victor Turner's Definition, Theory, and Sense of Ritual." *Victor Turner and the Construction of Cultural Criticism*. Ed. Kathleen Ashley. Bloomington: Indiana UP, 1990. 141-46.

Lacan, Jacques. *Ecrits*. Trans. Alan Sheridan. New York: Norton, 1977.

Leiss, William, Stephen Kline and Sut Jhally. *Social Communication in Advertising: Persons, Products & Images of Well-Being*. Toronto: Nelson Canada, 1990.

Sandwell, Bernard K. "The Laura Secord Story." Laura Secord Candy Company.

_____. "There Must Be Something in the Chocolate." Laura Secord Candy Company Scrapbook.

Turner, Victor. *The Forest of Symbols: Aspects of Ndembu Ritual*. Ithaca: Cornell UP, 1967.

_____. *The Anthropology of Performance*. New York: PAJ Publications, 1986.

FURTHER READINGS

Coffin, Will. *1812: The War and Its Moral*. Montreal: Printed by J. Lovell, 1864.

Curzon, Sarah Anne. *Laura Secord: The Heroine of 1812*. 1887. *Canada's Lost Plays*. Vol. 1. Ed. Anton Wagner. Toronto: Canadian Theatre Review Publishing, 1979.

_____. "Memoir of Laura Secord." *Laura Secord and Other Poems*. Toronto: C. Blackett Robinson, 1887.

_____. "The Story of Laura Secord." *The Lundy's Lane Historical Society.* 1891.

Denison, Merrill. *Laura Secord, Henry Hudson and Other Plays.* Toronto: Ryerson, 1931.

Jakeway, Charles. "Laura Secord." 1897. *The Fourth Golden Rule Book.* Toronto: MacMillan, 1915.

Land, R. E. A. "A National Monument to Laura Secord: Why It Should Be Erected." United Empire Loyalists Association of Ontario, 1901.

Machar, Agnes. "Laura Secord." *Lays of the "True North" and Other Canadian Poems.* Toronto: Copp, Clark, 1899.

Mair, Charles. "A Ballad for Brave Women." *Week.* Toronto, June 21, 1888.

McKenzie Ruth. *Laura Secord: The Legend and the Lady.* Toronto: McClelland and Stewart, 1971.

Stephen, Alexander Maitland. "Laura Secord." *Class-Room Plays from Canadian History.* Toronto: Dent, 1929.

Urquhart, Jane. *The Whirlpool.* Toronto: McClelland and Stewart, 1986.

Wallace, W. S. *The Story of Laura Secord: A Study in Historical Evidence.* Toronto: MacMillan, 1932.

Wood, Colonel. Review of "The Story of Laura Secord: A Study in Historical Evidence" by W. S. Wallace. *Canadian Historical Review* March 1932: 65-66.

CANADA POST'S *LE PETIT LISEUR* (THE YOUNG READER): FRAMING A REPRODUCTION

Loretta Czernis

Ozias Leduc was born in St-Hilaire, Quebec, in 1864. He lived in this small town most of his life and travelled outside it only rarely. He visited Paris once briefly in 1897, but he returned to his beloved St-Hilaire to reflect on what he had seen. He had a sense of community responsibility, serving as a school commissioner, church-warden and municipal councillor, and as a committee chairman for his local branch of the Society of St. John the Baptist. Leduc is said to have served his friends, family and town very well. He lived a long and active life, dying in 1955 at the age of ninety-one.

Leduc made his living by decorating churches, having studied church decoration under Adolphe Rho. His renown in Quebec rests on the thirty Catholic churches he decorated over a period of forty-nine years. Thousands have worshipped beneath Leduc's church mural designs, which are intended to inspire believers during reflection and prayer.

Ozias Leduc was, until recently, less well known as a painter of canvasses. The art historian and curator Jean-René Ostiguy has written of Leduc's style: "From 1900 on in his still-lifes, trompe l'oeil realism yielded to Symbolist suggestion" (101). Specific painterly influences include Edward Burne-Jones and Gustave Moreau. Leduc's canvasses were seen by those who went to commercial galleries and to art association and academy shows, but many more spectators saw his church decoration. There was an interesting dynamic in Leduc's professional life. He did "fine art" in his leisure time, creating art objects that were accessible to a very small audience during his lifetime. Those who would have had the opportunity to appreciate Leduc's paintings would have seen religious figures, still-life, landscapes and ordinary people in his canvasses, often illuminated by colours that imitated the effects of real life on stained glass. It is fine art objects that generally interest museums and art galleries. Such objects can serve to bolster and promote galleries, as well as other (related) government and/or corporate interests.

Le petit liseur by Ozias Leduc (1864-1955) National Gallery of Canada, Ottawa © Estate of Ozias Leduc/SODRAC (Montreal) 2001.

This essay highlights a "strip" from the ongoing state-based commodification of art. In this strip a Leduc painting entitled *Le petit liseur* appears to be more accessible by having been transformed into a stamp. Yet access is not the real issue. The painting has been appropriated for the purposes of promoting a version of Canadian culture as sponsored by the federal postal corporation. *Le petit liseur* was selected by Canada Post to become the first stamp in its commemorative series entitled Masterpieces of Canadian Art (1988). As developed by Erving Goffman, the concept of the strip refers to a segment of activity: "A strip is not meant to reflect a natural division made by the subjects of inquiry or an analytical division made by students who inquire; it will be used only to refer to any raw batch of occurrences (of whatever status in reality) that one wants to draw attention to as a starting point for analysis" (10).

Why analyze this particular strip? First, this study follows the traditions of earlier researchers dealing with mechanical reproduction (Benjamin), advertising (Berger) and promotional culture (Wernick). Their research can help us to track as well as to identify some of the ideological features of the reconfiguration of Leduc's painting to Canada Post's stamp. Second, *Le petit liseur* has been lifted out of its historical and artistic context by being transferred via engraving into Canadian stamp format, and it shows the effects of institutional commodification. Third, the impetus for such a stamp series is problematized by this analysis, since the new context in which the painting finds itself is primarily geared towards promoting a version of Canadian culture. The painting's place in regional debate is lost in the stamp, as are Leduc's artistic concerns.

The painting has been made famous by its engraved replica, but the engraved version is not and cannot be said to constitute an exact copy of the original painting. The engraving was designed to reinject body into the image when reduced to stamp size. Engraving is done by inscribing a hard surface using a sharp-pointed tool. In this case, an intaglio print—a printed relief—was the result, produced by means of photogravure, which is "a commercial printing process using resin—or bitumen—coated plates or cylinders, photographically etched or engraved in intaglio" (Lucie-Smith 93). Generating such reproductions involves a significant amount of technical expertise.

Walter Benjamin first published "The Work of Art in the Age of Mechanical Reproduction" in 1936. This classic essay points to significant changes in many art forms as a result of the discovery of techniques of mass reproduction: "Around 1900 technical reproduction had reached a standard that not only permitted it to reproduce all transmitted works of art and thus to cause the most profound change in their impact upon the public; it also had captured a place of its own among the artistic processes" (Benjamin 219-20). Benjamin declared that the status, and even the very existence, of unique historical art objects was being transformed as a result of mass distribution of their replicas. In addition, new art forms were emerging in which nothing like an original could be said to exist. He argued that a replica can only *remind* viewers of an original by acting as its visual referent. It cannot entirely replace the original since a copy can never maintain the "aura" of an original work. The reasons that Benjamin gave for the inadequacy of reproductions also explain important aspects of what he meant by the aura of an original. Reproductions cannot sustain an aura because the original is permanent while copies are transitory, and the eye is unprepared both spatially and conceptually for the original, since it is difficult to access and therefore rarely seen. According to Benjamin, "every day the urge grows stronger to get hold of an object at very close range by way of its likeness, its reproduction" (223).

Benjamin saw positive consequences for art through reproduction, in the sense that it could be liberated from its dependent relationship to ritual. Artistic production would no longer rely upon the ceremonies and traditions that had sustained art while it resided in castles, mansions and churches. Once detached from these settings and their associated conventions, art had to

The Young Reader as a Stamp. *Le petit liseur* by Ozias Leduc. © Canada Post Corporation, 1988. Reproduced with Permission.

develop another valuative affiliation in order to continue to communicate social meaning. In Benjamin's argument, "instead of being based on ritual, it [artistic production] begins to be based on another practice—politics" (224). By "politics" Benjamin meant the shift to emphasizing "exhibition value." Benjamin was suggesting that a profound change was occurring at the level of value. Emphasis on exhibition value was compounding the "contemporary decay of the aura" (223). When the value of a work of art resides in its exhibition value, the public expects it to be accessible. Once it has been reproduced, the new version renders the original recognizable, or famous; the artwork is then considered exhibitable and interesting to view. Some artworks that are frequently reproduced are always exhibited, for example, *The Mona*

Lisa. (Artworks that are not frequently reproduced remain inaccessible; not being famous, these have been rendered invisible.) The exhibitable artwork has been commodified. This is how it achieves recognition in the marketplace.

Questions important to this investigation of the reproduction of *Le petit liseur* emerge directly from Benjamin's insights. How was this particular painting turned into a stamp? Was it considered easy to reproduce? Was it seen to have cultural potential? Benjamin posited that "the work of art reproduced becomes the work of art designed for reproducibility" (224). Benjamin saw that generating copies involved a concerted effort to downplay the significance of originality in relation to artworks and to suture a public aura to works rendered famous through reproduction. I will consider how this occurred in relation to *Le petit liseur* after it was made into a stamp.

John Berger also suggests that reproduction of original artworks transforms the originals themselves. He argues that "the uniqueness of the original now lies in it being *the original of a reproduction*" (Berger 21). Drawing upon Walter Benjamin's insight that works of art become disconnected from their auras when copies are made possible, Berger asserts that art objects now have been rendered artificially mysterious: "The bogus religiosity which now surrounds original works of art, and which is ultimately dependent upon their market value, has become the substitute for what paintings lost when the camera made them reproducible" (23). In part, the mystery of originals is associated with their new-found flexibility through reproduction. Sections of paintings, for example, are often isolated and enlarged or reduced in order to be printed upon postcards or T-shirts. Paintings and sculptures are also used as backdrops in contemporary advertisements. Sometimes a fashion model will strike an odalisque-like pose. Thus Berger believes that artistic traditions have been overwhelmed by "a language of images" (33). This means that many more persons can see art objects by way of their reproduction. But it also means that these same art objects can easily be appropriated for publicity, which serves specific interests.

Publicity directs specific messages at its consuming audience. It is a system that continually invites and entices the viewer to buy. There is always something new to buy, and consumers are constantly urged to buy; if we cannot always buy then we are exhorted to think constantly about buying; advertising promises that our lives will be enriched—even transformed. The rhetoric of publicity relies heavily on the visual language of oil painting. Berger proposes that oil painting traditionally celebrated private ownership. I would argue that oil painting is thereby a proto-promotional medium. Publicity uses historical references in order to attribute status to commodities. Such references are readily available in the traditions of painting. Berger demonstrates how the tactile immediacy of oil paint has been refashioned into glossy colour advertisements with the help of photographic innovation. He is quick to add, however, that the language of publicity is not the same as the language of oil painting. A painting embellished the environment of its owner and gave him a sense of satisfaction with his life. Traditionally, paintings depicted objects that male patrons wished to possess. Publicity intends that the viewer should feel dissatisfied and yearn to consume. *Le petit liseur's* reproduction also involved publicity, first and foremost because the painting was transmuted into a promotional object.

Andrew Wernick, in his book *Promotional Culture*, argues that an advertisement for any given product employs rhetorical strategies that "will generally seek to persuade us that the net utility of purchasing it is higher than what is foregone through purchase, and at least equal to the satisfaction to be derived from making alternative and equivalent expenditures" (27). The net utility of the purchase is assessed by determining the significance of the product. Advertising transforms the product into "a cultural symbol charged with social significance" (31). There is the produced commodity and also its signification. These are two separate dimensions that become fused in advertising—the object and its social meaning. Corporate ideology is a part of not only the meaning-making processes bestowed upon commodities, but also, as Wernick argues, the consumers' orientation to their desires and potential fulfilment.

Wernick suggests that the concept of promotion can be used as a typology, with each strategy acting out a discursive role: "A promotional message is a complex of significations which at once represents (moves in place of), advocates (moves on behalf of), and anticipates (moves ahead of) the circulating entity or entities to which it refers" (182). All consumer goods are engaged by promotional discourse as media speech, a form of communication taken for granted by consumers. The taken-for-granted character of promotional discourse has made it necessary for public institutions to, according to Wernick, "also generate their own forms of promotional discourse, whether, as in the case of university recruitment campaigns, because they have become indirectly commodified, or, as in the case of electoral politics, because they have a market form which is analogous to the one which operates in the market economy" (183). Public institutions, including Canada Post, have felt the need to become image-conscious.

Going beyond Berger, Wernick is talking about much more than advertising strategies. "Promotion has culturally generalized as commodification has spread, as consumer goods production has industrialized, leading to the massive expansion of the sphere of circulation, and as competitive exchange relations have generally established themselves as an axial principle of social life" (186). Wernick has discovered that promotion is a complex hegemonic practice that implicates both producers and consumers of commodified objects and information. He understands hegemony as Gramsci first used the term, to refer to power as requiring both coercion and consent. In the case of the adaptation of the Leduc painting as a stamp, the viewer is asked to participate in simplifying what is seen and known. The viewer is invited to agree that the painting has been reproduced merely in order to popularize it. The gap between institutional promotion and local and particular forms of creative interpretation has been obscured. Promotion is a very useful tool for blurring distinctions between local subjectivities and bureaucracies. This is, of course, one way of attempting to reinvigorate a stable Canadian identity. But if government-run corporations are setting the agenda, this is not a version of patriotism generated by citizens.

In the introduction to this essay, I referred to the concept of the strip as developed by Erving Goffman in his book *Frame Analysis*. The point of analyzing such strips is ultimately to learn something about their "frame." The principles used to develop an organized definition of a situation act as a framework within which events occur and are interpreted, according to the rules of the frame. Though integral to the maintenance of everyday reality, frames are fragile. We know that frames exist foremost because we feel odd when we cannot find one to help us define a situation. The customs and traditions, as well as the norms and values, of communities can be understood as frames. Leduc's conceptual frame is significantly different from the bureaucratic frame within which Canada Post functions.

In *Le petit liseur*, Leduc depicted an everyday occurrence—a young boy looking at a book while sitting at a desk. The model was, in fact, Leduc's brother, which adds to the familial mood of the work. The painting is both intimate and intriguing. Ostiguy describes the original work: "The title is ambiguous since the student does not appear to be paying much attention to his reading. The boy appears in fact to be trying to copy the reproduction that illustrates his textbook" (121).

Is the use of the word *"liseur"* (reader) in the title of the work ambiguous, or ironic? Is the scene meant to be whimsical? Is Leduc depicting his brother as copying an illustration when the boy is supposed to be studying? It is not possible to determine precisely where the boy's eyes are focused. The viewer also cannot discern whether the boy is holding a pen or a brush, since the tip is hidden by his forearm. So the viewer is given a gift of possibilities by the artist, out of which he or she can construct meanings for the painting.

However, clues for the viewer in another of Leduc's paintings suggest that this mystery could be, in Goffman's terms, one of frame ambiguity. Considering Leduc's work *L'enfant du pain*, the following statements are included in a National Gallery of Canada brochure: "In *Boy with Bread*, the light clearly illuminates the bowl and bread and the boy's ragged sleeve, all of which are painted in fine detail. The boy's face and harmonica, which the viewer expects to be the central focus, are cast in shadow. Unconsciously, we try to look at the boy and the bowl at the same time. This gives the image a mysterious tension" (Herbert 15).

Le petit liseur was created by Leduc in 1894, as were his *Le liseur* (private collection), *Liseuse* (Musée du Québec) and *Liseur* (private collection). In all of these works, Leduc juxtaposes everyday objects with human subjects. Their relaxed postures and homely garments are illumined with a glowing light in a manner that generates questions about the relationship between portaiture and the artistic use of colour and perspective. Thus viewers are presented with an intriguing interpretative challenge. The scenes display the ambiance of quiet small-town life, which Leduc loved and participated in sustaining. They were painted in Quebec and are products of Leduc's unique vision, and they have a regional quality about them that has been rendered generic through the reconstruction of *Le petit liseur*. How *Le petit liseur* operates for critics depends on their backgrounds and goals. J. Craig

Stirling has written that critics constructed an image of Leduc that rendered him an "isolationist, bohemian and hermit" (Stirling 141). Further, A. Gehmacher has argued that Leduc was embraced by both the progressivist and traditionalist movements in Quebec thought. Writers within each group interpreted Leduc's work to suit their own distinct interests, without realizing that his creativity thrived on elements from both of these schools of thought and others (Gehmacher 52). The progressivists celebrated individuality whereas the traditionalists valued duty to one's roots above all else: "On the one hand were those who promoted a clerico-regionalist ideology that embraced the traditional morals, customs and values of French-Canadian culture. This point of view was embraced in the time-honoured notion of *le terroir*, or rural tradition, and *la patrie*, the attachment to one's native soil" (Gehmacher 44).

The directors at Canada Post decided to develop a new stamp series in 1988 using Canadian works of art. The Philatelic Services' bulletin published along with the Leduc stamp indicates that the series featured "Masterpieces of Canadian Art. Researched in consultation with prominent art scholars, the series will depict a surprising, forceful and diverse array of works of art from across the country" (*Commemorative Stamp Bulletin* 1987, 1). Georges de Passillé is the manager at Canada Post responsible for adapting selected artworks to the stamp format. He has also been responsible for selecting experts from across the country to assist him in determining which artworks are most appropriate for the stamp series. Canada Post has developed a corporate policy regarding the selection of stamp themes. There is a Stamp Advisory Committee composed of ten experts from a wide variety of disciplines who meet biannually to discuss proposals. The committee members must adhere to the following five criteria:

(1) Persons may not appear on stamps until at least ten years after death (except for the reigning monarch).

(2) No subject may be commemorated more than once within a twenty-five-year time frame. There is also a limit on the number of anniversaries that can be acknowledged with a stamp issue.

(3) There must be a balance of regional and cultural material: broad categories are used to assist with balance that include heritage, social, cultural or economic themes, customs, or recognition for individual excellence.

(4) The stamp format also influences the type of subject matter that can be chosen. Commemorative stamps may appear in sets, in series or as singles (depending upon their thematic significance).

(5) Once the type of issue has been determined, research begins for content. For example, the Masterpieces of Canadian Art series has chosen work from a variety of artistic media, from many parts of Canada and from different periods in Canadian art history (Ellis et al. 3-5).

The committee then annually submits recommendations to Canada Post's board of directors, which makes the final decisions. The time between proposal and decision may take up to three years. De Passillé's group decided not simply to produce a printed copy of *Le petit liseur* for the first stamp, but rather to initiate an art print process: "To produce stamps worthy of these masterpieces, Canada Post has chosen, for the first stamp in the series, the most exacting of traditional stamp-printing processes, steel engraving, in combination with photogravure" (*Commemorative Stamp Bulletin* 1). M. de Passillé explained in an interview that the engraving technique was necessary when shrinking the original because too much of its detail was lost using other forms of reproduction. In addition, the dimensions of the original painting had to be adjusted in order to conform to a vertical stamp format. The painting is 36.7 cm x 46.7 cm (horizontal). The engraving proof of the image for the stamp is 30 mm x 23 mm (vertical).

Benjamin's insights come into play with the transformation of *Le petit liseur* into an engraving. Designed by Pierre-Yves Pelletier and executed by Gregory Prosser, the engraving was the prototype for millions of stamps that stand in for the original art work, even though they are not exact copies. The engraving is a replica created in another medium for the purpose of high-quality stamp production. The engraving proofs made for the stamp are now catalogued in the National Archives. Not only has the painting been physically transformed, it has been lifted up into the bureaucratic apparatus, such that, since its issue in stamp form, many reproduction requests have come to the attention of the National Gallery's Curatorial Archives. Copyright permission has been given to a number of publishers for book covers, to accompany an article on the National Gallery, to the Postage and Philatelic Products division of Canada Post, and to the National Postal Museum. The National Postal Museum sought permission to create "a large format colour reproduction as a highlight of the art in the stamps section" (Curatorial file).

It seems that the post office and its affiliates have no compunction about shrinking and enlarging reconstructed art objects to suit their ideological purposes. Philatelic Products asked for fifty reproductions of the Leduc stamp. These were to be framed as gifts for dignitaries and "other promotional efforts" (Curatorial file). So the stamp version of *Le petit liseur* has changed the original to accommodate official purposes. The stamp refers to the original artwork as its public persona.

The stamp version of *Le petit liseur* has become a promotional commodity that helps Canada Post to present a carefully crafted image to the public. Commemorative stamp series are always of value to collectors, but the visual themes that are selected send a message to the general public. Series on native people, wildlife, women's history, regional and Canadian art tell the consumer that Canada Post is attentive to cultural, political and ecological concerns. In such a case, according to Wernick, "the boundary between sign and object is blurred" (184). Canada Post sells services, competing with courier, fax, e-mail and telephone services for business. To choose stamp subjects that indicate a sense of social responsibility on the part of a crown corporation demonstrates promotional savvy and "top-down" official Canadian culture.

Engraving is an expensive venture; I suggest that in the case of *Le petit liseur* it was done for promotional purposes. In order to produce a stamp that would be attractive and inspiring to consumers, and one that would communicate that Canada Post cares about Canadian art, much time was spent on the intaglio process to "bring out the detail of the original," says de Passillé. This was done in an effort to give the miniature recreation some depth. If you look at the stamp with a magnifiying glass, you can see the tiny strokes made by hand cutting in the surface of the engraving plate. Following upon Berger, the high-quality copies refer back to, but also rely upon, the original in order to become artistic stamps. Furthermore, the stamps are glossy colour versions with silver borders not unlike many magazine advertisements.

How does all of this relate to Ozias Leduc? Leduc is known as a religious and symbolist artist, who also taught the influential artist and theorist Paul-Émile Borduas. His paintings contain visual ambiguities that stimulate reflection in the viewer. Leduc used muted tones, and the source of light in his paintings is not obvious. He painted themes such that viewers could see how he was inspired by rural Quebec culture.

The art stamp series invites the consumer-citizen to buy a piece of Canadian culture for fifty cents. The painting's shape and medium have been changed, lifted out of its local Quebec context and relocated as a Canadian masterpiece by experts working for Canada Post.

Why is Leduc's work held in such high regard in Quebec? What did he do to merit a special place in "the pantheon of our painters"? Leduc found a way to communicate intimacy using the medium of oil painting. According to Gilles Corbeil, "intimacy is one of the hardest things to capture; it can elude the most sensitive temperament, the keenest mind. The painter can do it only by suggestion, and in Leduc, for all his subtlety, the power of suggestion is particularly strong" (7). The intimate interaction that Leduc sets in motion does not foster a relationship between objects or figures on the canvas and the viewer; rather, the intriguing placement of the objects is a key that can stimulate a dialogue between the artist (through his work) and the local viewer, who still knows of the importance that religion has played in the lives of the Quebec people and the building of their culture. His artworks are not dissimilar from his religious icons. It is largely this ability of an original painting to engage the viewer intimately that Benjamin was reflecting upon when he wrote about the aura of art. In pointing out the decay of the aura through reproduction, he was also predicting the loss of intimacy as well as the cultural and regional context of artwork.

The stamp version of *Le petit liseur* does not engage consumers in a relationship with Leduc's art. A stamp is not a spiritual icon; it is a political one. The purchase engages buyers in an economic-patriotic relationship with Canada Post. Through this special promotion, the intended hegemonic exchange is presented in a sensitive and caring "high art" frame, as Canada Post's promotional brochure states: "The Young Reader is the first in an exquisite series of stamps....To create stamps worthy of the masterpieces themselves, stamp printing techniques have been pushed to the limit" (Ellis et al. 11).

Le petit liseur has received recognition as a result of its stamp replica. The demand for copyright permission has increased dramatically since the stamp was issued. The acclaim comes with promotion, which arbitrarily connects a new aura to the work. Like the commemorative stamp, the newly established mystique is a transformed version of the original. The reprocessing of *Le petit liseur* for bureaucratic purposes has generated frame ambiguity, wherein the artist's interests and federal strategies have become blurred. Moreover, the ambiguity is submerged in promotion. This results in two visual tactics used in the commodification of art; the first makes it difficult to distinguish wide-ranging political motivations from artistic concerns in a cultural context, and the second makes it difficult to see the Canadian stamp as anything other than a mere copy of the original Leduc painting. Bureaucratic versions of Canadian identity blur distinctions between regions and do not address local concerns, which cannot be easily incorporated under a simplistic unity canopy. Distinct cultural production is unfortunately seen to subvert the project of Canada as one nation. The social context of Leduc's art presents an interesting challenge to any homogenizing bureaucratic project because he was operating within a unique milieu and worked in Quebec during a time when debates between progressive and traditional thinkers were building momentum. The naive features and unselfconscious posture of *Le petit liseur* bring a serenity to the artwork that seems very distant from struggles between politicized groups who wanted to guide the course of Quebec's history. Yet these debates eventually pervaded all levels and all sectors of Quebec society.

The citizen who purchases the stamps enters an agreement with the post office which extends beyond a payment of fifty cents. By participating in artistic stamp appreciation, the citizen acts as a patron of reproduced and miniaturized artworks. But the patron-citizen also agrees not to think critically about this form of participation and not to problematize artistic reproduction. Critique could generate questions about (among other issues) access. The patron-citizen has no access to the original *Le petit liseur*, only to his tiny understudy.

Works Cited

Benjamin, Walter. *Illuminations*. Trans. H. Zohn. Ed. and Intro. H. Arendt. New York: Schocken, 1969.
Berger, John. *Ways of Seeing*. London: BBC and Penguin, 1972.
Bourdieu, Pierre, and Loic Wacquant. *An Invitation to Reflexive Sociology*. Chicago: U of Chicago P, 1992.
Chilvers, Ian, and Harold Osborne. *The Oxford Dictionary of Art*. Oxford: Oxford UP, 1988.
Commemorative Stamp Bulletin. Ottawa: Canada Post, 1987.

Corbeil, Gilles. "The Still Life Paintings of Ozias Leduc." *Ozias Leduc 1864-1955.* Ottawa: National Gallery of Canada, 1955. 5-7.

Curatorial file: Leduc 18023. Archives Section, National Gallery of Canada.

Davis, Ann. *The Logic of Ecstacy: Canadian Mystical Painting 1920-1940.* Toronto: U of Toronto P, 1992.

Ellis, Louise, Thérèse Alié-Aubé and Catherine Lortie. *Souvenir Collection of the Postage Stamps of Canada 1988.* Ed. G. Longand and C. Lortie. Ottawa: Canada Post, 1988.

Gagnon, Maurice. *Peinture moderne.* Montréal: Ed. B. Valiquette, 1940.

Gehmacher, Arlene. "Authenticity and the Rhetoric of Presentation." *Ozias Leduc: An Art of Love and Reverie.* Montreal: Musée des beaux-arts de Montréal, 1996. 43-52.

Goffman, Erving. *Frame Analysis.* New York: Harper Colophon, 1974.

Lucie-Smith, E. *The Thames and Hudson Dictionary of Art Terms.* London: Thames and Hudson, 1984.

Herbert, Mary Ellen. *A Self-Guided Tour.* Ottawa: National Gallery of Canada, 1992.

Maurault, Olivier. "Monsieur Ozias Leduc homme—artiste." *Arts et pensée* (juillet-aout 1954): 175.

Mellen, Peter. *Landmarks of Canadian Art.* Toronto: McClelland and Stewart, 1978.

Ostiguy, Jean-René. *Ozias Leduc.* Ottawa: National Gallery of Canada, 1974.

Stirling, J. Craig. "Evolution of Critical Thought on Ozias Leduc." *Ozias Leduc the Draughtsman.* Montreal: Concordia UP, 1978. 136-45.

Wernick, Andrew. *Promotional Culture.* London: Sage, 1991.

FURTHER READINGS

Becker, Howard. *Art Worlds.* Berkeley: U of California P, 1982.

Crary, Jonathan. *Techniques of the Observer.* Cambridge: MIT P, 1990.

Duvignaud, Jean. *The Sociology of Art.* Trans. T. Wilson. London: Paladin, 1972.

Horkheimer, Max, and Theodor Adorno. *Dialectic of Enlightenment.* Trans. J. Cumming. New York: Continuum, 1993.

Jhally, Sut. *The Codes of Advertising: Fetishism and the Political Economy of Meaning in the Consumer Society.* New York: St. Martin's, 1987.

Steiner, Wendy. "Intertextuality in Painting." *American Journal of Semiotics* 3.4 (1985): 57-67.

Veblen, Thorstein. *The Instinct of Workmanship and the State of the Industrial Arts.* New York: A. M. Kelly, 1964.

Weber, Max. *The Theory of Social and Economic Organization.* Ed. T. Parsons. New York: Free Press, 1957.

Wolff, Janet. *The Social Production of Art.* London: Macmillan, 1981.

DILEMMAS OF
DEFINITION

Will Straw

When Joni Mitchell wailed "Oh Canada" back in 1971, the word evoked landscapes both emotional and geographic, wide and wild. In a series of quavering notes, she imbued those three syllables with homesickness and loss. Yet Canada remains forever neutral, even undifferentiated, to most U.S. minds. It's a hard place to feel specific about, except to note that some native speakers unfurl beautifully attenuated O's and moody girl singers grow on trees up there.
—Katherine Dieckman, "Paperbacks: Northern Lights"

In the introduction to their book *Mondo Canuck*, Geoff Pevere and Greig Dymond suggest that, "far as we know, no Canadians have yet died from a lack of cultural identity" (Pevere and Dymond ii). We might challenge this claim, of course, noting that a weakened sense of cultural identity sometimes produces social and personal crises whose consequences, in aboriginal communities and elsewhere, may be devastating. Most anglophone Canadians, nonetheless, regard the question of Canadian cultural identity as one that is of little urgency but irritatingly persistent. Few of us will die from a lack of cultural identity, but this does not absolve us of ongoing anxieties over the legitimacy of our own tastes and cultural habits; it does not diminish the federal government's conviction that its own legitimacy depends on the strength of a certain kind of Canadian culture. And, perhaps most importantly, the non-urgency of the cultural question in Canada does not remove the sense of ethical incompleteness that makes most of us wish, much of the time, that we were a little more interested in the films, novels, paintings and other products of English-Canadian culture (Miller xi).

I have endeavoured, in these few pages, to wend my way through some loosely connected themes borrowed or developed over several years of teaching courses on Canadian culture to undergraduate students. All of those courses were taught in English, at English-language universities, and this essay is mostly about English-Canadian culture, with all the messy imperfection which that term cannot shed. Indeed, the English language has no more status here than one of those languages of convergence of which Charles Taylor has written; it is a language that links citizens and immigrants, who may speak other languages at home and with their friends, to pre-existing Canadian cultural institutions and complexes of interlocking cultural phenomena.

ECONOMIC AND ETHICAL ACCOUNTS OF CULTURAL WEAKNESS

Over the years in which I have taught courses on Canadian culture, the average level of commitment by students to the ideal of a strong and distinct English-Canadian culture has remained surprisingly high. This commitment has gone hand in hand with the conviction that English-Canadian culture is weak, though specific explanations of this weakness have come in and out of fashion. A few years ago, students readily accepted the argument that structural conditions had produced and perpetuated this weakness. These structural conditions included the domination of our culture industries by companies based, for the most part, in the U.S., and the complicity of our own governments in maintaining that domination. With time, I have noticed, the appeal of an analysis framed in geopolitical, economic or structural terms has declined. Instead, students seem more and more willing to pose the problem in ethical, individualistic terms. If English-Canadian culture is weak, a new consensus seems to suggest, this is because we lack, as individuals, the moral strength that might compel us to seek out that culture's products and support them. Instead, we yield too readily to the temptations offered by those cultural phenomena which come from somewhere else.

There are, perhaps, valid historical reasons for this shift. English-Canadian culture no longer seems to be characterized by conditions of scarcity, conditions which once could be easily blamed on the production and distribution structures of multinational capitalism. It is no longer the unavailability of Canadian cultural artefacts that perturbs us, some might suggest, but their inescapable omnipresence, and the unfulfilled duties of which they now remind us. We may now buy Canadian fiction or musical recordings in chain superstores; the films of Atom Egoyan or the National Film Board are easily found on video cassette; and a dozen specialty TV channels now recycle several years' worth of Canadian television drama. While we continue, much of the time, to resist these phenomena, we now blame this avoidance on our own failings, for which we feel guilty. We are less likely to see this avoidance as the effect of lingering structural conditions that conspire to keep English-Canadian cultural artefacts marginal.

If students increasingly diagnose the weaknesses of our culture in ethical terms, academic writing on cultural policy has likewise come to place greater emphasis on the ethical dimensions of cultural consumption. The first wave of histories and analyses of cultural policy in Canada tended to regard the government's own claims about the need for a strong national culture as simply platitudinous, if not fraudulent. The true function of cultural policy, scholars suggested, was to protect the dominant interests in a particular industry, or to produce the ideological gloss that rendered palatable the Canadian government's complicity in our economic subservience to the U.S. (e.g., Raboy). Governments might summon us, as citizens and ethical subjects, to support a national culture, but scholars asked us to recognize that they were doing so in bad faith, masking the sellout of our cultural sovereignty, which economic policies and a failure of political will had made possible.

Recent scholarship has been more willing to take seriously the notion that the need of governments to intervene in the cultural field is genuine, rendered so by the imperative to shape the sorts of citizens that a state requires in order to perpetuate its legitimacy. In an influential book on cultural citizenship, Toby Miller has argued that states devise cultural policies, not simply to mediate between competing economic interests, but "to produce a sense of oneness among increasingly heterogeneous populations at a time when political systems are under question by new social movements and the internationalization of cultures and economies" (Miller xii).

Writing more specifically of Quebec, Allor and Gagnon suggest that the cultural field emerged, since the Quiet Revolution of the 1960s, as the principal realm through which the Quebec government seeks to legitimize itself (25-26). New thinking about the function of public cultural policy is less and less likely to emphasize the ways in which that policy might be subservient to the imperatives of multinational capitalism. Rather, it stresses the dilemma of governments whose legitimation is threatened by that capitalism, and their need to form citizens with an ethical commitment to national cultural development. Culture offers the most effective realm for linking citizen to state and ensuring the legitimacy of the state. The military and economic realms have either lost their mobilizing power or become immune to direct public intervention.

AMBIVALENCE AND ANXIETY: THE ENGLISH-CANADIAN CULTURAL CONSUMER

For a long time, English Canadians have allowed themselves the conceit that their involvement in U.S. popular culture is multi-layered. We are able, we believe, to move freely between the pleasures of participation, for which our profound understanding of U.S. popular culture has trained us, and the self-satisfaction of those who need not feel complicit with that culture. This ambivalence is often taken as proof that we are skilled negotiators of cultural resistance, possessed of the insider's intimate understanding of the culture that dominates us and the colonized subject's talent for subversive mimicry. The double registers that mark our relationship to U.S. popular culture are seen to shape both our habits of consumption and many of the cultural practices at which English Canadians seem to have excelled. (One of the most convincing uses of these ideas may be found in attempts to explain the character and success of English-Canadian sketch comedy [e.g., Pevere and Dymond].)

There is much that rings true in this account, but our ambivalence may take other, less noble forms. In the field of popular music (the focus of much of my own research), English Canadians are often torn between a smug sense of superiority over those excesses (of emotion or belief) that we observe elsewhere, and an ongoing anxiety over the sense that we have no important or heroic role to play. Canada is one of those mid-sized countries, like Australia, which, while developed and prosperous, nevertheless devotes most of its cultural life to artefacts that are produced somewhere else. That *somewhere else* is usually the United States, of course, and, in the case of popular music, the United Kingdom. At no point has a specifically or exclusively Canadian subculture figured in the histories of youth culture or popular music; in no instance with which I am familiar has a distinctly Canadian subcultural movement been copied or adapted elsewhere in the world.

This does not mean that we have no subcultures, of course, or that the energies which have presided over the formation of subcultures elsewhere have not found expression in Canada. This situation invites us, nonetheless, to examine the ways in which countries like Canada receive and assimilate avowedly oppositional and transgressive cultural artefacts whose origins are elsewhere. Because none of the genres that have marked post-war popular music in important ways are distinctly Canadian, almost all the musics we consume have been within forms whose historically privileged or more apparently pure moments transpired elsewhere—from rock 'n' roll through punk and hip-hop. This has shaped the status of the political within Canadian musical culture, as it has in dozens of other countries around the world. Artefacts for which socio-political claims may be made, whether these be gangsta rap records or drum-and-bass tracks, enter Canada within an economy of scarcity and legitimacy whose principal effect is to render them cherished and precious. We admire these musics as much for the marks of exotic origin they bear as for the vital energies they are seen to express, and the channels through which they enter our national cultural space are, typically, connoisseurist and cosmopolitan in character. Speed-garage dance singles from the U.K.—to invoke a recent example—are brought to Canada by individuals intimately connected to the circulation of information on an international level; they presume cultural capital of the most basic kind, such as that which tells you where to find British music magazines in Montreal or Regina, or what an imported record is and where to find it. The principle audiences for these artefacts, within Canada, show an interest in the already authenticated and the scarce. The often urgent social and political contexts of origin of these artefacts mark them in ways that serve to authenticate them, but these contexts have little controlling influence on the uses to which these artefacts are put in Canada or the meanings that come to circulate around them.

This is, of course, an obvious point. It's long been claimed that reggae, punk or trip-hop, for example, come to Canada only to be picked up by those ignorant of the circumstances in which they took shape, of the social energies and conflictual circumstances that presided over their emergence. This is one of the ways in which the legitimacy of our own versions of these subcultures is undermined. What is less often considered is the economy of objects and artefacts that structure the cultural sphere in a country like Canada, the role of scarcity and economic marginalization in producing a social cartography of tastes. Dance music culture in Canada, for example, is shaped by infrastructures that operate at two extremes: between the connoisseurist culture of imported twelve-inch vinyl singles sold only in independent record stores, at one end, and the market for domestically pressed CD compilations of cheesy Euro-house dance music at the other. There are few of the mediating institutions and little of the commodity production that would sustain fine gradations of taste and connoisseurship between these two extremes. There are virtually no locally pressed vinyl twelve-inch singles anymore, no dance singles to be found in major record stores at reasonable prices, a weak market generally for CD singles. This gulf exaggerates the fetishistically connoisseurist character of imported, underground dance music just as it nourishes the perception of the rest (i.e., those CDs produced in Canada) as abject and degraded.

One effect of this situation is that commodities that, in the context of their origin, bear the marks of oppositionality or authenticity are most readily brought into Canada by those with the skills and cosmopolitan connections to recognize the marks of connoisseurist value. Few dispositions in a country like Canada are more adaptable than those that hover at the borders and focus on imported records or other artefacts of avowedly oppositional cultures: these dispositions (and the credibility of the individuals who deploy them) can survive the transitions from punk to synth-pop to house to rave to electronica and on through recent revivals of easy-listening music and swing. Because most subcultural forms enter Canada through the gateway of connoisseurship, a taste for them has tended to cluster within the middle class, reinforcing longstanding associations between cosmopolitan bohemianism and a taste for the transgressive and genuine. The energies and social forces that have fuelled the emergence of certain kinds of music (or painting or cinema) are generally displaced, as these things enter Canada, by an overvaluing of their status as genuine, as cherished products of those places where the truly heroic moments in popular cultural history unfold.

What this means, of course, is that the field of popular music in Canada is, much of the time, marked by a high level of anxiety and status panic. Our decisions to favour certain kinds of music are mixed up with our uncertainty over whether we have accurately diagnosed their place within hierarchies of legitimacy that take shape somewhere else. As emotional, affective responses, anxiety and status panic are much less heroic than the sorts of subversive, resistant forms of consumption that subcultural theory (or cultural studies more generally) has claimed to uncover. They are, nevertheless, at the core of what it means to engage in cultural life in a country that lies just beyond the centres of cultural power.

English Canada's place within the international flow of cultural objects and influences has left us well equipped to contribute to broader, contemporary debates over globalization. Themes that are prominent in recent globalization theory—the unrooting of cultural artefacts from their places of origin, the fetishizing of local origins as the basis of cultural value, the commodification of nature within a global tourist economy, and so on—have long been addressed by Canadian scholars, critics and cultural activists. Cultural practices within English Canada unfold with a keen awareness of their place within international systems of cultural value; each grapples with the question of whether its origins are to be disguised or trumpeted.

MEASURING CULTURAL DISTINCTIVENESS:
THE DILEMMAS OF DEFINITION

In 1985, the Federal Task Force on Broadcasting Policy (or Kaplan-Sauvageau Commission), like government commissions before and since, addressed the problem of Canadian television and its relationship to a national culture. In particular, the task force confronted the complaint that much of the dramatic programming on Canadian television—programming made with public subsidies or used to meet Canadian content requirements—did not seem Canadian in any obvious sense. Programs were certified as Canadian according to the origins of the individuals and firms involved in their production, but such criteria did little to deter producers from making programs blatantly imitative of American models, or from disguising Canadian locales to suggest that they were in the U.S.

A research study conducted for the task force (by myself and two colleagues: Bruck, Straw and O'Sullivan) took up the question of how one might judge the Canadianness of television programs. The challenge was to devise a method of evaluation that would possess conceptual rigour and lend itself to practical application within government cultural policy. One might, for example, evaluate programs based on the extent to which they included cultural markers of Canadianness: recognizable locales, key signifiers of national location (such as licence plates or flags), rituals (such as curling matches) and so on. A system of rewards for the use of these markers might counteract the widely noted tendency of producers to disguise their fictional worlds in order to pass off Canadian films or television programs as American. Nevertheless, while one could imagine complicated systems for allocating points based on the presence of such markers, this would obviously trivialize the issue. It would reduce national cultural expression to a catalogue of tokens of Canadianness, many of them blatantly stereotypical.

Other possible criteria for evaluating Canadianness possessed more intellectual substance, but were no more appealing as possible elements of a cultural policy. While there is a widespread belief that Canadian films and television programs offer a distinct (i.e., more restrained) tone than those imported from the U.S., insistence on a Canadian tone as a requirement for certain kinds of public support seems both ludicrous and unnecessarily authoritarian. (The parallel example often invoked here is that of Australian film policy, which, it is claimed, gives additional support to films that manifest an Australian look.) More to the point, a valorization of tone risks enshrining, as the expression of a national cultural sensibility, an aspect of Canadian films or TV programs that might simply be an effect of their lower budgets and production values.

The Federal Task Force on Broadcasting Policy undertook its work after at least two decades in which critical discourse on film, literature, television, music and painting had offered influential arguments about the thematic consistency of English-language and French-language Canadian culture. The relationship of this work to cultural policy, however, has always been uneasy. Cultural policy within Canada has not, as in many other countries, been founded primarily on an abstract enterprise of democratization or geared towards the moral improvement of the citizenry. Rather, it has rested on claims about the distinctiveness of our culture and the importance of that distinctiveness as a basis for building or maintaining national cohesion. As a result, cultural policy has been compelled to flirt with the project of defining a national cultural character, even as it has bumped up against the obvious risks in doing so. As the very least, this has resulted in some conceptual slippages, such as those that occur when the characteristics of public broadcasting (similar as they often are across a number of different countries) are taken as the expression of a genuinely Canadian character.

The impulse to define national cultural traditions within English Canada was strongest from the late 1960s through the early 1980s, when it fuelled the effort to strengthen the place of English-Canadian culture within university curricula in the humanities. The critical position that dominated during this period is one which, somewhat reluctantly (since the term has become so explosively provocative in contemporary cultural theory), I will call the essentialist position. This position presumes that there are thematic traits common to works of Canadian culture, and that it is the job of the critic to find these amidst the variations of surface detail that might make such works seem unrelated. Perhaps the best known of these critical claims was Margaret Atwood's argument that the essence of the Canadian character could be found in the simple drive to survive, a drive which provided the thematic substance of Canadian literature in both English and French (Atwood 1972). This preoccupation with survival was evident in the number of literary characters who were victims; it could be seen in the preoccupation of Canadian authors with landscape and the general hardship of life.

Other versions of this argument took shape across the humanities. In his influential book *Movies and Mythologies*, Peter Harcourt found a thematic unity for English-Canadian cinema in a crisis of character motivation. Looking at the scattered feature-film tradition of the 1960s and early 1970s, he noted that the heroes of Canadian films were typically trapped in a real òr emotional adolescence. Later, Geoff Pevere would write of the stubbornly worrisome character of English-Canadian films, regarding this as the appropriate response of one national culture to a powerful neighbour whose own films were marked by the constant exhortation to be happy (Pevere). In the field of popular music, it was argued that the essence of a Canadian style was to be found in its interweaving of rural and urban influences, in an open sound of the sort found first in the folk revival of the late 1960s (Neil Young, Gordon Lightfoot) and, subsequently, in the open, expansive rock music of Blue Rodeo or The Tragically Hip (see, for example, Brown). Writing on Canadian television, Morris Wolfe argued that the essence of Canadian television was its slower, more restrained pace, its reliance on a lower number of jolts per minute than was typical of U.S. television (Wolfe). In her analysis of the visual arts in Canada, Gaile McGregor claimed that Canadian artistic practice was marked by a preoccupation with landscape, by an ambivalence towards nature that wrestled with both its beauty and its terror.

Those engaged in mapping the thematic preoccupations of English-Canadian culture rarely did so in an explicitly prescriptive sense, as if these inventories of thematic concerns were to be used forever after to judge between the genuinely and the falsely Canadian. Like any attempt to define a national tradition, however, they invited us to see certain works as more central or peripheral than others within the emergence of a coherent, national culture. The dangers inherent in an essentialist approach should be obvious, and need not all be rehearsed here. With time, the claim that Canadian fiction was principally about survival, or that its music was essentially a synthesis of rural and urban traditions, ran up against new waves of writing from immigrants to Canadian cities like Vancouver, or the recognition accorded rap production teams from Toronto or Halifax. Essentialist critical positions have figured as implicit influences on cultural policy—shaping ideas about what constitutes artistic value in the Canadian cinema, or about the appropriate formats for creative collaboration in popular music—but they can no longer figure unproblematically within public statements of government policy.

A second position in the debate over a Canadian culture is what I would call the *compensatory* position. This argues that Canadian culture possesses no distinctive essence, or that, at the very least, it is not the purpose of public policy to discover an essence and devise the means by which that essence should flower. Rather, the argument goes, Canadian culture typically compensates for those gaps that the cultural products of the U.S., Great Britain and France have left open. At one level, Canadian culture moves to fill these gaps in a strictly strategic sense, through the identification of open and underserved markets. Less obviously, Canadian culture will fill these gaps as a result of the more informal and unconscious processes by which those undertaking creative careers in Canada adapt to the possibilities available to them. The character of English-Canadian cultural artefacts, then, is not expressive of a deeply rooted, distinctive sensibility. Rather, it is produced in the ongoing effort to find distinctive means of producing and marketing cultural goods in an environment dominated by players and products whose origins are elsewhere.

If we have specialized in certain kinds of literature, or film, or television, this position suggests, it is because other sorts of cultural commodities with wide appeal are produced more successfully by the cultural industries of the U.S. and other countries. Seeing no point in competing with these industries directly, we have gone after the internationally dispersed markets for cultural goods that bear the mark of a certain quality—typically, goods which manifest a gentility and restraint of the sort treasured by cosmopolitan, connoisseurist audiences. Thus, if the best-known Canadian filmmakers make low-budget, somewhat arty films about loser figures, this is not (or not merely) because they are expressing essential qualities of the Canadian character. Rather, it is because loser figures are part of the dramatic vocabulary of the international art cinema, one way in which that cinema distinguishes itself from Hollywood blockbusters. Our television programs are not as flashy as those made in the U.S. because we depend, increasingly, on sales to overseas markets in which flashiness is not so highly valued. We have specialized in certain kinds of popular music (such as Maritime folk or Albertan country) because we know that ours is a world in which the markers of regional authenticity are the principal hook through which marginal musical forms may build an international audience. The Cirque du Soleil, Imax films and K-Tel compilation records were all devised in Canada, it might be argued, because we have become adept at producing idiosyncratic variations of longstanding and successful cultural forms.

The compensatory position on Canadian culture is easily adapted to the language of cultural policy. Public policy, it suggests, should direct resources to those Canadian cultural producers who might succeed in commercial terms. We have convinced ourselves that the support of more marginal cultural phenomena is, in fact, a realistic way to succeed in international markets, catering to specialized tastes that are often underserved by the products of Hollywood or multinational publishing conglomerates.

The advantages of the compensatory position on English-Canadian culture are many. It is both a humble and a realistic position, acknowledging that Canadian culture exists within a world culture dominated by the Americans, and that, however unfortunate this fact may be, it is largely irreversible. The culture we deem distinctly Canadian, then, is a culture which has filled in those gaps that American culture has left behind. If Canadian films appear to seek out a human scale unlike that of Hollywood, and if our television programs appear more thoughtful and caring, this is because film and television are funded, in Canada, in ways that encourage these qualities, and devised for audiences and markets that welcome them.

The risk of the compensatory position, its detractors will argue, is that it encourages the development of an English-Canadian culture that is wilfully marginalized. If we expect English-Canadian culture to fill the cultural spaces unserved by American-dominated commercial interests, then we have given up the fight to produce domestic products that will be massively popular and widely shared. (We will all watch *Friends* or *The Sopranos*, then divide into a dozen smaller audiences to watch the more specialized Canadian programs that follow.)

INFRASTRUCTURES AND IMAGINARIES

In an important critique of Canadian cultural policy, Maurice Charland makes the point that the Canadian emphasis on communications infrastructures and technological links across vast geographical distances has given rise to what he calls a technological nationalism (Charland). Canadian governments have been so concerned with the building of connections, he suggests, that they have paid insufficient attention to what will travel along them. The semantic and emotional glue required to hold a national culture together was absent from the design of these systems; that glue was provided by the popular culture of the U.S., which has used our communications infrastructures for its own dissemination. Communication technology, Charland writes, heralded as the means of promoting Canadian statehood and nationhood, paradoxically offered those in Canada a common national experience that included cultural commodities from the United States (210).

Charland convincingly suggests that the Canadian state's emphasis on building media infrastructures has weakened our national imaginary, if only by creating effective pathways for the distribution of U.S. culture within Canada. An emphasis on the channels through which culture travels, rather than the substance that such channels convey, has produced that peculiarly Canadian dilemma: we have one of the world's most efficient communications infrastructures and, at the same time, a national culture widely regarded as one of the world's most colonized and weak.

Nevertheless, the strengths of English-Canadian culture (both popular and high) are likewise rooted in the richness of the links and networks which have sustained that culture. The traditional concern of cultural critics with the thematic substance of culture has blocked attention to the patterns of interconnection and lines of solidarity that give a culture its rich texture, and which root it in the practices and movements of everyday life. These linkages and networks will often have, as the content that travels along or through them, little that fulfils long-standing criteria of Canadianness. The great achievement of the Canadian system of artist-run centres, set in place since the early 1970s, lies much more in the lines of collaboration and communication that this system has enabled and encouraged than in a recognizably distinct (and Canadian) body of work produced as its legacy. In the field of popular music, styles and practices that are not indigenously Canadian in any notable sense (such as the disco music produced in Montreal in the 1970s) have been the pretexts around which networks of cultural affinity, and complex relations between the local and the global, have taken shape. In these, as in so many other cases, culture is to be found in the ongoing activity through which people build institutions, join together in collaboration or activist militancy, and circulate the products of their creative labour.

WORKS CITED

Allor, Martin, and Michelle Gagnon. *L'État de culture:Généalogie discursive des politiques culturelles québécois.* Montreal: Research Group on Cultural Citizenship (Concordia University), 1994.

Atwood, Margaret. *Survival: A Thematic Guide to Canadian Literature.* Toronto: Anansi, 1972.

Brown, Laurie. "Songs from the Bush Garden." *Cultural Studies* 5.3 (October, 1991): 347-57.

Bruck, Peter, Will Straw and Denis O'Sullivan. *Performance Programming in the Canadian TV-Broadcasting System*. Research report commissioned by the Federal Task Force on Broadcasting Policy (the Kaplan-Sauvageau Commission), 1985.

Charland, Maurice. "Technological Nationalism." *Canadian Journal of Political and Social Theory* 10.1-2 (1986): 196-220.

Dieckman, Katherine. "Paperbacks: Northern Lights." *Village Voice*. Literary Supplement. (April) 1994: 32.

Elder, R. Bruce. *Image and Identity: Reflections on Canadian Film and Culture*. Waterloo: Wilfrid Laurier UP, 1989.

Harcourt, Peter. *Movies and Mythologies: Towards a National Cinema*. Toronto: Canadian Broadcasting Corporation Publications, 1977.

Lofgren, Orvar. "Scenes from a Troubled Marriage: Swedish Ethnology and Material Culture Studies." *Journal of Material Culture* 2.1: 95-113.

McGregor, Gaile. *The Wacousta Syndrome: Explorations in the Canadian Landscape*. Toronto: U of Toronto P, 1985.

Miller, Toby. *The Well-Tempered Self*. Baltimore: Johns Hopkins UP, 1993.

Pevere, Geoff. "On the Brink." *Cineaction* 28 (Spring 1992): 34-37.

Pevere, Geoff, and Greig Dymond. *Mondo Canuck: A Canadian Pop Culture Odyssey*. Scarborough: Prentice-Hall Canada, 1996.

Raboy, Marc. *Missed Opportunities: The Story of Canada's Broadcasting Policy*. Montreal: McGill-Queen's UP, 1990.

Taylor, Charles. "Deep Diversity and the Future of Canada." 1997. <http://www.uni.ca/taylor.html>.

Wolfe, Morris. *Jolts: The TV Wasteland and the Canadian Oasis*. Toronto: Lorimer, 1985.

Wright, Robert A. "Dream Comfort, Memory, Despair": Canadian Popular Musicians and the Dilemma of Nationalism, 1968-1972. *Journal of Canadian Studies* 22.4 (Winter 1987/88): 27-43.

TELEVISION

READING CANADIAN "POPULAR" TELEVISION: THE CASE OF *E.N.G.*

Jim Leach

The analyst of Canadian popular culture is faced with texts that rapidly disappear and with problems that never seem to go away. In the case of television, the problem of the ephemeral text has been alleviated by the advent of the VCR, but there will always be a gap between the text chosen for analysis and the current programs with which the reader is likely to be familiar. In these conditions, it is tempting to forego close readings in favour of rehashing the all-too-familiar problems facing Canada's "cultural industries." But these enduring problems can only be tackled on the basis of an understanding of how texts work in their cultural contexts, so I intend to explore some of the issues at stake through a close reading of an episode of the television series *E.N.G.*

Although this series was cancelled in spring 1994, it had attracted relatively large audiences over the previous five seasons. By analyzing an episode from the first season (1989-90), I will outline the tensions and possibilities involved in the production and consumption of "popular" texts in a Canadian context. While the episode may have passed into the limbo of the video archives, the questions remain, and my aim

Notes on page 125.

is to encourage readers to test my findings against their own experience of more current television productions.

Unlike most Canadian television shows that have received critical attention, *E.N.G.* was neither produced nor broadcast by the CBC, the public network, which has a mandate to support Canadian productions. *E.N.G.* was produced independently by Alliance Entertainment and broadcast on the private CTV network.[1] It was, however, often compared with the CBC's long-running series *Street Legal* (1987-94): both series sought to become "popular" by drawing on the proven formulas of American television series and adapting them to recognizably Canadian situations and settings, and both centred on the personal and professional lives of characters caught up in the everyday crises of newsmaking (in *E.N.G.*) and the law (in *Street Legal*).

In Defence of Popular Culture

In his influential work on popular culture, John Fiske has argued forcefully against theories (such as those associated with the Frankfurt School) that regard spectators as "cultural dupes" unable to resist the ideological messages conveyed by the media.[2] Fiske claims that, since commercial television programs must attract the largest possible audience, they must be open not only to readings in line with the dominant ideology but also to other readings that meet the needs of those groups whose cultural backgrounds place them outside the mainstream. These texts are thus not simply vehicles of a dominant and homogeneous ideology but unstable structures within which different meanings and pleasures compete with each other.

What Fiske calls his "optimistic skepticism" emphasizes the productive ways in which "the people" practise "the art of making do with what the system provides" (*Understanding* 31, 25). His account of popular culture is attractive and often persuasive, but it does run the risk of simply substituting a total acceptance for the total rejection that characterized many earlier cultural theories. The implications of his argument are especially urgent in relation to the problem of defining the "popular" in the Canadian context. As Fiske himself recognizes, "what the system provides" throughout the world is, increasingly, "commercially motivated mainstream television," which tends to be "made in America," either literally or through imitation of

American genres ("Moments" 75). He implies, however, that this situation does not threaten other cultures since the ideological meanings of "popular" texts are always subverted in their reception, noting that Australian Aborigines manage to wrest their own meanings from *Rambo* (Fiske, *Understanding* 57).

This argument calls into question the need for any form of cultural protectionism or public broadcasting. According to Fiske, "the commercial imperative" may result in "a closer relationship with popular social experience than the more distantly theorized political-moral-aesthetic position" of those supporting alternative kinds of television ("Moments" 75). In the Canadian context, some critics have drawn similar conclusions from the apparent "indifference of the Canadian viewer" to the kind of television supported by "Canadian nationalists celebrating the refusal of American values" (Collins 344).

The Canadian cultural environment has historically been saturated with images and fictions originating south of the border, while alternative Canadian images have needed the support of government institutions and have often been associated with "high" rather than "popular" cultural traditions. Fiske's theory would suggest that legislation to ensure Canadian content is futile and counterproductive, since "the people" will produce their own meanings in any case (meanings which will be "Canadian" only if people want them to be). Political interference will only ensure that Canadian programs will be associated with "them" rather than "us."

Fiske's arguments owe a great deal to the concept of "flow" introduced into television studies by Raymond Williams in 1974. According to Williams, previous cultural forms (novel, drama, film) were experienced as single events, whereas television offers a sequence of interrelated sounds and images no longer contained within the boundaries of single programs. Images and sounds, from quite different sources, are brought together through the sequence of scheduling or through channel switching; commercials and other materials are inserted into programs. Williams proposed that the apparently random patterns thus created could be analyzed to reveal "the flow of meanings and values of a specific culture" (Williams 118).

Fiske extends this idea by arguing that television does not depend on the linear and logical structures of written language but instead encourages "associative relations" that are "far freer than logical ones," opening up gaps and contradictions that allow the people to construct their own meanings, thereby creating what he calls "a semiotic democracy" (*Understanding* 109; *Television* 95). Williams was, however, less "optimistic" than Fiske, and he argued that the semiotic effect of the flow is far from democratic in that it is dependent on "the production habits of a majority of professionals" that set "limits to actual insights and perceptions" while ensuring "a certain confidence of address." This "confidence" is often located in the intrusive voice of the "expert" commentator but also in the trend towards programs dealing with "the rushed and anxious lives of professionals" in which "the connections to any wider life" are "made by the conventionally mediating figures of doctors and policemen" (O'Connor 53, 82).

The implications of the flow effect have rarely been discussed in relation to Canadian television because of the urgent need to identify specifically Canadian qualities in programs or to challenge the dominance of U.S. programming. However, Williams's discussion of the way in which television addresses viewers was echoed in an influential article by Peter Harcourt, first published in 1976. Comparing the forms of Canadian film and television with those of Britain and the U.S., he insisted that Canadian works are not inferior to the products of more highly regarded cultural traditions but that they operate in their own mode, which is "often more tentative, less sensational, less able to create a density of characterization than either the American or the British models." In effect, Harcourt argued that the Canadian mode lacks the "confidence of address," grounded in professional codes, which Williams found in British television (Harcourt 373).

This Canadian mode continues to be a factor in film and television production; its major achievements in television include drama anthologies like the CBC's *For the Record* (1976-85) and series like *Wojeck* (1966-68) that blend documentary and fiction techniques to confront (but not resolve) complex social issues. Professional attitudes are not completely absent from this tradition (Wojeck, after all, was a coroner); but it is clear that the "different" qualities of Canadian popular culture have often been perceived by audiences as signs of inferiority. In Fiske's terms, it might be argued that works within this tradition have not become "popular" because they do not offer the dominant values with sufficient authority to allow the viewer to construct resistant meanings. While government regulation and "high culture" rhetoric may associate the Canadian media with "them," the tentative address and modest production values create the impression of an amateur approach. There are clearly as many tensions at work here as Fiske finds in the popular culture of the U.S., Britain, and Australia, but the "popular" remains a highly problematic category in Canada.

MEANINGS IN THE FLOW

The episode I have chosen is called "The Souls of Our Heroes" and was first broadcast on 1 March 1990.[3] Its central story concerned media coverage of the massacre in Tiananmen Square in June 1989, and it followed the basic formula of the series by placing this "hard" news story in the context of other stories dealing with professional and personal relationships in and around the newsroom. In later seasons the personal lives of the newscasters became more prominent, but the tension between public news and private lives remained a distinctive feature of the series. *E.N.G.* frequently raised issues of how public and private meanings are constructed within the cultural and institutional constraints of Canadian television; and its allusions to actual news stories foregrounded questions about how the meanings circulated in the flow relate to a sense of a reality beyond the television discourse. Its view of the activities of media professionals suggests that the flow effect has expanded beyond television to the whole of postmodern cultural experience.[4] In our media-saturated cultural environment, all texts are read in relation to other texts, and read differently in different contexts. Television, which has been called "the postmodern medium par excellence," thrives on this instability of meaning (Joyrich 192).

Television offers a kind of endless text or, as Nick Browne has suggested, "supertext," in which many discourses (entertainment, advertising, news, sports, religion) are woven together (Browne 588). My "text" will thus consist not just of a single episode of *E.N.G.* but of all the material, including commercials, broadcast during that hour.[5] In the absence of clear or permanent boundaries, the analyst must artificially "freeze" the flow, while remaining alert to the intertextual play extending beyond the boundaries established for analytical purposes. The aim cannot be to discover *the* meaning of the text, and, since the practice of close reading is opposed to the casual and distracted quality of most television viewing, there can be no claim that the meanings identified will be consciously perceived by most viewers. But it is not a case of imposing meanings on a meaningless flow of images and sounds; the goal is "to trace out the contradictory and multiple readings that already exist within the fragmented text" (Joyrich 193). Reading *E.N.G.* becomes a way of exploring, in the Canadian context, how television represents and constructs the relationship between individuals and their social and cultural environments.

E.N.G.: Formula and Flow

E.N.G. did have one foot in the Canadian docudrama tradition, often using documentary techniques and rarely resolving the social problems uncovered by the news workers. Yet the major project of the series was clearly to deliver the pleasures of "popular" television, using a formula that owed more to the melodramatic codes of the daytime soaps than to the suspicion of "crisis structures" in the "Canadian mode" identified by Harcourt.[6] A number of loosely connected stories are interwoven, offering viewers a variety of characters and situations, but also inviting them to make connections among the stories, to draw on their memories of earlier episodes, and to make comparisons with other similar series.

While formulas provide producers with a framework that accommodates the hectic production schedule of a weekly series, they also help to organize spectatorship by setting up appropriate expectations. The pleasure then derives both from the fulfilment of these expectations and from the variations that must also be found in each episode to provide novelty and suspense. Since these formulas derive from the U.S. series that dominate Canadian airwaves, a Canadian series that attempts to become "popular" in this way is faced with the question of whether it can, or wants to, create a specifically Canadian inflection of its formula. While *E.N.G.* never denied its Canadian origins, and most episodes included visual or verbal information that identified the city as Toronto, it might be more fruitful to look for specifically Canadian qualities in the way the series handled the balance of formula and flow.

PROFESSIONAL CODES AND SEMI-IDIOTIC THEORY

Like most episodes of *E.N.G.*, "Souls" weaves together three "stories" (a particularly apt term for a series that deals with how events are turned—or not—into news stories). The main story in this case involves a dispute over the meaning of the events in Tiananmen Square when the Chinese government used force against students demanding democratic reforms. One of the station's reporters (Clarke) obtains an exclusive interview with a visiting Chinese businessman (Woo), who claims that the student movement was disorganized and that no real massacre took place. When a Chinese student (Li) sees the interview, he contests its account, revealing that he was an eyewitness, but is reluctant to challenge Woo on air because of fears for his life. As the news workers try to deal with the implications of this dispute, the executive producer (Ann) also has to cope with the sudden arrival of an old school friend (Arlene) and her children. The third story offers some comic relief in its depiction of the attempts of a producer (Mac) to enliven the public service "Crime Catchers" segment of the news program.

The interweaving of the stories invites the viewer to make connections between them. The basic premise is that any connections are coincidental: these events happen to take place at the same time in a typical period of hectic newsroom activity. As Fiske suggests, however, the flow effect encourages the viewer to construct meanings through association, based on the perceived similarities and differences in the stories and their development. While the meanings constructed will vary according to the viewer's own interests and needs, it is possible to identify the kinds of connections that the text (drawing on its cultural context) is inviting the viewer to make.

As always in *E.N.G.* and many similar series, the stories in this episode are introduced in a pre-credits sequence (or "teaser"). The opening of "Souls" deviates from this basic formula by only indirectly introducing what will turn out to be the main story, but the other two stories are set up in the expected way. Mac is shown filming a "Crime Catchers" segment about an assault, and the sequence ends when Ann is shocked by the sudden appearance of Arlene and her children in the newsroom. In between, a reporter (Dan) and cameraman (Jake) cover a demonstration at a daycare centre, and another reporter (Terri) complains that she is going to lose her story because Clarke has taken the only available camera operator. There is no reference to Tiananmen Square, but Li is introduced at the daycare centre, and it will soon become clear that Clarke is working on the interview with Woo.

The opening does set up the episode's concern with the effects of dramatizing the news and with how to determine the "truth" in the face of rival accounts of a single event. The first shot, in which a man climbs through a bedroom window to attack a sleeping woman, is suddenly interrupted when Mac jumps in front of the camera to deliver a public service message. We discover that the segment is being taped in the studio, but the attack initially looks like the dramatic opening to an episode dealing with a "real" case of violence against a woman. The momentary confusion raises questions not only about the effects of mixing fiction and news but also about how *E.N.G.*'s fictions relate to the problem of finding the "truth."

At the daycare centre, Dan and Jake complain that the demonstration is a "dull story." Li interrupts to suggest that, if it is a dull story, the "signifiers should correspond"; in other words, they should not try to make it seem interesting. The journalists dismiss this as "semi-idiotic theory," but the student's jargon does introduce the basic semiotic idea of coded meaning. From the professional point of view of the journalists, Li's suggestion is simply impossible, given the need to capture the viewer's attention to compete with other stations. The problem then is that issues like the need for adequate daycare are not seen as newsworthy despite the needs of women like Arlene, and that news programs are placed under great pressure to become more entertaining. Ironically, the daycare demonstration has been organized to attract attention, but it fails because such methods have become "dull" through repetition. The male news workers simply do not see daycare as a "political" issue, and Dan's lack of interest in this highly visible domestic demonstration will be contrasted with his efforts to find out what really happened in Tiananmen Square.

Since this opening "teaser" is designed to "hook" the audience in order to discourage channel switching during the credits, the need to engage the viewer's interest is already at work in the episode's own use of the formula. After we adjust to the revelation that the assault has been staged, there is a sudden cut to a black-and-white close-up of a baby's diaper being changed, as if seen through the monitor on Jake's camera (a frequent device in the series). These images, in Li's terms, offer signifiers that, because of a lack of context, we are briefly unable to attach to appropriate signifieds, thus drawing us into the process of constructing meanings; they also testify to the series' investment in the professional concern with keeping the viewer interested, which Li's semiotic theory questions.

My argument about how the opening works does not depend on whether the audience "gets" the brief reference to semiotics. Even the viewer unfamiliar with semiotic theory will grasp that Li is questioning the need to make the story "interesting," and later Li does explain more about semiotics to the slow-witted news reader (Seth). After Li claims that the "weight" of the composition of an image will affect the way in which viewers respond to it, Seth thinks that a change in camera position might compensate for the failure of his diet. The humour cuts both ways: the professional demands of newsmaking undercut the theoretical claims of semiotics, but semiotics challenges the ideology of professionalism.

Selling the News

As usual, the pre-credits sequence ends with a suspended question designed to maintain the viewer's interest during the credits and the first commercial break. In this episode, Ann's troubled look at Arlene leads into the credits, which are, of course, always the same and designed to establish the show's "image" (*E.N.G.*'s credits were fairly conventional, with dramatic music, shots of the characters at work, and black-and-white stills of the main actors). The credits are followed by a "CTV News Update" during which the network's primary newsreader (Lloyd Robertson) reads three headlines.[7] The insertion of "real" news into a fictional program about newsmaking suggests the way that the flow works to blur distinctions: it implies a confidence that any questions about newsmaking raised during the program will not affect the "integrity" of the network's own news operation or the "reliability" that its publicity claims for Robertson.

The news becomes part of the flow. Robertson's promise to be "back after this" embeds the following commercial within the news-break, and then he returns only to invite the viewer to stay tuned for the full news program later in the evening. In fact, the *three* news items introduced in the "News Update" function as a "teaser" for

CTV's "national news" in much the same way that the three stories introduced in the pre-credits sequence do for this episode of *E.N.G.* Although this "News Update" was a regular feature, the news items included were obviously different each time and apparently unpredictable. Yet only certain kinds of events are likely to make the headlines, and during the broadcast of "Souls," the headlines dealt with quite familiar topics: the Canadian bank rate, a hotel fire in Egypt, and a sexist remark made by a male cabinet minister about a female member of the Opposition. Since one of the basic myths of news coverage is that it cannot be planned, any relationship among these items, or between them and the fictional "stories," must be seen as coincidental. Yet connections can be made, and coincidences may come to seem significant, as when a news story on sexism in politics underlines the attitudes towards women that are at stake in Mac's "Crime Catchers" segment and in Ann's encounter with Arlene.

As with the choice of news items, the actual placement of commercials at any given point may be random, but the range of likely commercials is fairly limited. During the first season of *E.N.G.*, the commercial embedded in the "News Update" was usually for Esso, whose sponsorship of the news affirmed the company's image as a responsible corporate citizen. In the commercial shown during "Souls," lights gradually go on in a dark building as an unseen male commentator describes Esso's increasing commitment to "research" and assures us that "the future is looking bright." While Esso's claims gain credibility through association with the CTV news, the commercial offers reassurance in relation to the "crisis structures" that are built into the practices of both CTV's and *E.N.G.*'s news workers.

IMAGE AND REALITY

According to Derrick de Kerckhove, television "provides an intermediate level of social discourse, neither exclusively public nor really private; neither frankly fictional, nor reliably real" (de Kerckhove 207). *E.N.G.* explored the tensions created by the medium itself as it transforms the cultural landscape and comes into conflict with traditional values that depend on clear distinctions between public and private, fiction and reality. The constraints and negotiations involved in putting together a news program become the primary evidence of the cultural impact of the electronic media, and their exposure undercuts the myth of "objectivity" that, according to the professional codes of traditional journalism, links "the credibility of news" to the idea that it is shaped by "the flow of occurrences" rather than by news workers (Tuchman 115). Although CTV's publicity for "Souls" described the episode in terms of these codes by claiming that "the *E.N.G.* team" tries "to separate truth from fiction in reporting the massacre at Tiananmen Square," the actual effect is to insist that news is always, to some degree, fiction.

From the perspective of the news director (Mike), Mac contaminates the public realm of newsmaking by attempting to introduce subjective effects that belong only in works of fiction, like *E.N.G.* itself. When Mac uses a tracking shot to get "the bad guy's point of view," someone remarks that he is making a "homage to Hitchcock." Later he is seen at his desk with blood streaming from his mouth, but the blood is revealed to be a make-up job, part of his attempt to dramatize the news. However, when he appears with a black eye, his colleagues admire the special effect, but the injury turns out to be "real," the result of an altercation with a man identified by his wife as the assailant in the opening dramatization.

The association of make-up with fictional codes, which should not spill over into the news discourse, plays on our awareness that *E.N.G.* is a fictional series about newsmaking, since we know that even Mac's "real" black eye is "really" only make-up. Yet make-up does have its place in presenting the news: we see Li being prepared for an interview, and Arlene is able to take advantage of the studio's resources to get a new make-up job. In a commercial for Clarion cosmetics that promises "personalized" make-up by computer, make-up mediates between technology and personal identity. The suggestion that cosmetics can combat the dehumanizing effect of modern life contrasts with the program's uneasy treatment of make-up as the site of a tension among news and fiction, image and identity.

Newsmaking is presented as a constant struggle between the demands of reality and the construction of images, a struggle that extends to the relationship between the program and the commercials. For example, the commercials offer a series of images in which technology and nature are seen to be harmoniously related. In particular, a Bell commercial, which presents the image and sound of a loon as a metaphor for the "long distance clarity" provided by the telephone company, contrasts with the complexities of modern communications in *E.N.G.*'s urban environment.

Similar tensions develop around the depiction of family life in the commercials and in the program. Two commercials for breakfast cereal show families getting up in the morning; a McDonald's commercial draws on the news discourse as it shows children (in a daycare centre?) discussing their wishes for the future; a Chef Boyardee commercial shows enthusiastic children running through sunlit streets. In the program itself, the family motif is introduced in the demonstration at the daycare centre, and then we see Arlene trying to cope with her children as they create disorder in Ann's apartment and in the newsroom. The tensions within family life are also revealed by the effect of "Crime Catchers"; but Arlene does decide to return to her husband, and the program is immediately followed by a commercial for Knorr soups that celebrates "the perfect marriage."

TENSIONS IN THE NEWSROOM

Although the station was clearly a commercial one, the interaction of news and advertising was never dealt with explicitly on *E.N.G.* In this episode, however, Mike does defend the integrity of news programming against what he calls Mac's "showbiz" approach, which, he claims, belongs with the "beer commercials." The commercial context of newsmaking also affects the main story when Dan claims that Woo is working for the Chinese government in order to protect business interests affected by the adverse publicity. Mike affirms the professional codes of newsmaking, reinforced by CTV's presentation of the Robertson persona, but the opening has already shown how these codes are challenged by the need for programs, news, and advertising to compete for the viewer's attention without radically disrupting the accepted formulas or the flow effect.

Because of the stress on personal conflicts in the newsroom, the focus is shifted from the question of the "truth" of what happened in China, although this remains the key issue for CTV's publicists and the onscreen news workers, to the implications of this dispute over "facts" for Western news practices and the ideology that supports them. An international story like this would not normally be covered by a local news operation, but Clarke claims that his interview with Woo will throw new light on an old story. Mike agrees to run Li's version of events because of the need for "balance," and he tells an angry Clarke that news is not a question of "either/or." Clarke retorts by asking whether it is now "multiple choice" and accusing Mike of not having the "guts" to make a clear decision. Although Mike has taken a stand against the "Crime Catchers" experiment, the contradictions involved in his defence of traditional standards emerge clearly in an argument with Ann. After he has criticized her for unprofessional behaviour in allowing Dan to intervene in Clarke's story, she accuses Clarke of not following professional codes, to which Mike lamely replies that the only rule is "getting the job done."

The issues at stake are underlined in a final exchange between Clarke and Dan, after Li has sent Dan a videotape and gone into hiding. As Dan is editing his report, Clarke surprises him (and us) by telling him that he "did good," but he then explains that he is praising Dan for pushing Li until "you got what you wanted." Dan seems taken aback and accuses Clarke of being as "jaded" as Woo; but his claim that his own motive was to give the students "respect" is not entirely convincing, especially given his own earlier "jaded" response to the daycare demonstration. The final image is a freeze-frame of Dan, in front of a monitor showing a Chinese tank, holding a T-shirt autographed by students in Tiananmen Square. The reality of the massacre is reduced to a frame within a frame. It can be known only through news practices that are caught between the "expert" opinion of a supposedly detached observer (a "legitimated" but not necessarily unbiased news source) and an "eyewitness" account that may be, as Clarke suggests, distorted by emotion.

While the problem of understanding Tiananmen may owe something to enduring myths of the "mysterious" East and to the undemocratic practices of the Chinese government, it is primarily a matter of the constraints built into the codes and practices of Western newsmaking.[8] Thus, when Ann tries to convince Li of the need to fight for a "free press" in his country, the implication of Western superiority is—to some extent, at least—undercut by an awareness of *E.N.G.*'s concern with the many ways in which the Western media are not "free." The incorporation of an actual event into a fictional narrative and into the commercial flow may be open to charges of exploitation and trivialization, but the tensions that result do expose contradictions that raise questions about the construction of "popular" meanings.

Any text involves some kind of tension between the diverse materials of which it is composed and the form that the text imposes on them, but this is especially the case with regard to the televisual flow in which formal structures are both clearly defined (formulas) and subject to a wide range of distractions and disruptions. In "Souls," however, this tension is especially pertinent because all of the "stories" in the episode deal with the relationship between freedom and order. It centres on Woo's assertion that there was "anarchy" in Tiananmen Square and on the role of a "free press" in reporting these claims. The social and political implications of dramatizing these issues are complicated by the insertion of commercials that promise a freedom which does not threaten the dominant order, most notably one which offers "freedom from manual labour" to those who buy a Mazda car.

The interweaving of the stories also contributes to the development of this motif. Dan and Jake's search for Li, a victim of the suppression of political freedom in China, is intercut with a drinking session in which Arlene speaks of the lack of freedom in her life while Ann reflects on the terms on which she has gained her own relative freedom. All this is contained within the hectic activity that—as in all episodes of *E.N.G.*, but here intensified by the presence of Arlene's children— leads to the more-or-less successful construction of the organized meanings of a news broadcast out of the chaos in the newsroom. Such a process echoes the viewer's construction of meanings out of the apparent "anarchy" of the flow.

CONCLUSION

Any conclusion reached on the basis of a single text must remain as provisional as the order that the *E.N.G.* news team imposes on the rumours, messages, and sensations that flow through and around the newsroom. What the analysis of this particular text does suggest is that Fiske's account of popular culture as a "semiotic democracy" has much to offer in the analysis of Canadian popular culture. Yet the tensions and contradictions that contribute to the semiotic complexity of *E.N.G.* also suggest that, as the communications environment becomes increasingly global in the age of electronic media, we cannot just go with the flow if the experience of the "popular" in Canada is to involve more than wresting our own meanings from *Rambo*.

NOTES

1 The series was rerun in a late-night slot on some CBC stations and then
   on the Showcase cable-TV channel. *E.N.G.* was shown in the U.S. on the
   Lifetime cable network and in Britain on Channel 4.
2 For an illuminating survey of the Frankfurt School approach to "mass culture" and the "culture industry" and of recent reactions against the "elit-
   ism" of this approach, see Jim McGuigan, *Cultural Populism* (London:
   Routledge, 1992).
3 Written by Don Truckey; directed by George Bloomfield.
4 For an accessible and thorough treatment of theories of postmodernity,
   see Steven Connor, *Postmodernist Culture: An Introduction to Theories of
   the Contemporary* (Oxford: Blackwell, 1989).
5 My analysis is based on the program as broadcast by CFTO in Toronto;
   the commercials may have differed on other CTV stations, but this would
   only underline my central argument that the cultural meanings of popular
   television must be seen as provisional and shifting within certain relatively predictable limits.
6 R. Bruce Elder, for example, argues that Canadian *cinéma-vérité* filmmakers avoid the "crisis structure" that characterizes their U.S. counterparts. See his *Image and Identity: Reflections on Canadian Film and
   Culture* (Waterloo: Wilfrid Laurier UP, 1989), 104-107.
7 In later seasons, the "News Update" was moved to the final commercial
   break.
8 The role of the Western media in representing the events in Tiananmen
   Square as a "news story" is discussed in David L. Altheide and Robert P.
   Snow, *Media Worlds in the Postjournalism Era* (New York: Aldine de
   Gruyter, 1991) and in McKenzie Wark, *Virtual Geography: Living with
   Global Media Events* (Bloomington: Indiana UP, 1994). The leading role
   played by several women in these events is masked by the gender politics
   of *E.N.G.* in which this political "story" is treated as an all-male affair in
   contrast to the "private" story of Ann and Arlene's difficult reunion.

WORKS CITED

Browne, Nick. "The Political Economy of the Television (Super) Text."
    Television: The Critical View. Ed. Horace Newcomb. 4th ed. New York:
    Oxford UP, 1987. 585-99.
Collins, Richard. *Culture, Communication and National Identity: The Case of
    Canadian Television*. Toronto: U of Toronto P, 1990.
de Kerckhove, Derrick. *The Skin of Culture: Investigating the New Electronic
    Reality*. Toronto: Somerville, 1995.
Fiske, John. *Television Culture*. London: Methuen, 1987.
_____. "Moments of Television: Neither the Text nor the Audience." *Remote
    Control: Television, Audiences, and Cultural Power*. Ed. Ellen Seiter,
    Hans Borchers, Gabriele Kreutzner, and Eva-Maria Warth. London:
    Routledge, 1989. 56-78.
_____. *Understanding Popular Culture*. Boston: Unwin Hyman, 1989.

Harcourt, Peter. "Introduction to *Film Canadiana Yearbook 1975-1976*," *Canadian Film Reader*. Ed. Seth Feldman and Joyce Nelson. Toronto: Peter Martin Associates, 1977. 370-76.

Joyrich, Lynne. "Individual Response." *Camera Obscura* 20-21 (May-September 1989): 190-94.

O'Connor, Alan, ed. *Raymond Williams on Television: Selected Writings.* Toronto: Between the Lines, 1989.

Tuchman, Gaye. *Making News: A Study in the Construction of Reality.* New York: Free, 1978.

Williams, Raymond. *Television: Technology and Cultural Form.* New York: Schocken, 1975.

TWO LAWYERS AND AN ISSUE: RECONSTRUCTING QUEBEC'S "NATION" IN *A NOUS DEUX!*[1]

Sheila Petty

I n the macrocosm of North American television, the Quebec television industry offers a singular opportunity for critical study because
it is charged with the preservation of a vibrant Francophone popular
culture in a predominantly Anglophone continent. The language issues
underlying the situation figure largely in Quebec's non-reliance on
other cultural practices for visions of itself. It has been argued, for
example, that the majority of Québécois will not view American series
in their original version, and even if a dubbed American series is programmed at the same time as a Québécois series, the latter will win out
in Quebec.[2] Thus, Quebec's indigenous television productions are singularly self-reliant in that they have developed unique ways to challenge and transform popular television forms to suit their cultural
imperatives. In view of this phenomenon, it is not surprising that by
1990, *TV World* declared that "there are more French soaps in Quebec
than there are in all of French-speaking Europe combined" (Lavers 20).

Ever since the Société Radio-Canada broadcast its first images in
1952, Quebec has produced indigenous work that has both looked to its

Notes on page 138.

historical past and its cultural present. There is a multitude of television serials in a variety of genres from historical drama (*Duplessis, Cormoran, Les filles de Caleb, Blanche, Montréal P.Q.*) to current-affairs-driven serials (*A nous deux!, Scoop, Lance et compte, Chambres en ville*), offering a range of perspectives on contemporary and historical Quebec society. This paper will concentrate on the contemporary *téléroman* (soap opera), and consider the way in which current-affairs issues are appropriated by and transformed in these popular texts.

The *téléroman* has evolved as one of Quebec's most popular storytelling forms. Born as an adaptation of the classic novel form and an extension of the *radioroman*, the *téléroman* matured as an art form when some of Quebec's greatest writers—Claude-Henri Grignon, Roger Lemelin, Claude Jasmin, Victor Lévy-Beaulieu—began to write for television. Whether one considers the *téléroman* to be a reflection or a construction of society, one thing is certain: Québécois television serials possess their own singularity, drawing on both the American and European serial formats, but developing original, local preoccupations (Véronneau xviii).

An excellent example of this process can be drawn from *A nous deux!*, a low-budget, state-financed and -produced *téléroman*, co-authored by Suzanne Aubry and Louise Pelletier and first broadcast by Société Radio-Canada on 3 January 1994. Of particular interest is the co-authors' stated goal of critiquing a certain Québécois nationalist discourse based on race and the Catholic Church,[3] and how this leads to a deconstruction of Quebec's "national memory" as they take slices of Quebec's history, transfer them into an ideological/entertainment context, and produce new articulations of "nation."

The narrative of *A nous deux!* begins with Simone Vaillancourt, a young Montreal lawyer with strong principles, but no money, as she takes on a sexual harassment case. The case brings her face to face with Philippe Bertrand, a bourgeois lawyer, who represents the harasser and is her ideological opposite. Eventually, Simone and Philippe become partners, and the *téléroman* evolves around their cases, their families and their friends, providing *A nous deux!* with the multiple plot lines of true soap-opera form. However, the co-authors transcend the boundaries of traditional soap opera by foregrounding certain critical issues that have been both problematic and central to Quebec and Canadian history, in order to forge an ideological construct.

At first glance, *A nous deux!* would appear to fall into the category of "open" serial form, in which, according to Robert C. Allen, no one central character reigns, but in which a large community of characters is set in relationship to one another through multiple plot lines. Allen further argues that open serials such as American daytime soaps "trade narrative closure for paradigmatic complexity," which in turn carries implicit ideological values, attitudes and behaviours, rather than expressing a particular ideological "message" (18, 21, 22). Thus, while the serials might occasionally refer to contemporary social issues such as AIDS, adult illiteracy and sexual harassment, or even adapt current-affairs stories, these references to "reality" only function ultimately to permit a larger margin for narrative excess (Spence 184, 185).

One of the most distinguishing features of American soap-opera form is that the narratives thrive on a tension between reality and fantasy in which hyperbole, exaggeration and pure coincidence operate as driving elements in the plot structure. Although this tension exists to a certain degree in *A nous deux!*, fantasy is largely mitigated through extensive incorporation of Québécois current affairs into the structure of the text (one issue per two episodes), resulting in an explicit ideological component that is only present in American soaps in an implicit sense. In American soap-opera structure, the fantasy component is the overriding consideration, and while controversial social issues might be raised, the characters involved seldom, if ever, face realistic consequences. In *A nous deux!*, a character may win out in the arena of social injustice, but this "win" is mediated realistically in that miraculous change in the dominant culture is seldom accomplished, and, thus, the struggle must continue.

This focus on "local preoccupations" or ideological concerns is reflected in the televisual aesthetics employed in the text. Like American daytime soaps, *A nous deux!* is shot on enclosed sets on video with a multiple camera set-up. However, similarities in the production context are outweighed by different narrative concerns, and this is easily demonstrated by contrasting their televisual aesthetics. Since ideology in American soaps is an implicit structure read as a subtext beneath a construction that only appears to be primarily psychologically driven, aesthetic elements that reinforce emotional suturing, such as extreme close-ups and zooms, become foregrounded in the text. *A nous deux!*, however, is explicitly focussed on ideas, concepts and constructions of Quebec as a nation, necessitating the development, on the part of the *téléroman*'s creators, of televisual aesthetics designed to "intellectually" suture the viewer into the text's ideological concerns. This text emphasizes the exchange of ideas rather than emotions, thus the need for extreme close-ups or other emotive visual devices is reduced. Close-ups are used sparingly and are generally intended to underscore important ideas instead of emotional reactions. The text is centred on the creation of debate, and this is reflected aesthetically by the frequent use of neutral angles, balanced composition and a predominance of medium and medium-long shots, according the viewer the emotional distance required to weigh the ideological concerns offered by the text. This does not suggest that emotion is completely absent from *A nous deux!*: the visions of Quebec imparted by various characters are passionately held and expressed. However, the role of the "personal," so vital to American soap structure, is downplayed in *A nous deux!* in favour of the political.

In order to underscore this process I will examine the "Marguerite Lechêne" plot line and its visual expression as developed over episodes fourteen and fifteen from the beginning of the second season (September 19 and 26, 1994). The plot line concerns the character of Marguerite Lechêne, a young Haitian woman, who seeks legal counsel from Simone and Philippe after the offices of her newspaper, *L'echo d'Haïti*, have been vandalized. She shows Simone and Philippe threatening letters that she has received and at their prompting suggests that controversial talk-radio-host Michel Dion might be inciting the attack because of their past conflicts.[4]

Here the co-authors demonstrate their ability to pull together issues from Quebec current affairs, and combine and reconfigure them into instruments suitable to their fictional, ideological debate. The above plot line focusses on the difficulties in determining the line of demarcation between freedom of speech and the dissemination of hate as viewed through the lens of contemporary race relations in Montreal. The story line was inspired by the "Affair Alliance Québec," which occurred at the end of December 1988 (and carried well into 1989). Royal Orr, then president of Alliance Québec, was wrongly accused by the press of victimizing his own cause by setting fire to the Alliance Québec headquarters, following the political party's court case over Bill 178 (Québec's language law). This incident became the focus of a vicious debate among members of the media concerning the right to freedom of speech and the duty of journalists to be responsible for the accuracy of their coverage.

The co-authors take the central premise of "blaming the victim" and combine it with the freedom of speech issue, but go beyond the scope of the Royal Orr incident by intertwining a third issue: the troubled relations between Montreal's black communities and the MUC (Montreal Urban Community/Communauté Urbain de Montréal) police. In the 1990s, there were a number of alleged improprieties and outright questionable actions by the police against members of the black communities (including trigger-happy behaviour resulting in the deaths of innocent blacks), leading to ongoing charges of racism.[5] These events have created an environment of deep distrust, and racism has become a highly sensitive public issue.

This "combination" of issues allows the co-authors to explore the roles of the state and the police in the lives of minorities in Quebec in a way that would not be credible if represented by an Anglophone. Furthermore, the co-authors demonstrate a sensitivity toward injustices endured by blacks in Quebec by not attempting to link their plight to the French-versus-English "colonial grudge-match" (Dodge 10). Marguerite Lechêne, as the character placed in a recontextualized fictional situation similar to that of Royal Orr, is shown as a member of a distinct Haitian community (as opposed to a black homogeneity) that is at once separate from, but also linked to, "pure laine" Québécois society by sharing its language and authority structure.

The co-authors expose the splintered nature of a contemporary Quebec in which no single community shares a common history. The narrative situation is set up and simultaneously deconstructed through the presentation of a multiplicity of voices, ideological positions and points of view concerning the vandalism and arson, through Marguerite's innocence or guilt, and through her defamation and harassment. In the process, Aubry and Pelletier present an explicit debate on the state of Québécois society without appearing to privilege one point of view over another, at least in terms of screen time. The task of choosing sides is left to the viewers, who can sample the arguments offered by the characters and negotiate their own individual positions within the debate.

An example of this occurs in episode fourteen, just after the firebombing of Marguerite Lechêne's newspaper. Simone and Philippe

enter their office in the midst of a spirited dispute concerning the interrogation of Marguerite Lechêne by the police. Two ideological positions are constructed: Philippe takes the stand that the police are only
doing their jobs by interrogating anyone connected with the newspaper, and Simone espouses the belief that they are victimizing
Marguerite by attempting to blame her for the bombing because of her
racial background. In American soap tradition, one would expect to
see the disparity between Simone and Philippe's positions reflected in
high and low angles respectively. As well, the intensity of the argument as it progresses would generally see a movement from medium
decor shots to extreme close-ups in order to underscore the emotional
context of the argument. This is not the case as the scene under discussion is shot in a combination of medium-long two-shots and
medium shots. The individual medium shots of Simone and Philippe
function to some degree as close-ups in that they specifically foreground each character's position. However, the use of neutral angles
for both renders the positions equally valid, and the lack of clear resolution at the end of the scene allows the viewers to consider the pros
and cons of each. This structure becomes a recurrent device throughout the two episodes and is reprised each time the plot line delves into
an ideological debate of the issues.

In the "Marguerite Lechêne" plot line, the co-authors posit Philippe
as an embodiment of the dominant hegemony. He is a moderately conservative white male Francophone and possesses the viewpoint that
patriarchal dominant authority will act with benevolence and justice.
Philippe is not a central character in terms of screen time, the usual
determinant for such a designation. As a character embodiment of
Québec's status quo, Philippe's ideological positions become a magnet
for debate. As the characters constantly challenge Philippe's ideology
with their marginalized positions, the co-authors are able to foreground
the tensions and debates in contemporary Québécois society.

It is through Philippe that the police impropriety is drawn into the
narrative thread. Philippe suggests that they approach his former colleague, Lieutenant Robert Héroux, for Marguerite's protection, and a
meeting is arranged between Héroux and the two lawyers. Like
Philippe, Héroux also shows evidence of a paternalistic attitude
towards Simone, but unlike Philippe, he downplays the significance of
the vandalism: "Vandalism....That's a big word for some broken win-

dows and graffiti" (Vandalisme....C'est un bien grand mot pour des fenêtres brisées et quelques graffitis). Irritated, Simone replies without missing a beat, "Especially when it happens to visible minorities" (Surtout quand ça arrive aux minorités visibles). Héroux declares that the police are taking every precaution possible to sensitize the force to "minority problems." Paradoxically, however, as he is about to leave the office, he complains that he has reports to write because, now that the chiefs have become so "politically correct," every arrest must be justified. This seems to imply that "justification" for an arrest has not been necessary in the past.

Héroux asks to take the threatening letters with him to assist in the investigation. It becomes evident shortly, when Michel Dion's talk-radio invective against Marguerite intensifies, that the police are indeed leaking sensitive material to him, particularly in view of the fact that exact phrases from the letters received by Marguerite are used by Dion in ridiculing her charges of racism. Furthermore, Dion uses the letters to bolster his charge that Marguerite is responsible for the vandalism and arson. When Philippe confronts Héroux about the leak, the viewer is given the opportunity to consider the police position as Héroux attempts to defend himself.

Clearly, the co-authors are demonstrating the power of the "old-boys' network" as this important discussion between Philippe and Héroux precludes Simone and Marguerite. Furthermore, Héroux seems less outraged by the accusation itself than he is by Philippe's show of personal distrust by making it. Another example of this occurs during the "old boys" discussion between Philippe and Claude Paquette (Dion's defence attorney and Philippe's former law partner), who visits Philippe at his home with the intention of talking him out of prosecuting his client. It is significant that Paquette offers personal reasons (past friendship) as well as professional reasons (Dion could lose his job) as incentives to drop the injunction. Here, the co-authors implicitly critique the notion that connections are as important as the validity of one's case. For example, the very fact that this discussion takes place suggests that Philippe and Claude could have come to a private "agreement" that might have had serious consequences for Marguerite's case, consequences that would have been decided without her presence or voice. This inference is reinforced by the setting for the discussion: it takes place not at the office, but at Philippe's home, in his private space.

The above discussion has centred on those characters situated on the ideological right, in which all participants are linked by their relative positions of power in the dominant order. On the ideological left are the arguments or positions antithetical to the dominant, and these are primarily embodied by Marguerite, Simone, and Federico Marquez, the Chilean landlord/caretaker who owns the building in which the law firm is housed. All three characters directly challenge the veracity of established authority. For example, the character of Marguerite serves as a device to expose how police treat minorities: they refuse to believe their complaints; they make light of damages incurred by minority victims; they try to claim that all the incidents are isolated; and they eventually turn the situation around and blame the victim. Marguerite, who is obviously a victim, must fight to establish her own innocence even where Philippe is concerned. In a meeting with Simone present, Philippe advises Marguerite not to file an injunction against Dion but to wait and to trust the police and the system to vindicate her. Marguerite is incensed and she exclaims bitterly, "As far as everyone is concerned, I'm guilty" (Je suis coupable pour tout le monde).

However, despite Philippe's resistance, Marguerite drives forward with her intention to silence Dion's defamation. Aubry and Pelletier's Marguerite defies victimization because she recognizes the validity of, and defends, her rights by using the dominant apparatus to her best advantage. This is reflected visually, as the camera work does not linger on the emotional consequences of her victimization. And despite the vitriolic attack on her person by Dion and the police harassment, she does not back down, but sees the injunction to its conclusion even though success is uncertain. She never questions the correctness of her actions or displays fear in the face of authoritarian persecution; even when two of her colleagues are named as agitators by the police, she does not hesitate to defend them and her cause. Ironically, Marguerite's colleagues are considered "agitators" because they attended a rally in support of Jean-Bertrand Aristide.

Simone represents working-class, feminist, liberal Montreal and is highly suspicious of all authority structures. Although she is dismissed by Philippe on more than one occasion, she continues her independent inquiry into the affair, accepting Marguerite's concerns as valid and openly challenging the "official" version of events.

A thread of gender discourse is woven through the plot line. Marguerite, for example, is dismissed as "a hysterical woman" by the police when she tries to lodge a complaint regarding the vandalism. Simone's concerns are also dismissed, not just by Philippe but by Héroux as well, at their initial meeting. Ironically, the only figure of authority who validates Simone and Marguerite's concerns is the judge, also a woman.

Simone's purpose in the narrative is to challenge Philippe's comfortable assumption that the dominant authority is equally benevolent to all. There is a marked contrast between the way in which Philippe and Simone network. His contacts are all white males of equal social status whilst Simone is depicted networking with people who, by virtue of race or social status, are marginalized on the fringes of "pure laine" dominant society. She is ultimately responsible for exposing Dion's surreptitious connection to the police, but she does not develop this information in a vacuum; Simone offers her hypothesis to several characters, inviting their critiques. By having Simone consult characters on the periphery of the dominant group, Aubry and Pelletier in effect create a sounding board for ideological positions that might not otherwise receive dramatic expression.

The minority characters in *A nous deux!* have a far clearer perception of the dominant order's mechanism than does Philippe, who presumably belongs to it. After being dismissed by Philippe, Simone finds herself discussing the situation with Federico. Marquez, as an immigrant, immediately understands the issue Simone is grappling with, and he bolsters her position by agreeing that the police are obviously collaborating with Dion in his defamation of Marguerite.

Marquez provides the most important plot insight in the narrative, and this is not just by coincidence. Unlike Philippe, he is in a position to examine society from outside. Rather than having been born into a relationship with the established authority, Marquez has had to negotiate in much the same way that Marguerite has, and somewhat in the way Simone has had to negotiate a position with the "old-boys' network." It is Marquez's insight that ultimately spurs Simone in the direction of discovery: Simone and Marquez are in the office listening to Dion's program on the radio when Marquez comments that it is a strange coincidence that Dion's information regarding Marguerite is coming from the police. When Simone asks if Marquez thinks that the police are involved, he replies, "That's always what they do when they haven't done their work, blame the victim" (C'est toujours ce qu'ils font quand ils n'ont pas fait leur travail, blâmer la victime). Marquez's observation contributes to Simone's realization, in a later scene, that Dion is quoting verbatim from Marguerite's letters; therefore, only Héroux could have leaked them to him.

The final confrontation occurs in court and the arguments are laid out in the bold strokes of legal discourse, in an act of summation. Most interesting here is not the summation itself, but the new information that is revealed during Philippe's cross-examination of Héroux. During the questioning, Héroux is forced to concede that the police have never had grounds to consider either Marguerite Lechêne or her colleagues as suspects in the arson. When Héroux reveals this, the camera cuts away to a two-shot of Paquette and Dion; both appear surprised by Héroux's admission. This surprise is important because it implies that Dion as well as Marguerite have been victims in a larger police agenda. Aubry and Pelletier use this expository device to mitigate Marguerite's eventual victory. When Paquette confronts Simone and Philippe after the ruling, he points out to them that his client was an easy target but that the real instigators of Marguerite's defamation were the police, who, of course, go unpunished.

This is not the only ambiguity offered by Marguerite's victory. Certainly, the question of racism becomes subsumed by the legal issue of defamation, and it is significant that the judge's ruling steers away from both this issue and the issue of possible police impropriety. Aubry and Pelletier resist providing a miraculous cure for society's injustice, unlike in American soap opera, where the viewer is left feeling that the victory will be effective in achieving permanent change. The resolution is left deliberately ambiguous, enabling the viewer to ponder the larger implications of the issues. There are a number of questions implicitly raised and left unanswered by the text: are Philippe's views of benevolent authority validated by winning the case, or does Marguerite win the case because Philippe (as a member of the dominant order) and Simone are there to speak for her? Does Marguerite win the day because the case is just and she has the wherewithal to use the system? Certainly, from Dion's attitude in the courtroom, it is clear that this is a single battle won in a continuing war that is far from over. This lack of clear resolution reflects a cynicism toward authority in general, suggesting that if social change occurs, it will do so only in the face of persistent action by those who suffer injustice. Philippe himself addresses this directly when responding to Simone's charge that Héroux, and by extension the police, should have been their rightful target rather than Dion; he points out to her that a lawyer's role is not to reform society, but, rather, to bring a little justice into a world that is fundamentally unjust. This is not answer enough for Simone who regards this position as "cowardly."

If *A nous deux!* does not offer a tidy ideological resolution, it is because critique and debate are inherent to its structure. What the text does ultimately offer through explicit ideological discourse is a multiplicity of constructions of Quebec as a "nation." The characters of *A nous deux!* all share Quebec as a nation, but experience that nation in distinctly different ways.

This is the crux of Quebec's internal struggle to define its culture. As Martin Allor has observed, "Our collective history, however imagined, is less in question than the more personalized problem of identity in difference; *l'identitaire* is a hybrid, unstable figure. What is at stake then is the production of a cosmopolitan community; to be both a people (*le sujet-nation*), and therefore the ground of a state, and at the same time, to exceed the limits of this national-subjectivity: to not be identical with it" (70). Québécois television, from its inception, has played an exemplary role in the dissemination of these debates and in codifying and expanding notions of Quebec's cultural identities by virtue of its ability to communicate to a wide popular audience. *A nous deux!*'s significance in this tradition arises from its invitation to the viewer to actively participate in the redefinition and rearticulation of contemporary Quebec society in the face of the world.

ACKNOWLEDGEMENTS

Research for this essay was funded by the Social Sciences and Humanities Research Council of Canada. My thanks to Suzanne Aubry, Louise Pelletier, Maude Martin and Pierrette Villemaire for providing valuable background information on *A nous deux!* I would also like to thank Royal Orr for providing information regarding the "Affair Alliance Québec." Special thanks to V. Borden, D. L. McGregor and C. Cunningham for engaging with such enthusiasm and offering so many creative comments.

NOTES

1 "A nous deux" literally means "to the two of us." However, a more figurative and hence appropriate rendering of the title in English is "face to face."

2 According to Louise Cousineau, "the Quebec public doesn't often watch American series in their original version. But if TVA [Télé-Métropole] or TQS [Télévision Quatre Saisons] were to acquire the French version of one of the two series and broadcast it during *Emergency*, viewers would automatically make comparisons. However, the Quebec product, with local stars, will always have the upper hand" [Le public québécois ne regarde pas beaucoup les séries américaines en version originale. Mais si les réseaux TVA ou TQS allaient acheter la version française d'une des deux séries et la diffuser pendant *Urgence*, le public ferait automatiquement des comparaisons. Encore qu'une oeuvre québécoise, avec des gens d'ici, aura toujours le haut du pavé]. Cousineau is referring to the American series *Chicago Hope* and *ER*.

3 Conversation with Suzanne Aubry and Louise Pelletier, Montréal, 18 May 1995.

4 In Season 1 of the *téléroman*, Marguerite Lechêne is fired from her teaching job because of defamatory comments made by Michel Dion. She takes legal action and Dion is forced to pay some compensation.

5 "On March 13, 1992, more than 2,000 Montreal policemen, most of whom could barely tell the difference between a Rastafarian and a Sikh, marched in the streets to protest against a report made public by their police chief. The report blamed them for intercepting an innocent unarmed black, Marcellus François, in his car and killing him. The 24-year-old François was confused for another black suspect" (Dodge 10).

WORKS CITED

Allen, Robert C. Introduction. *To Be Continued...Soap Operas Around the World*. Ed. Robert C. Allen. London: Routledge, 1995. 1-26.

Allor, Martin. "Cultural *métissage*: National Formations and Productive Discourse in Quebec Cinema and Television." *Screen* 34.1 (1993): 69-75.

Cousineau, Louise. "La fascination du bon docteur." *La Presse* 24 September 1994, E3.

Dodge, Bill. "Black History, Bright Future?" *Mirror* 9.36 (1994): 10.

Lavers, Daphne. "Quebec: A *savon savant*." *TV World* 13.1 (1990): 20.

Spence, Louise. "'They killed off Marlena, but she's on another show now': Fantasy, Reality, and Pleasure in Watching Daytime Soap Operas." *To Be Continued...Soap Operas Around the World*. Ed. Robert C. Allen. London: Routledge, 1995. 182-98.

Véronneau, Pierre. "Introduction: La vie est un téléroman." *Répertoire des séries, feuilletons et téléromans québécois de 1952 à 1992*. Ed. Jean Yves Croteau. Québec: Les Publications du Québec, 1993. xiii-xviii.

FURTHER READING

Allen, Robert C. *Speaking of Soap Operas*. Chapel Hill: U of North Carolina P. 1985.

_____. "Melodramatic Identifications: Television Fiction and Women's Fantasy." *Television and Women's Culture: the Politics of the Popular.* Ed. Mary Ellen Brown. London: Sage, 1990. 75-88.

Barbatsis, Gretchen, and Yvette Guy. "Analyzing Meaning in Form: Soap Opera's Compositional Construction of 'Realness.'" *Journal of Broadcasting and Electronic Media* 35 (1991): 59-74.

Butler, Jeremy. "Notes on the Soap Opera Apparatus: Televisual Style and *As the World Turns.*" *Cinema Journal* 25 (1986): 53-70.

Cantor, Muriel, and Suzanne Pingree. *The Soap Opera*. Beverly Hills: Sage, 1983.

Collins, Richard. *Culture, Communication and National Identity: The Case of Canadian Television*. Toronto: U of Toronto P, 1990.

Feuer, Jane. "Melodrama, Serial Form and Television Today." *Screen* 25.1 (1984): 4-16.

Fiske, John. *Television Culture*. London: Routledge, 1990.

Marshall, Bill. "Gender, Narrative and National Identity in *Les filles de Caleb.*" *Canadian Journal of Film Studies* 2.2-3 (1993): 51-65.

Nguyên-Duy, Véronique. "Du téléroman de cuisine au supermarché médiatique: L'evolution du téléroman québécois depuis 1980." *Québec Studies* 18 (1994): 45-62.

Schneider, Cynthia, and Brian Wallis. *Global Television*. New York and Cambridge: Wedge and MIT P, 1988.

STRAIGHT UP AND YOUTH
TELEVISION: NAVIGATING
DREAMS WITHOUT
NATIONHOOD

Joan Nicks

In the article "Unhiding the Hidden," first published in 1974 and reprinted in an anthology committed to "the immense diversity of post-colonial theory" (Ashcroft, Griffiths and Tiffin i), Robert Kroetsch traces a pattern in modern Canadian literature. His focus is the adaptation of language to subjective experience and its liberating effect on the imaginations of fictional characters who circumvent the cultural imperatives of official, or familiar, Canadian boundaries. His observations remain timely and useful for the critical analysis of "deviance" in popular culture, and they are applicable to CBC-TV's (late) series *Straight Up* (Back Alley Films Productions/Alliance) and its approach to prime-time youth television. Processes of demythologizing Canadian authority structures underlie the contemporary narratives and televisual style of this now defunct CBC series, much like Kroetsch's identification of a paradox in Canadian literary fiction to "un-name...uninvent the world" through personal rites of passage: "In recent years the tension between this appearance of being just like someone else and the demands of authenticity has become intolerable—both to the individu-

Notes on pages 155-57.

als and to the society. In recent Canadian fiction the major writers resolve the paradox—the painful tension between appearance and authenticity—by the radical process of demythologizing the systems that threaten to define them. Or, more comprehensively, they uninvent the world" (394). As example, Kroetsch writes of Margaret Atwood's female protagonist in the novel *Surfacing*: "[She] must remove the false names that adhere to her experience. The terror of her journey is not that she…almost drowns; it is rather that she surfaces. The terror resides not in her going insane but in her going sane" (394-95). Comparing Atwood's and Robertson Davies's narrative strategies for expressing this paradox, Kroetsch elaborates: "Where the larger process of uninventing, in Atwood becomes a journey into the wilderness, in…Davies [*The Manticore*], it is a journey to the old civilizations, the sum of our ancestry. And yet, for both these novelists, the condition of pre-history is necessary to valid and authentic birth" (395).

Straight Up's contemporary television teens are drawn along the non-compliant lines that Kroetsch calls "rituals," and against the Hollywood teenpic model that Charles Acland analyzes to demonstrate how this genre takes "the perspective of the adult as it views the 'not-adult.'" The youth movie, he argues, "is rife with the gaze of the fully socialized" adult perspective in command (Acland 117). Even when a film's point of view is authentic of youth—"either intended for a young audience or about young people"—it is always adult-driven, with youth represented as "that which is watched" (Acland 117). As a television series, *Straight Up* is absorbed in the visceral experiences of teen characters who uninvent themselves by travelling the night city of its narrative worlds in a process I would describe as "navigating dreams without nationhood." That is, without rights and legitimacy attributable to adult cultural players, but, importantly, within youth's deviance from adult expectations and social norms. Narratively, adults are generally absent, and only rarely are they interested watchers of youth. ("Witnessing" adults are discussed below in my analysis of the episode "Small Bang Theory.") Through slippage from both formula television and popular youth codes, the teens get lost in the social cracks, bypassing official boundaries. Their imaginative experience has its own exploratory logic in dreaming and acting out: to test points of view that official culture and authority structures don't allow; and, effectively, to delimit the adult agendas of teen genres in film and television.

Dreaming here should not be confused with the tradition of blind escape and delusion inscribed into those adult-male examples of arrested development and avoidance in English-Canadian cinema.[1] In *Straight Up* the teens' journeys remain local, within Toronto, but are not predictably Canadianized or driven by social or moral agendas or topicality. The scripts and visual strategies open out personal domains for youth television as a category through the teens' subjective forays into symbolic parallel worlds. As decentred characters, they immerse themselves in ritual experiences that position youth's imaginative risk taking and that formally deviate from the plot progress and realist settings of the series' episodes. Such strategies both employ and circumvent a typical narrative/series format in television that pivots on the plot device of a dilemma to be solved and a lesson to be learned—as with the various (late) *Degrassi* series. Despite its circumvention of some aspects of format, even director Jerry Ciccoritti acknowledges *Straight Up*'s resemblance to television-anthology drama, although he commented in an interview that "the CBC pretty well gave me a free hand."[2]

Straight Up was the "first venture into episodic television"[3] for co-creators and executive co-producers Janis Lundman and Adrienne Mitchell, who were instrumental in shaping the goals for the series. Applying their documentary background—they produced the films *Talk 16* (1991) and *Talk 19* (1996)—to the research, they interviewed teenagers to gather real stories as a social basis for *Straight Up*'s dramatic constructions. The initial six episodes (1996 season) ran in the so-called adult prime-time slot—specifically from 9:30 till 10:00 p.m.—on Monday evenings following the sharp media/cultural satire *This Hour Has 22 Minutes*. Both series—albeit different in genre, form, content and target audiences—are marked by critique and deviance. The CBC's back-to-back programming of the two shows suggests that the network was keen to test whether *Straight Up*'s relative formal and narrative maturity and sophistication as youth television would appeal to adult viewers[4]—though *Straight Up* was dropped from the CBC's regular scheduling at the end of the 1998 season.[5] However, as a strategy, it might be argued that there is a constructive logic in the CBC's pattern of six-episode seasons (sometimes complete series) in the late 1990s, which may have benefited cutting-edge programs such as *Straight Up* as a hedge against declining into the formula common to long-running series.

When *Straight Up* returned as a series in 1998 with new episodes, the *Globe and Mail*'s television critic, John Allemang, observed that, as television, *Straight Up* was "deliberately designed to be a show looking for a fight": "Mainstream U.S. networks wouldn't touch its raw documentary-style storytelling, and even the looser MTV reportedly balked at [an episode] where a taxi driver masturbates in front of his drunk female passenger" (Feb. 25, 1998). What Allemang misses in his favourable commentary is how important the series' visual style is to constructing such sensational scenarios. *Straight Up*'s youths imaginatively and serendipitously occupy spaces that can be scanned, felt, penetrated, tested and, in Kroetsch's terms, uninvented to reveal something subjective, primal and apart from peer, parental or social scrutiny. Narrative imagery is personalized in teen characters who are exceptional (for better and for worse) and whose points of view and desires are visualized in a strong, sometimes disorienting manner that challenges even alert viewers. In key dramatic instances, the characters' subjectivity entails a reach for sublime experience that defies mainstreet city culture as well as suburbia. In other words, in parallel domains that are constructed to look both surreal and raw—through strategies that borrow from cinema and that also exploit televisuality—the cultural conditions of marginal figures who are not acknowledged as citizens or even as infamous outcasts must be "read" through the visual reflexivity of the socially incisive productions.

John Caldwell's concept of "televisuality" in his analysis of American television aids in understanding the stylistic excess that applies to *Straight Up* as production and programming within the CBC:

> [T]he term "televisuality"…describe[s] television's presentational manner…defined by excessive stylization and visual exhibitionism. In no way does this terminology mean a kind of Kantian aesthetic essence or spirit of the age principle. Rather, televisuality has become an active and changing form of cultural representation, a mode of operating and a ritual of display that utilizes many different individual looks. Televisuality, as I have been using the term, is less a defining aesthetic than a kind of corporate behaviour and succession of guises.…The workings of the televisual image are far from innocuous or inert. They help make up the very heart of television's engagement with viewers. (352-53)

Narratively, parallel domains in the case of *Straight Up* afford the personal discovery claimed in Kroetsch's literary trace: the youths' found moments, the uncovering or usurpation of uncommon insights. *Straight Up*'s teens *do* consume the products of popular culture (fast food, arcades, alcohol, movies, television, popular music). But they look beyond material gratification for something interior and individuated within their need to escape suburb, city and adult jurisdictions. Their modes of deviance temper the wholesale consumption of popular culture; that is, deviance as use, misuse, tailoring, questioning and circumvention of offerings from among mass culture's neon-lit products, pastimes and consumer attractions aimed at containing youth. So the constructions of the teens' escapes into parallel domains must be stylistically excessive and exhibitionistic as television—undermining the teenpic code of youth as only "that which is watched" (Acland). John Caldwell argues that television's exhibitionism can be found in the historical development of the medium:

> With increasing frequency, style itself became the subject, the signified, if you will, of television. In fact, this self-consciousness of style became so great that it can more accurately be described as an activity—as a performance of style—rather than as a particular look. Television came to flaunt and display style....In short, style, long seen as a mere signifier and vessel for content, issues, and ideas, has now itself become one of television's most privileged and showcased signifieds....The process of stylization rather than style—an activity rather than a static look—was the factor that defined televisual exhibitionism. (5)

Straight Up's initial (1996) six-episode footing in televisuality was exploited to serve a bolder youth-television scheme than prior CBC youth series, which, of course, paved the way for producing this denser teen-based drama. To begin with the implications of the series' title, it is unlike the specific site-naming of previous Canadian youth-television series. The numerous *Degrassi Street* and *Degrassi High* series, which were stretched into the young-adult spinoff *Liberty Street*, became subject to formula over the long production run. They were grounded in place names, with dilemma-solving narratives occurring in and about each series' designated coming-of-age territories of school, home, family, peers. *Northwood* (CBC-TV) and *Madison* (Global-TV), both produced in British Columbia (early through mid-1990s), followed similar paths as youth series, tailoring their narratives to their regional locales.

Straight Up's title signals something more undiluted than a specific locale, like the midnight hour when both hands of the clock reach twelve and honesty and transgressions become legitimized (Beale 438). This fits the series' excessive televisuality. For its teen outsiders, the boundaries of behaviour and memory loosen to an "after hours" condition, much as the lyrics of that jazz song by Thelonious Monk tell us that "memories always start 'round midnight / 'round midnight." This jazz comparison is not an incidental point, as the youths' imaginative flights into parallel worlds can be likened to the improvisation that liberates the jazz musician from a familiar melodic line, to get "in the groove" (pleasure and risk) of musical free-flight, creating colour and personal style through deviation from theme or pattern.[6]

The series' very title evokes the corrective potential of the individuated imagination. Characters are constructed to uncover both risk and insight through ritualized escapes from the straight (social) world, with the implication that they are acting without adult points of view and moral admonishments to "straighten out" or "straighten up and fly right." I am not arguing that adults did not "drive" the creation of *Straight Up*, but rather that their preproduction and production processes were consistent with their intentions of constructing a youth television series of integrity and voice for its teen subjects. This points to *Straight Up*'s uninvention of youth television—as far as that is possible, even within the CBC as a public network competing with other networks for audiences.[7] The teens' deviations—the "straight goods" from a "bent" point of view—into parallel domains are closed to adult institutional figures (police, parents, teachers, more conventional teens). The stylistic "play" of conventions, likened to jazz, within the formal structuring of each episode allows for internal narrative elasticity and layered characters, including the city's dark character.

The freewheeling subjectivity of the teens' deviance assumes that youth-television audiences either possess or are developing solid viewing tools to understand and enjoy drama that isn't transparent or that panders as empty entertainment. This is evident in the surreal rendering of the series' realist settings, made televisual through devices of lighting, slow motion and colliding imagery, signalled in the hard-edit, jump-cut, computer-jigged title sequence. The title sequence is constructed to look the way rap and hip-hop music sound: staccato narrative and imagistic "bites" for astute audiences in touch with the fragmented flow of music videos, computer technology and the formulas of much commercial television.

Straight Up places its teen characters in a Toronto core that is never directly named, but alluded to as urban-familiar through visual anchors (The Pickle Barrel, Sam the Record Man), thematic motifs (the ubiquitous arcades, a Yonge Street, fast-food hang-out named A-J's that appears to operate round the clock), and the settings of prior CBC series (*Degrassi*, *Street Legal*). These narrative settings suggest two functions: the establishment of an urban ground for the series, but without place-naming; and a realist departure point for the teens' stylized journeys into parallel domains. To effect these exhibitionistic departures, Ciccoritti explains that for every episode of *Straight Up* he insisted on at least two "cinematic moments." Within the twenty-one-minute structure, these ciné-moments wrench the dramas from the urban-familiar settings, creating the formal, personal imagery of the narrative trajectories at the heart of each episode.

Television's common formula of dilemma-driven narratives is altered by Ciccoritti's interest in what he referred to as making "a Robert Altman movie for kids," which expresses his wider cinematic ambition for this series as an edgy intervention into youth television's linearity and genre formulas. He noted that he does not care for the (now conventional) free-form, Steadi-cam shooting popularized in the American cop show *NYPD Blue*. A point I would emphasize here is that Ciccoritti's cinema-inflected dramatic and visual style stands apart from most television, a medium that rarely fulfils its potential to make popular art. The preproduction and production processes (research, writing, acting and shooting practices) that inform *Straight Up* indicate methods aiming for popular art.[8] The CBC's production history of playing with dramatic forms is many and varied (Miller 265), and certain contemporary similarities can be found in the production of *Straight Up*: for example, in Sydney Newman's observation that CBC "television [in the 1950s] never had time for experimentation....When original programs came along, it was simply because the person in charge had a personal view he was able to express without the heavy hand of knowledgeable control over him. Usually, one did things on the run, and marvellous things happened" (as quoted in Miller 289).

In the episode "Small Bang Theory," the featured female character "lacks" the entertaining appeal of protagonists in such CBC feature dramas as *Anne of Green Gables* (1986) and its sister series, *Road to Avonlea* (late 1980s-1996) and is a colder portrayal than even the most problematized *Degrassi* youths. When the alienated Simone swigs booze from a bottle in a stark public washroom, the slow-motion ciné-effect doubly emphasizes the deliberate power of her action and her potential to be an abusive alcoholic. Drunkenly unattractive, she is surly with her friends and willingly lost for the moment in terms that ritually echo Kroetsch's notion of "unhiding the hidden." She lives with her single father, an understanding parent. But her greater presence is as a contemporary rebel chasing ideals through deviant behaviour. Thus the series constructs her as a "true grit" visionary with a sense that outer space holds the promise of unbounded culture: she even wants to live among the stars.

At one point, Simone walks out of a party at a bar where a male peer is heard to comment about "closing the god-damn borders." Her physical withdrawal from this remark expresses a smart teen-rebel's disdain for bigotry and negative attitudes to immigration in a purportedly liberal, multicultural society. Simone's imagined parallel world has open boundaries, coded in the star-lights that dot the ceiling of her bedroom. An overachiever with near-perfect grades who is "into space," Simone tells her dad, "I'm going up [into outer space]. There's nothing…here for me.…If I don't go…make sure I die." Her dad, a single parent, stays up all night sewing a leather bungee harness that effectively takes Simone on an imaginary flight shaped by her personal imagery. The episode ends with Simone ducking through the open frame of a garage under construction, a site that initially defined her father's project but that becomes transformed by her gravity-defying manoeuvres from the exposed beams. We see her train for her free-flight dream (the stars)— a "Roberta Bondar" slipping through the constraints of social structures, at least for now.

In gender, class and imaginative terms, Simone's character is written and portrayed against the youth codes of Hollywood film; for example, *Clueless* (Heckerling, 1995), in which fifteen-year-old Cher (Alicia Silverstone) plays at rebellion by fetishizing consumerism in a parody so candy-coated in stereotype it effaces its own critique of shallow, class-bound Americana. The spinoff television series of the same name continued the stereotype of vacuous female youth. *Straight Up* works against this kind of American film-to-television formula, as well as against the codes of the TV soap-melodrama genre popularized in *Beverly Hills 90210* and *Melrose Place*: by not depicting youth as either shallow or predictable; by avoiding a slick visual veneer in both casting and style; and by engaging the ideas and words of its teen actors in its scripts. Even the progressively rebellious female teens of the *Degrassi* series (Playing With Time Productions, in conjunction with the CBC) were largely constructed to accept conventional values, however socially appropriate the moral lessons of the thematically topical dramas might be: a nice white girl dates the "wrong" boy (parental prejudice and miscegenation in "Black and White," *Degrassi High*); a working-class teen given to "punk" dress gets pregnant, has the baby and struggles to be a student while raising baby (Spike of the various *Degrassi* series). In the later *Degrassi Talks...on sex*, the actor (Amanda Steptoe) who had played Spike acted as host, cautioning Canadian youth about sexual risks and taking responsibility for teen pregnancy. Employing moral lessons may serve the social good, but it rarely liberates the imaginative potential of youth.

Though sex, alcohol and pregnancy are conventional to the soap's popularized escapist roots (e.g., *Beverly Hills 90210* and *Melrose Place*), there is no common imaginative, narrative or moral trajectory that the teens of *Straight Up* must "obey" as series characters. Few formulaic codes of series conduct or stereotype subsume them for the kinds of value lessons that shape the topical themes of the four *Degrassi* series. Twenty-something games of romantic deception operate in certain episodes of *Straight Up*, but are not softened as in *Liberty Street* (mid-1990s), the last of the *Degrassi* spinoffs until *Degrassi: The Next Generation* premiered on CTV in October 2001. The TV-soap cliches often found in *Northwood* are avoided; so too the Hollywood-style "pretty faces" and postured acting of *Madison*.

Straight Up altered the youth-television genre considerably in creating a series that privileges exploratory characters who transgress topical boundaries and popular formulas. Though alienated and moody, the series' youths are not abnormal. They are "problem youth," negative and self-destructive, but also productive in their liberating uninventions. They drink, hang out and cross paths with the consumer culture of McDonald's (A-J's) but are not dumbed-down as popular television fodder. They project intellect and control of language within colloquial, teen rhetoric; they speak of studying, books, reading, science, poetry and philosophy, but without obvious moral lessons about being studeous or knowledgeable. There is no Joey Jeremiah among them, *Degrassi*'s self-satisfied if appealing underachiever. They witness drive-by shootings by disaffected youths with pellet guns, and the intimidation of black teens by rifle-toting police. They form a loose community on the streets—youth inhabits mainstreet, but doesn't "own" it—yet police officers walk through their conversations like prison guards checking a general threat to public space and order.

In the episode "Big Time," the edgy and short Murray recalls James Dean's alienated male youth in *Rebel without a Cause* (Kazan, 1955). He bites the cap off a beer bottle then asks his buddies that familiar question that bonds Canadian boys and men: "Did you guys see that Leafs game last night?" Contrary to formula, his pals, Ed and Steve, are absorbed in debating heady concepts of time, "without," as Ed states, "any external device...no watch...nothing." Beer and hockey imagery give way to a dialogue on time and space, to concepts of unexplored parallel worlds:

Ed: One beer takes half an hour. Two take an hour—unless you want to call beer an external device. A hockey game takes five beers, overtime, six.

Steve: You wanna talk parallel worlds? You know we're in 'em—every waking moment.

Ed: You can't *see* a parallel world!

Steve: Did you ever think there was *no one* else?

This dialogue plays out the umbrella theme for the first six episodes, which Ciccoritti identified as "language and communication." In the scene described, the dialogue sets up Ed, Steve and Murray's movement into back alleys, looking for a rave (not a hockey game or a television set).[9] Rave rituals pivot on dancing until your batteries (or drugs) give out—something of a "going insane" ritual as discussed by Robert Kroetsch (395). Televisually described by his pals, Murray is dubbed "our navigator...like that TV bunny." That pink TV bunny with the reflexive outward glance is familiar to viewers as an endless traveller who crosses the boundaries of television flow, namely, the geographies of competing commercial genres and ads, much as he (or is it "she" behind those Ray-Ban "shades") blurs sexual definition.

Unlike the Energizer bunny, Murray loses his way in the web of alleys, has memory lapses and encounters the imagery of poverty and marginality hidden within the looser ethos of this scary underground milieu. He pauses before an abandoned car inscribed with the graffiti message, "Come as you are." Passage in the underground does not require a passport or a rigged identity but it does cue what Kroetsch terms "the tension between this appearance of being just like someone else and the demands of authenticity" (394). That is, in Murray's case, the tension between playing to the teen-rebel stereotype and having to be a "real loner," which frightens him. His character gets lost in the alley, and so without posturing or peer pressure, Murray reacts to express his fears and frustrations. Coming upon two tall cardboard cartons, stationed side by side, he assumes his pals are tricking him by hiding inside. The word "morphine" is scrawled on the adjacent brick wall. The formality of the shot creates a visual/textual paradox in the juxtaposition of cardboard cartons and graffitied brick wall. The camera's framing never allows us to lose sight of this word—"morphine" as both lure and dead-end, but without driving home a moral lesson about drugs. Murray vents his anger and fear by beating the cartons, flailing against a barrier that signifies his sense of isolation from the popular. The night city feels like an outpost of conflicting boundaries in the flimsy cartons and rigid wall, a profoundly visceral experience for Murray. There are no apparent signifiers of any official society here to entice youth, only the "going insane" underground ethos that tests his mettle. The graffitied wall is a prominent reminder of an unstable, disenfranchised culture, with youth among those at the fringes of society, neither kids nor adults. Steve's earlier retort ("Did you ever think there was *no one* else") seems prophetic and haunts Murray's isolation in this scene.

Themes of the death of culture are rife in *Straight Up*, but so is the survival of youth—and thus the breaking of television formula. In the episode "Dead Babies," Rory, a youth who likes to babysit, in this instance with baby Parker, is visited by his three pals, Murray, Ed and Steve (characters discussed above). They invent scenarios about "having a kid and coming home and finding it dead," prompted by Rory's reading of his own poem in class. Rory's poem begins with the imagery of basketball and goes on to enfold the imagery of dead babies who will never reach the hoop: "Little dead babies / hovering in the trees /…trying to swish from thirty feet / They watch like leaves /…never get to play."

While the four friends discuss how easy it would be to kill a child, sounds of baby Parker upstairs intervene through the nursery intercom; the receiver sits in the living room, in the form of a red plastic clown, replicant of Ronald McDonald, consumer culture's surrogate caregiver. On the television set, F. W. Murnau's silent film *Nosferatu* (1922) plays, a sign of youth's aesthetic and film literacy gleaned from beyond Canadian boundaries and Hollywood's claim on the horror genre. The house is decorated in the manner of a *Toronto Life* pictorial on middle-class success: wall-to-wall whites, upstairs and down; benign art prints on the walls. Lily the Goth keeps phoning, asking if she can come over. Upon her arrival, Murray, Ed and Steve leave. Lily, who earlier identifies herself as an atheist, possesses a solidity that defies her claim and appearance: she wears black head-to-toe, eyes made up in the manner of the stylishly undead, and carries a casket-shaped purse. Though enigmatic, she is devoid of the familiar masochism that, for example, marks film director David Cronenberg's otherworldly women characters.[10] What follows upon her arrival is an inversion of what we might expect: *not* a social replay of a horror narrative (no threats to baby Parker), but rather the imagery of grief and disclosure in the intimate discussion between Lily and Rory about existence.

Here is the paradox: in the modern home, an emblem of the material distractions of adults, Lily the Goth and Rory the sitter appear to be a social safety net against modern lifestyle culture. Their different viewpoints and imaginative insights control the scene, intervening into the upscale, suburban family imagery surrounding them. In slow motion, Rory is shown carrying the baby into the living room. Lily takes the baby, caresses him, feeds him. She looks like a black madonna, as suited to maternity as any suburban woman or TV mom. Rory picks up a small shoe. In slow motion, this gesture of caregiving is stretched, suggesting the fragile journeys of all children, emphasized by baby Parker's little shoe. Baby Parker is put to bed upstairs, Rory kisses him, Lily listens on the intercom. The contradictions between the normal, the absurd and the profound make this an unsettling and revealing sequence.

Lily presses Rory to explain his poem: "What part's real?" The question frees Rory to talk about the children his mother "tried" to have: "I got born, the others didn't. What makes me special?" Tension ensues and Lily decides to leave. The art prints on the walls depicting classical/mythic female figures appear to turn translucent with her movement to the foyer. Carrying her casket-shaped purse, Lily displaces these icons of femininities past, to survey her contemporary difference in a full-length mirror. Lily is no vampiristic femme—no signifier of the undead. She perceives her reflection as clearly as we do, as her visage and penetrating gaze command both the narrative mirror (the framing object/prop located in the hallway) and the television screen (youth's command of televisual space). She is characterized by televisuality and becomes the core of a highly stylized ciné-moment.

The extreme close-up on her eye emphasizes her canny gaze. Her informing vision is human not supernatural (not the "evil eye"), and she visibly blinks before confiding to Rory, "Two years ago I lost a baby...nine weeks...just when it starts opening its mouth." Lily's revelation is as luminous as her name, framed by the sharp black-out that formally blots out the living room (adult material space) behind her. This part of the scene is intercut with Rory's black and white memory-flash of Lily holding baby Parker. The isolation of physical and mental spaces occupied, of gestures remembered, constructs an empathetic link between life, loss, identity, desire and the imagination. Grief without family melodrama. Imaginative exchanges without lessons about teen pregnancy. In Kroetsch's terms, the scene's memory-flashes are a kind of prehistory, visual jolts of insight. Rory comments, "You would have been, like, young." A close-up of their clasped hands marks off this ciné-moment, which is sustained by a freeze-frame that has the further effect of suppressing the cliché in a momentary gesture of closure.

This dramatization of the examined life is sealed at the levels of experience, intimacy and insight, forged from the sitter's dark poetry and the Goth's self-styled otherness. Their handclasp is also a telling image of the narrative efficiency of television drama that fuses Rory's literariness (his poetry) and Lily's visualness (her questing look at herself as more than a visual spectacle). As viewers, we are pulled into the offbeat human engagement of individuals who are called "weird" by Rory's male chums, but who enlarge the signifying boundaries of youth television beyond its customary formula.

In *Straight Up*, I take "weirdness" to be a necessary lens for imagining uncommon humanness and necessary rebellion, and for expanding popular constructions. The effect is to unbind youth television and, in a wider context, to explore a more inclusive sense of culture than the terms "Canadian," "nationhood," "regional," "local," "urban" and "marginal" imply. Looking for a rave, practising free-flight, reaching for hoops (not only placating landscapes, e.g., *Anne of Green Gables*), retrieving "dead babies" in the mind's eye while tending to life: these are poetic processes of "going insane" and, at the same time, of breaching genre categories. They decolonize the mind and so facilitate a more trenchant youth perspective within television production. At the conclusion of the episode "Small Bang Theory," Simone's father is positioned and scripted to acknowledge that the adult perspective is present but not *the* authorative voice, as he and an interested neighbour (a woman) watch the teen spin through the air. "Yah, nausea, vertigo, loss of equilibrium—sort of the idea," he observes. "Kinda suits her," the woman comments, then walks away, as if the sight before her is—or ought to be—how the witnessing adult might reconsider youth's deviance as navigation outside familial and social regulation. In this positioning, deviance is the norm, for as the woman withdraws, the image of the flying female teen returns to command the screen—to take up televisual space. The shot spins outward to show the earth as but a dot within the universe, a radical shift from the two adults' observations at the sidelines. This is Simone's view, an imagined realization of her dream state.

In analyzing the contemporary teenpic for its devices and ideology, Charles Acland rightly locates subversions of "the disciplinary gaze of the adult" in certain teenpics, but with a propensity to depict what he describes as "the enticing nature of the spectacle of wasted youth" (118). Adults and officials (parents and police) are neither central nor peripheral in *Straight Up* but form a subtle part of the human landscape and surreal imagery. The series is constructed to evoke youth's negotiations with surveillance. In "Dead Babies," Lily is surveyor of her own image before the corridor mirror, not out of vanity but as scrutineer of a more complex teen figure than is generically popular in television and film. In "Small Bang Theory," Simone is sole witness to her own weakness, peering at her drunk reflection in the bathroom mirror as if only she can know it clearly. In "Big Time," the diminutive Murray alone confronts the graffitied underground and recovers from his hysteria without the scrutiny of either peers or adults.

Charles Acland's observation that deviant youth is a "crucial trope" that "helps patrol the boundaries" between normal and abnormal, adults and youths (133), can be fruitfully linked to Kroetsch's concept of imaginatively "unhiding the hidden" through "going insane" rites of passage. Such rites in *Straight Up* erode the assumption that the gaze of youth is fixed on self-absorption, without imagination and mindless of the social pressures and consequences of acting anti-socially. They enable navigation into parallel experiences and are not mere Canadian production vehicles to promote "our" culture, or to deliver social lessons alone in palatable, popular narrative form (e.g., "good-for-you" television) and thus keep a lid on errant youth and TV viewing.

If television can be said to have a media language, then *Straight Up* is what John Caldwell would term "textually messy." While pointedly American in his analysis, he makes an important argument for the continual rethinking of television as a popular medium engaged not only with exploratory forms, but also with audiences:

> Unlike classical Hollywood cinema, television had no centered gaze from the very start, and seldom had any seamless or overarching narrative. Multiple narrational modes issued from the same works, and audiences were constantly made aware of television's artifice and embellishment. In these ways, then, television has always been postmodern. Television has always been *textually messy*—that is, textural rather than transparent. (23)

"Textually messy" television can declassify genre and viewership. *Straight Up*'s striking exploitation of televisuality in constructing highly stylized ciné-moments shifts the common practices of youth television, and can be seen in retrospect as an advanced project in media literacy and popular culture for savvy audiences.[11]

Author's Acknowledgements

I am grateful to Jerry Ciccoritti for engaging in a telephone interview (summer 1997), and to Mary Jane Miller for her useful comments on an earlier draft of this paper.

Notes

1 For example, Pete and Joey (*Goin' Down the Road*, Shebib, 1970), "The Marshall" Dillon (*Paperback Hero*, Pearson, 1973), Toby and Chino (*Between Friends*, Shebib, 1973).

2 Though a relatively young director, Ciccoritti has broad directing and writing experience, across theatre (co-founder of Buddies in Bad Times Theatre Co., Toronto), television and film. His television direction

includes anthology drama, and the finely characterized CBC drama special, *Net Worth*. In 1997, he won "best directing" Gemini awards for both *Straight Up* and *Net Worth*. Ciccoritti and writer Andrew Rai Berzins are important to the dramatic, textured and writerly backbone of *Straight Up*'s first season. Berzins is credited with the series' development along with co-creators and executive co-producers Janis Lundman and Adrienne Mitchell. Others—Karen Walton, Kris Lefroe, Drew Birch, Michael Melski—also wrote strong episodes for the 1998 season. This is not a norm in television, a medium that thrives on genre redundancy and values producers over writers and directors.

3 CBC Web site.

4 The CBC has been increasingly subject to external and internal pressures (severe government funding cuts; criticism from without and within) as well as poor ratings, undermining the production of drama. John Allemang notes that despite the "more tolerant time of 9:30 p.m." the 1996 *Straight Up* episodes "still took a lot of heat for their mature themes" (*Globe and Mail* Feb. 25, 1998).

   The series' televisual style and youth centredness continued in the CBC's 2000 teen series, *Drop the Beat*, also created by Mitchell and Lundman, which occupied the 8:30 slot preceding *This Hour Has 22 Minutes*. Its focus: two black youths, Dennis and Jeff, both characters carried over from *Straight Up*, and the internal tensions and infighting of running a campus community, hip-hop radio show.

5 In the 1997 schedule, *Straight Up* was nowhere in sight, presumably part of the public broadcaster's survival strategies. Ciccoritti explained (interview) that seven new episodes had been ordered by the CBC for the 1998 season; six of this lot were directed by him, and one was directed by executive co-producer and co-creator Adrienne Mitchell. Due to the Winter (Nagano) Olympics, the CBC did not begin broadcasting these six new episodes until February 25, 1998, in the 8:00 p.m. slot on Wednesday nights, with a "14+" viewing code.

   John Allemang writes that these new episodes were ready for broadcast in the summer of 1998, and claims that producers Lundman and Mitchell were granted their choice of the 8:00 p.m. time as "compensation" for the programming delays (*Globe and Mail* Feb. 25, 1998).

6 Except for Sarah Polley, most of the series' actors are non-professionals, which Ciccoritti preferred, favouring improvisational strategies over the obvious acting of teens with performance experience (interview). Cinematographer Barry Stone explains that Ciccoritti "was casting 90 per cent of the roles with unknowns and first timers" (CBC Web site). Ciccoritti's comments on the actual processes: "All you have to do is work on WHO YOUR CHARACTER IS…listen to the other actor and REACT, NOT ACT.…Movie acting is recreating that state but with a small cheat—we know what our line is going to be. The idea is to try to creatively 'forget' that line.…I didn't want to teach them 'proper' acting technique…it would turn them into TV actor zombies.…The cast was totally up to that. We wanted to catch lightening in a bottle and I think we did" (CBC Web site).

7 On the eve of *Straight Up*'s late February 1998 return, John Allemang reported that the CBC claimed "to be nervous about premiering new shows

in the fall, when there is so much competition from the publicity machines at the U.S. networks and their Canadian simulcasters" (Feb 25, 1998).

8 *Straight Up*'s cinematic visuals owe much to the conjunction of lighting, shooting and editing techniques. Cinematographer Barry Stone describes the shooting: "We were shooting 90 per cent of the shows on location...Yonge Street day and night...interior/exterior just north of Wellesley....We attempted to do a lot of the longer scenes in 'oners' so that even if we had to cut, we would still maintain that active verite [*sic*] feeling....The camera style and movement for each episode was discussed and planned quite extensively in prep, and Jerry added...a specific colour to each show" (CBC Web site).

9 Initially a rave was a music/dance impromptu that went all night and occurred in or about abandoned urban buildings, or "cans"—that is, until the rave moved out of the underground to become an alternative system ("name" dj's, planned events), and into such visible and controllable city spaces as the public grounds of Toronto's Science Centre.

10 For example, as constructed in Cronenberg's early film *The Brood* (1979), through his mid-career film *Videodrome* (1982), to *Crash* (1996).

11 Canadians are weaned on American television, as programming, viewing demographics and ratings indicate, whatever loyalty audiences have had, and many continue to have, to the CBC, to Canadian drama generally, and to specific series (Miller 256-63, 346). Thus it is instructive to read the many viewer responses to *Straight Up* (CBC Web site). Viewers (mostly, but not only, teens) highly valued the series and commented on *Straight Up*'s authenticity in its representation of contemporary youth (some fondly recall the *Degrassi* series similarly, and also the American series *My So-Called Life*); its effective style, strong narratives, and gritty street textures; its Canadianness, in opposition to the obvious shallowness of certain American series (*Beverly Hills 90210* was specifically named by several viewers).

WORKS CITED

Acland, Charles R. "The Body by the River: Youth Movies and the Adult Gaze." *Youth, Murder, Spectacle: The Cultural Politics of Youth in Crisis.* Boulder: Western, 1995. 115-33.

Allemang, John. *Globe and Mail*, February 25, 1998. C2.

Beale, Paul, ed. *A Concise Dictionary of Slang and Unconventional English.* New York: Macmillan, 1989.

Caldwell, John Thornton. *Televisuality: Style, Crisis, and Authority in American Television.* New Brunswick: Rutgers UP, 1995.

Kroetsch, Robert. "Unhiding the Hidden." *The Post-Colonial Studies Reader.* Ed. Bill Ashcroft, Gareth Griffiths and Helen Tiffin. London: Routledge, 1995. 394-96.

Miller, Mary Jane. *Rewind and Search: Conversations with the Makers and Decision-Makers of CBC Television Drama.* Montreal and Kingston: McGill-Queen's UP, 1996.

POPULARIZING HISTORY:
THE VALOUR AND
THE HORROR

Jeannette Sloniowski

The lure for the public is that of mastering a dossier—by leafing through it.

—Pascal Bonitzer, "Silences of the Voice"

*T*he *Valour and the Horror* (Brian McKenna, 1992) has been one of the most controversial attempts in the history of Canadian media to create a popular and accessible account of some of the Canadian military's more disastrous moments in World War II. Immediately upon its release Canadian veterans condemned it for, from their point of view, a lack of objectivity and numerous errors of fact. Brian and Terence McKenna, its creators, responded, in typically journalistic fashion, defensively and with considerable outrage at what they perceived to be an attack upon freedom of the press and the autonomy of the CBC. This debate became extremely heated and ended finally in the courts, where the veterans tried, unsuccessfully, to sue the McKennas for libel.

The issues raised by *The Valour and the Horror* debate are important ones for the Canadian media. Crucial questions arose during the debate about the program and the status of popular media as translators of his-

Notes on pages 172-74.

torical "facts,"—questions concerning who has the right to recount history, or whether objectivity is possible in the retelling of a complex historical event, or, indeed, whether historical "facts" are malleable enough to support any interpretation of an event. As well, there was considerable discussion over the effects of reality TV and tabloids on the rather staid institution of CBC-Television documentary. Central to this debate was the role of the CBC—a publically funded corporation—in creating popular history. This essay is an attempt to put *The Valour and the Horror* into the context of popular television documentary and reality TV. Close analysis of parts of the series is combined with an overview of how the conventions of television shape the recounting of history—all the while acknowledging that the Canadian media do not operate in a cultural or aesthetic vacuum, but in fact compete with, borrow from, and recast the conventions of an increasingly globalized popular culture.

Television, with its penchant for sound bites and short time slots, is a problematic medium for the serious analysis of history. The conventions of television documentary or docudrama and historiography must be analyzed to assist in understanding the strengths and weaknesses of *The Valour and the Horror*. For the most part, historical analysis on television suffers from a kind of crude empiricism that seems to imply, as Colin McArthur has argued, that "any collection of 'facts' will produce their own interpretation, leaving out of account the predispositions of the observer categorizing them as facts in the first place" (McArthur 7). Virtually all television history is invisible. That is, it does not reveal itself as a constructed view of a few purposefully selected events. *The Valour and the Horror* shows and tells us "the facts" and then draws what by then have become the inevitable moral conclusions arising from those "facts." All of this is achieved with virtually no opposing view presented, or indeed any revelation that its argument is just one of the many arguments that surround a complex historical event. This approach to history might be considered a rather backward one in which, as John Caughie argues, "the past is understood as having a fixed and immutable existence rather than being the site of a constant struggle in the present" (Caughie 312). It is as though history is just sitting there waiting for us to discover "how it really was," (Arthur Ranke, qtd. in McArthur 8) rather than being constructed for the ideological needs of the present.[1]

Thus *The Valour and the Horror* is not necessarily well-argued history. But it is terribly persuasive, moving, and revealing to the degree that it documents the much-neglected feelings of the ordinary military personnel who were on the battlefields, in the planes, and in the prisoner-of-war camps. It is also a dissenting view from officially broadcast versions of the war, and very valuable as such. Aesthetically pleasing, its affectively charged combinations of image and music are hard to resist emotionally. One of the greatest strengths of film and television in the recreation of historical events, or one of these media's greatest faults, depending on one's point of view, is their ability to absorb the audience into an intense visual spectacle, allowing them very little time to think over what they have seen. The television image flows past us at a pace that makes reflection difficult at best. The rhetoric of a well-constructed film or television documentary, like the *The Valour and the Horror*, is extremely powerful, and is difficult to dispute without detailed knowledge of the events under examination—a knowledge possessed by few Canadians during the war, or in the present day.

The Valour and the Horror, a postmodern hybrid documentary-docudrama, consists of three separately broadcast, two-hour programs. One, "In Desperate Battle: Normandy, 1944," deals with the slaughter of Canadian troops at Verrières Ridge; another, "Savage Christmas: Hong Kong, 1941," with the mistreatment of Canadian prisoners of war by the Japanese in Hong Kong, and the last, "Death by Moonlight: Bomber Command," the blanket bombing of Germany by Canadian Lancaster bombers. All three segments are visually complex, consisting of colour footage shot in the present day in France, Hong Kong, Britain, and Germany, black-and-white archival footage from the World War II, archival still photographs and paintings, and colour dramatizations of letters written by various veterans. It is organized for the viewer by a "voice-of-God" narration that both describes and interprets various aspects of each campaign, and also structures the commentary, the interviews with Allied and German survivors of the war, and the scripted re-enactments of letters and memoirs originally written by Canadian and British military personnel. The sheer volume and variety of the images and sounds, and the authoritative way in which they are narrated by Terence McKenna, give evidence of a significant amount of research and a highly organized and definitive explanation of the issues. Compared with, for example, a documentary segment of CBC's *The National* or the usual run of televisual documentaries, its visual and aural complexity are impressive.

Through all of this complicated material the McKennas attempt to prove a number of things: that Canadian servicemen suffered a great deal in the war and many died needlessly; that some Canadian and British generals were incompetent and Canadian troops poorly trained and armed; that the Canadian military hierarchy spent their time currying the favour of their British masters and not worrying about the enormous casualty rate suffered by their troops; that the British tended to look down upon colonial troops and wasted their lives in futile manoeuvres; and that the bombing of civilians in Germany was both an act of terrorism and, in the long run, counterproductive. While one might argue that these are crucial issues that need to be examined, in the end *The Valour and the Horror*, by neglecting the context of the war and oppositional arguments, merely substitutes one immutable, emotional, and mythological view of the war for another, previously existing one. In accordance with the conventions of popular historiography, complexity of argument is sacrificed to sensationalism in a medium increasingly given to excess and tabloid-like news coverage.

One of the peculiarities of documentary narration is that as the narrator speaks, the pictures seem to prove the validity of his or her case. Pictures have a rather ambiguous nature. They can seldom stand on their own as evidence. (This ambiguity was clearly brought into focus by the variety of opinion surrounding the Rodney King case in Los Angeles.) But when pictures are contained by a narration, they become definitive. For this reason, they are a powerful but questionable way to advance a historical argument. One example in *The Valour and the Horror* is its use of that most common but questionable documentary convention: if the camera goes to the place where an event really happened, then what is said must actually be true. This does not make much sense, but consider the number of televisual documentaries and news reports that make a fetish out of going to the scene of the crime— as though that scene can speak for itself, or lend authenticity to what is being argued by the narration. As Keith Tribe notes in "History and the Production of Memory," "this history is…recognized as Truth by the viewer not because of the 'facts' being correct, but because the image looks right. This recognition effect 'that's the way it was' is a product not of the historicity of the plot but because of the manipulation of the image" (Bennett et al. 324).

One of the most important invisible features of *The Valour and the Horror* is the act of narration itself and what it implies. At the beginning of each episode the veterans reply to audible questions posed by the narrator, but the narrator himself is not visible onscreen. Later the narrator asks other questions of the veterans, which we do not hear. Thus the veterans' participation is structured not around their interests, necessarily, but his, for the most part, invisible questions. The documentary implies that we hear the veterans' stories, but in fact we hear their answers to his questions. Thus their story really becomes fodder for his overall argument, whether they agree with him or not. Because we never see the narrator, and never get to look at his facial expressions, it becomes extremely difficult to disagree with him, given that he has the voice, music, and all of the pictures on his side. Many cinematic documentaries, with greater and lesser success, have abandoned or questioned this "voice-of-God" narration in an attempt to get away from its authoritarian implications. But the male "voice-of-God" narration is conventional in most television documentary. And in the case of *The Valour and the Horror*, Terence McKenna's voice organizes all of the visual and aural material that is presented. All of the visuals work toward demonstrating the "inherent" truth of his argument, and because we never hear his questions in the "interviews," we are unable to evaluate his participation in the structuring of the veterans' stories.

The availability of filmed images often determines what documentary can historicize.[2] Documentary is an overwhelmingly visual form, and if there are no visual records of a historical event, a filmmaker may get into the controversial area of recreations and re-enactments. There has been some speculation that one of the reasons for the McKennas' failure to discuss the firebombing of York and Coventry, as part of the rationale for the bombing of Munich and Nuremberg, is that the British government refused to allow photographs of the thousands of civilian casualties because they thought it too demoralizing.[3] No photographs, therefore no visual history. This is, of course, one of the possibilities, but I would argue that *The Valour and the Horror* is so full of recreations that one more would not have been any more difficult for the audience to accept. It appears to be part of the McKennas' rhetorical strategy to leave out the context of the bombing. It might well be that

The Valour and the Horror seeks to convince the audience that the bombing of civilians is immoral regardless of context. A similar position was taken in *Death Row* (Bruce Jackson, 1980), a documentary on prison inmates, where the filmmaker refused to tell the audience what crimes his subjects had committed, because he felt that the death penalty was immoral for any reason. However, by neglecting context and argument in *The Valour and the Horror*, the McKennas depart from the realm of serious historical analysis into rhetoric, and by doing so, run the risk of trivializing history.

Music is another controversial documentary convention. There are those filmmakers, like Frederick Wiseman, who would argue that music should not be used in a documentary unless it happens to be playing naturally during the filming. Properly chosen music can affect the viewer's emotions, and some would argue that this is too manipulative a trick for documentary as it does not necessarily promote critical awareness. Fiction films relied upon this convention even in the silent-film era, when musicians would perform with films to help engage the emotions of the audience. The music in *The Valour and the Horror* is extremely moving and carefully chosen. Fauré's *Requiem* is repeated in all three episodes. It is solemn and sad, and the solos are apparently sung by a young man—presumably in harmony thematically with the emphasis the McKennas place upon the youth of the soldiers and the graveyard setting of all three episodes. Overall, the music creates an atmosphere of sadness, grief, and mourning for the dead, and relates the sense of victimization and loss so central to the thematic concerns of the McKennas' dramatization of the events. Despite the repetitiousness of the *Requiem* over the six-hour run, it is skilfully integrated into the documentary at moments when particularly terrible events are shown or recollected, like the description of the effects of the bombing of Dresden in the "Death by Moonlight" segment. After a time, I would argue, the audience becomes conditioned by the music, and is prompted to respond emotionally whenever it is heard.

Anyone who would make a television documentary, including the McKenna brothers, must work within a number of institutional constraints, and conventions, imposed upon them by the aesthetic, economic, and ideological structures of the medium. For example, a television documentary is only one item on a menu of television programs designed to give the audience "an evening's entertainment" (McArthur 13). In other words, a television documentary must compete with everything else that is on television that night. This includes other documentaries, but also sitcoms, tabloid news programs, game shows, and rock music videos. Thus the television documentary is not merely a source of information, but also a source of popular entertainment. As such it thrives not only on dramatization, but the selection of events that lend themselves to dramatic representation. The subject of most drama is conflict and human suffering, and television documentary makers are therefore attracted to events like war, revolution, political intrigue, and controversial people or celebrities. Many of the crucial events of world history, like detailed theoretical discussions about policy, are not easily dramatized, are seldom recorded on film, and thus appear to be unsuitable for television—even though they are, arguably, at least equally as important as individual battles or the dramatized recollections of "great men."[4] Also, the sound-bite characteristic of what passes for verbal argument on television does not lend itself to the complex and lengthily argued historical analysis necessary for a better understanding of the issues at hand.

Drawing on the affective potency of dramatization, *The Valour and the Horror* personalizes history. This makes for many highly charged moments, but tends to create a dearth of useful analysis—analysis that is essential if the audience is to rationally reassess the events of the past. A number of commentators have argued that the empirical method of unproblematic "fact" gathering has often been associated with stories of great or villainous men, and in the end with the imposition of moral judgements upon their behaviour (McArthur 8). But Colin McArthur argues that the narration of history tends to become lopsided when "experiental phenomena are given primacy over equally real, but not directly observable, deep structures" (McArthur 13). However, these experiential phenomena make fertile ground for television dramatizations since the realist televisual text thrives upon stories about individuals to create both identification and emotional response, with the conventional, and ideologically correct, poetic justice in the end.

This personalization of history, which is an essential characteristic of the dominant, popular historiography, begs a number of crucial questions—particularly questions of class. By pillorying several individuals, *The Valour and the Horror* refuses to analyze the attitude of the British and German military hierarchies towards colonial troops and enemy civilians—attitudes that appear distressingly similar. When the incompetent or villainous generals die, their deeds die with them. A more thorough class analysis would have bypassed individuals and noted that Western military hierarchies have a lengthy history of "de-housing" civilians; in Vietnam the process was called "urbanization," and in the Gulf War, "collateral damage." Thus the personalization of history, characteristic of television, might make for good drama, but it also tends to trivialize history and create comfortable mythologies around systemic and class-based attitudes toward colonials and enemy civilians.

It would be a mistake, I think, to underestimate the effect upon *The Valour and the Horror* of American television genres such as the tabloid news programs and what has been called, strangely enough, "reality TV"—programs such as *America's Most Wanted* and *Rescue 911*, and, more importantly, the confessional/therapeutic discourses of American television, recently discussed by Mimi White. In a discussion of *The Valour and the Horror*, which appeared in *Saturday Night* magazine in May 1993, Brian McKenna said that, "I have this feeling that there's this Jungian subconscious in this country that has all this pain, all these stories of war passed on genetically—this pool of suffering and horror that we've never really tapped....The soldiers come home and the macho world of the military says you don't talk about it, you lock it away" (qtd. in Collins 47) These pools of suffering are precisely what television's therapeutic discourse dives into daily through *Oprah, Montel,* and *Sally Jesse Raphael*. Indeed, one might see *The Valour and the Horror* as a therapeutic plumbing of memories repressed by the veterans, or "survivors," who now relive their pasts in the televisual confessional.[5] But, more importantly, the memories revealed are those that have, from the McKennas' point of view, been forcefully suppressed by the official record of the war.

Confessionally and therapeutically, *The Valour and the Horror* attempts to return "the repressed" to cultural memory. At the extraordinarily moving conclusion of the episode "Savage Christmas," after all of the horrors have been revealed, one of the veterans says, "I didn't tell my own mother everything. I just wanted to forget it." This clearly uncomfortable moment of confessional television indicates the clash between the narrator's need to show "everything" over the veterans' need for privacy. The final scene in this episode shows the two veterans who have been interviewed throughout the episode in a Hong Kong veterans' cemetery, summing up their experience of revisiting the past. Both men have been stoic throughout the recounting of their terrible ordeal; both are enormously dignified in trying to set the record straight. In this final scene both break down, and both seek to escape the camera's invasive and voyeuristic presence. However, the camera is not so easily eluded in this tabloid-like confessional moment, as it pursues them, showing them in large close-up, even though they attempt to distance themselves from its intrusive eye. There is a very moving moment as the two struggle to retain their composure, not knowing that these kinds of highly charged confessional, teary moments are the stock in trade of daytime talk shows, tabloid programs and reality TV.

The McKennas attribute much of the hostility toward *The Valour and the Horror* to the pain caused by this return of the repressed.[6] Indeed, one of the issues that has troubled the debate between the veterans and the McKennas has been over what is now called "post-traumatic stress syndrome." In previous wars this condition was known as "shell shock" and it was sometimes considered shameful—an exhibition of weakness or even malingering. Some of the veterans argue that the McKennas' concern with this condition, and victimization generally, in *The Valour and the Horror* is a reflection of their seventies, post-Vietnam bias. Colonel Jack English, a vocal contributor to this debate, has even referred to Brian McKenna as "a petulant flower child" (qtd. in Collins 74). The idea of confession and therapy is thus seen, by some of the veterans, as a revisionist imposition upon World War II by two journalists whose sensibilities were formed by the angst surrounding Vietnam.

However, in another sense, this manner of conceiving of the past as a repository of repressed memory to be purged by therapeutic confession is indeed a modern phenomenon and largely conducted on television. T. J. Lears has argued that in our era, through television and advertising, "the expression of the Protestant ethos of self-denial was reconfigured in favor of therapeutic self-revelation" (qtd. in White 12). It is likely that the McKennas' "post-Vietnam" desire for this therapeutic self-revelation colours their assessment of the history of World War II—an ideological move that is not made clear in the documentary itself.

Michel Foucault, in another context, has argued that, "confession is a ritual of discourse in which the speaking subject is also the subject of the statement; it is also a ritual which unfolds within a power relationship, for one does not confess without the presence (or virtual presence) of a partner who is not simply the interlocutor but the authority who requires the confession, prescribes and appreciates it, and intervenes to judge, punish, forgive, console and reconcile" (61-62). Foucault also notes that the role of an interlocutor—in the case of *The Valour and the Horror* it is filled by the McKennas—is also a hermeneutic or interpretive one (67). That is, the visual and spoken material in *The Valour and the Horror* is organized by the interlocutors to support their view of the event, and indeed they intervene here, as Foucault argues, to judge and to punish the Canadian and British military, and to console the veterans by revealing their status as survivors. The power is on the interlocutors' side. In this case, the veterans' stories tend to become confessions about their past sufferings and "sins." Indeed, the McKennas' use of the veterans' statements, and their interpretation of them in scripting the dramatizations, has become another bone of contention between them.[7] The veterans in this case do not recognize the authority of the interlocutors to judge their "sins." One might argue that the North American media generally have taken on the role of public interlocutor, and in the case of *The Valour and the Horror* they work to chastise the misdeeds of the military hierarchy and the government.[8] The confessional discourse becomes a site of conflict between two hegemonic cultural groups who are battling over the interpretation of the past. In the long run, of course, *The Valour and the Horror*, although it brings to light certain "errors" on the part of the government, still supports the very structures that it appears to critique through its acceptance of the conventions of the dominant popular historiography.

Furthermore, the use of recreations, so controversial in *The Valour and the Horror*, are conventional in "reality TV." Recreations have been sparingly used in cinematic documentary. It is almost as though filmmakers have regarded this as somehow falsifying the evidence or creating a fictionalization of the events. This is a most complex issue. Although many documentary makers refuse to use recreations, in a very basic sense many of them recreate events without actors. Robert Flaherty, the first influential documentary filmmaker, did not use actors. He did, however, have his real people re-enact long-dead traditions like harpooning seals and building igloos. Yet Flaherty did not feel that he was engaging in fiction or falsehood. Rather, he felt that he was showing the essence of Eskimo life. (More, or as pertinent, in a Canadian context, Québécois filmmaker Pierre Perrault's *Pour la suite du monde*, 1963, did the same.) Presumably, the McKennas have tried to provide the audience with the essence of the ordinary Canadian servicemen's experiences by using actors to represent them. They have argued, correctly, that this kind of information is seldom part of the official record. These recreations are clearly marked as such in *The Valour and the Horror*, but the clever choices of actor, camera position, and setting in many of the recreations are clearly rhetorical and show the McKennas' interpretations of individual behaviour.

One controversial recreation stands out in particular, that of Bomber Harris—and he is given short shrift. Overall, he is depicted as an obsessed man who caused the deaths of thousands of civilians and wasted the lives of his own men. This ad hominem argument, characteristic of this kind of historical analysis, is at its strongest in the depiction of Harris. The actor who plays him does so in a most unattractive manner. He is forceful and arrogant, and the camera, more often than not, moves into extreme close-up, distorting his face and making him seem excessively unfeeling. One key edit explains his character to us: onscreen, a retired German fireman describes the bombing of Munich and its aftermath. When he explains that a plague of rats invaded the city to feed on its death, there is a quick cut on the word "rats" to an extreme close-up of Harris's face. This edit is a pointed editorial comment designed to create distaste for the villainous Harris.

One can easily see the problem of including recreations in documentaries. Although they are clearly marked, subtle rhetorical effects can be directed to the audience in an unobtrusive manner. Words can be inflected and given meanings they might not have had in the original letters and interviews. Tele-documentary makers like the McKennas use fictional modes to compete with "disease of the week" movies, tabloid shows, and the evening news. They seek out controversy with which to entertain the audience—a practice the *Globe and Mail* critic John Haslett Cuff has called "dumbing down" the news and documentary. The ad hominem attack upon Harris is ultimately unsatisfactory, since Harris is never seen as a member of a powerful military elite whose behaviour seems to have changed little since the forties, even though the nature of the war is vastly different.[9] Despite the fact that *The Valour and the Horror* opens up some of the ideological contradictions in our culture, in the end, the personalization of history tends to help paper over these ideological cracks. And, indeed, the defence of Harris, versus the interrogation of what lies behind the charges levelled by the McKennas, has coloured the debate surrounding these issues.

The limited time available on network television also constrains the retelling of history. Tele-history strives for clarity, simplicity, and an unambiguous representation of historical events. The fact that the interpretation of history is seldom simple, clear, and unambiguous seems not to trouble the writers of popular history. In their three episodes the McKennas took about six hours to examine some very complex historical situations. "Savage Christmas" is arguably the most satisfactory episode, despite its subtle racism, because it is about the least complex of the three events, concentrating mainly upon personal experience and the terrible suffering of Canadian prisoners of war.[10] Two hours (or in fact 104 minutes minus commercials) is clearly not enough time to examine complex military history. Some time ago theoretician Pascal Bonitzer argued that documentary knowledge is generally shallow knowledge, and that we all know that true knowledge comes from long hours of study and thought. Knowledge, he argues, "exists as the effect of a labor of inquiry...of placing the object in perspective and investigating its form" (Bonitzer 321). This kind of knowledge is seldom gleaned from two hours in front of the television set. And yet Canadians get most of their knowledge of both current and past events from television drama, documentary, and newscasts. Bonitzer categorizes this, not as true knowledge, but as "the impression of knowledge" (321).

Another issue, which is very troubling, is the confusion created by the McKennas and the CBC between documentary and journalism. Despite what a sometimes naive audience might believe, documentary filmmakers seldom claim the objectivity claimed for them by many viewers. A documentary film is an opinion, an argument, and sometimes a work of art. It is subjective. It is not, as Terence McKenna claims, at the beginning of *The Valour and the Horror,* "the truth."[11] It is McKenna's take on the truth. Documentary is often, but not always, based on a real event or personage. It is always the filmmaker's opinion about that event or personage. A documentary filmmaker is under no obligation to be objective. Documentary can be seen as a form or rhetoric or argument, and every filmic device available to the fiction filmmaker is available to the documentarian.

Journalism, on the other hand, claims objectivity and balance for itself. This is, of course, a mythical but highly valued belief held by journalists.[12] Journalists often attempt to present two sides of an argument. They typically select a number of people who hold opposing beliefs, and assume by doing this they have covered the range of opinion and that the truth lies somewhere in the middle of the two opposing views. It appears to be a journalistic convention that the opposing sides must be allowed to speak; think, for example, of *Nightline*, the ABC series news show, where Ted Koppel tries to cover a range of usually rather conservative opinions. The McKennas allow no opposing views in *The Valour and the Horror*—and there clearly are opposing views; as documentary filmmakers they are not required to do so, but as journalists they probably are. What confuses the issue here is that most Canadians associate the McKennas with their work on the CBC's flagship newscast, *The National/The Journal*. This association is a problematic feature of *The Valour and the Horror* which can lead to both misinterpretation and baseless criticism.

The Valour and the Horror is one of those hybrid forms produced by television—neither documentary, nor docudrama, nor journalism—that John Caughie labels "uneasy" (342). The issue of televisual documentary was discussed thoroughly in *Screen* in the mid-seventies, where both its dangers and "progressive" potential were argued. Progressive because the mixture of documentary and fiction seems to problematize representations of "the truth" and, as Caughie notes, make the audience "skeptical of the other representations that tv has to offer" (300); dangerous because it can lead to failures of analysis and the proliferation of mythologies. It is curious to note that the critique of *The Valour and the Horror* undertaken by Canadian veterans is virtually the same as those levelled at British docudramas such as *Days of Hope* (Loach, 1975), *Cathy Come Home* (Loach, 1966), and the extremely interesting *Death of a Princess* (Thomas, 1980).[13]

The public discussion surrounding *The Valour and the Horror* has unfortunately not been particularly enlightening. Rather than discussing the important issue of the role of television as historiography, and, crucially, a rational, public examination of the McKennas' charges, there have been calls for punishment and censorship. In the end one has to assess the progressiveness of *The Valour and the Horror* on the basis of its reconstruction of the recent past. Is *The Valour and the Horror* progressive because it challenges the dominant view of the war, or is it television that is marked by what Caughie calls an "extension of the easy liberal discourse which appropriates and consumes unease and contradiction" (329)?

I would argue that it is some of both. By challenging the official record of the war and telling the personal stories of Canadian veterans, *The Valour and the Horror* educates younger Canadians about the sacrifices and suffering of their grandparents. But by unproblematically adopting the conventions of the dominant popular historiography, *The Valour and the Horror* does not equip that audience to rationally reassess the events of the past. Furthermore, it appears to me that the McKennas have taken the past and used it for the ideological needs of the present. These needs include the requirements for popular television; but the situation of the servicemen depicted in *The Valour and the Horror* also strikes me as similar to the problems faced by Canadians in 1993. Consider the basic narrative situation of *The Valour and the Horror* as the following: decent, but poorly trained and armed Canadians face two enemies, a larger, stronger, and better-trained German Army, and a Canadian government that appears intent upon betraying them by currying the favour of an important ally. Read this way, one might argue that Canada's difficulties with free trade and recession in the early nineties lie at the heart of *The Valour and the Horror*. An overwhelmingly powerful U.S. and the Mulroney government, whose major interest appeared to be courting the favour of the Reagan/Bush administrations, form the background of *The Valour and the Horror*. If Caughie and McArthur are right and history is the site of a continuous struggle for meaning in the present, and historiography is not "a process of reconstructing the past but of acting upon it for the present" (McArthur 8), then *The Valour and the Horror*'s painful reappraisal of the past could be seen as a grim reflection of the Canadian present rather than "the truth" about World War II.

NOTES

1 An earlier version of this paper was presented at a colloquium at Brock University. After all of the papers had been presented a veteran in the audience stood up and asked why anyone who wanted to know about the

war didn't just come and ask the veterans, since they are the ones who know what it was all about. The McKennas' position does not seem significantly different than the veterans' in this regard.

2 See McArthur for a more extensive discussion of this issue.

3 This fact is taken from Dick, "History on Television."

4 Colin McArthur writes in his exemplary examination of television and history that the dominant historiography, in fact, "favoured a kind of linear narrative history whereby 'facts' and 'great men' were assembled in chronological order and suitable moral judgements made about their interrelationship" (8).

5 The idea of the survivor is extremely important on programs like *Oprah*. Usually they are women who have survived spousal abuse, incest, or a violent crime. Indeed, Oprah is herself a survivor of childhood sexual abuse. The idea of surviving may indeed be one clue to the affective potency of many of these programs, which appear to be aimed at a working-class female audience.

6 Brian McKenna even goes so far as to speculate that the violence that he experienced as a child at the hands of teachers who had served in the war "came out of their silenced war" (Collins 47).

7 The veterans' protests against what they felt were errors of fact, but also of interpretation of their letters, memoirs, etc., may be found in *A Battle for Truth: Canadian Aircrews Sue the CBC over "Death by Moonlight": Bomber Command*, published by the Bomber Harris Trust, 1994, and "Flarepath," a newsletter also published by the Bomber Harris Trust. I am grateful to the Hon. J. Roderick Barr, Q.C., for giving me access to these and other materials concerning the veterans' response to *The Valour and the Horror*.

8 There is a religious aspect to a number of the televisual confessionals. It is almost as though celebrities such as Tonya Harding and O. J. Simpson are put in the stocks and their sins displayed for all to see. In the case of the talk shows the panellists are often held up to ridicule before the audience. Both the host and the audience question panellists and castigate them for their sins. In an increasingly secular society, these programs can be seen as enforcing a kind of public morality upon "sinners."

9 The recent behaviour of the Canadian military in Somalia tends to support this view.

10 The McKennas imply in "Savage Christmas" that the kind of behaviour exhibited by the Japanese in Hong Kong was institutionalized in their culture. Nothing is said of German cruelty, and in the Normandy episode German soldiers are on record expressing remorse at having slaughtered so many of the Canadian Black Watch. The Japanese are treated very differently in *The Valour and the Horror* than the Germans. Germans are competent and civilized, the Japanese are cruel and indifferent to human suffering.

11 McKenna, in fact says, "This is a true story. In some cases actors speak the documented words of soldiers and nurses. There is no fiction."

12 See Hall for a discussion of the ideas of "objectivity, neutrality, impartiality and balance" (345) and the way in which these ideas support hegemonic positions within the mass media.

13 For an interesting discussion of these and other docudramas, and the issues that surround them, see Goodwin.

Works Cited

Bennett, Tony et al. *Popular Television and Film: A Reader*. London: British Film Institute, 1981.

Bonitzer, Pascal. "Silences of the Voice." *Narrative, Apparatus, Ideology*. Ed. Philip Rosen. New York: Columbia UP, 1986. 319-34.

Caughie, John. "Progressive Television and Documentary Drama." *Popular Television and Film*. Ed. Tony Bennett, et al. London: British Film Institute, 1981. 327-53.

Collins, Ann. "The Battle Over *The Valour and the Horror*." *Saturday Night* 108 (4) May 1993: 44-49.

Dick, Ernest. "History on Television: A Critical Archival Examination of *The Valour and the Horror*. Unpublished.

_____. "*The Valour and the Horror* Continued: Do We Still Want Our History on Television?" *Journal of the Association of Canadian Archivists* 35 (Spring 1993): 253-69.

Foucault, Michel. *The History of Sexuality*. New York: Pantheon, 1985.

Goodwin, Andrew et al., eds. *BFI Dossier 19, Drama Documentary*. London: BFI, 1983.

Hall, Stuart. "Culture, the Media and the 'Ideological Effect.'" *Mass Communication and Society*. Ed. James Curran et al. London: Edward Arnold, 1977.

McArthur, Colin. *Television and History*. London: BFI, 1980.

White, Mimi. *Tele-Advising: Therapeutic Discourse in American Television*. Chapel Hill: U of North Carolina P, 1992.

MUSIC

IN THE GREAT MIDWESTERN
HARDWARE STORE: THE
SEVENTIES TRIUMPH IN
ENGLISH-CANADIAN
ROCK MUSIC

Bart Testa and Jim Shedden

PREFACE

Since 1995, Canadian rock musicians have shone dramatically from a position of unprecedented prominence in the North American music industry. Leading the way, Alanis Morissette won four Grammy Awards (the high prizes of the U.S. industry) for her album *Jagged Little Pill*, whose sales, by the fall of 1996, rivalled those of the top-ranked American pop diva Whitney Houston. Alongside Morissette, other Canadians, especially Bryan Adams, enjoyed unprecedented continental prominence. Céline Dion's impact on the 1996 Grammies and her booming record sales more than confirmed the decade's trend. This mid-1990s florescence of Canadian rock contrasts sharply with its sorry status a generation earlier. In 1970, Canadian radio stations adamantly refused even to play records made by Canadian musicians until they were compelled to do so, starting the next year, by the

---

Notes on pages 212-15.

Canadian Radio-Television Commission (CRTC) (Yorke 1-11). The
recording industry was then dominated by British and American firms
who rarely signed Canadian rock musicians and, when they did, never
adequately developed or supported their careers. The same record
companies are still in place today and, if anything, multinational control of the recording industry has further concentrated through corporate mergers (Straw, "Sound" passim). But their attitudes toward
Canadian rock musicians have undergone fundamental changes.

This paper examines the commercial rise of rock music in English
Canada from the mid-1960s to the present day, concentrating on the triumphant breakthrough years of the 1970s. Our historical sketch is out-
lined in the third section. Divided into six "moments," this essay pro-
ceeds from the installation of the CRTC's Canadian-content regulations
and concentrates on the 1970s, though we also briefly discuss the 1980s
and 1990s. Overall, we argue that Canadian rock is best understood in
socio-economic and geographical rather than aesthetic terms, and we
eschew the conventional Canadian nationalist-cultural interpretation.
That is why we begin by opposing two critics who hypothesize the
project of creating a unique and national Canadian rock sound on cultural-nationalist aesthetic grounds. This paper will then focus on signal
moments and analyze selected careers to exemplify a socio-economic
history of Canadian rock that has yet to be written.

AGAINST CANADIAN CULTURAL NATIONALIST INTERPRETATION

In the article "'Across the Great Divide': Imitation and Inflection in
Canadian Rock Music" (1986), Barry Grant paints a picture of
"*Canadian* rock and roll" (Grant's emphasis) whose main feature is an
aesthetic strategy: irony. He claims that irony effects a "generic subversion" of American rock forms. Grant interprets particular records,
like the Toronto group The Diamonds' "Little Darlin'" (1957), to argue
that certain Canadian rockers subvert American rock-musical-and-lyri-
cal idioms. Grant connects Canadian rock to the spirit of Canadian
comedy instanced by the skit-comedy TV show *SCTV*, which spoofed
American network television, and to ironizing tactics of English-
Canadian documentary films like the NFB production *Lonely Boy*
(Koenig and Kroitor, 1961), which depicted Ottawa-born teen-idol
singer Paul Anka. Manifestations of this ironic bent Grant takes to

exemplify a Canadian subversive posture toward American pop-culture forms. Authentically Canadian rock shares this tendency toward ironic subversiveness, and so, for Grant, it serves as a distinctive national-cultural trait. It also serves him as an evaluative measure, and so Grant regards most commercially successful Canadian rock bands, notably Bachman-Turner Overdrive and Rush (126), to be American copycats because he cannot discover ironic inflections in their music.

The appeal of this interpretive approach is considerable. It sets out a demonstrable aesthetic difference in Canadian rock and connects that difference to similar aesthetic tactics in other Canadian pop-cultural production. However, Grant would be hard-pressed to discover more than a handful of popular Canadian rock musicians for whom irony is a distinguishing feature of their music. We add to Grant's examples a few more, like Rough Trade's "High School Confidential" (1980) and Kim Mitchell's "Patio Lanterns" (1986), that fit his model well. Nonetheless, most Canadian rock ironists would have to be regarded as cult—and not popular—figures, like Stringband, Mendelson Joe, or Nash the Slash. The trickle of Canadian rock irony does not offer much national-cultural distinction when we compare it with the steady flow of parody underwriting American rockers since the 1950s period of Little Richard and Bo Diddley through the corrosive 1960s American rock genre-benders like Frank Zappa and Captain Beefheart, and outlandish British ironists like Arthur Brown and Mot the Hoople. It is likely, in other words, that rock is a pop-culture genre inclined to ironic *self*-subversion without respect to national cultures. Irony cannot, then, be a convincing sign of Canadian cultural difference in rock music.

In the article "Dream, Comfort, Memory, Despair: Canadian Popular Musicians and the Dilemma of Nationalism," Robert Wright claims that a "golden age" of Canadian rock occurred in the years 1968-72. He argues that important Canadian musicians reflected the background of rural folk music and actively foregrounded both a "back-to-the-land" sensibility and a protest-song trend (Wright 283-301). Wright interprets such Canadian musicians as Gordon Lightfoot, Bruce Cockburn, Joni Mitchell, and Neil Young claiming that their preference for folk-music forms was distinctly Canadian. Wright brushes aside the inconvenient fact that the same folk and protest forms also underwrote U.S. pop music in the 1960s by proclaiming that Canadians "co-opted and preserved an earlier American folk-protest tradition" into the next decade, the 1970s (284).

Wright's chronology of "co-option and preservation" here is dubious. As a folkie, Lightfoot had his closest contemporary colleagues in Americans like Tom Paxton and Tim Hardin. Similarly, Mitchell established herself as a notable 1960s songwriter through covers of her songs recorded by American folk-diva Judy Collins (and so, by the way, did Leonard Cohen). But Mitchell's star rose later through the recording of her "Woodstock" (1970) by the rock group Crosby, Stills and Nash. The originally Winnipeg-based rocker, Neil Young, was recognized as a singer-songwriter with protest-folk credentials only *after* his association with the California rock group Buffalo Springfield and its successor, Crosby, Stills, Nash and Young. Wright's cohort of Canadian musicians "co-opted and preserved" nothing American musicians did not continue to develop similarly and simultaneously, and these Canadian musicians evolved in close counterpoint with them as well. As for "preserving" a protest-song tradition into the 1970s, it could hardly be said to have been abandoned by Americans to any greater degree than by Canadians. Lightfoot's greatest successes were love ballads made in the 1970s (e.g., "If You Could Read My Mind" [1971]) accompanied by strings, and his role as Canada's songwriter laureate (i.e., songs like "Canadian Railroad Trilogy" [1967] and "Alberta Bound" [1971]) corresponds to Lightfoot's flagging commitment to protest and to his mutation from folk singer to commercialized "singer-songwriter" on the model of James Taylor and Cat Stevens. Mitchell's career soared in the same fashion when she switched to pop songwriting and pop arrangements on her LPs *Blue* (1971) and *Court and Spark* (1974). As for Canadian latecomer folkies like Murray McLauchlan and Bruce Cockburn, the former's minor success arose from distinctly urban material (i.e., "Down by the Henry Moore" [1975]) while the latter remained stalled as a cult figure until he very belatedly transformed his image under the influence of punk, rocked-up his instrumentation, and recreated the protest song with "If I Had a Rocket Launcher" (1985).

Wright's interpretation of the nationalist-cultural ethos to which he seeks to link these musicians raises further problems. It rests on the claim that the Canadian national character is more embedded in ruralism than the American. This claim was prominent in the 1960s as a component of a Canadian cultural nationalism, but it never matched the socio-economic or cultural facts. Canadians were overwhelmingly urbanized and at work in industrial manufacturing long before the 1960s; and many historians date the urbanization-industrialization of Canadian society to as early as the 1920s. The cultural-nationalist construct of a rural Canada as authentic Canada must be regarded as a 1960s bourgeois-leftist-cultural-nationalist confection that served to fantasize Canada—and here Canadian musicians—as "not-Americans."

The conceptual problems we see with Grant's and Wright's cultural-nationalist interpretations lie, first of all, with their restrictions. Both critics fundamentally, if discretely, strive to carve out Canadian musicians' differences from rock so that they can evaluate them *above* it on behalf of Canada's cultural identity. While conceptually attractive, in practice, Grant provides too little scope for accounting for Canadian rock. Interpretively unpersuasive and historically dubious, Wright's claims are flimsy attempts to draw distinctions between national cultures. Our broader disagreement, however, concerns the way these critics assume rock to be an already decided *American* genre, as if the essence of rock were immediately apparent and could be assigned to a national culture on aesthetic grounds. We want to turn to this broader second issue now.

ON NOT DEFINING ROCK: CHRONOLOGIES AND MOMENTARY AUTHENTICITIES

Rock critics reflexively cast their definitions of the music by resorting to some kind of chronology (see, for example, Marsh 272-73). We'd like to indicate why this reflex carries important insights. Rock arose as a hybridized musical form and continued that way. Rock 'n' roll appeared in the 1950s as an amalgam of C&W, R&B, jazz, and pop-song forms. In its hybridizing aspect rock resembles other popular-culture forms, such as movie genres, radio formats, musical theatre, comic books, mass-produced cuisine, and so on. Pop-culture hybridizations are events (or, rather, series of events) that do not yield stable essential forms. This peculiarity characterizes popular culture in almost every instance, and so assumptions of, and critical quests for, essences of pop-culture forms miss the point of their material creation and development over time. They misconstrue popular culture's dynamics as aesthetically normative and wind up deforming them in a misguided attempt to grasp their supposed essences (Jarrett 68-182). This misconstruing, we want to emphasize, is different from a critic indulging his or her taste. A critic can prefer one period of a film genre or comic books over another. A critic can use any rock period as a taste measure, but we cannot suppose that there is an aesthetic essence disclosed in this exercise of taste. And a critic should not confuse his or her enthusiasms for essence—much less *national* essence. This is what Grant and Wright do, for they believe they have defined "Canadian rock" against "American rock," which they assume to manifest the essence of the rock genre in national-cultural terms.

There have, nonetheless, constantly been plenty of heated debates about rock "authenticity." What rock critics, fans, and musicians indicate in such debates is that rock has made an unusually high investment, for a pop-culture form, in its "self-truth," and it serves pervasively as a taste criterion. But, authenticity in relation to what? How can one speak of a musician being authentic when the music's hybrid nature makes its essence, or "roots," impossible to define? It proves impossible to answer this question, and all claims to "self-truth" in rock are locked in a contradiction. This contradiction is not static, however, but dynamic, and it accounts for the notorious instability of rock music manifest in short career arcs, serial stylistic diversity, mercurial fan support, and the tendency toward irony we already noted. Or, to put it more positively, rock music's recurrent renewals, its grasping at innovations, returns to "roots," and so on, arise from the contradiction between investment in authenticity and the fact that there is nothing really to be authentic about. Rock's contradiction is destined to play out repeatedly and provide the underlying dynamic of rock chronology. The contradictions cannot be resolved but only rehearsed over and over.

Take as an aspect of rock's instability the musicological aspect, the myth of roots, or the "real origins" that yielded 1950s rock 'n' roll and sometimes are invoked as the defining source of the music. Rock's origins, as we recalled above, were a first hybridization of "race records" made by black R&B musicians and C&W. Rock thereafter is a readily hyphenated term that admits of serial amalgamations with other forms like folk-rock, soul-rock, or jazz-rock. These hyphenated sub-generic terms semantically admit rock music to be constantly and serially hybridized. Some critics have argued, as does David Shumway (119), for these as well as other reasons, that rock represents a "cultural practice" on the other side of a historical rupture in culture, and that this rupture defines modern popular culture generally.[1]

Like most pop-cultural forms, but more intensely than perhaps any other, rock relies on a *participation mystique*. By this we mean the engagement of fans with the energy and perceived expressive self-truth of the music. Rock is what the fans/critics say it is, and nothing is more obvious than that what rock is in these terms changes often, and often wildly.[2] A tension exists between rock and its "early user" listeners and its delivery-marketing systems (radio, record companies, critical organs, etc.) that constitute the music industry. The fans who first hear and enthusiastically champion a band or group of bands at local clubs (Street 257) engender a participation mystique, and then "marketing" takes over to distribute the music in the form of recordings, radio airplay, organized tours of performers, and publicity. It is the tension between participation mystique (the passing moment of felt authenticity) and the music industry (the distribution of the music) that characterizes the rock cycles that serially concretize the contradiction of rock's authenticity and its material existence as a pop genre. Rock, then, is a cyclical story in which the *local* (or *regional*) origination of musicians and their fan-base and wider industrial marketing continuously overlap, intersect, separate, and so on, with all kinds of uneven distributions of power, control, and energy, and over short spans of time. Such a dynamic militates against generic stability and precludes coagulation of any aesthetic essence.[3]

Each new redistribution of rock's energy and appeal arose from an initial *localized* participation mystique and corresponds musically with sub-generic invention, revivification, and innovation. These processes succeed one another usually through contradictions of stylistic preferences, but each claimed to be recovering rock itself and each seemed soon to betray rock. This is how the fundamental contradiction of rock authenticity played itself out for the more than four decades between the mid-1950s, when the music first appeared as a popular-culture scandal, and the mid-1990s. Once assimilated into the music-business delivery systems, radio, records, publicity, and concert tours, rock's participation mystique crosses a barrier into something different, but its intense engagement enjoys a strong *half-life* as a more widely enjoyed recorded and/or touring music, until that decays and is displaced by the next, often contradictory outbreak of energy and authenticity, assimilation and circulation. The only historical constant between 1958 and 1968, approximately its first decade, is that rock kept growing as a music-industry force. So, authenticity, as the working definition of rock at a given moment used by fans and critics, is labile and, quickly relocated musically as well as in terms of its "cultural" posture, racial positioning, and even usage-consumption (i.e., a local club, a car radio, a large rock festival, a basement rec room). Doubtless, the main social factor is the speed with which rock fans pass through their adolescence. The next "generation" (or even the next graduating class) requires fresh rock musicians and styles to elicit their commitments and, therefore, to inflect the music's authenticity.

We need to add a note specifically on radio for two reasons. First, in general, radio is historically rock's premier delivery system. Second, radio has played an even more critical role in Canadian rock, often a matter of life and death for basic economic reasons. The population of Canada is so small and distances between population centres so great that musicians must generate a market base for record sales quickly to support concert tours, which by themselves cannot usually sustain even a low-cost rock outfit. Until very recently, in the absence of secondary supports, like a viable rock press or television exposure, radio was the only medium available to Canadian bands. This is why the CRTC Canadian-content regulations proved to be such a crucial benchmark in the development of Canadian rock music.

Initially, rock radio arose in the 1950s as a format designed to play the Top 40 (or even Top 20 pop hits). These were single songs and not album tracks. AM radio aptly suited rock's economies of scale by targeting relatively specialized audiences (in comparison to movies, much less TV) and delivering doses of rock in three- to four-minute bites through the 45 rpm single. By 1970, with the opening up of the FM band and the achievement of stereo capability, FM rock stations defined themselves against Top 40 AM rock stations that played only hit singles by expanding their playlists into non-hits and album backtracks. Simultaneously but gradually in the 1970s, the record industry redesigned the unit of rock-music consumption from the 45 rpm single to the LP. The radio and LP nexus corresponded to rock music's proliferation and augmented it further. Numbers of recordings and touring bands greatly increased, and, paced by concert tickets and record sales, rock music became a large-scale industry phenomenon for the first time. Radio reacted to rock's market growth and FM stations resumed Top 40 playlisting, but within sub-generic limits (still leaving AM to purely generic pop "singles acts"), so that interpreting the brute sales figures of record charts (themselves multiplying to reflect sub-generic sales patterns) was finessed to meet the somewhat specialized rock-music tastes of target audiences (Barnes 16-25). We return to discuss the longer-term consequences of this trend in the 1990s in this paper.

It was in the late 1960s that the ideal of a national Canadian rock music was first entertained seriously, which led to the Canadian-content regulations. It was not a wholly fortuitous moment for this to have happened, for this was the period when FM radio and the LP began to assume the importance they would have in the next decade. Record companies in the 1970s assumed that musicians would have to be systematically supported with promotional and touring subsidies while they built up a fan-base over several LPs and tours. Companies expected limited album-track FM airplay long before record sales produced a profit. In this strategy, the big radio-hit 45 rpm single became the cap of a graduated promotional process, not the primary goal. Now the LP was regarded as the commercial unit of measure. Internationally owned record companies dominating in Canada refused to invest in the development of Canadian bands at anywhere near the levels that would become the industry standard in the 1970s.

CANADIAN ROCK AND REGIONALISM: OUTLINING A HISTORY

As our argument above indicates, the chronological premise, modelled on how rock's evolution is usually written, is that it consists of serially arrayed North American and British sub-generic forms. We now want to add a *geographical* premise that will be directed to the discussion of Canadian rock. Rock sub-genres arise simultaneously but heterogeneously in numerous North American regions—regions that often cross national boundaries in terms of musical styles and their popularity. Rock sub-genres, however, burgeon serially in terms of market popularity. This is to say that in Louisiana or Texas, for instance, a rock style may simmer locally without having any impact on the wider music industry at the same time very different styles dominate the airwaves. Then, the local style bursts from the local scene and, for a time, achieves popularity through recordings, radio play, and touring. This has happened at various times to locally favoured musicians of Detroit, New Orleans, Macon, Austin, and Seattle.[4]

Musical developments in rock will, then, often be a chronology of *regional local-listener* excitement and innovation followed by the rise through acceptance into national marketing conduits. This model is different from the model of formation of a stable national rock sound in the U.S., Britain, or, for that matter, Canada. In our argument, the privileged geography for the crucial part of the story of 1970s Canadian rock is the North American industrial midwestern region surrounding the Great Lakes.

Above we assumed parallels between rock and other pop-cultural forms. However, in one crucial respect, rock differs from movies, print publishing, and television: it has never been centralized. Even though major record companies have their headquarters in Los Angeles, New York, or London, rock music has no production centre akin to Hollywood. While its marketing is corporately centralized, rock music rarely arrives at the industry centres—a Los Angeles or a London—without already having been materially produced by its musicians—the songs written, the band sound evolved, the image established.

If rock's production is geographically decentralized, its history is unique in popular culture in being both an episodic and a geographical story of local eruptions arising at a remove from the centres of popular culture and only later channelled through centralized marketing systems. This is no less the case of Britain and Canada than of the U.S. More dramatic contrasts between metropole and local region may be invoked by contrasting Atlanta, Georgia, and Los Angeles, Austin, Texas, or Seattle, Washington, and New York, than contrasting, say, Winnipeg and Toronto. However, the impression that the centre is everything in Canadian rock is an error arising from a tendency to insist on a "Canadian" national culture (for movies, publishing, and TV, and, therefore, for rock music) rather than the right focus on the role of localities in rock. In fact, regional cities such as Winnipeg and Vancouver, Sarnia, Calgary, and Kingston have originated cutting-edge Canadian rock no less than a metropole city like Toronto. Indeed, we will argue that the triumphs of Canadian rock in the 1970s arose from, and travelled through, regional scenes, and that musicians linked up, again region by region, *across* the national border with the U.S., most significantly with other places in the Great Lakes area—with, in other words, the greater industrial middle west of the continent.

Nonetheless the story of rock is not the same as the story of the music industry despite their constant interaction. We thoroughly agree with writers like Grant that Canadian rock must be seen in relationship to a hegemonic American music industry. Until the 1990s, sustained success in Canada was predicated on success in the U.S. market. For the reasons we mentioned above—and these come down to great distances and small population—the financial requirement to sustain even a compact Canadian rock band requires it to reach beyond its immediate locality with records and concert tours. That reach has been provided only by internationally owned record companies and radio. The consequence of this is that no local scene within Canada really mattered until the possibility of entering marketing conduits, and that meant getting on Canadian radio.

Once we move beyond tales of short-lived local scenes (and their mystiques—Toronto's or Vancouver's in the 1960s, or Toronto's Queen Street in the punk era), Canadian rock history is the harsh chronology of rock acts either making it stateside or (more usually) not enduring at all. These tales contribute to issues that involve the "institutional" as well as market realities of rock in Canada. For these reasons, the founding of the CRTC (1968) and the implementation of Canadian-content regulations for radio (1970-71) are watershed institutional events.[5] With them the Canadian federal government changed the market set-up in which Canadian rock musicians operated. Prior to the CRTC's formation, Canadian rock acts were commercially successful only insofar as they moved their careers to the U.S. (e.g., Neil Young, David Clayton-Thomas, Joni Mitchell, and Steppenwolf). The quintessential, but highly idiosyncratic, case in point during this period, and the one that we develop below, is The Band.

In this study we will divide the chronology of Canadian rock into six moments. The first moment consists of the few R&B groups, like The Diamonds and The Crew Cuts, and pop singers, like Paul Anka, successfully exporting themselves to the U.S. during the 1950s and early 1960s. The second moment consists of musicians like Neil Young and The Guess Who who repeated this either by moving to the U.S. (Neil Young) or hitting the charts there (The Guess Who) without preliminary success in Canada.[6] The third moment arises directly from the "Cancon" regulations that paved the way for Crowbar, A Foot in Cold Water, The Poppy Family, Lighthouse, and others. The fourth moment involves rock bands that were able, for the first time in Canadian rock, to sustain careers beyond radio-hit singles. These bands were success-ful in touring, album sales, and American popularity, and the signal groups here were Bachman-Turner Overdrive, April Wine, and Rush. The fifth moment marks the rise of managers, especially Bruce Allen, and the consolidation of a music-industry infrastructure that worked—and continues to work today—behind Corey Hart, Loverboy, Trooper, and Bryan Adams. This moment continues to the present. However, by the mid-1990s, a greater diversity in musical directions emerges, exem-plified by Sarah McLachlan, Blue Rodeo, The Tragically Hip, Barenaked Ladies, The Dream Warriors, and Alanis Morissette, and these constitute a contemporary sixth moment.

Transcending the Second Moment: The Imaginary Pilgrimage of The Band

> The Band—four Canadian rockers held together by an Arkansas drum-mer—staked their claim to an American story from the beginning. The story had its veils, but the fact of the story was plain. "This is *it*," my editor Marvin Garson said in the spring of 1969, as he sent me off to cover The Band's national debut in San Francisco. "This is when we find out if there are still open spaces out there." (Marcus, *Mystery Train* 43)

Of all the Canadian rock musicians who departed for the U.S. to achieve success in the late 1960s, The Band would prove to be the most idiosyncratic and also the most suggestive rock ensemble of all. While Neil Young must be recognized today as rock's most durable and mercurial eccentric, at the same time he was smoothly inserting himself into the Los Angeles scene. Young blended well into Buffalo Springfield, then into the "supergroup" Crosby, Stills, Nash and Young. The Band's gestation was uncommonly long, and the impor-tant phase of their career was remarkably brief. The players were first assembled as The Hawks, a backing group for Ronnie Hawkins. An Arkansas shouter whose compatriot, drummer Levon Helm, accompa-nied him to Toronto in 1958, Hawkins settled there to become a per-manent godfather figure. He played a Southern-style roadhouse ver-sion of rock 'n' roll. Although he initially had a string of hits that established his stature, Hawkins was, by the early 1960s, already a relic, albeit a rambunctious one. Initially, the young Hawks were typical Toronto rockers of their era, white R&B players apprenticing in Yonge Street saloons behind visiting American singers. Hawkins, a rocker with a particularized Southern idiom, took them on for long-term employment in 1961.

Then, in 1965, they were recruited by Bob Dylan as a nameless touring electric backup band. The collaboration between the Hawks and Dylan was notoriously intense and extremely successful. It lasted beyond the concert tours when the group's members retired with him to the neighbourhood near Woodstock, New York, after Dylan's motorcycle accident temporarily curtailed his career. To this point in what was a decade-long apprenticeship under very controlling front men, the group that would become The Band still had no name and the members remained unknown to the public. They secretly worked with Dylan on a set of homemade recordings (a portion much later released as *The Basement Tapes*, [1975]); they laboured with him on the material that would become the singer's comeback album, *John Wesley Harding* (1968), which Dylan recorded without them; and their own first LP as The Band, *Music from Big Pink* (1968), was named for the house where they and Dylan had assembled.[7]

When The Band released this record under their calculatedly generic name and made their concert debut, in 1969 in San Francisco (their second concert was at Woodstock that summer), their music was at odds with the flamboyance and instrumental virtuosity of sixties rock. A virtually acoustic ensemble, the group featured raw-boned group vocals (Helm and bassist Rick Danko were the main singers). The members looked and dressed in photographs like well-worn homesteaders who had wagoned in from a winter's solitude to kick up their heels a bit at a church social. Most songs were set in a dragged medium tempo, a few in a slightly accelerated waltz, usually with a layered keyboard sound recollecting the church and barroom in about equal measure. Aspects of the sound, notably the tempi and vocals, derived from Dylan, whose stamp was evident in the songwriting as well. But The Band's musical style, and the myriad sources on which it drew, was extraordinary in its allusive range as well as in the sense of a hard-to-locate past. These were not ersatz cowboys, or rural hippie innocents, or good ol' boys on a C&W toot. The Band eluded these nostalgic stereotypes and did so with an ambiguity that made them seem at once foreign and uncannily familiar.

They were instantly a critical success, and by the time they released their second LP, *The Band* (1969), a mainstay of the then-new FM rock radio stations. However, they had no major hit singles and *Music from Big Pink* never became a gold record. Then, within about seven years, The Band bowed out, quite majestically, with a 1976 concert, The Last Waltz, filmed and released as a feature-length concert documentary (1977) directed by Martin Scorsese.[8]

What is perhaps most interesting to our discussion of Canadian rock is that The Band cannot readily be called an American band and yet seemed to critics like Marcus an archetypal American band. Aside from the Southerner Helm, the members were Canadians, and Robbie Robertson and Richard Manuel were the principal songwriters. But, in fact, it is Helm's presence as vocalist and drummer that opens the critical question of The Band. Their music is evocative, often pointedly so, of a *regional* North America, rather than of the *nations* of Canada and the U.S. The distinction is important. The stories their songs tell— like Dylan's, the Band's songs often deploy elliptical narratives—are sometimes Deep Southern, sometimes Far Northern or Maritime. But most often they seem to arise from an ambiguous place that has no definite location, that has no official version of itself and is therefore unlocatable. The same ambiguity pertains to the songs' times, which do not belong to a known history, but only to those small and forgotten times that nations do not recall, but localities remember, vividly if elliptically, as happening "down the river," "up the creek," or "over to her house," that happened during that "bad winter" or after "the year the harvest failed." In some songs, these things are more specifically historical, as in "The Night They Drove Old Dixie Down" and "Acadian Driftwood," but most of even their epic songs—"The Weight," "Chest Fever," "King Harvest (Must Surely Come)," "Unfaithful Servant," "Across the Great Divide"—paint ambiguous and almost wholly imaginative landscapes.

And so, too, the music The Band weaves continuously echoes sounds associated with regional origins and historical periods of popular music, but in mixtures that can be located only by vague types and not as historical sources and references. There is as much early jazz as folk, as much Canadian East Coast as American Southern, as much of the Baptist church as the Brownsville brothel. All that the listener feels sure of is that The Band plays music long obsolete and that it remains so even after they have revisited it, but that, on the other hand, no one ever played or heard it like this before.

Reconstructing The Band's music by its sources—doubtless possible—would confirm that it amalgamates an imaginary regionalist plurality of, and especially the sense of a musical-narrative conversation between, Canada's East and North, and the U.S. South and Midwest. This is finally made explicit on their last studio LP, *Northern Lights–Southern Cross* (1975). These interpretive claims are summarized by Marcus in the theme and title of his essay "Pilgrim's Progress." Marcus interprets The Band to be an eccentric rock-music recapitulation of the antique Protestant ethos for which John Bunyan's allegory *Pilgrim's Progress* long served as the prototype. There is a powerful connector across the great diversity of regional allusions encompassed by The Band's music, and it is the mythos of an old American (but it has to be North American) experience. It is a mythos of biblical—at times millennial and tragic—Christianity. Such a strong and mythically rich connector across national borders also explains in part why The Band's imagined circulation of music and tales can actually make listeners see vividly what we already know: that the scattered regions of the continent have exchanged and communicated pieces of their cultures for two centuries now. This connector, this deep old mythos, made us receive as meaningful a popular culture of songs, story fragments, musical metres, vocal intonations, and odd moral fantasies that do tie far-flung regions of the continent together culturally.[9]

If we have paused to elaborate an interpretation of The Band it is because their music seems to us to exemplify in a highly imaginative and idiosyncratic fashion an important practical feature of popular music, and so of rock music, in North America: that connections are more often drawn between regions than countries. Among the Canadians who left to pursue musical careers in the U.S. in the 1960s, the members of The Band used their unique way of being a Canadian group, one first backing Hawkins's obsolete American Southern rock and then driving Dylan's magisterially odd amalgam, to become the archetypal American rock group. And, yet again, The Band was, in everything that mattered, thoroughly eccentric to the rock music surrounding them on both sides of the border. The radical idiosyncrasy of The Band must be understood to include no rock authenticity as the music almost always demands. There was no local "scene" from which they sprang, no "early users," in effect, no "fans." The Band was one of the extremely few rock groups that created itself purely from imagination and memory and that made the decentralized character of rock the source of an unsurpassingly evocative music—evocative, that is, of multiple lost localities and pasts.

Now, we are speaking here of The Band's music, not its place in the rock-music business. In industry terms, The Band constituted a footnote, at best, to sixties rock. The Band appeared at the moment, right in the euphoria of Woodstock, when rock music came to be absorbed into a greatly expanding music industry in a new way. The era of "arena rock," of best-selling "concept albums" (whose prototype is The Who's *Tommy*), in short, of rock's hypertrophic staging of its own intensity, was about to define the next decade. The Band was the oddest possible prelude to the 1970s, which would frenziedly market "heavy metal" and "art rock," "glitter rock" and "glam rock," and "disco." And yet, for us, The Band represents, for Canadian rock music, nothing odd at all, but something exemplary: the imagination of regional connections that would, in the 1970s, under radically less imaginary and immeasurably more brutal conditions of play, mediate the sudden and unexpected triumph of Canadian rock, rising from the most unpromising and incongruous of quarters—the suburbs of Toronto, Windsor, Winnipeg, and Calgary.

The Third Moment: False Starts

Many of the artists of the third moment had achieved minor local success in the late 1960s, often under other band names. The new Cancon radio regulations pushed these musicians into new prominence through the vehicle of Top 40 singles. It was U.S. success that initially proved how productive the federal regulations were. Nonetheless, there are reservations about this third moment, and they begin with the music itself: it was pre-formed and derivative. The bands were past their prime inspiration (which was limited in the first place), and what resulted was predictably a cycle of one- and two-hit singles bands. Stylistically, the rock played by these early 1970s Canadian bands resembled second-tier but popular American rock hit-singles groups of the period, like Three Dog Night, The Doobie Brothers, and Chicago, among which The Guess Who were to be numbered. All these bands served an institutionally opened marketing niche, but they lacked the capacity to expand it. Typically, Lighthouse, formed by drummer Skip

Prokop and composer-keyboardist Paul Hoffert, initially as a preten-
tious sixteen-member ensemble complete with string section, swiftly
pared itself down to the level of a second-string Chicago and then hit
with "One Fine Morning" in 1971. Such Canadian bands never developed into groups that could sustain LPs and concert careers. This
proved critical. By 1970, the major units of rock consumption, and
therefore of reputation and career momentum, were becoming the LP
and the concert tour. This third moment is best described either as a
holding action or a false start.

THE FOURTH MOMENT: CANADIAN TRIUMPH (BACHMAN-TURNER OVERDRIVE AND RUSH)

By the mid-1970s, a type of rock arose that was album-oriented and con-
cert-based, and that held wide appeal for young audiences in the suburban and ex-urban terrain of the continent's industrial heartland. Hard
rock initially had little music-industry caché and none with a rock press
still looking to the 1960s for its models of authenticity. Hard rock would
doom the dominance of the Canadian singles-style acts that first arose in
response to Cancon regulations. A band that sprung from the most
famous of these singles acts, The Guess Who, was Winnipeg's Bachman-
Turner Overdrive (BTO). They exemplified the sound and image of this
hard rock. Virtually indistinguishable from American bands possessing
the same appeal, BTO was also the most successful Canadian second-tier
rock group of the period, the early 1970s. They marked the transition
from short-lived hitmakers like the Poppy Family and Lighthouse to the
more durable triumphs of album-oriented rock (AOR) that came later in
the decade with Rush. As with its parent group, sustained success for
BTO in Canada was predicated on success in the U.S.; once again, like
The Guess Who, BTO was mainly a singles band, but one that became a
very successful concert attraction on both sides of the border.

   Hard rock defined itself as appealing exclusively to the very young,
and, while it continued the oppositional posture of 1960s rock, it was
not really against anything, and certainly not the "Establishment." BTO
were consummate businessmen and they made no secret about their
marketing savvy in their lyrics or statements in the media. Parents and
teachers (and older siblings) hated BTO's hard rock, but not because of
the meanings it conveyed. On the contrary, it was intentionally mean-

ingless. It was apolitical and yet insisted on being antagonistic. It was
utterly unpretentious in its lyrics and delivery, and bereft of serious
emotional tenor. Departing from the often elaborate song forms of sixties rock, hard rock was simplistic, though it still retained the cult of
virtuosic guitar playing. Some hard rockers, like the Michigan-based
Bob Seger, still drew upon soul-music roots and reflected the R&B traditions of the Midwest. But the more typical strain consisted of bands
like Brownsville Station, Alice Cooper, Deep Purple, Thin Lizzy, REO
Speedwagon, and Kiss. This was BTO's cadre.

The title of the single "Gimme Your Money Please" might best
exemplify the ethos of BTO. But there is nothing cynical about it. In
fact, BTO's ground-tone would always be cheerfully open-handed and
their attitude was nothing if not transparent. Indeed, the band exemplified how easily the demands of the expanding music industry could be
reconciled to the postures of rebellious rock authenticity during the
1970s. What this meant was that early in that decade, hard rock lost its
pretense to be about anything (politics, erotic liberation, religious or
poetic vision) and expressed nothing but the glamorization of the rock
"lifestyle" itself. BTO was exemplary of these trends in every respect.
Consider this final stanza of the band's signature tune, "Takin' Care of
Business" (1974):

There's work easy as fishin'
You could be a musician
If you can make sounds loud or mellow
Get a second-hand guitar
Chances are you'll go far
If you get in with the right bunch of fellows
People see you havin' fun
Just lyin' in the sun
Tell them that you like it this way
It's the work that we avoid
And we're all self-employed
We like to work at nothin' all day.

"Takin' Care of Business"
Written by: Randy Bachman
Ranbach Music/Sony/ATV Songs LLC
All rights on behalf of Sony/ATV Songs LLC, administered by Sony/
ATV Music Publishing, 8 Music Square West, Nashville, TN, USA 37202.
All rights reserved. Used by permission.

Unlike other hard-rock bands, high-living was not part of the BTO scenario. No sex, no drugs, just rock 'n' roll. Yet, despite the clean living espoused by Bachman (a practising Mormon), the message BTO broadcast is the same as most hard rock of the decade: work hard, play hard. The form this message took was the recurring paean to rock itself. And, despite claims to a basic Canadian character of the group (Pevere and Dymond 70-73), BTO's musical style and message and appeal were identical to that of their Midwestern American counterparts. The meaning, while intended to be empty, actually possesses a utopian aspect not hard to interpret. BTO obsessively evoked the "good times" to be had by average working-class suburban and ex-urban youth. While the banality of the pleasures BTO's songs enumerate are a radical diminishment of the fantasies of 1960s rockers like Jim Morrison or John Lennon—who dreamed of touching God, or more often the Goddess; or the ecstatic liberation after overthrowing the American empire—the shell idea of unfettered freedom remained. As utopians of a plainer hue, BTO fantasized a collapsing of pleasure and work into the rocker's job. This was a job without bosses because the worker-musician now owned the business, for "we're all self-employed." BTO's was a wakeful utopia involving trucks rumbling down the highway, and beers enjoyed later among the boys leaning on tailgates after the band's show. This is a fantasy with a backdrop coloured differently from rock's outlandishly dreamy 1960s pleasure dome, but its shape and function were familiar, and its appeal broadened demographically.

Rock in the 1960s was the fantasy indulged by an unprecedentedly affluent middle-class youth culture centred in San Francisco and Los Angeles. By comparison, 1970s hard rock was the fantasy of working-class youth living in the middle of the continent who could, and did briefly, imagine the permanent release into a lifestyle where labour and fun were the same. This was a moment just prior to the recessionary cycles begun with the oil crises of the 1970s, which would soon severely damage this class cadre, impoverish its industrial base (the steel and automotive industries), and foreclose on the easy glee of the hard-rock sub-genre. While it lasted it was a fantasy that had no centre, no equivalent to Haight-Ashbury; its domain was virtually everywhere. Its fantasy was mobility and constant repetition possessed of an industrial élan that BTO's album covers rightly emblematized with vans and trucks—i.e., with working-men's industrial vehicles—and accompanied by a music so simple it *could* serve as the soundtrack of constant motion. It expresses, at root, a late-industrial utopia. This rock arose in BTO's own neighbourhood, the regional terrain looped around Winnipeg, then Calgary, Sarnia, Windsor, and soon proved readily transportable when BTO lapped circuits of touring and radio play around the whole industrial Midwest. In the most important demographic and economic respects, BTO showed that Winnipeg was hardly different from Windsor, Flint, Duluth, or Butte.

The diminution of rock fantasy between the 1960s and 1970s corresponded to a spread in both the sociology and geography of rock's listeners. The spread moved inward from the decidedly coastal counterculture of the middle-class and college/university-destined young to the middle-American mass of the young in general. The spreading rock of the 1970s included the working class and lower middle class of the less-affluent but, for the moment, well-paid and secure population of the industrial belt of the middle of the continent. The broadening of rock's audience is no mystery; in the 1970s, rock became big business for the first time and did so without apology. Robert Duncan points out that the "half a million strong" referred to in Joni Mitchell's "Woodstock" was "an accountant's epiphany too" (37). He adds: "And, indeed, for all the noise, the music business of the sixties was a mere infant—squalling perhaps, but tiny—by comparison with the brute of the post-Woodstock 1970s. In the 1970s, in fact, the music business finally grew up—like some kind of thyroid case—to become the music industry" (37).

Rock was now a product. Although rock music was still a tool of youth identification, the 1970s young, now a hugely engorged demographic cohort, were rebels without causes except for an occasion to rock out. BTO typified the consequences: hard rock's root formalism was sixties rock stripped down and reshaped as an easy commodity. And BTO made the conditions of rock's consumption their utopic theme and trimmed the musical style to fit a life that would be lived wholly between work and the enjoyment of tailor-made commodities that celebrated a simple "lifestyle" condition, one drained of imaginative surplus. It was the band's perfectly generic genius to warp that dull, diminished truth into a still-utopian paean to rock itself.

It is commonplace in cultural studies to understand demographics in terms of class, nation, race, gender, and sexual orientation. It is perhaps more instructive in the instance of considering rock on this continent to consider geography as well, as we have begun doing. We take geography in two senses: first, to mean region (the South, the Midwest, the East Coast, etc.); second, to indicate patterns of local development (e.g., "rural," "urban," "ex-urban/industrial," "suburban," etc.). The early success of a rock sub-genre can happen in a specific region and, then, after local success, the popularity of the band or genre can spread to other locales with similar patterns of development. For example, in the 1970s, the initial and regional success of "Dixie rock" bands like the Ozark Mountain Daredevils, Black Oak Arkansas, and Lynyrd Skynyrd in American-Southern suburban/ex-urban regions prepared for the sub-genre's widening popularity in developmentally similar suburban/ex-urban regions throughout North America. Our account of BTO is such an example of how Canadians arose from a regional outpost like Winnipeg and achieved success continentally, with its particular base of support in the Great Lakes, Midwest region.

Rock's sustained market success is predicated on its ability to communicate, past the local participatory mystique, to audiences with a shared demographic background. There has been wholesale neglect of the geographical homologies across restrictedly regional sites of reception. The demographic situation relevant to 1970s rock was that regional and class sensibilities among the young across a much-widened class range were intensified and let loose within the channels of cultural consumption represented by rock. BTO's success was geographical in both our senses as well as class-based (and race, age, and gender-based: this was music embraced by white working-class and lower-middle-class boys). BTO's success was a forerunner of things to come, which, in the form of another band, Rush, it did very soon. As Pevere and Dymond argue:

> Rush has earned one of the most eccentrically successful positions in the global musical market....[By] positioning themselves outside of vogue and fashion, touring with the relentless tenacity of a Canadian winter, baldly fetishizing technical virtuosity and pop metaphysics, Rush connected with those kids who'd grown up with bikes, torn jeans, paperbacks and strip malls just like the boys in the band. When you consider the countless thousands of square suburban miles in North America, Europe and the U.K., it becomes quite clear why Rush found itself the band of choice for millions upon millions of kids. (184)

Rush represents the great triumph of Canadian rock. The connection Pevere and Dymond draw between Rush and their fans has endured for more than twenty years. The Toronto-based trio of Geddy Lee (bass, vocals), Neil Peart (drums), and Alex Lifeson (guitar) is the most successful Canadian rock band of all time. Formed in 1968, they were a popular Yonge Street bar band at the Gasworks and the Abbey Road Pub. They released a cover of "Won't Fade Away" in 1973 and their self-titled debut album in 1974, and enjoyed minor success touring Southern Ontario until a DJ at WMMS in Cleveland began to play their music. After tours of large stadiums, opening for hard rock bands like the Texas-based ZZ Top, they were signed to Chicago's Phonogram Records and released *Fly By Night* (1975), which reflected their heavy-rock/bar-band stage. In the following year, with *2112,* Rush established their own hybridized style. That style can be characterized as hard-rock "power chords," virtuoso guitar solos associated with heavy metal, relentless percussion, epic lyrics derived from fantasy literature, extended song length, and, for a rock band, complex musical structures. But this description does not yet account for the key differences Rush's stylistic amalgam made, and which made the major difference for Canadian rock.

Hard rock in the early 1970s, as exemplified by BTO, was still based on hit singles, consumed on the radio, and simply confirmed in concert. BTO expanded upon the first wave of Cancon acts by becoming a successful concert attraction and by packing their LPs with more hit singles than usual, but their style remained rooted in the short radio-centred song. Meanwhile, in the U.K., two rock sub-genres were emerging, "heavy metal" and "art rock" (the latter soon amalgamated with "progressive rock"), both of them "album-oriented." Heavy metal evolved across albums by Pink Floyd, Emerson, Lake and Palmer, and The Moody Blues and fell into a close alignment with "progressive" bands like Genesis, Yes, and King Crimson. Although exclusively British in origin, both heavy metal and art/progressive rock held huge appeal for North American listeners soon equal to, then surpassing, hard rock. The main difference was that this newer 1970s rock did not depend at all on hit singles. The preferred format stretched into extended-song forms, and these bands made the LP format their own; and the LP was rapidly becoming the standard, rather than exceptional, music-industry unit of consumption.[10] What airplay art/progressive rock and heavy metal received came through FM stations, which, by choice (most U.S. stations) or regulation (e.g., the CRTC in Canada), did not play hit singles.

Very young audiences flocked to see this British rock music performed—it took well to large sports arenas—and listeners likewise bought large quantities of albums by bands like Yes, Led Zeppelin, Black Sabbath, Queen, and Emerson, Lake and Palmer. However, no successful American bands played progressive or heavy-metal rock. It seemed exclusively a British franchise. In Canada, however, the situation was soon strikingly transformed. Canadian bands absorbed both heavy-metal and art/progressive styles and produced their own hybrid from them that spearheaded Canadians' unprecedented success in the North American market. What we want to argue is that this so-called "art-metal" Canadian hybrid, which is what Rush perfected, is the only instance of a distinctly Canadian form of rock to emerge. When bands like Saga (Toronto), Prism (Vancouver), Max Webster (Sarnia), and Rush fused the hard rock with art rock, they brought together the straightforward guitar-bass-drums style that appealed to young listeners in the Great Lakes industrial middle-west—the Canadian bands' home ground—with the expanded LP format/extended virtuoso synthesizer-keyboard-guitar art rock of British bands. The result was the first uniquely Canadian hybridization, one that never had an equivalent in American or British rock.[11] If BTO's success was predicated on rock's expanding reach into the youth of the industrial suburban and ex-urban class in the early 1970s, Rush consolidated its hold on the same audience. If BTO exemplified a diminution of sixties-rock aspirations to liberation, Rush represented two things: a thematic reinflation and an explicit shifting of the intellectual and political milieu of hard rock.

The relation between the two Canadian bands was suggested by a 1978 *Maclean's* cover story whose January 23rd headline read "The Rush Revolution," and, inside, "To Hell with Bob Dylan. Meet Rush. They're in it for the Money." Rock may have become big business in the 1970s, but the big-capitalist ethos of the music industry coexisted with contradictory postures of surviving and still very popular "hippie era" rock bands, like Crosby, Stills and Nash and Jefferson Starship. Heavy metal and progressive rock would change this, and Rush proved crucial to collapsing the contradictions of 1970s rock culture.

Rush's appeal was partly comparable to BTO's, as Pevere and Dymond argue, because it cohered with the mid-1970s' "*nouveau riche* suburban work ethic, according to which 16-year-old kids who didn't have part-time jobs were losers" (186). Will Straw's account of the rise of heavy metal provides needed economic perspective on Rush. When the LP replaced the single as the crucial consumer format, it transformed the music industry's economics: "the break-even point for album sales went from 20,000 to 100,000 copies" (Straw "Characterizing" 370). This meant that (as we noted above) record companies had to think more strategically and long term to ensure considerably greater longevity of rock groups, who would have to build a following rather than expect the quick (but lower cost-recovering and quickly fading) success of hit singles. These considerations, observes Straw, "made more important an audience segment that had been somewhat disenfranchised by movements within rock of the late 1960s—suburban youth. In the 1970s, it was they who were the principle heavy metal constituency" (373).

Straw's analysis is mainly geographical, and, though it is not without the familiar race-class-gender dimension of cultural studies, when he compares the rise of heavy metal to the rise of disco music, its 1970s contemporary, it is the *where* that counts more heavily than the *who*. Straw observes: "the demographics of disco showed it to be dominated by blacks, Hispanics, gays, and young professionals, who shared little beyond living in inner urban areas" ("Characterizing" 373). He goes on to argue:

> Suburban life is incompatible for a number of reasons with regular attendance at clubs where one may hear records or live performers; its main sources of music are radio, retail chain record stores (usually in shopping centres), and occasional large concerts (most frequently in the nearest municipal stadium). These institutions together make up the network by which major-label albums are promoted and sold—and from which music not available on such labels is for the most part excluded. ("Characterizing" 373)

The story of Rush's success is the tale of their manipulating these "institutions" to reach the suburban and ex-urban youth audience. The early career of Rush was typical of local hard-rock outfits, and they were jokingly called "Led Zeppelin Jr." for awhile. With *2112* (1976), Rush distinguished itself musically and lyrically and from this point reached great commercial success. Comparisons between the Canadian band and British progressive-rock groups like Yes now became commonplace. The resemblance was not mysterious: Rush played complicated instrumental solos; they evinced sophistication with the newest recording techniques; they composed lyrics saturated with mythological fantasy that permitted them to piece together thematically unified LPs, closer to suites than single songs. These features were all hallmarks of British progressive rock, though Rush's instrumental attack was much tougher and louder, and brought them onto terrain previously owned by American Midwestern hard rock. Not long after their success was secured, comparisons to other groups ceased and Rush gained their peculiar reputation as the "thinking man's" rock band, a position they continue to hold—along with very high record sales—in rock magazines' reader polls.

In contrast to the young fans, rock critics responded negatively to heavy metal, and Rush's "art metal" was no exception. Straw observes that critics disliked such bands because they seemed "unauthentic." Critics "adopted more and more of the terms of journalistic film criticism, valorizing generic economy and performers' links with the archives of American popular music" ("Characterizing" 375). By the late 1970s, rock criticism had become professionalized; one consequence was that its practitioners became "historians," and another was that they also became, against rock criticism's best reflexive insights, rock essentialists. Heavy metal, art rock, progressive rock, and Rush's "art metal" were all defiantly "non-historical" sub-genres. They were divorced from black music sources and familiar song forms, and disregarded aesthetic virtues associated with rock such as brevity, leanness, and laconic lyrics. This rock was unapologetically white, developed pretentiously operatic extended song forms, was long winded, overblown, and immensely wordy. Overall, "rock-historical" inauthenticity ruled. However, this is what makes it paradoxically authentic: that is, writes Straw, its "non-invocation of rock history or mythology in any self-conscious or genealogical sense" ("Characterizing" 375) declares it to be *de nouveau*. Its devoted young fan-base gave this 1970s rock its own participation mystique. We insisted above that rock authenticity is *not* a historical category, but just as often requires rockers to break with the past. Rush's "art metal" place in the chronology of rock music does not require an adjustment in that position any more than the advent of The Beatles or Motown does.

Professionalized rock critics took sixties rock as the benchmark for rock's cultural ambitions, believing the political and pseudo-religious ethos of the later years of the 1960s to be a hallmark of thematic seriousness. In very general terms, rock's appeal, and not just for critics, can be partially explained by its intellectual pretensions. Rock has sometimes provided a simplified but seductive entrance for the young into the world of ideas and culture. Bob Dylan opened the ethos of the Beats to a wide public. Jim Morrison and the Doors introduced figures as diverse as Nietzsche, Antonin Artaud, Norman O. Brown, Aldous Huxley, and Bertolt Brecht to the 1960s generation. Patti Smith directly exposed the punk generation to the names of Rimbaud, Verlaine, Baudelaire, and Rilke. William S. Burroughs remains a touchstone figure for countless rockers, major and minor. Such authors are obvious canonical fare from the perspective of those with a sophisticated literary education. But for the young whose intellectual circumference is a suburban high-school curriculum, such authors can constitute a passionately sought out "underground literature," an alternative reading list of names discovered from allusions on album sleeves or song lyrics. The values of sixties rock extolled by critics who cast unsympathetic eyes on the rock of the 1970s include such literary cultural values. And while heavy-rock bands like BTO erased such values, the general stylistic reinflation of art/progressive rock and heavy metal included a new expansion of lyrical ideas into literary terrain once again.

Rush's references are extraordinarily wide ranging: from poets like Coleridge ("Xanadu" on *A Farewell to Kings* [1977]) and Eliot ("Double Agent" on *Counterparts* [1993]) to scientists like Carl Sagan ("Cygnus" on *A Farewell to Kings*). The band has tended to map its albums on literary bases, even though not all its recordings are "concept albums" (i.e., thematically unified suites). However, it was the influence of Ayn Rand that was definitive and certainly most controversial. Rand's right-wing libertarianism (which she called "Objectivism") has been cited by drummer Neil Peart, the band's main lyricist, and vocalist-bassist Geddy Lee on numerous occasions. Rand is credited on *2112* because of the similarity between her novel *Anthem* (1938) and the narrative conceits of the LP. In some ways, she seems a peculiar taste for a rock band, since Rand began publishing in the 1930s. However, her popular heyday was the 1970s. It was then that she appeared on the underground reading lists of suburban high-school students. Rand's virulent anti-communism and pro-capitalist individualism saturate all her writings, but they achieve programmatic force in *Anthem*, a dystopian fiction set in a totalitarian society resembling a Leninist Soviet Union in which individuality is outlawed. The same tale is told on *2112*. Here is Rush's portrait of the album's communitarian society:

> We've taken care of everything
> The words you hear the songs you sing
> The pictures that give pleasure to your eyes
> It's one for all and all for one
> We work together common sons
> We are the Priests, of the Temples of the Syrinx
> Our great computers fill the hallowed halls.
> We are the Priests, of the Temples of Syrinx
> All the gifts of life are held within our walls
> Look around at the world we made
> Equality our stock in trade
> Come and join the Brotherhood of Man
> Oh what a nice contented world
> Let the banners be unfurled.
>
> "Temples of Syrinx" by Geddy Lee/Alex Lifeson/Neil Peart
> © 1976 Core Music/All Rights Reserved.
> Used by Permission from the Rush album *2112*.

The difference between 1960s anarchistic rock longing for freedom and a virulently anti-communist libertarian source in *2112* was not lost on critics. They harshly attacked Rush for the political position their songs supposedly expressed. Most rock critics already held heavy metal and progressive rock alike in measured disdain, and Rush's monumentalizing amalgamation of both styles seemed even worse. But it was their lyrics that drew particular condemnation. While it is perfectly true that Rush's totalitarian target was fantasized and abstracted to such a degree that no specific political regime could be secured as its historical referent, it should not have been difficult—but it was for critics impossible—to grasp why Rand's radical individualism would hold great appeal to suburban youth, beginning with Canadian youth. They were, for all practical purposes, living in the geographical twilight zone where "we've taken care of everything," namely, the white suburbs girdling the middle cities of North America. Given that the 1970s was a decade during which the social concerns that directed the young of the 1960s into socially conscious individuation were supplanted by the "Me Decade's" overwhelmingly private preoccupations, an LP like Rush's Rand-derived *2112* provided the perfect fantastic scenario of teenaged individualism inflating to heroic proportions.

Moreover, when Rush achieved their distinct hybridized musical style with *2112*, they no longer sounded like farm-league Led Zeppelin, and the break with the sounds and lyrical accents of the late 1960s also meant a break with the hippy counterculture. This break proved extremely productive for the band. Suddenly, as *Maclean's* reported, Rush "found themselves speaking on behalf of a large segment of rock fans without spokesmen, a group who, despite a love for loud, violent music, were highly conservative and certainly self-centered" (*Maclean's*, 23 Jan. 1978).

Similar celebrations of individuality are evident throughout Rush's career, and often take on the Nietzschean character of a self-centred yet heroic non-conformism, later expanded (on *Hemispheres* [1979] and *A Farewell to Kings*) into cosmologies, theories of the bicameral mind and the dialectic of Apollo and Dionysius. Although the musical style they developed became increasingly technological in its aural land-scaping, Rush's lyrics are inclined toward imagery derived from "sword and sorcery" fantasy and science fiction. Musically, too, Rush's music mirrored movements in pop-cultural phenomena of the late 1970s. Rush's musical style evinced the turning-inward of the North American young across the class spectrum. The capacity of the music itself to provide escapist fantasy was likely more significant than the lyrical content. We have already argued that there was a niche market for the amalgam of heavy metal and art rock: this appeal lies in the syn-thesis of rock's masculinist show-of-force tendencies, on the one hand, and a fascination with technological wizardry, on the other. The appeal of Rush's music can be seen in the same context as the appeal of the arguably right-wing fantasies of *Star Wars* (1977) and *Close Encounters of the Third Kind* (1977) in movies; in science fiction Michael Moorcock's Jerry Cornelius novels (1968-77) and the endur-ing cult of Robert Heinlein's *Stranger in a Strange Land* (1961); the renaissance of fantasy-based comic books; and the early rumblings of role-playing video games. All of these phenomena represent the increasing role of fantasy, escapism, and solipsism in popular culture during this period. Rush's music, like that of their British heavy-metal and art-rock companions, created for its audience a futuristic, technologically hyperbolized, post-industrial soundscape, at once utopian and dystopian in its synthesis of classical music (*2112* was meant to invoke Tchaikovsky's *1812 Overture*, two hundred years after the fact), and a nightmarishly cold, robotic, mechanical sound.

By the time Rush made *Permanent Waves* (1980), the band was, for all practical purposes and as the album's title suggested, a permanent fixture on the rock scene. And with them, so was Canadian rock music, whose likewise enduring international breakthrough the band had spearheaded. For those desiring an indigenous Canadian rock-music industry, the moment of Rush's triumph is the defining episode. Their success, moreover, was symptomatic. Canadians not only took control over a significant segment of its own rock music market, but Canadian bands had forged a unique form of rock. Like so many Canadian cultural highlights, it was a synthesis of the American form—hard rock—and a British variation on it—art rock. There was no stylistic parallel to Rush, Max Webster, or Prism in the U.S. These bands not only depended for their survival on stateside success, as usual, but they now had defined that success with their own sub-genre. What is most interesting is that Rush bypassed the Cancon pathway to success: it was achieved without significant Canadian or American radio airplay. Their audience was built instead on concerts and steadily increasing album sales—precisely on the model of other rock bands of the 1970s. This was a model that worked mainly in the Great Lakes industrial region, then served as the springboard for continental and then international success.

THE FIFTH MOMENT: CONSOLIDATIONS IN THE 1980S

By the early 1980s, Toronto had imported punk from London and New York. The effects on Canadian rock were slight. At first, Canadian punk seemed to correspond to the late 1960s in terms of cultural rebelliousness and, in Toronto, to a local rock scene defined by a downtown neighbourhood: Queen Street in the late 1970s echoed Yorkville Avenue in the late 1960s. Indeed, it turned out to be rather like Yorkville, a celebrated "scene" that produced no rock music that connected with listeners. Even faster than Yorkville, moreover, Queen Street was transformed into a trendy shopping and dining district.

Toronto's punk-forerunner band was Rough Trade, fronted by Carole Pope, which evolved from The Bullwhip Brothers to become a mildly notorious Toronto club band in 1974 (its initial fan-base consisted of nightclubbing gays and lesbians). The band went unrecorded until 1980, when it belatedly signed with CBS/True North and enjoyed a short run of slick LPs following the hit single "High School Confidential." The other signal band was Martha and the Muffins, formed in 1977. After a preliminary gig in Toronto—tellingly at the Ontario College of Art, which served as Toronto punk's gene pool—the band recorded its first LP, *Metro Music* (1980), in Britain, under the paternal sponsorship of Robert Fripp, of the British art-rock group King Crimson. The album yielded the international hit "Echo Beach" (1981). There were several further LPs then quick dissolution. Martha and the Muffins' sound was derivative of British New Wave pop (XTC's "Making Plans for Nigel" is comparable), which greatly blunted and softened punk and made it radio-playable. Indeed, Martha and the Muffins would become the prototype of the Toronto punk that would make any mark, faint as it was. The Spoons, Payola$, and Parachute Club were lightly likable one-hit bands despite considerable press attention. Harder Toronto punk—The Diodes, the Mods/News, the Viletones, Teenage Head, the Battered Wives, etc.—made no impact whatsoever. Canadian punk was a case of rock that was local in origin with highly intense participation mystique that achieved no music-industry half-life.

Punk characterized itself as the antithesis of "corporate rock," as heavy-metal and progressive rock came to be regarded by the end of the 1970s. Punk's no-nonsense, straight-ahead production values and abrasive poses of artistic integrity were intended to be the counter-revolution against the dictates of rock music as a calculated, over-decorated commodity. However, in Toronto (and in Vancouver as well), the punk effort arose from an art-school cadre of "avant-garde" musicians; what they sought to do was to put rock back into the bottle of their own bourgeois, art-college-youth tastes in politics and music. Theirs was a late effort to generate an elite urban rock aesthetic to oppose a suburban and ex-urban one. This effort would prove prescient in some fundamental respects, but its immediate effects on Canadian rock were negligible.

Coincident with the rise and rapid fall of Canadian punk was a consolidation of all that punk opposed. The most successful chapter in

Canadian rock history continued unopposed under the guidance of Vancouver-based manager Bruce Allen. Despite the exceptional longevity of the band itself, the musical synthesis Rush represented was a short-lived phenomenon, and it flourished only between 1975 and 1980. Nevertheless, the market breakthrough the band, and those in its trail (e.g., Saga and Prism), accomplished proved durable, and others were building on it. By 1980, BTO's manager, Allen, signed Prism, Trooper, and Loverboy and maintained the BTO/Rush momentum by working radio-friendly variations on an updated hard-rock style. Allen realized that success has little to do with seeking a distinct Canadian rock sound but that it is wrapped up in exerting control over the music industry, and that this involved "artist development" of a systematic kind. Allen excelled at it.

After coaching BTO, Allen's guidance of Prism, Powder Blues, Lisa Dalbello, Tom Cochrane's Red Rider, Susan Jacks, and Loverboy in the late 1970s and early 1980s proved his strategy sound. Allen's most successful act, the most commercially successful Canadian rocker ever, was Bryan Adams. Allen took the advantages offered by Cancon regulations to new heights, and Adams is the decade's archetypal performer in this regard. After a tumultuous start in the failed band Sweeney Todd, Adams formed a songwriting team with Jim Vallance of Prism, and then Allen retooled Adams as a solo performer. Adams was soon dominating album and singles sales alike with hits that included "Cuts Like a Knife," "Heat of the Night," and "Everything I Do (I Do It For You)." He had the best-selling Canadian rock album in 1983, 1985, 1987, 1991, and 1992. Allen and Adams proved their ability to manipulate Cancon when Adams's album *Waking Up the Neighbours* was disqualified as Canadian content (because it was co-written with the U.K.'s Mutt Lange and, therefore, only satisfied one of the four areas of qualification). Adams threatened to boycott the Juno Awards; the CRTC changed the rules, and the album was declared Cancon; Adams won the Best Entertainer and Best Producer of the Year awards. The episode revealed both that the protective scaffolding of Cancon had done its job and had become irrelevant. The musicians it had enabled were now stronger than the rules themselves.

If BTO and Rush were part of the expansion of the rock market to include suburbia and ex-urbia, Adams exemplifies rock's expansion not just of a demographics of class and geography, but also of age. The

1980s saw rock albums so middle-of-the-road that the music ceased to be exclusively youth-oriented, and rock swamped pop music altogether. Older generations may have continued to listen to rock before, but in the form of nostalgia for their own youth music. Now, Adams joined the international cohort of Madonna, Prince, Abba, Bruce Springsteen, Tina Turner, Sting, Michael Jackson, Whitney Houston, Dire Straits, and many others in creating music for all markets. The telling cap was Adams's providing the soundtrack tune for so mainstream a Hollywood film as *Robin Hood, Prince of Thieves* (Reynolds, 1991).

What matters in our account is that the triumphant aspect of the fifth moment represents a turning-away entirely from the desire to create a distinctly Canadian rock. The national-culturalist objective was never more than a hopelessly vague critical ideal. Canadian musicians had pragmatically figured out how to occupy the higher tiers of the international industry both musically and commercially and did without it. They had, starting in the 1970s, played out an economic destiny and succeeded against great odds to conquer the music market through the channel of regional rock sub-genres. Canada's enduring capability in rock chronology becomes, by the 1990s, the regular capacity to generate rock records that slot smoothly into all radio and wide-reaching concert venues.

THE SIXTH MOMENT: CONCLUSION—THE DIVERSIFIED OTHER IN THE 1990S

The sixth moment is characterized by an extraordinary dispersion of musical styles and fragmentation of the rock audience. That this would occur simultaneously with the success of artists like Adams and Dion needs explanation. The sixth moment was foreshadowed by punk. Punk bands produced their own EPs and cassette tapes and fanzines, and developed rough-and-ready (if also very short-lived) rock-club scenes and low-budget styles of concert promotion (instanced by the early Police tours and Lollapolooza, and lately by Lilith). Punk's strategic prescience had great lasting influence over localized media-savvy and mercurial styles of promotion, both of which were simulated by Canadian rock television in the form of MuchMusic, which began broadcasting in 1984. In Canada (and elsewhere), the possibility arose of postponing, even of bypassing, formerly indispensable industry conduits. In fact, delivery systems for rock were now multiplying: rock-video television exposure, rock dance clubs, and other exposure media now reflect unprecedented fragmentation of the rock audience. These innovative delivery systems would not bear fruit until the later 1980s (at the earliest), but by the 1990s, the major record labels, unable to rationalize rock's growing pluralism of sub-genres into successive blockbuster LPs or dominating trends the way they had in the past, began to regard all "alternative rock" as a species of research-and-development.

In this conclusion we indicate that, by the 1990s, this sixth moment necessarily changes how to consider Canadian rock and its future prospects. As the rock industry enlarged in the 1970s and 1980s, it became more corporate and international, especially in terms of the conduits of distribution. One would have perhaps expected a greater and greater degree of music homogenization in the rock produced to coincide with this consolidation. The success of Bruce Allen and other managers and producers like him throughout the international industry certainly points to this. However, Will Straw persuasively shows that, for a number of reasons—and the decline in radio airplay as the dominant delivery system is the most obvious—"audiences for performers have come to be built on what everyone in the industry now calls the grassroots level" ("Sound" 113). The music industry now, more than ever before, recognizes that its commercial life's blood flows through local and regional scenes and their participation mystiques, and not in "mainstream" rockers like Bryan Adams. The sixth moment in Canadian rock coincides with an explosion of many points of "authenticity," experienced as so many simultaneous sub-generic movements and scenes of local origination: e.g., the Seattle, Chapel Hill, Austin, Hamilton, and Halifax scenes; the new rise of Britpop, the revival of krautrock, alternative, grunge, punk, hardcore, thrash, hip-hop, acid jazz, trip-hop, trance, old school, jungle, and techno. The list of simultaneous sub-genres now assumes a dizzying variety. Paradoxically, however, these multiplying sub-genres now achieve high degrees of commercial distribution earlier and with an unprecedented ease.

This situation requires analysis and emphasis because, in effect, it changes the long-term conditions and assumptions under which Canadian rock has struggled since the 1960s. Put bluntly, *for the first time ever*, it is possible to imagine an indigenous Canadian rock music succeeding within its local market and there alone. Previously, Canadian rockers had to succeed in the U.S., and, to do so, had to hook up with tendencies prevailing there. This is how BTO and Rush succeeded. They did so on their own terms. But they also recognized that their home ground shared the great industrial Midwest. The new situation is not so simple. Canada continues to parallel European and American trends closely. However, a band like Kingston-based The Tragically Hip, the most successful new Canadian band in the mid-1990s, sold more copies (200,000) of their 1994 CD in Canada in the first four days of its release than they sold of all their previous albums in the United States over the past five years (Straw, "Sound" 114-15). In other words, the band is successful in Canada without making significant inroads in the U.S. There is no discernible reason, moreover, why The Tragically Hip would be unsuccessful in the U.S., since its sound is congruous with many bands on the so-called "alternative" scene there, such as R.E.M. and Soundgarden. The phenomenon is occurring, too, at the same time as the huge North American success of Alanis Morissette (herself a perfect match for "alternative" female vocalists in the U.S.) and the continued success of Adams and another huge hit album by Rush. What is new in this situation is that bands like The Tragically Hip do not *need* to follow Morissette or Adams into the U.S. market to flourish.

We began this paper arguing that Canadian rock music is best understood in socio-economic and geographical rather than aesthetic terms. With the peculiar exception of Rush, it would be erroneous to argue that a distinctly Canadian rock sound has ever emerged. Moreover, we argued that even Rush's unique Canadian "art metal" hybrid was more significant for demographic and geographical reasons than for national-cultural "aesthetic" ones. That is, the Canadian national-cultural significance of Rush will always, in our view, be elusive, though for different reasons from The Band's significance. The Cancon regulations of 1971 cleared the ground and made it possible, finally by the mid-1980s, for Canadian music acts to prosper and thrive. None of this, however, ensured that a uniquely Canadian style or approach to music would develop. Nonetheless it did, with Rush, although the current plurality of Adams, Morissette, et al., and the more restricted success of The Tragically Hip, et al., show that such a national-rock sound need not develop, and none since Rush has.

Two additional factors merit brief analysis, and a fuller examination different from the present study, because the 1990s situation is now different. Straw has isolated these factors and made suggestive assertions about them ("Sound" passim). The first is a basic transformation of rock's delivery systems. Radio play has diminished in importance as a current-rock promotional tool, now that broadcasters have elected to pursue an older audience more attractive to advertisers. Radio now relies increasingly on rock's backlist of recordings and the blander kind of pop-rock exemplified by Madonna, Adams, Dion, etc. This ensures massive sales for high-tier acts working within a middle-of-the-road style but scant exposure for upcoming and "alternative" acts.

Additionally, radio has withdrawn its focus from what Straw terms the "discourses" associated with rock ("Sound" 108-109). The music played no longer has the connection with the broadcast formats it once did when at least FM DJs offered some commentary on records or concerts or associated "lifestyle" matters. In place of radio, music-dedicated television stations, and especially MuchMusic in Canada, now provide this focus. MuchMusic's impact goes even further than that of MTV in the U.S. It provides Canadian rock with something it always lacked, an equivalent to a rock press. Featuring interviews with musicians, rock-related news, regularly centred on local scenes across Canada, and "lifestyle" segments, MuchMusic resembles a rock-magazine format, just what Canadian rock fans never had before, though these were familiar apparatuses in Great Britain and the U.S. thirty years ago. It is the rock press (and not radio) that is the main vehicle of celebrity. Because its staple is the look-dominated rock-video clip and a somewhat less restrictive playlist than radio, rock television reflexively favours stylistic pluralism. Segments are devoted to different sub-genres, and being directed at a younger audience than radio, rock television inclines to "alternative rock" in a way just the opposite of radio's gravitation to "mainstream rock." But for Canada most importantly, MuchMusic spreads this powerful promotional apparatus over the entire country, which radio, always local, never did.

The second factor pertains to the music industry and its marketing apparatus. The recording industry recognizes that "alternative" and sub-generic categories sell in a cumulative way more than "mainstream rock" does as a whole. Niche sales have become aggregately more important to the record industry than popular "mainstream" acts

(Straw, "Sound" 96). A site where the consequences of this "welcome pluralism" is physically apparent is the record store, which now must be large enough to contain and display a massive inventory of relatively slow-moving, highly variegated rock. Hence, the record "megastores," such as those built by multinational firms like HMV, Tower, and Virgin, have tended to displace the previous retail chain stores, a circumstance accounting for the quick demise of two of the major Canadian chains, A & A and Discus, in the 1990s.

This transformed retail situation corresponds to the changed strategies of major record labels. Previously, as we explained above, record companies sought to cultivate select acts for a long period, seeking to build a large audience that might eventually enable a band to reach "superstar," which was also break-even, status. This is the route that Rush travelled, for example. Major labels often off-loaded the early stages in this process to small independent labels that they would buy up when one or more acts on their roster seemed to be maturing in the market. In the 1990s, this system decayed, and major labels now sign bands much earlier, after they have built up a grassroots—most often very local—following through homemade recordings and touring. This is how the legacy of punk rock has been actualized. Overall, this industry change has transformed what was formerly Canadians' music-industry "marginality" into a new "capillary" arrangement that has become normative in industry terms internationally. The era of monumental promotional instruments of "arena-rock" concerts and saturation hit-radio airplay have now passed. "Mainstream rock" is effectively a meaningless designation. So now too is "alternative rock." The massive success of *Jagged Little Pill*, a recording that came from nowhere—a dismal and unknown pop singer who transformed herself into an "alternative" diva—is best understood as dramatizing this new situation.

NOTES

1   Rock provides a famous scandal of that rupture. The first hybrid that yields "rock 'n' roll" in the 1950s was a triple scandal: of the musical genre whose roots are a suspect amalgam of white and black musical forms; of a musically impoverished, vampiric genre that commercially assimilates every other popular musical form; and of a chimerical musical type that won't settle upon a generic essence of its own. Rock did not define itself historically—the enduring cult of Elvis Presley notwithstanding—but as a cultural practice of serial amalgamations. Fragmentation and successions

of styles in rock, and the surfacing of its subordinate sub-genres to momentary pre-eminence, were preordained. After the initial and brief "rock 'n' roll" scandal, the dynamic was set by the permanent social factor of post-war adolescents becoming independent consumers, *plus* the fresh intrusions of Afro-American and white musical idioms unmediated by pop-song decorum, and hybridized differently.

2   In what follows we depend a good deal on Steve Jones, "Recasting Popular Music Studies' Conceptions of the Authentic and the Local in Light of Bell's Theorem" (Straw et al., 1995), especially 171-72.

3   By 1958, rock 'n' roll's original scandal, had faded. New stars were groomed by management firms and launched by television's *American Bandstand*, and its energies channelled by a series of inane dance crazes, like the Twist. Rock fell to a very low level of local origination. The Beatles and the other groups forming the "British Invasion" (1962-64: The Animals, The Rolling Stones, The Swinging Blue Jeans, The Dave Clark Five, etc.) crashed into this situation with great force. Their music involved a renewed roughness that represented a high level of local origination (Liverpool and London were very local scenes) and a high degree of listener participation. The Americans responded to the British with rock forms possessing local origination on two fronts, one black (Memphis, Detroit, etc.), the other white (the second, New York, stage of the folk and blues revival exemplified by Bob Dylan, Tim Hardin, the Paul Butterfield Blues Band, John Hammond Jr., and Tim Buckley). The black "soul sound" was generated the first time that urban black musicians predominated on the record charts. Folk-rock, in turn, excited local city scenes in San Francisco (The Grateful Dead, Quicksilver Messenger Service), New York (The Youngbloods, the Velvet Underground), Macon, Georgia (The Allman Brothers), and Los Angeles (The Doors), which engendered American "acid rock." The British replied with another adaptation of black sources, in this instance an instrumentally virtuosic treatment of blues (e.g., Jeff Beck Group, Cream, Ten Years After) rooted, again, in local English club scenes. A new and powerful hybrid, "sixties rock," was also quickly to become a hugely successful marketing rationalization. However, its half-life extended through the 1970s, when "sixties rock" became 1970s "arena rock" until the fierce reaction of punk, localized in New York, then in London, and other cities—some of them notably regional, like Akron, Ohio, Washington, D.C., and Toronto. The period of the 1970s prior to punk corresponds to the first important moments of Canadian rock music.

4   Hence, for a Canadian example, in the 1950s and 1960s, Toronto can be seen as part of the North American middle-west and was a city receptive to R&B, not unlike other Great Lakes industrial cities, e.g., Chicago or Detroit. R&B cover groups made up of white Canadian musicians, like the Diamonds and the Crew Cuts, were successfully launched from Toronto into the U.S. market in that era.

5   In the late 1960s, a cultural-nationalist, somewhat anti-American fervour swept Canada. Between the formation of the CRTC and 1970, there were unsuccessful efforts to get commercial radio stations to showcase a percentage of Canadian talent. But Canadian radio avoided Canadian rock

talent to the point that, in early 1969, Winnipeg's The Guess Who had a million-seller in the U.S. with "These Eyes," but Canadian radio stations still refused to play the band (Yorke 8). In February 1970, at the prompting of individuals like Walt Grealis (publisher of the Canadian music trade magazine *RPM*), and to the shocked disbelief of the broadcast industry, the CRTC announced Canadian-content ("Cancon") guidelines. Beginning in January 1971, Canadian AM broadcasters would have to program a minimum of 30 percent Canadian content.

6　The 1960s in Toronto have sometimes been recalled differently, as they are by Wright, for example. The standard accounts include glowing recollections of Yorkville Avenue, Toronto's hippie axis. For example: "It was not unique but Yorkville Village through the sixties and early 1970s had more impact on Canadian music than any other factor [except the Cancon rules]....It was a scene, like Greenwich Village in New York and Haight-Ashbury in San Francisco, that drew many creative people, especially in the music field, within its influence" (Melhuish 65).

　　In fact, the best-known musicians associated with this "scene" were those who would move to the U.S. (Young, Clayton-Thomas, Mitchell, etc.) while those left behind never became major figures. Many, like Al Cromwell and Mike McKenna, remained decidedly obscure. The only real lasting claim that could be made for comparison to Greenwich Village was the basement folk club The Riverboat, which booked important American folk acts into the 1970s.

7　See Marcus's *Mystery Train* for a masterful book-length analysis of this period.

8　In fact, The Band's third LP, *Stage Fright* (1970), began a long decline in the quality and resonance of its recorded work. The concert repertoire strayed little from material from the first two LPs. Eventually, The Band recorded eight studio LPs, but it also released five compilations and concert LPs, not counting 1974's *Before the Flood* reunion tour concert LP with Dylan. The group's period of florescence was no more than five years. The melancholy exception was the original group's final studio record, *Northern Lights–Southern Cross* (1977). Various versions of The Band were assembled later and in 1993 a reunion album, *Jericho*, was made.

9　This is the focus of Marcus, *Mystery Train*, chapter four, 87-126.

10　The LP format was only exceptionally important in the 1960s as with The Beatles' *Sergeant Pepper's Lonely Hearts Club Band*, The Who's *Tommy*, and the Rolling Stones' *Satanic Majesty's Request*.

11　The role of English-Canadian youth's anglophilia is inestimably important here but it has never been studied. Anecdotally, however, we note that in Canada, which had no rock press of its own, British rock publications like *Melody Maker* and *New Music Express* competed with U.S. magazines like *Rolling Stone* among rock fans. This is a situation simply inconceivable in the U.S. By the same token, British bands often enough decided to launch their tours from Toronto. Some, like Supertramp, built their initial North American fan-base in Canada. Because of Canadian academic critics' obsession with the dominance of the U.S. products on TV and film, they have assumed exactly the same to be true of popular music, and the important and distinctive role British rock played and continues to play in Canada has been woefully overlooked. Yet the triumph of Rush and other bands—not to mention the later developments of punk and reggae in Canada—is incomprehensible without taking the anglophile factor into account.

WORKS CITED

"To Hell with Bob Dylan: Meet Rush. They're in It for the Money." *Maclean's*, January 23, 1978. <http://www.worldwidewebtour.com/~lakesidepark/interviews/content/1970s/1978-01-23-macleans>.

Barnes, Ken. "Top 40 Radio: A Fragment of the Imagination." *Facing the Music*. Ed. Simon Frith. New York: Pantheon, 1988. 8-50.

Duncan, Robert. *The Noise: Notes from a Rock'N'Roll Era*. New York: Ticknor & Fields, 1984.

Grant, Barry K. "'Across the Great Divide': Imitation and Inflection in Canadian Rock Music." *Journal of Canadian Studies* 21.1 (Spring 1986): 116-27.

Jarrett, Michael. "Concerning the Progress of Rock & Roll." *Present Tense: Rock & Roll and Culture*. Ed. Anthony DeCurtis. Durham and London: Duke UP, 1992. 167-82.

Jones, Steve. "Recasting Popular Music Studies' Conceptions of the Authentic and the Local in Light of Bell's Theorem." *Popular Music–Style and Identity*. Ed. Will Straw, Stacey Johnson, Rebecca Sullivan and Paul Friedlander. Montreal: Centre for Research on Canadian Cultural Industries and Institutions, 1993. 169-72.

Marcus, Greil. *Mystery Train: Images of America in Rock'N'Roll Music*. New York: Dutton 1976.

_____. *Invisible Republic: Bob Dylan's Basement Tapes*. New York: Holt, 1997.

Marsh, Dave. *The Heart of Rock & Soul: The 1001 Greatest Singles Ever Made*. New York: New American Library, 1989.

Melhuish, Martin. *Heart of Gold: 30 Years of Canadian Pop Music*. Toronto: CBC Enterprises, 1983.

Pevere, Geoff, and Greig Dymond. *Mondo Canuck: A Canadian Pop Culture Odyssey*. Toronto: Prentice-Hall Canada, 1996.

Shumway, David. "Rock & Roll as a Cultural Practice." *Present Tense: Rock & Roll and Culture*. Ed. Anthony DeCurtis. Durham and London: Duke UP, 1992. 117-34.

Straw, Will. "The English Canadian Recording Industry Since 1970." *Rock and Popular Music: Politics, Policies, Institutions*. Ed. Tony Bennett, Simon Frith, Lawrence Grossberg, John Shepherd and Graeme Turner. London: Routledge, 1993. 52-65.

_____. "Characterizing Rock Music Culture: The Case of Heavy Metal." *The Cultural Studies Reader*. Ed. Simon During. London: Routledge, 1993. 368-81.

_____. "Sound Recording." *The Cultural Industries in Canada: Problems, Policies and Prospects*. Ed. Michael Dorland. Toronto: Lorimer, 1996. 95-117.

Street, John. "Dislocated? Rhetoric, Politics, Meaning and the Locality." *Popular Music–Style and Identity.* Ed. Will Straw, Stacey Johnson, Rebecca Sullivan and Paul Friedlander. Montreal: Centre for Research on Canadian Cultural Industries and Institutions, 1995. 255-64.

Wright, Robert. "'Dream, Comfort, Memory, Despair': Canadian Popular Musicians and the Dilemma of Nationalism, 1968-1972." *Journal of Canadian Studies* (Winter 1987): 27-43. Rpt. in *Canadian Music: Issues of Hegemony and Identity.* Ed. Beverley Diamond and Robert Witmer. Toronto: Canadian Scholars, 1994. 283-301.

Yorke, Ritchie. *Axes, Chops & Hot Licks: The Canadian Rock Music Scene.* Edmonton: Hurtig, 1971.

REELIN' 'N' ROCKIN': GENRE-BENDING AND BOUNDARY-CROSSING IN CANADA'S "EAST COAST SOUND"

Nick Baxter-Moore

Take it downtown, get it plugged in
Turn it on, turn it up on ten
The piper's paid and now its time to go
Reel'n'roll! Reel'n'roll! Reel'n'roll! Reel'n'roll!
—from "Reel'n'Roll" by Rawlins Cross

The first verse of "Reel'n'Roll," the opening track and title song of the third album by Canadian East Coast band Rawlins Cross, situates the singer in his day job, waiting for his shift to end, when he will be able to join the other members of the band to make music ("All day punch a time clock / We get to play when the work is through"). Then it's downtown to some bar, plug in instruments and amps, and let it rip ("Turn it on, turn it up on ten"). It's a song of fours—four-line verse, four-line chorus ending with the four-times-repeated injunction to "reel'n'roll," played in standard (4/4) rock time. It is, in many respects, a classic self-reflexive bar-band song, about being a part-time musician, about working days and making music at night. There are echoes

Notes on pages 239-41.

here of Bob Seger, or Bob Seger wannabes, reinforced by the timbre of Joey Kitson's rough-edged vocals. Alternatively, in its reflexivity, and to some extent in its rhythm and recursive hooks, "Reel'n'Roll" is also reminiscent of the Dire Straits song "Money for Nothing," albeit without the latter's self-effacing irony.

What saves "Reel'n'roll" from sounding derivative, however, is the instrumentation—signalled in part by the multiple-resonant line "The piper's paid and now it's time to go"—which lends added meaning to Dave Panting's lyrics. Instead of featuring a Mark Knopfler-style guitar in call-and-response pattern with the vocalist, the spaces between the words are filled by Ian McKinnon's highland bagpipe, while the standard rock rhythm sound of drums, bass and guitar is supplemented by Geoff Panting's piano accordion, played through a MIDI interface so that sometimes it sounds like itself and sometimes like a Hammond organ. And, instead of an extended virtuoso guitar solo, the instrumental bridge features brief eight-bar leads from the pipes and unenhanced accordion. Only in the last verse and coda do we hear something that sounds like electric lead guitar, but it actually comes from Brian Bourne's Chapman Stick, which also doubles as the bass.[1]

Not only is this a variety of rock music played on unconventional instruments, but the foregrounding of different players serves to demonstrate the communal nature of this musical enterprise, more like a folk session than star-fronted rock band. As a result, when the lyrics speak of the band's intention to "Try to link both the young and old," they may refer to the potential audience, but also seem to signal the band's distinctive sound and musical philosophy—striving to combine the rhythms, timbres and technology of modern rock ("the young") with instruments and playing conventions of traditional Celtic folk music ("the old") in a blend of musical styles that is, of course, encapsulated in the song's title and refrain—reel'n'roll, indeed.[2]

The Celtic-rock fusion of Rawlins Cross is one example of a new and exciting sound that may be labelled the "East Coast Sound." It is a style of music that originates largely, but not exclusively, in Atlantic Canada, and its principal feature is a blending of the conventions of traditional Celtic (or Gaelic) folk music with those of contemporary forms of popular, or "rock," music.[3] As evidenced in the growing popularity across the country of artists such as Rawlins Cross, Ashley MacIsaac, The Barra MacNeils and The Rankin Family, among others, the East

Coast Sound has broken out of its regional roots and is becoming established as a form of national popular music. This article investigates the development and characteristics of this "sound" and attempts to place its emergence within a broader conceptual framework for analysis of the evolution of contemporary popular music in Canada.

Canadian Popular Music as Miniature Replica

Notwithstanding the much-publicized (in Canada, at least) success of Canadian artists at recent Grammy Awards, it may be fair to suggest that for much of the last forty years most people unfamiliar with the Canadian music scene would find it hard to differentiate English-Canadian rock and popular music from their American counterparts. Canada lacks an indigenous rock-music tradition, in part, it has been argued, because "the experiences, the roots, which have given shape to rock music's various forms...are wholly American" (Grant 118). Moreover, the growth of an indigenous rock music has been further hampered by the relatively small size of the Canadian domestic market, the close proximity and cultural affinity of Canada to the United States, and the latter's dominant position in the Canadian popular-culture industries—in television, film and magazines, as well as record production and distribution (Berland and Straw; Straw). The Canadian recording industry is largely a branch-plant operation and much of its popular music product is indistinguishable from that produced by the parent corporations.

To the extent that there is an "official" definition of what constitutes Canadian music, it is "music made by Canadians." The Canadian-content regulations imposed by the CRTC (Canadian Radio-television and Telecommunications Commission) on domestic radio stations and music-television channels determine what music is "Canadian" largely in terms of the citizenship of the principal performer, lyricist or composer of the music.[4] Hence, for these purposes at least, Canadian popular music is defined in terms of inputs into the production process, not by any distinctive characteristics of the music or lyrics.

Within the North American context, French-Canadian popular music has always sounded "other," in part because of the language of the lyrics and partly because it has absorbed musical influences from other Francophone societies. But, according to John Shepherd, "[o]nly once has a seemingly distinctive English-Canadian musical culture emerged and this during the period 1968 to 1972," when a number of singer-songwriters in the contemporary folk genre (Leonard Cohen, Gordon Lightfoot, Joni Mitchell and Neil Young, among others) gained "international reputations without 'losing' their national identities as Canadians" (Shepherd 189). Many of their songs, such as Lightfoot's "Black Day in July" (1968) or Young's "Ohio" (1970), implicitly contrasted the civil strife and state-sanctioned violence south of the border with Canada's "peaceable kingdom," and they were heralded by Canadian nationalists, lent new fervour by the national mood in the wake of the 1967 Centennial celebrations, as harbingers of a burgeoning sense of Canadian cultural identity.

However, if one accepts, as Shepherd does, Robert Wright's critical analysis of this period in Canadian popular-music history, even this apparent exception loses its significance. According to Wright, far from being distinctively "Canadian," these singer-songwriters were successful in the U.S. as well as Canada because, first, they had a strong affinity for, and drew heavily upon, established American folk-music traditions, and, second, their estrangement from "official" America was shared by many Americans of the Sixties generation (Wright 37, 39). Their ambivalent stance towards American politics and popular culture, part insider, part outsider, allowed them to identify and articulate through their songs what many Americans already suspected about their own society. But, while the substance of their lyrics may have betrayed them as Canadians, their songs were nevertheless expressed through the conventions of an established American musical form.

To the extent that such a thing exists, therefore, Canadian, or rather English-Canadian, rock is often seen as a regional, and derivative, form of popular music, as a kind of "miniature-replica" of the American (or North American) original. In its most extreme form, this miniature-replica argument leads some critics to conclude that, as Michael Taft puts it: "A distinct Canadian popular music is 'historically groundless' and the search for such a phenomenon would be fruitless indeed" (208).

GENRE-BENDING: INFLECTION VS. IMITATION

In an important contribution to the understanding of Canadian rock music written in the mid-1980s, Barry Grant concurred in part with the "miniature replica" thesis. In the absence of an indigenous rock tradition and of an established Canadian music industry, Grant argued, for most Canadian artists there has seemed to be "little choice but to go south, to make it first in the US, and then return to Canada with an opening into the domestic market. And of course the best way to do this is to *sound* American, to be virtually indistinguishable from American music" (Grant 122, emphasis in original). As a result, he suggested, "much Canadian rock fits comfortably within the [predominantly American] mainstream...and some tunes even sing the praises of capitalism and the American work ethic," for example, Bachman-Turner Overdrive's 1974 hit "Takin' Care of Business" (126). Nonetheless, from the earliest days of rock 'n' roll, Grant argued, some Canadian artists have sought to distinguish themselves from the dominant American sounds.

To provide a framework for his analysis, Grant borrowed from the field of film criticism the concepts of "imitation," the faithful replication of the conventions of existing artistic genres, and "inflection," a process of playing with, subverting or adopting an ironic distance from those conventions, a process that might also be labelled "genre-bending." Faced with a choice between imitating the conventions of American popular music and inflecting them with a Canadian "accent," Grant proposed, some Canadian artists have chosen the latter course.

Grant illustrated his thesis first with reference to hit records by two of the earliest Canadian groups to establish themselves in the (North) American market—"Sh-Boom" by The Crew Cuts (1954) and "Little Darlin'" by The Diamonds (1957). Hence, while "Sh-Boom" served to show that "Canadians can create the American pop product at least as well as the Americans themselves," according to Grant, "Little Darlin'" is a song that "pokes fun at its own tradition: it takes an ironic distance from the genre of the sentimental romantic ballad, the genre to which it apparently belongs, by playing with its conventions" (117-18).

Other examples of the *imitation* formula furnished by Grant include Paul Anka and Bobby Curtola (the first Canadian artist to "make it" in Canada without first going to the U.S.), both of whom faithfully replicated the dominant American "teenybop" style of the late 1950s and early 1960s. But he also identified a number of artists or individual recordings representative of the *inflection* strategy of playing with the conventions of American musical genres.[5] Thus, while The Guess Who's "American Woman" (1970) is based on a power-chord riff typical of electric blues-rock hits of the period, Grant argued that the lyrics subvert the "conventional figure of unrequited love" found in many such songs "by turning her into a *femme fatale* the singer actually wants to avoid....This woman with her seductive charms ('sparkling eyes that hypnotize') is nothing less than America and her seductive material abundance" (122). As another illustration of the ways in which inflection can work, Grant used the example of Rough Trade, the Toronto-based new-wave electro-pop band of the early 1980s, which drew repeatedly on the iconography of Hollywood and American popular culture, but invested these references with ironic and subversive overtones. In particular, suggested Grant, the lyrics of such songs as "High School Confidential" (1981) and lead singer Carol Pope's explicitly sexual but "gender-bending" stage persona challenge "the heterosexual ideology which informs the depiction of love and sexuality in almost all rock and pop music" (125). In conjunction with the connotations of the band's name, these devices may be seen as part of a broader genre-bending strategy of appropriating and subverting both the icons of American popular culture and the conventions of contemporary rock.

Grant's imitation/inflection framework may be applied to any collection of Canadian rock and popular music.[6] While the general pattern that emerges is the preponderance of imitative strategies, a sufficient (and, over time, growing) number of Canadian artists have engaged in various forms of inflection as to suggest the elements of a discernible Canadian style of music. Thus, Grant argued, "an essential characteristic of Canadian music is generic subversion. It is chiefly in this way that Canadian rock artists have attempted to make *Canadian* rock and roll" (116, emphasis in original).

But if an identifiably Canadian brand of music had thus emerged, Grant suggested that, even by the mid-1980s, there were no distinctive Canadian genres or "sounds." In contrast to the United States, where there have developed numerous genres or sub-genres of rock, often associated geo-culturally with particular cities or regions—Detroit's Motown sound, the Philadelphia (Cameo-Parkway) sound, the California surfing sound or the Seattle (grunge) sound of the early 1990s—there were no Canadian equivalents: there was "no distinctive Edmonton sound, or Ottawa sound, or Maritime sound" in Canadian rock music (119). This may well have been the case a decade or so ago, when Grant wrote his article; but it is no longer true today.

THE EAST COAST SOUND

On a Monday night in late January 1996, I was among a sellout crowd of around six hundred people packed into Isaac's, the student pub at Brock University in St. Catharines, Ontario. Outside, it was typical late-January weather, about minus twenty degrees Celsius and threatening more snow; inside, it was hot and stuffy, cigarette smoke and beer fumes suffused the air as the crowd of mostly university students mingled, talked and, perhaps, listened with half an ear to the usual musical fare of a student pub night—Nirvana, Nine Inch Nails, Green Day and other denizens of the contemporary, "alternative" rock scene in North America, along with the odd golden oldie and the occasional gesture to Canadian content. But these people hadn't queued for up to an hour in the cold and paid fifteen dollars each to listen to the DJ or his selection of music. Believe it or not, this largely college-age crowd from metropolitan Southern Ontario was waiting eagerly to see and hear a fiddle player from Cape Breton, Nova Scotia.

Admittedly, Ashley MacIsaac is no ordinary fiddle player, even from a part of the world that produces masters of the instrument. Born and raised in Creignish in Cape Breton's Inverness County, MacIsaac learned to step-dance at age seven, took up the fiddle at nine, turned professional at thirteen and at seventeen released his first album, *Close to the Floor* (1992), a reverential rendering of traditional Scottish, Irish and Cape Breton fiddle tunes, accompanied only by piano and acoustic guitar. Now, at twenty-two, he was the *enfant terrible* of Cape Breton fiddlers, Canada's pioneer of "Celtic grunge," a blending of traditional fiddle tunes and styles with the rhythms, instrumentation, timbres—and the attitude—of modern alternative rock.

Backed by The Kitchen Devils, a four-piece band featuring a conventional "rock" lineup of drums, electric bass, keyboards/synthesizer and guitar—less conventionally supplemented for some numbers by a bagpiper and by guest vocalist Mary Jane Lamond, who also played bodhran—MacIsaac took the stage at Brock wearing baseball cap (backwards, of course), dark glasses, T-shirt, kilt and Doc Martens, his naturally dark goatee contrasting starkly with newly dyed white-blond hair. Over the next two hours (during which, as usual, he shredded three or four bows), a step-dancing, stomping, never-still MacIsaac thrilled the crowd with his playing of jigs, reels, strathspeys and airs—some rendered relatively straight, but more often embedded in a subversive soundscape of punk, grunge, hip-hop and, perhaps for the few old-timers in the audience, even disco![7] In the process, he fulfilled the aspirations announced by Rawlins Cross in "Reel'n'Roll," placing "old" tunes in a modern setting and bringing them to a new, "young," audience.

For those who haven't seen him perform live, MacIsaac's 1995 album *hi™ how are you today?* is a wildly eclectic, often uneven, sometimes eccentric showcase for his talent. Backed by a variety of artists, including the chamber group Quartetto Gelato on "MacDougall's Pride," Halifax riot-grrrls jale on his vocal rendition of Bob Snider's "What An Idiot He Is," members of The Kitchen Devils and a number of musicians based in Toronto where the album was recorded in several stages using two different producers, MacIsaac blends fiddle tunes old and new with diverse rhythms, timbres and effects. For example, the first track, "Beaton's Delight," begins with a brief homage to pop culture, a sound check, a series of sampled sounds as if surfing the radio dial, before MacIsaac's voice: "Hello, this is Ashley MacIsaac," then a somewhat camp "Hi, how are you today?"; the solo fiddler plays a high-energy strathspey, one foot stomping, then slowly the band comes in and, one minute into the track, Donald A. Beaton's composition has been turned into industrial-strength music. The second track, "Sleepy Maggie," based on the traditional fiddle tune of that name with added Gaelic lyrics by Mary Jane Lamond, begins with a sound like a radio-telescope signal beaming into outer space, then the scratching of the needle in the endless groove of an old "78" lays down a circular rhythm; guitar (maybe dobro) and fiddle settle into the same groove, the drum machines kick in, synthesizer follows, finally vocals, and "Sleepy Maggie" becomes Celtic hip-hop. The album version of "Devil in the Kitchen," Cape Breton's "ultimate step-dance tune" according to the liner notes, is pure instrumental hardcore: fiddle, guitar, bass and drums played as fast and as loud as possible. In live performance, however, thrash metal meets Celtic rap as MacIsaac adds a frantic and irreverent recitation about a race between God and the devil to impregnate a farmer's daughter: God wins and the offspring is Cape Breton fiddle virtuoso Buddy MacMaster.

Ashley MacIsaac's particular brand of fiddle playing and his variety of fusions based on traditional, or neo-traditional, tunes may be unique, but he also represents the harder, more "alternative" edge of a broader musical movement that has emerged from Atlantic Canada to find a wider audience in the mid-1990s. From the more traditionally rooted electric folk and folk-rock of the Irish Descendants and Great Big Sea, through the Celtic-pop-country of The Rankin Family, the adult-oriented Celtic-rock of Rawlins Cross and The Barra MacNeils, and on to MacIsaac's alternative Celtic-grunge, the East Coast Sound appeals to a broad spectrum of musical tastes. What these artists all have in common, however, apart from their origin in a specific geo-cultural region, is their ability to blend elements of the Celtic-inspired traditional music of Atlantic Canada with modern rock and popular-music forms and idioms.

It may be argued that the East Coast Sound is neither new nor unique to Atlantic Canada. A similar blending of traditional and modern rock forms may be heard in the electrified folk-rock of British bands such as Fairport Convention and Steeleye Span in the late 1960s and early 1970s, or more recently in the music of Scotland's Run Rig, Ireland's Moving Hearts, or the Celtic-punk of The Pogues. Elsewhere in Canada, Vancouver's Spirit of the West started out in the mid-1980s as a Celtic rock/folk band before moving to a more mainstream rock/pop sound, and Stratford, Ontario-based Loreena McKennitt has produced a half-dozen albums of strongly Celtic-influenced ambient music (she rejects the term "new age") that have won her international acclaim. Even in Atlantic Canada, the Newfoundland-based band Figgy Duff (which for several years included Dave Panting, now of Rawlins Cross) had been playing electrified Celtic folk for nearly two decades until its breakup following the death of founding member Noel Dinn in 1993.

What is new about the East Coast Sound is the sheer number of bands and solo artists engaged in making this kind of cross-over Celtic traditional/rock/pop music in the Atlantic region. A second distinguish-ing characteristic is the fact that many of these artists have moved beyond the stage of inflecting traditional songs and tunes with modern electric instrumentation to the point at which they are writing new songs that combine conventions from both the new and old musical forms. Indeed, this appears to be a common career path. Rawlins Cross began as a trio (Ian McKinnon and the Panting brothers, Dave and Geoff), playing almost exclusively traditional music in St John's, Newfoundland, around 1987, but then they began writing more and more of their own music. On the band's most recent album, *Living*

River (1996), there is only one traditional piece, the instrumental "Mairi Nighean Alasdair," compared to four traditional tracks out of ten on their debut album, *A Turn of the Wheel* (1989). In similar fashion, The Rankin Family's first, eponymous album (1989) contained seven tracks (including medleys) of largely or exclusively traditional origin and only three of their own songs; by the time their fourth album, *Endless Seasons*, was released in 1995, the ratio of traditional to original, self-penned material had been reversed.

Finally, while this may not necessarily be the most reliable of indicators, the novelty of the East Coast Sound may also be assessed by the fact that mainstream purveyors of popular music have been unsure how to categorize the artists and their records. In an era of "narrowcasting," of increasingly specialized radio formats, this can sometimes serve as an obstacle to achieving wider exposure.[8] Thus, while Ashley MacIsaac's grungier sound has allowed him access to younger audiences on the MuchMusic video channel and on "alternative" or "new rock" radio stations, other East Coast bands have found airplay harder to come by outside Atlantic Canada, and their recordings sometimes turn up in strange places in record retailers—for example, in early 1996 one chain of record stores in Southern Ontario carried albums by Rawlins Cross and The Barra MacNeils in its "Country" music section.

BOUNDARY-CROSSING: "MAKING NEW MUSIC"

The music of Ashley MacIsaac, Rawlins Cross and other artists from the East Coast appears in many cases to go beyond "genre-bending," that is, subverting and inflecting the conventions of existing genres or sub-genres of popular music. Rather, this music actually crosses the boundaries between genres—in particular, those between traditional Celtic (Scots/Irish) folk music and various sub-genres of contemporary rock. It is therefore a music that "syncretizes" sounds and conventions of pre-existing musical forms while, at the same time, creating a new genre of popular music that has been labelled the "East Coast Sound." The concept of *syncretism* literally means reconciliation, in a blending or fusion of pre-existing elements. Its origins lie in theological discourse, where it signifies the attempt to reconcile different systems of religious belief; for example, through the appropriation of gods, adaptation of rituals and observances, or simply "selection of whatever seems best in each" (*Chambers's Twentieth Century Dictionary*). Applied to the realm of popular/rock music—which, of course, has its own pantheon of gods (as in "guitar gods"), high priests (writers and DJs) and ritual observances—syncretism implies the creation of new genres and sub-genres of music by blending or fusing vocal styles, instrumentation, rhythms and timbres from other, older forms.

In this sense, all modern forms of popular music are the result of syncretism.[9] Genres such as rock, pop and country, and their respective sub-genres, are the outcomes of a successive blending of various combinations of earlier forms—blues, hillbilly, gospel, R&B, cowboy and western swing, jazz, bluegrass, vaudeville/music hall, Tin Pan Alley, among others—and these in turn evolved out of fusions among even earlier musical traditions.[10] And so the process continues, as the rock/pop commercial mainstream has periodically renewed itself (when not in one of its "retro" phases) by co-opting lyrical, instrumental and rhythmic conventions from other musical forms and cultures. The late 1960s witnessed the development of folk-rock, the jazz-rock fusion of Miles Davis and Herbie Hancock, and the rock-opera (The Who's *Tommy*); the 1970s saw the embrace of Caribbean music, led by Bob Marley's reggae revolution and the neo-ska of Britain's "two-tone" movement; in the 1980s, the emergence of crossover country artists (later to become New Country) was followed by the incorporation of various traditional musics from Africa and Latin America into the so-called "world-beat" phenomenon, popularized by artists such as David Byrne, Ry Cooder, Peter Gabriel and Paul Simon.

Three conditions appear to be necessary for such syncretisms to take place in popular music. The first prerequisite is *eclecticism* since, as Michael Taft has observed, "the amalgamation of musical forms cannot occur without a variety of music available to the public" (Taft 198). Since much of his analysis is concerned with folk-music forms, however, Taft may overemphasize the significance of "public" availability of musical variety when it comes to analyzing the conditions for syncretism in more commercially oriented music such as rock. For example, it is unlikely that most buyers of Paul Simon's *Graceland* album (1986) had previously received much exposure to music and performers from the South African townships. Consequently, we should emphasize here the availability of diverse music traditions to performers/artists rather than the wider public, although, as will be suggested below, for syncretized music to become "popular" (that is, widely appreciated and consumed), it must indeed have a receptive audience.

The second prerequisite for musical syncretism would appear to be *cultural distance*, a sense of detachment from the cultural communities in which particular musical traditions originate. Every musical form carries with it a burden of "cultural baggage," a set of musical and social conventions relating to its production and consumption that defines what is pure or "authentic" about that form and which is likely to weigh most heavily upon members of the originating community. Note, however, that these conventions may also be reinforced by commercial considerations—for example, by record company executives' calculations of what will sell—or by critics.

If Grant's portrayal of the "imitation" formula implies that most Canadian artists yield to the combined pressures of cultural baggage and commerce to reproduce the conventions of American popular music, his version of the "inflection" strategy demands a degree of cultural detachment from a single hegemonic musical tradition, which allows artists simultaneously to pay homage to dominant conventions and icons while "pushing the envelope," as it were, stretching the boundaries defining existing genres of popular music without breaking them altogether. Likewise, Wright's conception of the ambivalence of Canadian singer-songwriters towards American society in the late 1960s suggests a similar degree of relative cultural detachment.

For syncretism to occur, however, it might be expected that an even greater sense of cultural distance is required from the originating communities, or from the guardians of authenticity, of each of the musical traditions to be fused or blended. It is perhaps for this reason that the creation of new genres or sub-genres through syncretism often seems to occur among outsiders or members of what might be labelled "marginal communities." For example, pioneers of commercial rock and roll such as Elvis Presley and Jerry Lee Lewis came from the poor white ("white trash") communities of the American South. And it is surely no coincidence that perhaps the greatest modern syncretizers of rural American musical traditions were The Band, who were four-fifths Canadian (plus one "Southern boy" from Arkansas), outsiders whose Canadian origins lent them cultural distance from the American musical forms on which they drew in creating their unique blend and provided for Robbie Robertson, for example, "a window to look through, so I didn't take things for granted" (Hoskyns 8).

Finally, as suggested above, *audience receptivity* constitutes a third prerequisite for syncretized musical forms to become "popular" music—at least, if we define "popular" in terms of widespread consumption as well as by the characteristics of the music's production and distribution.[11] Audience receptivity to new musical forms may be "primed" through advertising and marketing strategies or by taste-shapers such as critics and DJs. It may simply be a consequence of boredom with existing forms of mass music—for example, the receptivity of North American audiences to the British Invasion of the 1960s may be viewed in part as a consequence of the "blanching" of the indigenous rock 'n' roll tradition in the era of "the Bobbys."[12] Moreover, it may be argued that widespread audience receptivity to new music requires that at least some of the elements blended into the new syncretism be familiar. As Greil Marcus has observed of The Band's *Music from Big Pink* album (1968):

> The richness of *Big Pink* is the Band's ability to contain endless combinations of American popular music without imitating any of them....The Band's music on *Big Pink* is personal, their own invention, but not merely personal; it is an unpredictable resolution of common inheritance, something we shared in pieces. This was a new sound, but you could recognize yourself in that sound. (Marcus 48)

Hence, for all that they were largely of Canadian origin, The Band's unique synthesis of American musical traditions—many of them familiar of course to Canadian audiences—was still *American* music. In contrast, the East Coast Sound, emerging out of conditions largely unique to Atlantic Canada, draws upon Canadian traditions and represents a distinctively Canadian contribution to the North American music scene.

SYNCRETIZING SOUND: THE ATLANTIC "NEW WAVE"

All three conditions required for the syncretization of popular music forms—musical eclecticism, cultural distance and audience receptivity—are present to a greater or lesser degree in the recent emergence of the East Coast Sound from Atlantic Canada.

First, the region has long been home to an eclectic variety of imported musical forms. Traditional Anglo-Celtic and French/Acadian folk musics brought by the original settlers of this part of Canada coexist alongside the more modern North American popular idioms of rock, pop, blues and country. What is particularly important, however, is the fact that traditional "folk" forms such as Cape Breton fiddle music have survived as genuinely "popular" music—as dance music to be consumed and enjoyed—rather than as "heritage" music or historical artefacts to be preserved and revered in their original, "authentic" form. Hence the separation between folk or traditional music, on the one hand, and rock or popular music, on the other, is less marked among both performers and audiences in Atlantic Canada than in many cultures.

Furthermore, Atlantic Canada already has a long history of musical syncretism. Cape Breton fiddle music is itself a product of blending and borrowing from a number of fiddling traditions and styles in which Scots, Irish, Acadian and Appalachian influences have all made their mark. The later syncretization of traditional music originally from the British Isles with American western, swing and country resulted in the emergence of a phenomenon sometimes labelled "country & eastern." For most Canadians of a certain age, this is perhaps best typified by the "Down East" music of Don Messer and his Islanders, whose Maritime-swing is "recognized by folklorists and fiddle archivists...as a synthesis of Canada's diverse traditions" (Quill 156), while a further distinctive fusing of the same elements also took place in Newfoundland (Taft 205-206).

Second, in part because of this syncretic tradition and because of the survival of traditional-music forms as popular dance music, it may be argued that there is less cultural baggage, or a greater sense of relative *cultural distance*, attached to various musical conventions in Atlantic Canada than in the societies in which these forms originated. For example, according to Bob Hallett of Great Big Sea, the self-proclaimed "aggressive folk" band from Newfoundland: "The way the old singers in Newfoundland look at it, they don't draw any distinction between songs. They don't go, 'Well, this is a treasured folk song and this is not.' My old man loved Elvis tunes as much as he sang the old ballads, and he didn't draw any lines" (Winick 10). Time and space may well be important factors here. The major waves of Gaelic Scots and Irish settlement in the region occurred between 1760 and 1830, and there has been little modern immigration from these sources to renew the population. Thus, while the Gaelic language and Celtic music have survived (the former only just), they have evolved virtually in isolation from the originating cultures. At the same time, ethnic mix and geography combine to reinforce historical ties to the British Isles. The Atlantic provinces are the least "multicultural" part of Canada, and the region is on the margin of the North American continent, geographically remote from the major centres of population, although still subject to North American cultural influences via modern electronic mass media. It has also been an economically depressed region for much of the twentieth century, eking out a marginal existence from land and sea, or from government social welfare programs. Hence, given the earlier observation that there is a tendency for musical syncretism to be initiated by "outsiders" or among members of marginalized populations, which are more likely to be subject to eclectic musical influences unencumbered by cultural baggage, Atlantic Canada's history of producing new musical forms and styles may come as no surprise.

That some cultural baggage persists, however, is apparent even in the case of the East Coast Sound. As one of the more radical and more widely known innovators among the new artists from Atlantic Canada, Ashley MacIsaac in particular has felt its weight. After the first televised performance of his new rock-infused sound, MacIsaac received anonymous letters from "local fiddle zealots...berating him for his blasphemy to an old and dear tradition," and the president of the Cape Breton Fiddlers Association, Father John Angus Rankin, warned that traditional music will suffer if young fiddlers follow in MacIsaac's footsteps and "play for the money" (Bliss 41). For his part, however, MacIsaac claims that fiddle styles in Cape Breton have long been "dirtier" (grungier?) than the more formal playing that continues to predominate in the British Isles, again perhaps reflecting the already hybrid nature of Cape Breton fiddle playing and its use as dance music. Interviewed for the MuchMusic television program *Celtic Ceilidh*, he argued that Scottish/Gaelic fiddle music "lost its realness" when it ceased to be a music for the common people and became entertainment, performed by hired players, for the rich folk in the Lowlands: "That's what everybody at home is scared will happen....I believe that we've recognized what it was that was real and could be lost, and I like to play the old way just as much as I like playing with the band."

To demonstrate his commitment to the tradition, MacIsaac followed up his rock-infused 1995 album *hi™ how are you today?* with a return to more conventional arrangements of traditional tunes, featuring only his own fiddle and piano (with guest John Allan Cameron, a veteran promoter of Celtic music on guitar) on his third release, *fineᴿ thank you very much!* (1996). The new album is a response in more ways than one—the continuity in the titles perhaps suggesting that there is greater commonality between the two forms of music than his purist critics will admit. Nonetheless, on *fineᴿ thank you*, as well as on its less-reverential predecessor, MacIsaac takes a dig at the guardians of authenticity by emblazoning across the cover of the CD an official-looking logo bearing the words "CBDA approved"—for MacIsaac, "CBDA" equals the "Cape Breton *Diddlers* Association."

According to Ian McKinnon of Rawlins Cross, MacIsaac may be singled out for criticism by the traditionalists because the fiddle is the focal point of his performances ("the fiddle *is* the music") and because "he's coming from a purer tradition than we are" (interview, April 1996). In contrast, although he acknowledges that "one or two from the old piping community may have reservations," McKinnon has heard few complaints about his own use of the highland bagpipe in a Celtic-rock band, perhaps because the pipes are rarely front and centre: McKinnon plays several other instruments as well (tin whistles, trumpet, bodhran), and when the pipes are featured, they are usually heard as part of a multi-instrumental accompaniment and/or counterpoint to Joey Kitson's lead vocals. Nonetheless, it seems that, even for McKinnon and his fellow band members, the use of "traditional" instruments and conventions is not entirely free of cultural baggage: in contrast to MacIsaac, he emphasises, "we are more faithful to the tradition. We approach the music with reverence."

Consequently, while I have argued that a sense of cultural distance is one of the prerequisites for musical syncretism to take place, it is not absolute. While the musicians of Atlantic Canada may indeed feel a sense of detachment from the communities in which traditional Celtic music originated, there are still local conventions and authorities that cannot be entirely disregarded. Indeed, a number of the new East Coast bands make clear in album notes and acknowledgements, as well as by their playing of work by local composers, their debt to the traditional music of the region and to those who kept it alive. For example, the

Rawlins Cross song "Long Night" (also from *Reel'n'Roll*, 1993) was written by Dave Panting as a eulogy for the great Newfoundland fiddle player and raconteur, Emile Benoit, who died in 1992:[13]

Long Night	So this is what it all comes to
Long Night	This is what we all go through
Long Night	Another friend is gone
Long Night	Leaving us to carry on

Death is a mighty uniter
The defeat that comes to every fighter
Live on! The dawn will be brighter
Live on! Live on! Live on!

"Long Night" by Dave Panting
© 1993 Ground Swell Records
Used by Permission from the Rawlins Cross album *Reel 'n' Roll.*

The track opens with a slow lament on Ian McKinnon's pipes, over ethereal chords from Geoff Panting's synthesized accordion, then breaks into medium tempo rock, Joey Kitson's vocals backed by or interspersed with, it seems, the band's full range of traditional and modern instrumental variations—mandolin, guitar, Chapman Stick, accordion (with and without interface), tin whistle, bagpipes, drums, bodhran. And, in honour of the tradition, in the brief instrumental breaks between chorus and verse, Dave Panting's mandolin picks out a Benoit-like jig.

With respect to *receptivity*, the third condition for the emergence of the East Coast Sound as popular music, for audiences in Atlantic Canada, Celtic music has long maintained a place in the popular realm. But the receptivity of audiences elsewhere in the country to the new sound may be attributed to a number of developments in popular music, and in popular culture generally, over the last decade or so. As noted earlier, a significant trend in popular music in the late 1980s was the appearance of "world beat," which saw the co-optation or blending into mainstream rock music of a variety of musical forms indigenous to cultures outside of the Anglo-American societies in which rock's earlier adaptations had taken place. Paul Simon, for example, employed rhythms and performers from South Africa and Latin America on *Graceland* (1986) and *Rhythm of the Saints* (1990). Ry Cooder has recorded with musicians from West Africa (Ali Farka Toure, *Talking*

Timbuktu [1994]) and India (V. M. Bhatt, *A Meeting by the River* [1993]), fusing his guitar stylings with their indigenous musics. Canadian artists and audiences, however, have not had to look so far afield because, as in the British Isles, "exotic" sounds were to be found on their own doorstep in the form of music from the Celtic peripheries.[14]

As a number of artists interviewed for *Celtic Ceilidh* emphasized, the emergence of Celtic-rock in its various crossover forms is part of a broader reawakening of interest in Celtic traditional music and, more generally, in Gaelic culture and language. Some ascribed this to a resurgence of nationalism (especially in Scotland, for example), some to a need for people to rediscover traditional and local roots amid trends towards economic and cultural globalization, some even to the approach of the millennium. Certainly, Celtic has become "chic." Celtic symbols and designs have begun appearing in artwork, jewellery and high fashion, not to mention tattoos, and awareness of aspects of "Gaelic" history and culture has also been aroused by Hollywood blockbusters such as *Braveheart* (1995) and *Rob Roy* (1996). But, in contrast to this trendiness, what really appeals according to many of the musicians is what Ashley MacIsaac calls the "realness," and others refer to as "honesty," in the music—the fact that it is, perhaps, music *of* the people.[15] And the music can be fun, which is another reason for its appeal to younger audiences and performers. Thus, the lead singer of the Irish band Hothouse Flowers, Liam O Maonlaí, who has recorded with The Rankin Family (on the title track of their 1995 EP, *Grey Dusk of Eve*), suggested that as in Atlantic Canada, "traditional music is very alive here in Ireland. Young people play it not because it's a museum piece, but because it's 'Wow! Cool!'"

To some extent, it may be argued, the East Coast Sound draws upon the familiar because Celtic music has always maintained a presence even in other parts of Canada, if only largely among recent arrivals from the British Isles or, possibly, the descendants of earlier British and Irish immigrants. In the last three decades or so, it was kept alive in tours, concerts and televised performances by artists such as John Allan Cameron (father of Stewart Cameron, guitarist in MacIsaac's band, The Kitchen Devils), the novelty pub act The Irish Rovers and the original electric folkies from Newfoundland, Figgy Duff. For those who were interested, Celtic music could also be found on the folk circuit, in bars advertising "Irish pub night" and, in its traditional and/or military forms, at the Highland Games to be found in many parts of Canada in the summer. And, of course, hundreds (maybe thousands) of kids each week are sent to Scottish dancing classes: indeed, one of the unantici- pated delights of attending a concert by Ashley MacIsaac, for example, occurs offstage when a dozen or more trendily dressed teen- and twenty-somethings in the audience form a circle and start jigging and reeling, putting into practice steps vaguely remembered from their childhood Saturday mornings in a local hall.

Finally, the growing popular appeal of the East Coast Sound has been further promoted by, and is reflected in, the development of insti- tutional and commercially oriented support structures. Since its found- ing in 1989, the annual East Coast Music Association (ECMA) Conference and Awards has given an enormous boost to all kinds of popular music from Atlantic Canada and now receives national and international media coverage. The major record labels and distributors have "discovered" the region. As recently as 1992, there were no agents or management companies and no distribution system for independ- ently produced artists in Atlantic Canada—a vacuum that was filled in part by the establishment of Halifax-based Ground Swell Records, founded by Ian McKinnon to manage and to distribute albums by his own band, Rawlins Cross, as well as other artists, and by the growth of Duckworth/Atlantica in St. John's (Ian McKinnon, interview; MacDonald 19). Ground Swell signed distribution contracts with Warner Music Canada for its artists, including Rawlins Cross and Cape Breton fiddler Natalie MacMaster, while other emerging East Coast artists have also been snapped up by the majors. Last, the New Country Network (now Country Music Television) specialty music channel on cable TV, licensed in 1995, has provided a showcase for a wide variety of adult-contemporary rock, including the music of East Coast artists such as Rawlins Cross, The Barra MacNeils and The Rankin Family, who could not previously acquire national exposure on the more youth- oriented MuchMusic video channel.

As a consequence of all these factors, the Celtic-inspired syncretism of the East Coast Sound has transcended its original regional and eth- nic roots to find a wider national and international audience and has become recognized, at least within North America, as a distinctively "Canadian" contribution to the evolution of contemporary rock. And, as the audience has grown, so has the number of performers working in the new crossover genre. A second wave of artists from Atlantic Canada, led by Great Big Sea (chosen by public vote as 1996 ECMA Entertainers of the Year), Natalie MacMaster and Slàinte Mhath (featuring younger siblings of The Barra MacNeils, hence often called "the baby Barras"), have been joined by such bands as The Immigrants and Jimmy George from Ontario, Edmonton's Captain Tractor, and Mad Pudding and The Paperboys from Vancouver. In the mid-1990s the East Coast Sound has become a form of "national" popular music.

Conclusion

This analysis has attempted to place the emergence of the East Coast Sound, the Celtic-rock-inspired music of Atlantic Canada, within the broader context of the evolution of Canadian popular music. While historically, to the extent that it was recognized at all, a distinctive Canadian rock music has been distinguished by "genre-bending," or the "inflection" (rather than "imitation"), of the conventions of mainstream, largely American, rock music, the East Coast Sound is a product of crossing the boundaries between the pre-existing genres of rock and traditional music to create a unique blend. Such syncretisms, it has been argued, take place under conditions of musical eclecticism and cultural distance—conditions both found present to a greater or lesser degree in Atlantic Canada. However, it was also found that, contrary to initial expectations, artists working in the new genre had to contend with some surviving cultural baggage; hence, it may be the case that the most important prerequisite for syncretism is the coexistence of diverse musical forms within the popular realm, rather than cultural distance in any absolute sense. I also argued that, if it is to become "popular music" (in all senses of the term), a newly syncretized genre requires a receptive audience. In this respect, a number of trends in popular music and popular culture discussed in this article may be seen as contributing to the growing popularity of the East Coast Sound and its acceptance as a form of national popular music in Canada.

In conclusion, what is the larger significance, if any, of the emergence of the East Coast Sound? According to Barry Grant, whose framework for analysis of Canadian popular music provided the conceptual point of departure for this discussion, when a Canadian artist chooses the strategy of inflection and asserts, through lyrics or music,

"I am not American," this represents "a tentative but progressive step forward toward defining our own popular music" (Grant 126). But is this enough? English Canada has sometimes been labelled "Notland," a satirical term for a society that defines itself largely in terms of what it isn't (that is, English Canadians are not British, not French, not American). But just as this kind of "negative identity" may be considered an inadequate basis for the building of a national political community, so saying "I am not American" through inflection may be seen as only an intermediate stage in the development of a national popular music or any other field of cultural endeavour. In contrast, the evolution of new, distinctively Canadian genres or sub-genres of music, such as the East Coast Sound, represents a major step forward in the maturation of English-Canadian popular music in particular and, such is the power of popular culture, perhaps also of English Canada's sense of cultural identity.

POSTSCRIPT

This article was first conceived as a conference paper, presented at the Conference on "Boundaries" (hence, in part, the reference to "boundary-crossing" in the title) hosted by the Centre for Canadian Studies, Edinburgh, Scotland, in May 1996. At that time, the East Coast Sound was still at the zenith of its popularity, but one of the defining characteristics of popular music, like other forms of popular culture, is its "momentary," or ephemeral, nature. Tastes and styles are constantly changing; new and distinct genres and sub-genres of music emerge, become popular for a while, maybe even becoming "the next big thing," and then either fade away, perhaps surviving as a minority "cult" sub-genre, or are absorbed into the relatively undifferentiated mainstream. In the past four years, the "moment" that was the East Coast Sound has largely been and gone, and with it have also gone some of the artists and bands who pioneered this particularly Canadian musical form.

In September 1999, The Rankins (formerly The Rankin Family) announced their intention to part musical company to pursue individual careers. Four months later, in January 2000, founding member John Morris Rankin, much respected as a musician for his work with others as well as with The Rankins, died in a road accident. A few days after his funeral, the members of Rawlins Cross made it known that 2000 would be their last year together as a band: again, like the Rankin siblings, after six albums and numerous national and international tours in the past twelve years, band members wanted more time to devote to individual projects and, in some cases, to their families.

Following his meteoric rise to stardom as one of the leaders of the Celtic-rock new wave, Ashley MacIsaac has seemingly lost his way. After numerous unsuccessful attempts to record a new "contemporary" album, amid struggles with internal demons and drug dependency, MacIsaac effectively retired from the record business for a couple of years and was released by his major label, A&M. In November 1999, he made a much-anticipated return with *Helter's Celtic* for independent Loggerhead Records, but the new album is a "mixed bag," lacking the sustained innovative genius of *hi*™ *how are you today?*, and prospects for a comeback for the former *enfant terrible* of Celtic-rock were further jeopardized by negative publicity and a spate of cancelled bookings in the wake of his eccentric, outrageous "performance" at a Millennium Eve Concert in Halifax.

Some new faces have emerged. Gaelic singer Mary Jane Lamond (who formerly toured with MacIsaac) and Cape Breton fiddler Natalie MacMaster (niece of Buddy MacMaster) have established national reputations and respectable album and concert sales. In both cases, however, their music is largely traditional in origin, albeit sometimes accompanied by "contemporary" instrumentation and arrangements. Among more established East Coast acts, groups such as The Barra MacNeils and The Irish Descendants continue to tour extensively, but perform largely to older audiences more attuned to their traditional repertoires than to Celtic-pop or -rock fusions. Only Great Big Sea, among the bands featured prominently in this article, has retained a younger audience while continuing to find new ways of combining the two musical traditions.

The East Coast music scene, never entirely monolithic even at the height of the Celtic-rock phenomenon—think of Halifax rockers Sloan or jale, country artist Kim Stockwood, or "transplanted" Easterner and multiple East Coast Music Award winner Sarah McLachlan—has benefitted from the increased exposure lent to the region's music scene by the widespread popularity of the East Coast Sound even though the latter is no longer its driving force. Lured to Atlantic Canada, and especially to the annual ECMA Awards and Trade Show in search of the next Celtic-rock sensation, major labels found a vibrant popular music culture and a rich vein of "undiscovered" (or, rather, "unsigned") talent in a wide range of musical genres, including singer-songwriter Bruce Guthro and The Johnny Favourite Swing Orchestra.

Four years on, the East Coast *scene* continues to flourish, but the East Coast *Sound*—that unique syncretism, or blending, of the traditional "Celtic" music of Atlantic Canada with conventions of contemporary rock and pop—has, like many other preceding genres and subgenres, enjoyed its allotted popular-culture lifespan. However, its decline in popularity since the mid-1990s does not diminish its significance as a catalyst for artists and the music industry in the Atlantic region, as a key, formative stage in the evolution of Canadian popular music, or as a case study that enhances our understanding of the processes and dynamics of popular culture in general.

NOTES

Grateful acknowledgements are due to Richard Blaustein (East Tennessee State University), Brock University colleagues Terrance Cox and Barry Grant, and the editors of this volume for their comments on earlier versions of this article. I also thank Ian McKinnon, of Rawlins Cross and Ground Swell Records, for his assistance.

1　For those unfamiliar with this exotic-looking instrument, the Chapman Stick is an evolution from the electric guitar. It has ten strings, five treble (or melody) strings and five bass strings. Since the sound is made by "hammering on" (that is, pressing the strings down sharply onto the touchboard with the fingertips) instead of plucking or strumming, both hands may be used at once to play different sets of strings; one, usually the left, producing the bass line, the other playing chords or creating a melody.

2　Like Chuck Berry's rock 'n' roll classic "Reelin' and Rockin'," to which it seemingly alludes, "Reel'n'Roll" is a self-advertising song: the title denotes not only the activities described in the lyrics, but also the style of music the listener should expect to hear. In this and other respects, among all the new East Coast bands and artists, Rawlins Cross often appears to be the most self-conscious or self-aware about the innovative nature of the new sound. In addition to *Reel'n'Roll*, for example, other album titles include *Crossing the Border* (1991) and *Living River* (1996), the latter an allusion to the living tradition of Celtic/Gaelic culture in Atlantic Canada.

3　The terms "Celtic" and "Gaelic" are often used interchangeably to describe cultural (including musical) influences from parts of the British Isles. Strictly speaking, "Gaelic" is a language spoken, with some significant variations, only in parts of Scotland and Ireland (as well as in Cape Breton), while "Celtic" is a generic term for peoples and their cultures originating in all the western peripheries of the British Isles—including Scotland, Ireland, Wales and Cornwall—as well as Brittany in northwestern France. Note that, given the cross-fertilization of folk traditions among different parts of the British Isles, some writers use the term "*Anglo*-Celtic" in preference to either "Celtic" or "Gaelic."

4   To qualify as "Canadian content" under CRTC regulations, a piece of music must normally fulfil at least two of the following criteria: the music was principally composed by a Canadian; the principal artist performing the music or song is Canadian; the performance either took place or was recorded in Canada; and the lyrics were written by a Canadian. From the initials of these four components—Music, Artist, Performance, Lyrics—comes the very Canadian acronym MAPL, seen on many CDs and tapes to inform radio programmers and consumers that this recording qualifies as Canadian content.

5   In addition to the artists discussed here, Grant also includes The Band (the first part of his title alludes to their song "Across the Great Divide") among his examples of Canadian inflection (Grant 124-25). However, while some members of The Band did perhaps try to (re-)establish a Canadian identity in late career, for much of their history, as I argue later in this article, they played quintessentially *American* music.

6   Many of the artists and recordings discussed by Grant are to be found on the four-CD set celebrating the twenty-fifth anniversary of the Juno Awards, *Oh What a Feeling* (MCA, 1996). Readers may wish to spend some time applying the imitation-inflection framework to tracks on this collection, perhaps especially to those that postdate Grant's analysis.

7   In live performance, although not on record (probably for copyright reasons), MacIsaac segues from a traditional fiddle tune into a rendition of The Bee Gees' "Staying Alive," featured in *Saturday Night Fever*, the 1977 "disco" film starring John Travolta.

8   See, for example, "Fusion Confusion," *Daily News* (Halifax), March 21, 1996.

9   On the "generic" nature of popular culture, and especially popular music, see Gendron.

10 For example, the original rock 'n' roll of the mid-1950s (Chuck Berry, Elvis Presley, Little Richard, et al.) was a product of blending black rhythm and blues (R&B)—in turn derived from blues, boogie and gospel—with white Southern country or hillbilly influences. For an interesting analysis of this process, see Hatch and Millward.

11 For a useful, if inconclusive, discussion of the many meanings of "popular music," see Jones and Rahn.

12 "The age of the Bobbys" is a slightly derogatory term for that period in the late 1950s and early 1960s when mainstream (read "white") American pop music was purged ("blanched") of most of the black music influences that had originally contributed to rock 'n' roll. Buddy Holly had died in a plane crash, Elvis was in the army, Chuck Berry was in jail and Jerry Lee Lewis was in disgrace after marrying his thirteen-year-old cousin. In their place the record industry promoted the "teen-idols," some actually called

"Bobby"—Bobby Vee, Bobby Vinton, even Canada's Bobby Curtola—while others, such as Fabian, Frankie Avalon and Paul Anka, might just as well have been. In this period, the principal strategy of the music business appeared to be one of "finding a pretty face and seeing if it could sing" (Ward et al. 203).

13 "Long Night" was subsequently co-dedicated to Panting's friend and former bandmate in Figgy Duff, Noel Dinn, who died of cancer in 1993. Other examples of honouring the tradition include the Rawlins Cross instrumental "Israel Got a Rabbit" on *Crossing the Border* (which is "dedicated to the memory of Rufus Guinchard"), Ashley MacIsaac's tribute to Buddy MacMaster in the rap-style voice-over in "The Devil in the Kitchen" (discussed above), and MacIsaac's "Brenda Stubbart," named after another famous Cape Breton fiddler (on *hi™ how are you today?*).

14 Canadian syncretisms between traditional and contemporary musics have also occurred in the case of another local but "exotic" form, the music of aboriginal peoples, as evidenced in recordings by Canadian artists Susan Aglukark, Kashtin, Buffy Sainte-Marie, Laura Vinson and some of the recent work of former Band member Robbie Robertson.

15 The attribution of "realness," or "authenticity," to commercially oriented popular music has long been viewed as problematic; see, for example, Frith.

Works Cited

Berland, Jody, and Will Straw. "Getting Down to Business: Cultural Politics and Policies in Canada." *Communications in Canadian Society*. Ed. Benjamin D. Singer. 4th edition. Scarborough: Nelson Canada, 1995. 332-56.

Bliss, Karen. "Ashley MacIsaac: Fiddler on the Edge." *Canadian Musician*, 18.1 (February 1996): 40-44.

Frith, Simon. "'The magic that can set you free': The Ideology of Folk and the Myth of the Rock Community." *Popular Music* 1 (1981): 159-68.

Gendron, Bernard. "Theodor Adorno Meets the Cadillacs." *Studies in Entertainment: Critical Approaches to Mass Culture*. Ed. Tania Modleski. Bloomington: Indiana UP, 1986. 18-36.

Grant, Barry K. "'Across the Great Divide': Imitation and Inflection in Canadian Rock Music." *Journal of Canadian Studies* 21.1 (Spring 1986): 116-27.

Hatch, David and Stephen Millward. *From Blues to Rock: An Analytical History of Pop Music*. Manchester: Manchester UP, 1987.

Hoskyns, Barney. *Across the Great Divide: The Band and America*. London: Viking, 1993.

Jones, Gaynor and Jay Rahn. "Definitions of Popular Music: Recycled." *Journal of Aesthetic Education* 11.4 (1977): 79-92.

MacDonald, Sandy. "Traditional Music Finding New Ears." *Canadian Composer* (Summer 1992): 18-19.

Marcus, Greil. *Mystery Train: Images of America in Rock 'n' Roll Music*. 4th edition. London: Penguin, 1991.

Quill, Greg. "Country and Eastern." Ed. Peter Goddard and Philip Kamin. *Shakin' All Over: The Rock 'n' Roll Years in Canada.* Toronto: McGraw-Hill Ryerson, 1989. 149-62.

Shepherd, John. "Value and Power in Music: An English Canadian Perspective." *Relocating Cultural Studies: Developments in Theory and Research.* Ed. Valda Blundell et al. London: Routledge, 1993. 171-206.

Straw, Will. "Sound Recording." *The Cultural Industries in Canada: Problems, Policies and Prospects.* Ed. Michael Dorland. Toronto: Lorimer, 1996. 95-117.

Taft, Michael. "Syncretizing Sound: The Emergence of Canadian Popular Music." *The Beaver Bites Back: American Popular Culture in Canada.* Ed. David H. Flaherty and Frank E. Manning. Montreal/Kingston: McGill-Queen's UP, 1993. 197-208.

Ward, Ed, Geoffrey Stokes and Ken Tucker. *Rock of Ages: The Rolling Stone History of Rock & Roll.* New York: Rolling Stone Press/Summit, 1986.

Winick, Steve. "Great Big Sea: Folk from the Rock" and "The East Coast Music Association Conference and Awards." *Dirty Linen* 64.1 (June/July 1996): 25-26.

Wright, Robert. "'Dream, Comfort, Memory, Despair': Canadian Popular Musicians and the Dilemma of Nationalism, 1968-1972." *Journal of Canadian Studies* 22.4 (Winter 1988): 27-43.

OTHER SOURCES CITED

"Celtic Ceilidh," program in the *New Music* series, broadcast on MuchMusic, July 23, 1996, produced by Scott Jardine for City-tv productions (Toronto, 1996).

Interview with Ian McKinnon, member of Rawlins Cross and president, Ground Swell Records (Halifax), April 1996.

FORCEFUL NUANCE AND STOMPIN' TOM

William Echard

The Present, Toronto, Fresh Shouts and Echoes

At the time I was researching and writing this paper, May 1995, what traces could be found of Stompin' Tom Connors in downtown Toronto?[1] Some were very fresh: the week before he was interviewed by Peter Gzowski on *Morningside* (CBC-Radio), and beside the stairway to the second floor of Sam the Record Man there was a large and recent portrait of Tom and Sam smiling, shaking hands.[2] A short walk from Sam's down Dundas Street you could see a huge mural of a cartoon Tom, foot stomping vigorously towards us as he loomed up a brick wall, the map of Canada receding spaciously behind. The mural had been there for a few years, but now it was obscured by construction. In the World's Biggest Bookstore, also just around the corner from Sam the Record Man, there was a special sale on the illustrated children's edition of some selected Stompin' Tom lyrics: the books were numerous, prominently displayed, and remaindered.

These were continuing traces and events in the neighbourhood of Toronto's Yonge and Dundas streets; easily visible and periodically renewed, they were evidence of Stompin' Tom as a forceful, lingering presence. And if you knew a bit of Tom's history there were other traces

---

Notes on pages 257-59.

and affinities to be seen, more faded and not renewed. Walking about fifteen minutes west on Queen Street you could see that the Horseshoe Tavern, his regular Toronto venue through the early seventies, was still in its original location. It was not a country-music bar anymore, but inside you could still see the decor that fills the concert film *Across This Land* (1973), strangely transposed.[3] The stage was bigger and in a different place, the spot where Tom and his band stood in the movie having been modified to house a small refrigerator and bar. But the wood tones were the same, and some of the furniture looked to be mid-seventies vintage, or a good approximation. Down by the lake, at Ontario Place, the Forum had been torn down. The Forum was the other regular 1970s Stompin' Tom performance spot, but through demolition the photos and reviews connecting Tom to this place have come mostly unmoored from the landscape, except for a strange familiarity in some of the surrounding hills and trees.

These are lines of force: effects that Stompin' Tom has had on the things to be seen in the neighbourhood of Dundas and Yonge, currents in the way we might see parts of Queen Street and the lakefront. He has had an effect on the physical environment, on the signs that make up the possible meanings of Toronto, and in some other parts of Canada—like Skinner's Pond, Timmins, Wawa—there are similar echoes and changes in the landscape. And of course his influence continues: he continues to record and perform on a regular basis.

Flowing along with and beside these physical echoes are the feel-ings of people who have been affected by Stompin' Tom: people who I have found eager to tell me how they met him in a restaurant in 1973, or hitchhiked across Canada because of his example, or who feel freer writing songs because he seems so free, or who feel more situated and proud because of what he has done. There are also the people, maybe equally numerous, who are irritated or embarrassed by his stridency and single-mindedness, who have told me that his sim-plistic view of nationality is dangerous and regressive, that he pan-ders to the lowest common denominator and ends up insulting every-body.[4] Again, strong echoes of the past flow into an ongoing experience and debate. Lines of force.

The history of Stompin' Tom's career to this point could be seen as a history of forceful impressions and actions, doggedly projected through and upon a simple, single-minded populist nationalism. It does not at first glance appear to be a realm of great nuance. But, as the title of my paper suggests, I think that in some ways it is.

The History, Slugging It Out[5]

"My ambition? I guess you could say it's to sing Canada to the world."
(Connors qtd. in Nowlan 31)

Tom Charles Connors was born to Isabelle Connors in Saint John, New Brunswick, on February 9, 1936. His father vanished shortly after-wards, and Tom never knew him. In 1939, Isabelle took Tom and left Saint John to hitchhike throughout the Maritimes. In 1942, Tom was taken away from Isabelle by Children's Aid and placed in St. Patrick's Orphanage in Silver Falls, New Brunswick, where he remained until he was eight years old. Tom speaks of the separation and his time at the orphanage as being highly traumatic: "[T]hey beat the hell out of me, and everybody else, with leather straps and bamboo canes…and if they couldn't find anything to hit you with they grabbed you by the hair.…I ran away from there every chance I got" (Nowlan 13).

In 1944, following another escape attempt, Connors was taken into foster care at the farm of Russell and Cora Aylward in Skinner's Pond, PEI. Although Connors seems to have fonder memories of this place than of the orphanage, and continues to keep in touch with the Aylwards, he still ran away frequently, and in 1949 he was moved to the Saint John Vocational School. Around this time Tom bought his first guitar, from his roommate, and began to accompany himself as he sang (he wrote his first song, "Reversing Falls Darling," in 1947). He has frequently stated that his main musical influences up to this time were Hank Snow and Wilf Carter, both yodelling-cowboy-style Canadian singers who had enjoyed considerable success in the U.S. (Carter under the name of Montana Slim, Snow by moving to the U.S. and renouncing his Canadian citizen-ship). He also speaks fondly of the house parties and old-time music-making at the farm in Skinner's Pond. Tom's life up to this point provides many of the powerful components of his image: a child abandoned by his father, close to but taken away from his mother, subjected to cruel or indifferent treatment in orphanages, but still clinging to his spirit, running away to seek his own space. It also tells us about his musical roots: old-time Maritime music and singing cowboys.[6]

In 1952 Tom ran away once again, this time for good, and found work on a coal boat making runs between New Brunswick and Newfoundland. The years 1952 to 1964 were spent hitchhiking and doing odd jobs around Canada and the U.S., often in the company of his close friend, Steve Foote. During this time, Connors continued to write songs about and for the people and places he visited, performing them on a casual basis. As he hitchhiked around the country, he was building on the styles that first influenced him, combining old-time music and a 1920s-30s style of cowboy singing with a deep commitment to Canadian people, places and folklore. This period provides the tropes of the second part of his image: a hobo citizen of the entire country, devoted to and singing about the daily life of people all across Canada simply for the love of it, but still suffering hard times and personal rootlessness, needing great determination and toughness to get through.

The Maple Leaf Hotel in Timmins, Ontario, is the venue where Tom Connors is usually said to have begun his career as a professional musician, and the story of how this came about is a frequently circulated piece of Stompin' Tom folklore. Apparently, he arrived in Timmins in 1964 as an amateur musician: "[H]e dropped into the Maple Leaf Hotel, found he had 35 cents in his pocket, and that beer was 40 cents. 'I asked the waiter if he'd make up the nickel for me, and he asked whether I could play the guitar I had with me. I said I could, and he said 'look, you sing us all a couple of songs, and I'll pay for the beer.' So I sang, and he went to fetch the boss, and...[he] asked me how I'd like to sing at the hotel for a week, for money.'" (*Canadian Composer*, "Stompin' Tom" 10, 46). As the story continues, Tom became quite popular and remained at the Maple Leaf Hotel for fourteen months. Also at this time he hosted a daily half-hour evening show on the Timmins radio station, CKGB. Using Timmins as a base, Connors (not yet called Stompin' Tom) toured extensively through Northern Ontario.

At this point, the final parts of his image began to come into place: the cowboy costume, an emphasis on humour and novelty (the novelty of the ordinary Canadian in a market saturated by images of Americanness), and a tendency for the media to emphasize his past as an abandoned child who found a home in the whole of Canada. Aside from his introduction to professional performing and broadcasting, the two events that propelled Connors into his popular persona were the invention of the name "Stompin' Tom" and his contract with Dominion Records.

The exact origin of the name "Stompin' Tom" is not clear, but a few themes emerge in various tellings of the story.[7] Connors was in the habit of stomping his foot as he performed, and he was also in the habit of wearing cowboy boots at all times. This proved hard on stages and rugs, and he began to use a plywood stomping board to protect the floors, to add a little more distinctiveness to the sound of his stomp, and to provide a memorable prop (at the end of a show he would loft the board above his head, dramatically dumping sawdust in a stream). It is usually agreed that it was in Peterborough, sometime around 1967, that this practice led to the name "Stompin' Tom" (some say the fateful words were spoken by a waiter, some say the MC, some say two old ladies in the front row). Also in 1967, Connors signed a contract with Rebel, a small Toronto label, and recorded two albums: *Northland's Own* and *On Tragedy Trail*.[8] These records show us Connors's style at the moment of his transition from a roving troubadour to a comedic, nationalistic icon. The name and cowboy image are in place, but the music is unaccompanied and predominantly serious, still looking back towards his roots.

In 1968, Connors signed a contract with Dominion Records, the recording branch of Canadian Music Sales. While working at Dominion, he met producer Jury Krytiuk, who became his manager. Between 1968 and 1969, the final touches were put on the distinctive Stompin' Tom persona. The stomping board was highlighted and the cowboy hat and boots became standard. He began to put more emphasis on his humorous material, to perform and record with a backing band, and he moved to Toronto to begin to make more serious inroads into the urban market.

Connors's first album for Dominion was *Bud The Spud* (1969). The title track was quite successful, receiving fair exposure on CBC-Radio and through word of mouth. Connors supported it with regular performances at The Horseshoe Tavern, as well as venues throughout northern Ontario and the Maritimes.[9] He became well-known as a colourful figure, a writer of catchy and funny songs about local people and places. He built on this basic impression in two ways: he continued to occupy the country-comedian persona, writing light, clever material, and he emphasized the nationalist and populist underpinnings of his repertoire.

In the early 1970s, it was unusual for songs with strongly regional
Canadian associations to receive broad exposure in the media. In general, Canadian performers who wanted mass acceptance moved to the
States and/or performed music that closely copied U.S. models.
Connors began to make himself into the head of a campaign to create
more room for Canadian themes in music broadcasting.[10] Some other
commercially viable musicians would sometimes perform explicitly
Canadian material (Gordon Lightfoot is one example, see Wright), but
no one besides Connors played *exclusively* this kind of material. As he
became increasingly well-known through songs like "Bud The Spud,"
"Big Joe Mufferaw," and "The Bug Song," Connors became insistent
that there was a deep and largely ignored need among Canadian popular-music audiences for material that affirmed a Canadian identity, and
he frequently berated country-music broadcasters for not programming
Canadian material.[11]

Along with this nationalist agenda came a strong populist tendency.
Connors and his management were explicit about wanting to make what
they considered simple music for ordinary people.[12] Connors's humour
drew heavily on well-worn themes like outhouses and "Newfies," and
his lyrics always maintained a loose, colloquial warmth.

I will describe Connors's music in some detail shortly, but for now
it can be noted that he stayed far away from the kind of slick, "countrypolitan" sound that was coming to be associated with Nashville, and
nurtured an unpolished but energetic directness in performance, along
with a writing style that perched squarely between memorable innovation and comfortable cliché.[13]

This strategy brought considerable success. In 1971 Connors formed
his own record label, Boot Records, and several related publishing
houses. His 1973 wedding was broadcast live on CBC-Television, and
the same year he performed for Queen Elizabeth II. By 1978 he had
won six Juno awards. But his single-minded brand of patriotism and his
tendency towards populist oversimplification also raised more than a
few hackles among many journalists who felt compelled to question the
ultimate value of Connors's rhetoric.[14]

This ongoing debate reached a head in 1978, with the most spectacular gesture of Connors's career. Along with his frustration at the lack
of air time given to Canadian material on radio, Connors had for some
years felt that the Juno awards were not being administered in a way

that gave fair chances to Canadians who chose to remain in Canada rather than move to the United States. In a press release of April 1, 1978, Connors claimed:

> It's not just this year but every year that there are Juno Jumpers who jump into the country for the Junos and then jump back out to their foreign jobs....In my opinion all nominees should have their principal place of residence in Canada and conduct their business affairs from a Canadian base of operations thereby keeping the Canadian Junos Canadian. (*Globe and Mail*, "Stompin' Tom" 32)

Connors invested a good deal of personal feeling into this issue, and his protest was backed by extreme action. He declined his 1978 Juno nomination, and returned all six of his previous Juno awards to CARAS.[15] In order to dispel claims that he was doing this as a publicity stunt, Connors announced that he would not record or perform in public for one year, so that he could not benefit from any publicity that might be generated by his protest. In fact, he actually remained out of the public eye for closer to 10 years.[16]

Since his comeback in the late 1980s, Connors has picked up exactly where he left off. He still supports the same populist vision of Canada, and he is still trying to encourage other artists to write more material that reflects their personal experience as Canadians, as well as to give such material more chance to succeed in the media.

POLYSEMY, OSCILLATION, AND NUANCE

> He shakes hands firmly, levels a steely, hawkish gaze and grumbles, "I'd like to say it's a pleasure to meet you, but I won't know that until I read what you write." Later, backstage, Connors lights one in a chain of cigarettes and offers an apology for the terse first meeting. "I got a little carried away back there and I'm sorry, but you've got to understand I'm sincere about what I'm doing...and if you turn this into some joke, honest to God, it will break my heart." (Potter C1, C4)

Even from this brief historical template, we can see how Connors's career and image are built from forceful elements: the myth of the orphan and hobo, the determined nationalist, the champion of ordinary people. By consistently living out, and aggressively marketing, these themes, Connors has garnered a reputation for consistency, sincerity, and passionate commitment to his beliefs. However, much of his commercial success also comes from his skill as a comedian and creator of novelty, which can undermine the ultimate seriousness of his political agenda. Humour is not necessarily antithetical to serious agendas (and is often an effective tool in communicating them), but Connors's anxiousness, evident in the quotation given above, demonstrates that the balance can be precarious. This tension between the "serious" and the "silly" is also evident in the need of some fans to negotiate between various parts of Connors's repertoire: "a lot of the music that he sang, and the songs that he wrote, were legitimate folk songs, they were about events, they weren't just stupid songs. He makes money on the stupider ones, but...a lot of the more serious ones he does were about events that nobody has captured in song like he has done" (Steve Pritchard, personal communication, 1993).[17] This conflict is a first shift in the monolithic lines of force. It is a site where we might look for subtle effects in the play between the serious and the absurd, the admirable leader and the affable clown, and most importantly in the way Stompin' Tom seems to oscillate continually between poles rather than settle in one place.

Generally, it is in this kind of oscillation that we can find *nuance*: subtle shades of meaning and function that enrich and motivate our relationship with the image, the rhetoric, the music. There are other such nuanced oscillations in Stompin' Tom. I have argued elsewhere (in "Inventing to Preserve") that the entire power of Connors's nationalism rests on an oscillation between innovation and traditionalism, between invented and inherited traditions. But before proceeding to analyze nuances in the music itself, I should point out that this kind of polysemy, oscillation, and openness to multiple readings is not unique to Stompin' Tom. In his writing on blue jeans, John Fiske has argued that *any* popular text must exhibit a polyvalence of this kind:

> The importance of contradiction within popular culture is [thoroughgoing]...but for the moment we can turn to a discussion of two of its characteristics:...that contradiction can entail the expression of both domination and subordination...[and] that contradiction entails semiotic richness and polysemy. It enables the readers of a text...to partake of both of its forces simultaneously and devolves to them the power to situate themselves within this play of forces at a point that meets their particular cultural interests. (5)

In a sense, then, the serious/silly oscillation we have detected in Stompin' Tom is one condition of his popularity: it is an opportunity for polysemy; it keeps audiences engaged and allows them to read themselves into the text. Another nuance, as I have suggested, is the natural/invented oscillation in his nationalism and traditionalism. Other oscillations that could be investigated include the tension between the populist and the star, or between Connors's strongly regional voice (centred in two places, PEI and Northern Ontario) and the claim that he can speak for all of Canada. In tracing these oscillations, we are in one sense just examining Stompin' Tom's particular engagement with what Fiske argues is a general feature of popular texts. But I would suggest further that some of Stompin' Tom's solutions in this regard are original enough to be considered unique personal traits, and that the overtly political dimension of his image requires that he actively *exploit* these oscillations in such a way as to maximize his potential audience (through polysemy) while simultaneously making himself seem utterly solid and naturalized (to maintain credibility).

Up to this point I have tried to establish two things. Firstly, the Stompin' Tom persona is constructed out of forceful elements, and has had strong effects on the physical and social environment in some parts of Canada. His forceful exterior and essentialist politics require him to project a monolithic solidity. But secondly, as with any popular text, the Stompin' Tom persona must remain somewhat open and display enough polysemy to reach the largest number of readers and to move along with transformative currents in the marketplace. This kind of openness and multiplicity I have called "nuance," since it leads to a large number of gradations in meaning and experience. By choosing the word "nuance," I hope to highlight the fact that the transformative flows and multiple strata are operative within an impression of a *single* object. The text must seem somehow fixed, or we would see a continuous transformation or a parade of new entities rather than the nuancing of a single entity. This is especially important in the case of Stompin' Tom, since his politics and traditionalist aesthetic require him to seem stable, unchanging and reliable.

These observations are only a starting point, a way into the material. As a musicologist, I will pursue them with respect to the music itself, the patterns of sound that Connors presents in recordings and concerts. One of the main tasks undertaken in my larger study of Stompin' Tom

(Echard, "Approaching") was to explore how the semiotic oscillations in the music are related to those in Connors's rhetoric and visual image, and how they form a single system of imagined and actual community. In the remainder of this paper, I will look more closely at how the music itself is nuanced, and how this nuancing relates to Stompin' Tom's musical forcefulness.

DISCREPANCIES AND NUANCE IN THE MUSIC

> Music, to be personally involving and socially valuable, must be "out of time" and "out of tune."...Put another way, wherever "lexical meanings" are various and ambiguous for a particular phenomenon, one can assume a lot of collective and individual unconsciousness and conversely a greater power for "speaker's meanings" [to] define situations....*Discrepant* is as good a term as I've been able to find for the phenomena that make music a peculiarly powerful vehicle for participatory consciousness and action...it is the little discrepancies between hands and feet within a jazz drummer's beat, between bass and drums, between rhythm section and soloist, that create the groove and invite us to participate. (Keil, "Participatory" 96-98)

In his theory of participatory discrepancies, Charles Keil is looking to find inviting semiotic oscillations in tensions (discrepancies) between elements of performed music. In his work on grooves in jazz ("Participatory"), for example, Keil looks at the way a drummer's cymbal tap pulls against the underlying beat implied by the ensemble as a whole, or at the way the drummer's time and that of the bassist pull against each other. In these fields of tension Keil senses a musical *process*, as opposed to a static syntax, and argues that this processual aspect of music leads to *engendered feeling, participation, groove.*

Keil's groove is an example of what I have called "nuance": a continual oscillation within a syntactic form that engages people and invites them to participate. By defining my terms in this way (groove as a kind of nuance, discrepancy as a source of groove and therefore also a source of nuance), I want to point out that there is no ultimate opposition between forcefulness and nuance, but a continual mutual formation. While a strong groove is more overtly forceful than some other kinds of nuance (for example, the quiet satisfaction that can arise from a subtle change of tonal colour), what they share is their common generation out of some form of semiotic oscillation or ambiguity, their fundamentally fluid and processual nature, and their ability to encourage participation. Keil's work on discrepancy can help us to understand the relationship between force and nuance in Stompin' Tom in at least two ways. Firstly, as I have noted, Keil demonstrates how nuance is fundamentally connected to force, clearing up in advance the possible confusion of conceiving these two aspects of the work as separate. Secondly, by highlighting discrepancy as one of the musical mechanisms that can produce groove, Keil has suggested a particular way to analyze musical details. In order to see how force and nuance interact in Connors's work, I will begin by looking at ways that discrepancies appear in specific formal details.

There are many discrepancies in Stompin' Tom's music. Elsewhere (Echard, "Approaching"), I have explored formal aspects of the music, showing that in his choice of harmonic material and phrase-structure Connors balances between a staunch, even clichéd traditionalism, and occasional radical innovation. Some of his formal schemes, such as those in "Muk Luk Shoo" or "Big Joe Mufferaw," are entirely novel and quite ingenious, whereas the majority stick to familiar sixteen- and thirty-two-bar country forms. In this case, innovative formal and harmonic trends pull against traditionalist ones in the repertoire as a whole. Similar discrepancies can be found between the stylistic connotations in some of his instrumental arrangements: for example, the somewhat extended seventh-chord harmony in the introduction to "Wop May" pulls against the straight triads of the rest of the song, and in "Bud The Spud" the tight country rhythm section pulls against the more improvisatory, rock-influenced electric guitars.

These examples are perhaps closer to what Keil would call syntax than what he would call process. But they are nonetheless discrepancies that open up a space for participation (for freer and more multiple readings). They also help to keep the overall stylistic connotations of Connors's work fluid. Many of the elements of his style have, through the commercialization of U.S. branches of the country and old-time music trees, come to be heavily American in their connotations. By breaking down these fixed connotative codes through discrepancies, Connors not only invites his audience to participate more actively in the reading, but he loosens the fixed, American associations of his sound, and reclaims some stylistic elements for his Canadian agenda.

But there is another type of discrepancy that is crucial to Stompin' Tom's sound, in what I call the texture of performance. By "texture" I mean the global impression that emerges from the way the timbre, rhythmic placement, and tuning of each instrument interact in a total fabric. The texture can be understood as the shape of the music as it blends with the ambient noise in the performance or listening environment. It is a general attitude in the way the music fills and interacts with acoustic and physical space. It is different from groove in that it is not primarily a rhythmic phenomenon, but it is similar in that different textures enact different relationships with the music, different modes of involvement. It is like a tactile texture in that it is a *general* feeling, a large surface for the listener's body and awareness to move on and through. The texture is the global shape you can sense when you let the individual pulsations and currents of the groove merge into their most general form.

The thing I notice about the texture of Connors's music through the 1970s (hear, for example, *Live At The Horseshoe* or *Bud The Spud*) is that it seems somehow "spread" or ragged. Connors has a propensity to sing ahead of the beat, slightly under pitch, and scoop up to the note. The instruments are often not perfectly in tune with themselves or each other, attack points are often not synchronized, and tempi tend to fluctuate within individual instruments and within the ensemble as a whole. The texture spreads out in at least three directions. Firstly, there are discrepancies with the "countrypolitan," Nashville sound that had come to dominate much commercial country music of the time. Secondly, the instruments deviate from each other (in tuning, rhythmic placement, and timbral blend). Finally, there are discrepancies within individual instrumental lines (a guitar might speed up or slow down, for example). And in the centre of this gnarly soundscape there is a strong energy, an intense groove.

This kind of texture is common in Connors's albums and live performances between 1969 and 1978.[18] Some writers and listeners have looked disparagingly on this soundscape, saying that the texture is simply a result of inadequacies in the performance, and that more care should have been taken.[19] But this is only a partial (and somewhat prejudicial) explanation. The albums by Connors's friend Stevedore Steve, for example, were recorded by the same companies with many of the same musicians, but they have a more focused sound.[20] And more importantly, the criteria for judging a "successful performance" depend on the intentions and desires of the performer and the audience. Connors frequently asserts that he does not work according to the Nashville scale of production values. His music has a different political and social purpose, and the openness and raggedness of the texture is an integral part of its effect.

When Connors talks about the role of music in his society, he often mentions performances for pleasure in people's homes (the old-time music tradition as he knew it growing up in PEI), and talks about his role in forming a bridge through which audience members can get to know each other better: "When I was out there I know for a fact that people in every room that I ever played, they became friends instantly because when I seen two tables sitting together and they weren't talking to one another, I'd introduce them right off the bat...and the next thing you know they put the two tables together and from that time on they're friends" (*Morningside*, CBC-Radio, December 27, 1988). In this role, as in a house party, the musicians must be participants in the total event, rather than stars separate from the audience. The loose, spread-out sound of Stompin' Tom's band can help to reinforce this image in two ways. Firstly, it blends in well with the ambient noise of a party or hotel. Noises made by audiences tend to be "spread" even when the audience is acting together. For example, when an audience claps along with a performer the attack points are widely dispersed, creating regions of intensity rather than a distinct marking of the beat. Other ambient noises, like conversation or breaking glass, are even less rigidly structured. When the texture of the band is spread, there is less acoustic distance between the sound of the band and the ambient noises in the performance space. To my ear, this allows the music to insinuate its way into the surroundings, coiling itself around and through ambient noises rather than competing with or overpowering them.

Secondly, and partly because of the first point, the spread texture softens the distinction between the performers and listeners by downplaying performance skill, which not everyone has developed, in favour of honest communal expression, which everyone is invited to explore. This is a fine balancing act. A certain amount of textural spread can help to lessen the potential gap between performers and listeners, but too much might cause the listeners to question the competence of the performers. I believe that one of Connors's greatest musical achievements is the way he situates the texture of his music right between these two possibilities, allowing him to be credible both as a professional musician and as just one of the crowd. In this way, Connors's sound downplays rigid discipline and difference, in favour of exploration and community.

CONCLUSION

The idea that the texture of Connors's music invites a certain kind of participation and community recalls Christopher Small's notion of *musicking*. According to Small's theory, a musical performance is a ritual in which all present participate equally, and which is geared towards producing, for the duration of the event, an ideal imagined society. My analysis of the texture of Connors's music as a nuanced, inviting, process-generating strategy certainly seems consistent with the idea that musicking serves to generate and maintain bonds within a social group. And the utopian notion that musicking is directed towards the production of an *ideal* imagined society seems consistent with Connors's relentlessly glowing, generally simplified portrayals of Canada and Canadian life. In other words, my analysis can be taken to show a few specific ways in which Connors's music acts to produce a vision of an ideal Canadian space.

However, this same energy can act in less positive ways as well. Although Keil does not explore it in this light, group action can be damaging and reactionary as well as nurturing and generous. The nuance generates force, which can then flow in any number of directions. Although my evaluation of Connors has been generally positive, I would be remiss if I glossed over the fact that his vision of Canada sometimes seems to veer from a comfortable "all for all" message into a more reactionary "all for one" sloganeering. The somewhat reactionary impulse seen in early songs like "Unity" (already cited) has in some ways deepened since Connors's return from retirement, for example, the recent song "Believe In Your Country," which suggests that those whose patriotic fervour is weak or ambivalent have a duty to move elsewhere.

The ideal society towards which the musicking is oriented, in a case like this, might not be entirely utopian. Although the nuance and force of a music flows out of the spaces and ambiguities that encourage individual participation, this same force can act to limit freedom and close down certain options. Running parallel to the circle of force and nuance there is a continuing and precarious negotiation between freedom and coercion.

I do not make this point in order to put Connors's achievement in a negative light, but only to place my analysis in a broader context. One of the more important effects of analyzing aesthetic nuance is that we can become more aware of how it participates in the *entire* flow of force in culture, from the most local to the most global level. The nuance generates the force, and the discrepancy generates the groove, gets people moving and feeling in particular directions: from the tapping toe, to the mural on the street, to voting, writing, and beyond. Stompin' Tom deserves our attention partly because he has moved so effectively through this matrix. He has deftly manoeuvred the currents between force and nuance, and has thereby become one of the most interesting and lively figures in the Canadian musical landscape.

NOTES

1 I situate this discussion in Toronto for two reasons: first, because this is where I have done my fieldwork, and second, because Toronto is the city where Connors has been most vigorously and consistently promoted.

2 *Morningside*, long hosted by Peter Gzowski, is a very popular CBC-Radio morning show. Sam's, located near Yonge and Dundas streets in downtown Toronto, is the main store of the Sam the Record Man chain.

3 *Across This Land*, 1973, directed by John Saxton, is distributed by Cinepix.

4 Throughout this paper, when I present these kinds of generalizations I am summarizing results arrived at through work on my M.A. thesis, "Approaching Stompin' Tom." I will occasionally expand these generalizations when I think it is essential to do so, but, in general, see the thesis for more extended explanations.

5 This is a very abbreviated version of the history presented in my M.A. thesis ("Approaching"). It combines a number of sources, including newsprint articles, radio archive materials, biographical and PR mailings from ACT records, personal interviews with fans and local broadcasters, and correspondence with Connors.

6 The term "old-time music" is a catchphrase for the traditional music of rural communities in North America from the beginnings of settlement to the advent of mass-distributed sound recordings. Bronner describes the style as a mixture of Anglo-American fiddle tunes, square dance music, play-party tunes, Victorian parlour songs, Native American and British ballads, sacred songs and minstrel songs. The term is usually used to refer to the fiddle-based dance music of domestic or public gatherings, such as house parties or barn raisings, and is generally thought to evoke associations of rural life, traditional values and communal well-being.

The "singing cowboy" style began with the work of Jimmie Rodgers in the late 1920s (although Rodgers was actually a "brakeman" rather than a "cowboy"). His relaxed ballad style and distinctive yodel, along with an explicitly Texas affiliation (much of the recorded country music prior to Rodgers was from the Southeast) inspired many followers, who produced a distinct sub-genre of country music (the singing cowboy). Two of the earliest, Hank Snow and Wilf Carter, were Canadians, and Connors cites them as his earliest and strongest musical influences.

7　See, for example, *Canadian Composer*, November 1970, 46; or *Maclean's*, August 1972, 44.

8　In general, discographic references in the text are abbreviated. See the discography for full citations.

9　The exact extent of Connors's commercial success in this period is hard to establish. He did not appear on any charts, but it is not unusual for a "success" in regional, Canadian terms to be numerically far below a general chart success. There are reports in the press of the local popularity of "Bud The Spud" (*Canadian Composer*, November 1970, 46), word-of-mouth recollections that it sold well, and the evidence of Connors's continuing success at the Juno awards. But the files of Boot and Dominion records have been unavailable since the mid-eighties, so this evidence is hard to quantify.

10　Connors was not entirely alone in this effort. The Canadian Radio-television and Telecommunications Commission (CRTC), as established by the Broadcasting Act of 1968, became increasingly interested throughout the 1970s in establishing Canadian content (CanCon) regulations for broadcasters. However, Connors often expressed the opinion that the commission was not doing enough to promote Canadian content.

11　Connors insists that Canadian material was infrequently programmed because broadcasters did not feel that material with a strongly regional flavour would be of interest to a wide listenership. Some broadcasters have claimed, however, that the real problem was that the Canadian material simply was not produced to professional standards, and that the American material was of higher quality. This position is summarized in the CRTC, *Country* 34.

12　In 1970, Jurk Krytiuk stated: "Most of the stuff these days, including C & W, is getting too sophisticated in order to appeal to the intellectual types, and the working man can't appreciate this stuff, so I'm giving them what they like" (*Canadian Composer*, May 1970, 37). Based on his work and rhetoric in the early 1970s, I assume that Connors shared his manager's sentiments at that time.

13　In the years following World War II, and especially in the 1950s, Nashville became the centre of country music production. A core of highly skilled studio musicians arose in the city, as did a number of sophisticated studios and engineers. The sound that emerged from this situation was polished, precise, and much more consistent than previous country music had been. It was explicitly engineered as a compromise between pop music and harder country sounds. Most energetically cultivated by (guitarist and producer) Chet Atkins, the style is variously called the Nashville sound, countrypolitan, the Nashville compromise, and the

Chet Atkins compromise (a good description of this style can be found in Malone 256-57). The Outlaw sound, exemplified by Waylon Jennings, Merle Haggard, and Willie Nelson, emerged as a deliberate challenge to the hegemony that the Nashville sound had achieved by the late 1950s.

14 See, for example, *Globe and Mail* August 5, 1974, 13; or June 4, 1975, 14; or *Toronto Star* September 27, 1974, E9.

15 The Canadian Academy of Recording Arts and Sciences has been the governing body of the Juno Awards since 1975.

16 It was between 1986 and 1990 that Connors gradually returned to public life: first with very limited recording activity to support special Cancon projects, then with a nationally broadcast *Morningside* interview on December 27 1988, and finally with a new Capitol Records recording contract in 1989 and a seventy-city comeback tour beginning on May 5, 1990.

17 Steve Pritchard, one of the consultants in my Master's research, is a freelance Torontonian country-music broadcaster and journalist. This statement is representative of a negotiation I have seen enacted by several of my consultants. For more details, see Echard, "Approaching."

18 Since his comeback and contract with Capitol Records, Connors's sound has been somewhat sanitized and tightened up.

19 See, for example, *Canadian Composer*, May 1972, 22; or *Toronto Star*, September 27, 1974, E9.

20 Two Stevedore Steve albums recorded by Connors's label, and featuring many of the same musicians as Connors's own recordings, are *Hard Workin' Men* (Boot, BOS-7102, 1971) and *I've Lived* (Boot, BOS-7111, 1972).

WORKS CITED

Bronner, Simon. *Old-Time Music Makers of New York State*. Syracuse: Syracuse UP, 1987.

Canadian Radio-Television and Telecommunications Commission. *The Country Music Industry in Canada*. Ottawa: CRTC, 1986.

"Can a Mynah Bird Gain Canadian Citizenship and Find Happiness as a Pop Performer?" *Canadian Composer* May 1970: 34-37.

"Catching the Charisma of Stompin' Tom Ain't Easy." *Canadian Composer* May 1972: 22.

Echard, William. "Inventing to Preserve: Novelty and Traditionalism in the Work of Stompin' Tom Connors." *Canadian Folk Music Journal* 22 (1995): 8-22.

_____. "Approaching Stompin' Tom: An Overview of the Early Work of Tom C. Connors." M.A. Thesis in musicology, York University, Toronto, 1995.

Fiske, John. *Understanding Popular Culture*. Boston: Unwin Hyman, 1989.

Keil, Charles. "Participatory Discrepancies and the Power of Music." *Music Grooves*, Ed. Charles Keil and Steven Feld. Chicago: U of Chicago P, 1994. 96-108.

_____."Motion and Feeling Through Music." *Music Grooves*. Ed. Charles Keil and Steven Feld. Chicago: U of Chicago P, 1994. 53-76.

Malone, Bill. *Country Music USA*. Rev. ed. Austin: U of Texas P, 1993.

Miller, Jack. "A Painful Journey with Stompin' Tom." *Toronto Star* September 27, 1974: E9.

Nowlan, Alden. "What's More Canadian than Stompin' Tom?" *Maclean's* August 1972: 30-31, 44-46.

Potter, Mitch. "Stompin' Tom." *Toronto Star* May 27, 1990: C1, C4.

"7,500 Fans Clap, Cheer, and Stomp for Canada's Musical Nationalist." *Globe and Mail* August 5, 1974: 13.

Small, Christopher. *Music of the Common Tongue*. New York: Riverrun, 1987.

"Stompin' Tom Awaits Industry Blacklist." *Globe and Mail* April 1, 1978: 32.

"Stompin' Tom Connors." *Canadian Composer* November 1970: 8-11, 46.

Wright, Robert. "Dream, Comfort, Memory, Despair: Canadian Popular Musicians and the Dilemma of Nationalism, 1968-72." *Canadian Music: Issues of Hegemony and Identity*. Ed. Beverley Diamond and Robert Witmer. Toronto: Canadian Scholars', 1994. 283-301.

SONGS CITED

All words and music are by Tom Connors. See discography for album information.

"Believe In Your Country." From *Believe In Your Country*.
"Big Joe Mufferaw." From *Stompin' Tom Meets Big Joe Mufferaw*.
"Bud The Spud." From *Bud The Spud*.
"The Bug Song." From *Bud The Spud*.
"Muk Luk Shoo." From *To It And At It*.
"Reversing Falls Darling." From *Bud The Spud*.
"Unity." From *The North Atlantic Squadron*.
"Wop May." From *My Stompin' Grounds*.

SELECT DISCOGRAPHY OF AVAILABLE ALBUMS

These are many of the albums currently available on CD from Capitol Records/EMI. For a complete discography of all Stompin' Tom recordings and information on the original labels, see Echard, "Approaching." The dates given are the original release year, but the catalogue numbers are those of the current Capitol CD release. As of August 2000, there is also a complete and up-to-date discography online at Connors's own Web site: <www.stompin-tom.com>.

Northland Zone (orig. *Northland's Own*). 1967. C-93044.
On Tragedy Trail. 1968. C-93045.
Bud The Spud. 1969. C-92974.
Stompin' Tom Meets Big Joe Mufferaw. 1970. C-93047.
Merry Christmas Everybody. 1970. C-93046.
Live At The Horseshoe. 1971. C-93048.
My Stompin' Grounds. 1971. C-92976.
Stompin' Tom Connors and the Moon Man Newfie (orig. *Love and Laughter*). 1971. C-92975.

Stompin' Tom and the Hockey Song. 1972. C-93049.
To It And At It. 1973. C-93050.
Stompin' Tom Meets Muk Tuk Annie. 1974. C-93051.
The North Atlantic Squadron. 1975. C-92977.
The Unpopular Stompin' Tom. 1976. C-93052.
Stompin' Tom at the Gumboot Clogeroo. 1977. C-92978.
Fiddle And Song. 1988. C-92921.
A Proud Canadian (anthology). 1990. C-80010.
Once Upon a Stompin' Tom (anthology). 1991. EMI C-97103.
More of the Stompin' Tom Phenomenon. 1991. C-95897.
Believe In Your Country. 1992. C-99599.
KIC Along With Stompin' Tom (anthology). 1993. EMI S289451.
Dr. Stompin' Tom...Eh? 1993. EMI E227225.
Long Gone to the Yukon. 1995. EMI 0-7243-835298-2-7.

"IT'S MY NATURE": THE DISCOURSE OF EXPERIENCE AND BLACK CANADIAN MUSIC

Rinaldo Walcott

The first half of the title of this essay is taken from Canadian rapper Devon's album *It's My Nature*. On the album, Devon performs a number of songs that point to the multiple influences of his unique rap as being Canadian by "nature." I explore the music of black Canadians in an attempt to engage with the discourse of experience as it is expressed in the lyrics of the music, its rhythms and the identifications that black Canadian artists make with diasporic black people elsewhere. The central concern of the essay is to shed some light on the usefulness of the discourse of experience while at the same time attempting to articulate some of the limits of such a discourse. In particular, because my focus is mainly rap music, my interest in questioning the discourse of experience is central to the music. Rap and its musicians have made much about the "realness" of their music (Toop; Rose, *Black Noise*; Potter). In the musicians' utterances rap gets its power from its ability to narrate "real" life experiences and to place those experiences in the public sphere for debate.

Reading black experiences in Canada largely through rap music and mainly male rappers, I am ambivalent about the discourse of experience as it is used for making sense of collective moments,

Notes on pages 275-76.

memories, desires, disappointments and pleasures. Rap musicians often articulate "realness" in an attempt to speak to collective experiences. My intent in questioning experience is to wrench it away from the position it currently occupies as "sacred" and to reframe it as a practice that is not assumed to be immediately transparent. I argue that experience as sacred has come to characterize individual foundational claims which are used as the basis for a singular collective narrative. In particular, the ways in which the deployment of experience and its telling have become sacred tend to close down contesting, divergent or other ways of seeing and knowing. Thus, I am interested in opening up the range of responses possible within the context of experiential discourses. I interpret black popular music in Canada as a way to point towards a different understanding of the deployments of the discourse of experience.

EXPERIENCE: A BRIEF HISTORY

The discourse of experience was quite important to the new social movements of the 1960s and after. Personal testimony opened the way for consciousness-raising and articulating important questions concerning the organization of post-World War II society. In particular, groups of citizens who had been "locked out" of institutional forms of power used the language and discourse of experience to lay claim to different and sometimes competing knowledge(s). These knowledge-forms and -claims, which were often discredited and subjugated, came to the fore through collective forms of affirmation of what was termed experience. By having individual experiences validated and affirmed by innumerable others, the procedures of institutional power arrangements increasingly came under pressure to admit to the flaws and inadequacies in hegemonic ways of knowing and to (re)arrange things differently. Thus experience as a discourse and a way of knowing worked to "overthrow" the idea that only formal institutional ways of knowing (largely male and white) were valid and valuable.

More specifically, the civil-rights and black-power movements, second-wave feminism and the gay and lesbian movement made important use of the language and discourse of experience to challenge and call into question institutional power. Personal testimony in the form of retelling a narrative of exclusion and its effects on the individual, which stood in to represent the collective experience, played a crucial role in these social movements. The discourse of experience was deployed by these social movements to demonstrate how discrimination worked and to delineate the constructedness of institutional objectivity as a form of power and as exclusion. This application of the discourse of experience was important for opening up institutional arrangements to questions from those who were "outside" the institutions.

The success of using experience this way made itself manifest in a number of important ways. Institutions were forced to recognize different experiences as ways of knowing that had much to contribute to the broadening of knowledge. By the 1980s and 1990s experience and the experiential has ascended to the realm of the sacred. That is, in many quarters, personal testimony has taken on the spectre of transparent truth-claims whereby questioning them suggests a kind of vulgarity on the part of the questioner. Therefore, the invocation of the language and discourse of experience has come to occupy a place that often carries the implicit demand that the experiential not be questioned. In fact, once experience is invoked by a speaker, writer or some other actor as the base of their knowledge-claim, affirmation is supposed to be the order of response. It is the deployment of experience and the assumption that affirmation is inevitable that I query in this essay.

QUERYING EXPERIENCE

Black Canadians' relations with their place and belonging in the nation stand out as one thing that can be used to discuss and demonstrate the importance of experience and the experiential (Walcott, "Voyage" 1997). It is to that "experience" that I shall direct what follows in this essay. My readings of the lyrics of the rap songs that follow are meant not as final statements on how to read black Canadian popular music, but rather as efforts to open up a tentative investigation into the ways in which we read experience (especially in rap) and use it both as validation and less than validation. I hope to offer a much more complex relation to the language and discourse of experience than we have come to expect.

Freud's notion of "common feeling" speaks directly to the way in which an identification with an experience can take place only in the psyche or the imaginary and therefore constitutes a feeling of sorts with the experience of the Other (43). Such feelings can constitute a collective response, but they cannot constitute a transparent collective knowing. The processes of identification are far too complex for identificatory practices to be entirely revealed or made transparent.

Yet, the experiential has a grounding in our social circumstances as well. Following Dorothy Smith, I want to suggest that the discourse of the experiential does not take its utterance only from various psychic sources (even though I believe those to be the most important), but also from how we understand and make sense of the social. Smith observes that:

> To begin from direct experience and to return to it as a constant or "test" of the adequacy of systemic knowledge is to begin from where we are located bodily. The actualities of our everyday world are already socially organized. Settings, equipment, environment, schedules, occasions, and so forth, as well as our enterprises and routines, are socially produced and concretely and symbolically organized prior to the moment at which we enter and at which inquiry begins. (23)

Smith's insight makes sense for reading Devon's song "Mr. Metro." The song is a narrative concerning police shootings in Canada, and more locally, Toronto. Devon's song is located in what Smith calls the tragic "actualities of our everyday world" (23). His experience and therefore his narrative, is "located bodily," following Smith (23), as he attempts to narrate a tale that plays itself out through the destruction (death) of mainly black male bodies:

> Metro's number one problem
> Is that no one trust them
> Causing all this tension
> For something I wouldn't even mention
> Pick up *The Star*, pick up *The Sun*
> Headline "Metro gets another one"
> And another one gone and another one gone
> And another one bites the dust
> ...
> No, no, no, no, LAPD; ease up RCMP; ease up
> Orange County; ease up
> No OPP; ease up 52; ease up
> Peel Region; ease up, don't shoot the youth
> "Mr. Metro" by Devon. Capitol Records EMI-Canada.

Devon's utterances in the song are largely framed within the collective "experiences" of black people in Canada. His attempt to articulate a narrative of collective experience for black people to identify with is given authoritative salience in its appeal to individual experiences that some people might have had and that others might have common feeling with, for various complex psychic reasons.

Despite Smith's claims and observations, it is useful to pose and make use of them in conjunction with Joan Scott's caution, in the essay "Experience," that the use of the term "experience" can often be foundational. Scott's project seeks to remove the experiential from the realm of the sacred and to ground it in the networks of contestatory knowledge claims and fractured (self?) representations. Scott writes:

> The evidence of experience works as a foundation providing both a starting point and a conclusive kind of explanation, beyond which few questions need to or can be asked. And yet it is precisely the questions excluded—questions about discourse, difference, and subjectivity, as well as about what counts as experience and who gets to make that determination—that would enable us to historicize experience, to reflect critically on the history we write about it, rather than to premise our history upon it. (33)

So, because Devon's song speaks to the reality of black life in Canada, its appeal to the experiential, the "nature" of being black in Canada, positions a particular kind of experience and narrative for blackness from which one might construct a history. Yet, Scott's warning is that such a history must be open to question and interrogation, be aware of its "foundations" or the limits of its claims, and be open to "critical reflection" of its telling and implications.

Thus experience and the experiential are not neutral utterances with uncomplicated consequences. I have chosen a song concerning the issue of policing to make this case because of its clear-cut implications for something called the black community. Clearly, police shootings seem to mark the black community, and to deploy those shootings as constituting the black experience can often lead to closing down debate at exactly the moment when it might need to occur. Police shootings can become "a conclusive kind of explanation" for black displacement in Canada. Such a position is manifest by the calypsonian whose chorus "they're supposed to serve and protect / not to shoot suspects" echoed

Devon's "Mr. Metro." The metaphor is taking hold as a communal experiential narrative. Therefore, when Scott asserts that to "understand the operations of the complex and changing discursive processes by which identities are ascribed, resisted, or embraced and...indeed achieve their effect because they aren't noticed" (33), other positions outside of the foundational experiential ones are invited. Thus, policing must not and cannot constitute the only narrative through which blackness in Canada is understood despite its salience and reality.

But, once again, to accentuate the ambivalence about reading experience as an all-or-nothing game, it is important to point out that experience comes to us from the world we inhabit. Smith argues: "If we begin from the world as we actually experience it, it is at least possible to see that we are indeed located and that what we know of the other is conditional upon that location. There are and must be different experiences of the world and different bases of experience" (25). While I am in agreement with Smith's general emphasis of being aware of how we are located in the world and how that location influences our relations with others, I must add that Smith fails to at least explicitly account for the psychic realm or the place of the imaginary. I want to suggest that it is the space of the imaginary that opens up interesting ways to read experience beyond the repetitions of the same.

To trouble and worry rap's narratives of experience or "realness" means that we must enter into the realm of the imaginary and extract from it the sites where the "social" and the "psychic" come together, collapse and are made possible and impossible. Rap music is one of those artifacts that allows us to read in multiple ways the important and immediate concerns of youth today—in particular black youth— especially at the level of the psychic. Black youth are my focus, not just because they invented rap and hip-hop culture, but because I believe that their subaltern status in North America renders the insights of their discredited and subjugated knowledges crucial to any pedagogy of liberation.[1]

THE SPACE OF THE IMAGINARY IN RAP

At the same time I posit that it is necessary to read rap music for the information and narratives that it conveys about the social lives of black North American youth. Such readings must not produce rap as constituting "protest" and realism" only. Thus, rap music must not be read only as constituting the "real" or "naturalistic" narratives of black North American lived experiences. Rather, a complex interplay must be achieved between "the real" and "the not real" of rap music. It is at the in-between position of the real and the not real that some moment of clarity might be seen/heard in rap. Given the narratives of rap music, it is sometimes possible to use those narratives to begin discussions that understand the music as a popular mirror of black North American experiences.

Following the social theorist Ann Game, who argues for a "different sociology," one that does not fall for the idea that sociological narrative can reproduce the real, I also call for a different socio-cultural reading. That different socio-cultural reading is one where the social is also understood as constituted through the imaginary and does not rely on the assertion of statistics and narratives that supposedly represent (mirror) real actors. As Game suggests, researchers need to recognize that the social reality that they claim to mirror in their narratives is a "fictional reflection" of the events encountered in the moment of research. Therefore, the requirement is to better understand temporality, exceptions to the rule and the imaginary as sites whose mapping is always contingent, fluid and crucial to the (re)telling. What was called "gangsta" rap is a good example. Social research might suggest that the narratives of gangsta rap seem to replicate real-life examples of violence. But when we consider that most rappers come from middle-class families we must rethink whether those narratives of violence are based upon a sociology of actual experience, or rather, whether they are propelled by fantasy and an assumption that we all share knowledge of an increasingly violent world.

Rap often makes use of the "economy of stereotype" to anticipate and manipulate our response to lyrics. Consider the above example of gangsta rap: rappers have continually exploited the stereotype of the fast-talking, tough and dangerous black man. Such use of that particular stereotype makes the commercialization of gangsta rap a reality. This use of the economy of stereotype is in fact related to psychic responses and the audience's actual and imaginary lives. At the same time, to read rap as constituting the "true to life" narratives of black Canadians would be to render the realm of fantasy—that is, the not real—as outside the scope and the narrative construction of rap music and its makers. Rap is not just a mirror or reflection of black Canadian experiences; it is also a mapping of desire, which is much more difficult to situate and pin down. Discussions of the imaginary have been lacking in rap criticism.

Robin D. G. Kelly has broached the subject in terms of gangsta rap and demonstrated that, while much of gangsta rap is violent and misogynist, the raps have a long history in black diasporic verbal play. His genealogy traces gangsta rap back to the "baad man" aesthetic and the blues tradition, citing working-class black male verbal play at the turn of the century as one source for making sense of gangsta rap. Kelly thus poses the question concerning which aspects of black culture will be supported and which will be called into question. From his position it is clear that the nihilism of gangsta rap must be called into question, and I concur:

> Given the central place that misogyny occupies in the gangsta/baadman aesthetic, it would be hard to trust a straight sociological answer to this question. Furthermore, I do not believe rap music can or ever intended to represent the true and complex character of male/female relations among black urban youth. Too many critics have taken the easy way out by reading rap lyrics literally rather than developing a nuanced understanding of actual social relations among young people, in all of their diversity and complexity. And there is no reason in the world to believe that any music constitutes a mirror of social relations that can be generalized for entire groups.[2] (216-17)

Kelly's observations are important because he speaks directly to the issue of the experiential and the ways in which some rap musicians and critics have been complicit in producing particular readings of rap. In particular, a nuanced reading would search for the arguments that refuse to pathologize black family life as the source for the production of troubling musical lyrics. The ghost of the Moynihan Report can haunt musical criticism. The insistence on needing rap as a representation of the experiential has limited what kinds of histories have been thus far written about the genre.

In a general discussion of Canadian popular music, Michael Taft makes the case for understanding Canadian pop music as "eclectic and syncretic" (197). His analysis of Canadian popular sound fits well with interpretations of rap music as a form. Rap music is what Gilles

Deleuze and Felix Gauttari would call a rhizome: "A rhizome cease-lessly establishes connections between semiotic chains, organizations of power, and circumstances relative to the arts, sciences and social struggles.…The rhizome includes the best and the worst" (7); "A rhizome has no beginning and no end; it is always in the middle, between things, interbeing" (25). The rhizomatic nature of rap is its ability to spread across wide expanses gathering everything in its way and making what it gathers its own. Let me elaborate. If we accept that rap is rhizomatic, then reading it as a mirror of a one-dimensional narrative of urban black experiences would be unnecessarily misleading. Desire and fantasy play key and important roles in rap that cannot be under-stood if the narratives of rap are viewed only as a mirror of the real. Despite rap musicians' appeal and insistence on the real, rap's narra-tives also articulate fantasies and desires, which, while posed in the lan-guage and discourse of experience and the real, are not representative of the real. We should resist reading all of rap's narratives as actual wants and needs: they are truly desires—that is to say, unachievable.

Let me demonstrate by way of a detour. The theme song of the popu-lar American sitcom *The Fresh Prince of Bel-Air* is a trope on North American obsessions with violence. The narrative of the song suggests that the Fresh Prince (played by Will Smith) is sent to live with his "aunty and uncle in Bel-Air" after a fight erupts on the basketball court. The song explains how a boy from the ghetto would end up living in Bel-Air and asks the audience to use our sense of "real" violence in the inner cities of North America to understand a scenario that is actually a pretty weak plot premise. Yet the song, and the resulting sitcom, works because it ushers in a fantasy: escaping to a wealthy enclave where one has only to worry about what kind of fun to have. As a song, then, "Fresh Prince of Bel-Air" inaugurates a fantasy, and, at the same time, as a trope it uses our imagined sense of "real" violence to capture us as an audience.

Rap musicians are what Jacques Attali would call the *jongleurs* of postmodern North America. In *Noise*, Attali describes the myriad ways in which the practices and actions of the *jongleurs* of the Middle Ages exceeded a simple category of music. The *jongleurs'* actions were rhi-zomatic in that their practices not only produced music, but moved into the realm of political stabilities and instabilities, which, he argues, were in effect music (14-20). Rap musicians' practices also exceed the too-easy confines of what commodified forms of music have come to mean. Let me elaborate by way of example. The turntable, which was initially of crucial importance to rap music, was in the late seventies and early eighties relatively cheap and on its way into the dump heap of technological history, as were vinyl records. The rise of the compact disc player and the CD made vinyl records almost obsolete. The accessability of vinyl records and blank audio tapes for recording made the initial dissemination of rap music easy for poor, urban black youths.

However, rap music made use of the refuse of post-industrial North America by reclaiming vinyl and the turntable and imbuing them with what is valued most in capitalist society—the capacity to produce desired commodities. Sampling and versioning pre-recorded music, layered over with their own words—often strident critiques of American capitalism and the decaying inner city—the "new" songs/sounds could be disseminated in black communities relatively easily and cheaply about twenty years ago, giving birth to rap. This capsule history of rap speaks also to its political significance. The invention of rap gestures to both its social and psychic relations: the fantasies of pleasure and the possible escape from poverty, and the resourcefulness of using one's social environment to give birth to an art form of immense political significance.

CANADIAN RAP: THE TENSIONS OF BELONGING

On the Dream Warriors' first album, *And now the legacy begins...*, they sample and rewrite the theme song of the once-popular Canadian television game show *Definition* (CTV, 1974-90). Their appropriation is interesting because of the ways in which their sample speaks to a much more complex history. Quincy Jones, the African-American composer and music impresario, composed the theme song of *Definition*. The song "My Definition of a Boombastic Jazz Style" is a rewriting by the Dream Warriors of what we have come to know as "Canadian," an identity that often has no place for imagining blackness within. The desire for a national homeland by diasporic blacks is always mythic and always unachievable. Even when Africa and returns to Africa stand in as the real representation, the national homeland remains an unachievable desire. Yet the Dream Warriors take what might be the most Canadian of artifacts and remake them to speak to a collective black experience of alienation from the nation and a desire for a possible national homeland. At the same time because of the nature of the song's composition the

Dream Warriors' appropriation worries any too rigid boundaries of nation, allowing them elsewhere on the album ("Ludi") to enter into identificatory relations with blacks outside Canada.

The appropriation of the *Definition* theme song is important because its use offers us (readers/listeners) an avenue for thinking more clearly about the language and discourse of experience. Particularly, this avenue can provide ways to question institutional power arrangements without a recourse to individual affirmation. By this I mean that the Dream Warriors are not involved in defining merely themselves but are concerned with definitions of who is in and out of the nation. Thus, the Dream Warriors' sample and version of the *Definition* theme song does not force us (Canadians) to focus our attention on individuals, but rather requires that we address the collective narrative of the nation whereby some presences are absented and must constantly assert their presence. But this rather abstract articulation of the Dream Warriors in what they call their "boombastic jazz style" has its counterpart elsewhere in a fashion that is much more clear-cut.

Maestro Fresh-Wes's third album title announces and makes clear his ambivalence about the nation. *Naaah, Dis Kid Can't Be from Canada?!!!* is hyper-commentary characteristic of rap musicians. The role of the experiential conditions the choice of the musicians but directs us to the collectivity, opening up important questions for our consideration. I have argued elsewhere that Fresh-Wes's title has to be read as doubled (Walcott, "Voyage"). This is so because he is not only speaking to his marginality in the Canadian nation, which he left to live and work in New York, but he is also launching a critique of the assumption that the best rap comes from the U.S.

What is particularly interesting about Fresh-Wes's hyper-commentary on his album is that he walks the thin line between reality and fantasy. The desire to achieve recognition is both real and a fantasy, and it is the twining of both of those tensions that occasions his move to the U.S. Fresh-Wes is aware that living in the U.S. can expose his music to a marketing machine, which might help in the process to fulfil his fantasy of musical success. His sense of not belonging is both state-imposed—lack of support for his type of music by radio stations—and a condition of how he sees himself in the world—as belonging to a diasporic group of people whose allegiances to nation are never entirely secure.

Following Michael Taft's above-mentioned reading of Canadian popular musical taste and listening patterns as eclectic, let me conclude this essay with music from another genre, jazz, in particular Joe Sealy's *Africville Suite*, an album of history, memory and resistance. Sealy remembers the destruction of Africville in Nova Scotia in haunting jazz rhythms and poetry.[3] His musical response to an attempt to literally erase a black presence is an important addition to the ways in which Canadian rappers have attempted to narrate such experiences. Yet, Sealy's music does not lend itself easily to foundational claims. Like rap, jazz is itself a rhizome, but the difference between jazz artists and rap artists is in the ways in which they make use of the discourses of experience, history and "realness" to construct their art.

Sealy engages in much of the border-crossing the rap artists engage in, but his border-crossing is situated differently both historically and experientially. Sealy's "rememory" of Africville is the story of the collective and communal common feeling and does not begin with the individual experiential claim to utter its narrative. Thus, while the destruction of Africville represents individual moments—all witnessed through an attempt at black erasure from the nation—*Africville Suite* resists making a foundational and defining "black" claim. Instead, the album gives the feeling or sensation that the story of Africville is just one story among others.

Sealy's *Africville Suite* is a collection of twelve poetic songs beginning with "Poem #1" and ending with "Song of Hope." Through the poetry of David Woods, the lyrics of Dan Hill and an ensemble of singers and readers like Jackie Richardson, Sealy attempts to bring Africville back to life in song. Songs on the album, like "Train's Comin'" and "Duke's in Town," speak to the vibrancy and excitement that existed in Africville, and act as a counter-narrative to reasons for Africville's destruction. "Duke's in Town" chronicles the arrival of Duke Ellington, whose second wife's relatives lived in Africville and therefore occasioned Ellington's visits. "Train's Comin'" speaks to the way in which the train played a major role in black peoples' lives, not only passing through their communities and dividing black communities from neighbouring white communities, but also in relation to employment for black men as porters, baggage handlers and so on. *Africville Suite* is an exemplary album because Sealy is able to combine a number of elements that speak to a cultural memory of oppression and, in this instance, sonic resistance without recourse to individual narratives of the experiential as validation for his project.

Black popular music is often caught between the individual and the collective (blues and calypso are good examples of this bind) trying to produce a narrative(s) that can speak to both but often obscuring one, with the other coming to stand for the sum. However, by continually querying the experiential we can avoid the pitfalls and blind spots of singular collective meanings. To question the experiential in black popular musics is to question how those musics have been traditionally read as anthropological statements about blackness. Black musics have come to be read as scripts that offer insights into black life in ways that other forms of representation might not. While it is correct that black musics offer insights into the economic, social and cultural events of individual and collective black lives, reading the musics as only insider knowledge subtracts from the ways in which music also plays an important role in fantasy, role reversals and other matters of the psyche. However, it is only through questioning the experiential and the narratives that encode experience and fabricate the assumptions of its certainty that we might arrive at a number of other and potentially more interesting ways of reading black musics. We must try to formulate reading practices of black musics that exceed the desire for insider knowledge of a black experience and attempt also to read the musics for the pleasures, fantasies and disappointments. Such a reading practice would take us beyond the confines of an experiential narrative of oppression to a place where a fuller appreciation of black musical genius might be understood.

NOTES

1   By referring to black youth as subaltern I mean to signal the ways in which mass culture represents them as different and alien. But more specifically I mean to call attention to their class positions and their relative lack of access to the resources of the society for making and renewing their lives. Black youth in the 1990s are the perennial not-quite-citizens of North America.

2   In this particular essay Kelly is at pains to point out the misogyny in some forms of rap, specifically gangsta rap. For further discussions of the debate concerning rap's misogyny see Williams, "Two Words"; Rose, "Black Texts" and *Black Noise*; and Davies, "Black Bodies."

3   The destruction of Africville in Nova Scotia was authorized and sanctioned by the Halifax city authorities. The demolition of Africville began

in the 1960s and was complete by the end of the decade. Most of the black residents opposed the decision to destroy their community. Africville had existed as a black homeland for more than 150 years. For information from the perspectives of the residents see *The Spirit of Africville*.

WORKS CITED

Africville Genealogical Society. *The Spirit of Africville*. Halifax: Formac, 1992.

Attali, Jacques. *Noise: The Political Economy of Music*. Trans. Brian Massumi. Minneapolis: U of Minnesota P, 1989.

Davies, Carole Boyce. "Black Bodies, Carnivalized Bodies: Afro-American Women's Struggles with Carnival's Meanings." *Border/lines* 34/35 (1994): 53-57.

Deleuze, Gilles, and Felix Guattari. *A Thousand Plateaus*. Trans. Brian Massumi. Minneapolis: U of Minneasota P, 1987.

Freud, Sigmund. *Civilization and Its Discontents*. Trans. James Strachey. New York: Norton, 1961.

Game, Ann. *Undoing the Social: Towards a Deconstructive Sociology*. Toronto: U of Toronto P, 1991.

Kelly, Robin D. G. *Race Rebels: Culture, Politics, and the Black Working Class*. New York: Freedom, 1994.

Potter, Russell. *Spectacular Vernaculars: Hip Hop and the Politics of Postmodernism*. Albany: SUNY, 1995.

Rose, Tricia. "Black Texts/Black Contexts." *Black Popular Culture*. Ed. Gina Dent. Seattle: Bay, 1992. 223-27.

_____. *Black Noise: Rap Music and Black Culture in Contemporary America*. Hanover: Wesleyan UP, 1994.

Scott, Joan. "Experience." *Feminists Theorize the Political*. Ed. Judith Butler and Joan Scott. New York: Routledge, 1992. 22-40.

Smith, Dorothy. *The Conceptual Practices of Power: A Feminist Sociology of Knowledge*. Toronto: U of Toronto P, 1990.

Taft, Michael. "Syncretizing Sound: The Emergence of Canadian Popular Music." *The Beaver Bites Back?: American Popular Culture in Canada*. Ed. David H. Flaherty and Frank E. Manning. Montreal: McGill-Queen's UP, 1993. 197-208.

Toop, David. *The Rap Attack: African Jive to New York Hip Hop*. London: Pluto, 1984.

Walcott, Rinaldo. "'Keep On Movin': Rap, Black Atlantic Identities and the Problem of Nation." *Black Like Who? Writing, Black, Canada*. Toronto: Insomniac, 1997. 71-94.

_____. "'Voyage Through the Multiverse': Contested Canadian Identities." *Border/lines* 36 (1995): 49-52.

Williams, Sherley-Anne. "Two Words on Music: Black Community." *Black Popular Culture*. Ed. Gina Dent. Seattle: Bay, 1992. 164-72.

DISCOGRAPHY

Devon. *It's My Nature*. Capital Records EMI of Canada, CA 99645, 1992.

Dream Warriors. *And now the legacy begins...* Island Records Ltd., 391310-2, 1991.

Maestro Fresh-Wes. *Naaah, Dis Kid Can't Be from Canada?!!!"* Attic Records Limited, ACD 1397, 1993.

Sealy, Joe. *Africville Suite*. Sea Jam Recording Inc., 100 1997.

"COWBOYOGRAPHY": MATTER AND MANNER IN THE SONGS OF IAN TYSON

Terrance Cox

With his 1983 release of *Old Corrals and Sagebrush*, Canadian singer-songwriter Ian Tyson began a second and idiosyncratic career in a branch of popular music that he calls "cowboyography." Over the next decade, he also remained a working rancher on the eastern slopes of the Rockies, raising cutting horses on land that royalties from his songwriting had enabled him to buy. Through the recording of four subsequent albums of cowboyographic songs, Tyson's two chosen vocations complement each other.[1] The resultant works comprise both a documentary of contemporary cowboy life and an instance of conscious myth-making as Tyson redefines the "cowboy-artist" for our times.

These recordings have been highly, if somewhat surprisingly, successful, with both intended audiences and beyond, winning awards and considerable sales.[2] They have earned Tyson bardic status within renascent cowboy-arts circles. The critical and popular acclaim given these works, locally and throughout North America, augments our notions of Canadian contemporary "alternative" popular music. As up-to-date in their conception and strategy as metafiction and narrowcasting, Tyson's songs are otherwise as unhip as waltzes and shuf-

Notes on pages 292-95.

fles or breaking colts to the saddle. They counter prevailing mainstream popular culture's celebration of the transient with an
archivist's aesthetic.

This paper presents critical analyses of representative songs from
Tyson's "cowboyography" in a discussion of major themes, recurring
practices and pertinent contexts. It argues for a coherent vision and purpose, apparent in the songs' prominent and constant elements, which
include the cowboy cultural allusions as metaphor; the particular focus
on other analogous artists; the use and adaptation of musical conventions; and the "northern" aspects of Tyson's "range." It concludes with
the consideration of a "master" song that incorporates the essentials of
Tyson's work in an extraordinary performance.

"Springtime," the first song on his album *Cowboyography* (1986),
may be heard as a concise introduction to Tyson's essential themes and
practices. It presents springtime's arrival on the eastern slope of the
Rockies, cataloguing particular signs of its "sighing all along the
creek" in the return of wildlife to hills made almost bare of snow by a
recent chinook. In this highly specific setting, Tyson refrains instances
of cowboys at work with seven variants on the phrase "Larry's pulling
calves at the Quarter Circle S," each one followed by the song's burden
line: "We made it through another on the northern range."[3] There are
two significant lyrical departures from the repetitions of the pulling-
calves chorus: in the third repeat, Tyson sings instead of a brood mare
asleep in the afternoon sun, shedding her hair, and alters the burden line
to comment that it is time for a change; in the final iteration, the song
becomes self-reflexive as it sings of a different kind of cowboy work:
"Ian's in the hills trying to write songs."

The music in all its aspects is exemplary of Tyson's songwriting and
performance. It is conventionally structured in theme and bridge stanzas and chorus, with an elegantly simple, ascending/descending
melody built on standard changes (in this case, D to G to A), with a relative minor bridge (to B minor and E minor) for the chorus. The opening verse and chorus are sung a capella by Tyson and background
vocalist Cindy Church. This verse is twice repeated, once with
weather-report lyrics and, then as a fully scored reprise, to close.
Accompaniment comes from the usual band of acoustic and electric
guitars, pedal steel, fiddle, piano, bass and drums, playing in a subdued,
balanced and gently rhythmic arrangement.[4]

Canonical elements of this song's lyrics include the specificity of its world: the wild and domestic fauna; the flora and weather signs: all the particulars of eastern slope and northern range, presented as both actual and as having mythic resonance. For instance, the chorus names of people and their outfits (George's T-Y, Waddie's Little E, Allan's Bar 4 Oarlock) all sound authentic. They are certainly not chosen for rhyme or mellifluous ease. One readily hears these as documentary, as naming Tyson's working cowboy neighbours, the "we" who survive together the unspoken-of winter. They share this chosen common life and place and serve as the primary audience for the very songs about their labour and locale that Tyson is trying to write. Two variants on the naming gesture place "Gary...at the old stampede" and "Lonnie...at the top of the world," in each case extending the range of activity in time and grandeur.

The structural devices that single out the brood mare and the song-writing "Ian" for emphasis reveal other constants in his songs: the prominent role given to animals, especially but not exclusively horses, and their presentation as analogously "other." In Tyson's songs, as in cowboy life, the horse is a ubiquitous figure, in actual and referential senses.[5] The horse is the cowboy's working vehicle in practical and metaphoric terms. It becomes metonymic of nature's spirit, tenuously allied to us. Tyson's horses, as here, are very often female. This brood mare, in the afternoon sun, asleep and shedding winter, embodies springtime in a companion animal; by juxtaposition with "Ian's...trying to write songs," it acts as an aesthetic totem, as a muse. Although it functions as an analogue to the cowboy-artist, the horse remains "other"; in the complex relationship between horse and human, recurringly present throughout these recordings, Tyson also finds insights into human bonds.

Placing the songwriter's craft and his muse amongst particulars of ranch life and work in contemporary southern Alberta, the song "Springtime" is overtly representative of Tyson's cowboyography; it is explicit about the methods and purposes coherently implicit elsewhere. All his songs document and celebrate, from within, a judiciously detailed, profoundly resonant, demandingly difficult and ironically beloved culture. This song's burden line attests to that culture's never-certain survival.

In "Springtime," as in numerous other songs, the protagonist-singer is obviously an autobiographical figure: he is recognizably the owner of the Tyson ranch, outside Longview, Alberta, seventy kilometres south of Calgary; a man of a certain age, born and partly raised on Vancouver Island; a man whose English father migrated to the Canadian West, drawn by the lore of Will James's novels, becoming, for a short while, a working cowboy. He is "Ian," a former rodeo rider (an experience recounted in his 1960s song, "Someday Soon") and, with ex-wife Sylvia Fricker Tyson, once an internationally successful folk musician, the man who is now in these Albertan hills, "trying to write songs."[6]

For other songs in the cowboyography series, Tyson assumes the persona of another working cowboy, always with specific contextual givens; indeed, he is sometimes an actual person (for example, in the songs "Claude Dallas" and "Ballad of Jack Link"). In several rodeo songs, among them the aforementioned "Someday Soon," "Non-Pro Song" and "Rodeo Road," the singer is one whose skills and purpose make sport out of cowboy work. The rodeo performer, like the cowboy artist, celebrates the culture by representing it on the public stage. These other working cowboys share with "Ian" an acute eye and ear for details and the opportunity and ability to reflect cogently on the life and work in demotic idiom and arresting imagery. Each shares a special affinity for horses and adopts the same "damned-fool" ironic stance towards all that is beloved: the land, its creatures, wild and domesticated, the vicissitudes of work and fellowship.

When Tyson engages that tradition of song dating from the troubadours, if not from Solomon, and essays a "love song," his romantic overtures retain an unusually prominent role for cowboy-culture particulars, as contextual details and sources of metaphor. Even while singing a lullaby for his daughter, Adelita Rose, Tyson wishes her dreams of "pretty little horses."

A figure much resembling "Ian" and his alternates appears elsewhere, as the narrator-protagonist in the nineteenth-century songs from the prairies/great plains cowboy tradition with which Tyson punctuates his otherwise largely self-composed recordings. These include such songs as "Windy Bill," "Leavin' Cheyenne," "Whoopee Ti Yi Yo" and even "Home on the Range."[7] In so doing, Tyson cites his sources and analogues and also asserts the continuity of "tradition and individual talent" within cowboy culture.

When Tyson sings these historical songs and when, on significant occasions, he writes songs set in the past, he leaves behind our moment and his usual procedures and emphasis. When such songs sound notes that may seem merely yearning or sentimental, Tyson perhaps succumbs to nostalgia. To present cowboy culture through wistful filters of longing, however, is antithetical to his artistic purpose. In most of his work, Tyson insists on the present-tense reality of cowboy life; it is not merely historical (nor fictional). The historical serves the present as a source of aesthetic analogues. This is especially apparent in a number of songs where parallels between the composer and the protagonist are even more telling, those where the subject is a historical cowboy artist, such as the painter Charlie Russell of "The Gift" and "the man they call Will James," the Québécois writer of Western fiction, and Tyson's father's inspiration.[8]

The song "Will James," from the 1984 sessions augmenting the original *Old Corrals and Sagebrush*, celebrates the virtues of James's craft, his imaginative grasp of a chosen world, and how these affect the singer, in his practical as well as his aesthetic life. The relationship between James and the singer presents a model of complex integrity between art and life. In its opening stanza, the singer recounts his father's gift of many books, recalling as his continuing favourites, even though he is now long past his childhood, Will James's "tales of wild and windy slopes." The second and third stanzas name the virtues of these works of western fiction, beginning with what the singer deems a "perfect combination" James had achieved by "living of his cowboy dreams" and so making direct links between his life and art. He notes that James's heroes were not so much the cowboys as their horses, comments on the realistic clarity of their drawing, such that "[o]n every page they'd come alive / And jump straight out at you." In a bridging chorus, the singer adds to his portrait of the other cowboy artist such aspects as coyote-like stealth and a taste for whiskey. He sings his esteem of James's works as "still the very best," and, bringing the song briefly into the present, addresses the audience: "So I've memorized those pictures, boys."

The last stanza "remembers back" more than three decades,[9] when he ("a city kid") was a feckless novice, breaking colts. Faced with a problematic task, the singer speaks the words "What would Will James do?" and places himself (and his song) in a continuum of correspondences between art and life, between writer and reader, singer and audience. In the last two lines, he assumes a voice of tall-tale summation

("And you know it was the damnedest thing"), which then, typically, resolves by understatement ("But it kind of got me through").

Tyson refers in this song to James's fiction as "pictures." Although James did indeed illustrate his stories with line drawings, it is also the case that the models of artistic process and purpose celebrated in Tyson's cowboyography share basic elements that are not determined by the form of their particular art, be it painting, fiction or music. His songs about other cowboy artists espouse *verité* aesthetics: directness; clarity; the vivid transcription of detail and specifics that creates memorability. Beyond the embrace of such principles, these songs exhibit little concern with theoretical issues of structure or mode; they assume, without question, conventional tropes and practices, from sunset rides to standard chord changes. Tyson's prototypes are presented as firm in their allegiance to artistic methods that continue established folk traditions, and he, in emulation of them, seldom shows interest in formal experiment or in expressing anxiety over the means and purpose of making art.

These artist-hero songs articulate a common vision of what art is for. Tyson's tribute to the nineteenth-century American cowboy painter Charlie Russell, "The Gift" (from *Cowboyography*), is most explicit in this regard. It presents art as having both a documentary and a mythic purpose. Art like Russell's records a present reality as accurately as possible, an entity valuable for its own sake, made more urgently so by its threatened loss to a forgotten past. But for the work of artists like Russell, the future does not know its origins, and subsequent artists have neither source nor models, no access to the archives of human existence, no context for contemporary experience. In such a conservative, if not old-fashioned, conception of its role, art is depicted as a "second nature," a parallel to natural creation, its making as a godlike gesture, no less so for revealing human foibles.

"The Gift" presents Russell's legend, one "every cowboy knows," from his St. Louis birth to an afterlife audience with God, and tells how "Kid Russell," in 1880s Montana, found a new home and his complementary vocations. The singer praises the detailed accuracy of Russell's paintings, from "light on horsehide shining" to "twisting wrist of the Houlihan throw," the thoroughness of his observation and the verisimilitude in its rendering. He is careful to establish that both Russell's subject and his skill are gifts: "God hung the stars over Judith Basin / God put the magic in young Charlie's hand."

God is also the protagonist of the interpolated choruses, the maker of "Montana for the wild man / For the Peigan, the Sioux and Crow." The singer judges God's greatest gift as having been "saved for Charlie." By the lyrics' deliberately ambiguous phrasing, that gift may be understood to be Montana's landscape, Russell's artistry and/or the specific charge God is cited as making: "Said get her all down before she goes—Charlie" because "she's bound to go."

In the final verse comes Russell's death and apotheosis; God gives the Kid his afterlife job: "You're in charge of sunsets up in old Montana / Cause I can't paint them quite as good as you." The mythic task is no sooner pronounced, in hyperbolic manner, than any hint of hubris is undercut by the verse's conclusion: "And when you're done—go out and have a few / And, Nancy Russell, make sure it's just two."

"The Gift" is but one of many songs where Tyson's other cowboy is American. Cowboy culture crosses the border, no less so than the cattle and cutting-horse trade and the rodeo circuit. Tyson's songs are matter-of-fact in their frequent use of American settings and characters. Taken as a whole, however, the works are also clear about their home "on the *northern* range." The many references to Canadian particulars are equally casual and unabashed. Among the songs are several that show prominent "Canadian consciousness," in both their matter and manner.

One song of Tyson's first songwriting career, "Four Strong Winds," the one that underwrote both his ranch and second musical career (when Neil Young included it on his highly successful 1978 album, *Comes A Time*), has indeed entered said Canadian consciousness. So thoroughly established in the popular Canadian canon is this song of permanent things, transient work and tenuous relations "way out there" in Alberta that it belongs on a very short list of alternative national anthems. Tyson records "Four Strong Winds" with his augmented studio band, extra fiddles and backup vocals, added mandolin and accordion, for *I Outgrew The Wagon*.

From the 1982 sessions for *Old Corrals and Sagebrush* comes the song "Alberta's Child," where issues of Canadianness and the border, implicit elsewhere, are specifically addressed. Its two verses directly contrast regional variants within cowboy culture, Texan and Albertan. The criteria are all cultural markers that "cross the Great Divide":[10] "Copenhagen chew" and Coors beer versus "too much damn wind and not enough whiskey"; "your lovers and your fighters, wild brahma bull riders" opposed to "up north" with "saddle broncs…hockey and honky-tonks"; the music of Waylon and Willie against "[o]ld Wilf Carter 78s." Attitudinal differences are noted: Texans "[a]in't a bit bashful about speakin' their minds" nor to "sing of her glories all in song;" Albertans make do with "[d]umb stuff like chores when it's twenty below." The contrasts establish clear differences in the two cultures and, by connotation, in their attendant values. In performance, the literal negatives on the Canadian side ("too much," "not enough") are heard as ironic; the singer's cultural preferences for the "dumb stuff" are unmistakable.

The music for these lyrically contrasting verses is likewise performed with differing timbres and arrangement, reinforcing the thematic burden of the song. The Texan verse gets an electric, somewhat raunchy, contemporary country inflection that may verge on parody; the Albertan verse is acoustically scored, subdued but augmented by old-fashioned extra timbres, such as prominent mandolin and fiddle.

The lyrical oppositions of value, echoed in the musical settings, suggest a conflict more between aesthetic than national issues. Tyson's songs are not "country"; they are "western." The hats his cowboys wear are not a costume in their "act"; their citizenship is irrelevant to their authenticity. Nonetheless, they do often speak with a recognizably Canadian inflection. For instance, this song's aggrandizing moment gets a familiarly Canadian ironic deflation in the last lines of the stanza, where the singer concludes that he will "always be Alberta's child" though "he may go to hell or even Vancouver"; in so saying, he expresses succinctly the attitudinal counterpart to the Texan bombast. The Canadianness of Tyson's voice can be heard in subtle accents that speak with notes of ironic distance from American boasts.

Tyson's oeuvre includes two versions of the paradigmatic love song, "Old Corrals and Sagebrush," on the so-titled first disc and, slightly revised, on the fifth and most recent, *Eighteen Inches of Rain*. Both performances bracket the erotic longing of the chorus ("I'd like nothing better / Than to lay these eyes on you") with verses listing other things the singer loves, which are, not surprisingly, specific icons out of cowboy culture and examples of its musical tradition. In the first category are the titular items, ponderosa pines, and "cowgirls in old pick-up trucks;" in the second, "old time waltzes / George Jones and Emmy Lou [Harris]."[11] Typically, the second verse brings together the beloved, with whom "[t]here'd be nothing sweeter / Than to spend the night," and memories of her singing the Bob Wills 1940 western swing classic, "Rose of San Antoine." The song's idiom requires enumerative listings of the singer's protestations of love, especially as attenuated by long absence. Tyson here augments such statements by placing the singer's depth of feeling for the beloved in the context of these treasures of cowboy culture, suggesting that her worth to him, so measured, is all the greater.

Often, Tyson's ostensible love songs seem to be as much for the cowboy life itself as for the beloved who happens to be along for the ride. Such a song is "Rocks Begin to Roll" from the second sessions for *Old Corrals and Sagebrush* and which he reprises for the 1991 CD, *And Stood There Amazed.* [12] An insight into Tyson's musical practices comes from considering some sonic differences between the two recorded versions. The 1984 original has the usual arrangement of conventional instruments, cowboy band and chorus, in the background, playing a moderate shuffle. In the 1991 version, the music sounds more to the foreground, with a piano and band introduction, two verses of guitar solos, and a piano coda; a more complex interpolation of instruments; crescendos and special effects (for example, an imitative tumbling drum roll that traverses the entire kit during the singing of the burden line); and a distinctly heavier backbeat rhythm.

These musical changes enhance resonances that the lyrics already exploit, the musical and sexual connotations of the phrase "rocks begin to roll." The song's title also serves as burden line, concluding its chorus. That chorus celebrates the destination "on the eastern slope" where the singer wishes soon to be, that place he is "going to travel on the gravel" towards. In the first verse, he journeys in the company of "sixteen broncs unbroken." In the second verse, he invites the beloved along; she is a woman with "a buckaroo heart." The chorus sings of a paradise "way out back of back of beyond" where the singer longs to be left ("to cope"), where "the circle stays unbroken / When the rocks begin to roll." This multi-allusive assertion of virtue in a beloved place suggests both continuity and new beginnings. The reference to the Carter Family's "Will The Circle Be Unbroken" lends notes of spirituality as well as of a musical tradition. While the phrase "rocks begin to roll" may recall the gravel of the escape road, or derive from obscure cowboy argot and lore, it also invokes the musical idiom of rock and roll. That term, like jazz before it, has been, since at least turn of this century, musicians' slang for sexual intercourse. It is with that resonance that the singer completes his invitation to the beloved to share his life and place in paradise: "you can rock and roll me," and, reflexively, the updated version of the song, uncharacteristically, rocks.

The significant link between timbre and connotation in Tyson's musical settings, apparent most obviously when he departs from standard procedures, as in the second "Rocks Begin to Roll," is nonetheless present in all the songs. The generic conventions of other musics are simply that—other. His works show little interest in formal experimentation or innovation. He assumes the instrumentation and presentation of the established western musical idiom, at least in part, as a targetting gesture; he narrowcasts his address to a known audience. These are the sounds, the rhythms and timbres of waltzes and shuffles, that his audience accepts as familiar, aesthetically satisfying, and/or perceives as fit to the milieu of cowboy culture, where these sounds are normative. When Tyson occasionally breaks from western musical conventions to reinforce his lyrics, it is clear that these departures likewise assume a resonance between musical idioms and specific cultures. For another succinct example, in the song "Old Alberta Moon," from *Old Corrals*, he has the band deviate from their honky-tonk manner only for the recurring line "Toronto may be rhythm and blues," where they play a passably funky line. With like purpose, for "Since The Rain," from *I Outgrew The Wagon*, he puts the chorus, with its burden line "It's like Africa tonight across the plain," to a loping reggae beat. Exotic transformation of the familiar landscape is echoed by Third World musical allusions.

In both his variance from the expectations of the popular love song by linking lore and eros, and in his occasional and sanctioned departures from musical orthodoxy, Tyson, most often, affirms the values of cowboy culture and its conventions of song. There is, however, one remarkable instance where conventional wisdom and standard procedure are subjected to challenge, with extraordinary results. The major themes and recurring figures of Tyson's work are all to be heard in the masterpiece of his cowboyography, the song "Irving Berlin (Is 100 Yrs Old Today)," from *I Outgrew The Wagon*. It reiterates the typical elements and goes beyond them.

The song presents a day in the life, a collage of apparently random events and observations, an innovative structure for a song, reminiscent of the George Martin and Beatles' masterpiece about another day in a different life. It is a notable day: the 11th of May, 1988, the centenary of the composer Berlin's birth. Amidst the "dryest spring in 91 years," the singer pauses from work, begun early "[b]efore the wind started blowin' too hard," for a moment that becomes the present tense of the entire song. That work is described as "start[ing] those fillies at the pen," presumably a reference to the process of breaking and training cutting horses.

A radio plays, over which he hears that "Irving Berlin is 100 years old today." This line forms the first half of the song's four-times-repeated chorus. The second choral line provides insight into the singer's emotional crisis, apparent in a marked gain of intensity in the music's arrangement and the singer's change from laconic to impassioned tone, about which the introductory verse gives no hint. It turns casual previous allusions to weather conditions into a pathetic image: "The wind's gone and blown my woman away."

As if heedless of the day's import and of his crisis, the singer turns his and our attention to those fillies: "You know, the buckskin and the bay." There is open affection in his description of the bay, who is "a lit-tle sweetheart...yeah she is / Pretty much like her mom," but it is the buckskin who has the rest of the verse. The literal sense of his first words of commentary are belied by the tone of admiration in their per-formance. She is "rank" and a problem: "took me 20 minutes / Just to put the hobbles on." She is highly able ("She's smart and she's fast") and determinedly other ("and she doesn't like people"). The singer's gaze registers one further compelling image of the buckskin filly before a swift transition to the chorus: "She trembles as she stands." An anec-dote of work, seemingly a rhetorical withdrawal from troubling issues of the chorus, leads to an apt "found metaphor," an image the singer's consciousness happens upon, as if by happy accident, that brings the complexities of situation, context and moment into harmony. Resonant in this image of the bereft cowboy "in denial," expressing empathy with a determinedly antipathetic female other, are answers to as yet unasked questions, to be voiced in the next verse.

The performance comes out of the second chorus without the pre-vious verse's return to subdued instrumental playing nor the singer's reversion to continued conversational discourse, seemingly with us as intended audience. With sincere complement of tone and burden, he pleads directly to his absent beloved, his outburst supported by swell of the band: "Good Gawd a'mighty, is it ever goin' to rain? / Are you ever coming home?" The juxtaposition of questions, where literal drought becomes metaphoric of its emotional counterpart, reprises the technique of the chorus. As noted, it also reconstructs the presumed relationship between singer and audience. It turns out we have been overhearing what we had heard as being spoken directly to us. By verse's end, our notion of the song's moment is further revised, as the singer presents himself, in the third person, as "a cowboy on the telephone." We are eavesdropping on a phone call to the absent beloved, a contact attempted, a gesture made of a workday's urgent moment, perhaps given pretext by news of the day, by Berlin's extraordinary anniversary.

In the next beat of this drama, the singer parenthetically addresses "old Irving Berlin," wonders if he "ever wrote a song / 'Bout blowed out country, a marriage gone wrong," and, in so doing, makes explicit the self-reflexive aspect of what has been, all along, this song with a songwriter in its title and chorus. Among many things, Tyson's song pays tribute to a fellow composer of popular music. In the fourth and final verse, the opening line makes the tribute overt as the singer wishes "Happy Birthday Irving" and alludes ("God bless you") to one of Berlin's anthems. As a multi-faceted oral structure, experimental in collage and jump-cut narrative, ambitious in expression beyond established means, Tyson's "Irving Berlin" is, for the cowboy-song idiom, verging on the avant-garde. In a genre deeply resonant and reverent of tradition, this song, with multiplicity of discourse, subject, situation and reference, is damn near postmodern. It can be deemed a meta-song. In its self-reflexivity, the song shares what Linda Hutcheon calls the "self-conscious or 'meta-' sensibility of our times" (x). In her study of Canadian postmodern novels, Hutcheon finds "novels that admit openly they are fiction, but suggest that fiction is just another means by which we make sense of our world" (x-xi). Tyson's manifest awareness of the intricate process of songwriting as presented in "Irving Berlin," and to a lesser extent in "Springtime" and elsewhere, suggests an aesthetic where song is "neither self-sufficiently art nor a simple mirror to or window onto the world outside" (2). In such a controlled display of "radical doubt," Tyson's aesthetics are closer to those of the late twentieth century than to those nineteenth-century certainties about art admired in the work of James and Russell.

Meanwhile, back at the ranch, the singer carries on. He contemplates the near future, lists available diversions ("The hockey game is on tonight from Boston") and strategies of denial ("Tomorrow I'm goin' to try and fix the tractor / And try and keep my mind off a you").[13] Tomorrow will be a version of today, without attendant resonances, though the movement from trying to break a horse to fix a tractor may suggest progress in the work, some insight gained, a rapprochement attempted.[14]

The metaphoric links that the song forges between marriage-gone-wrong, drought and workday anecdote are readily evident; they recast, with deft and striking vitality, conventional images. Their coherence with the recurring Berlin references is more conjectural. That Tyson received inspiration for the song on this particular day may be serendipitous, included in the resultant song as what in documentary film is incorporated as a "privileged moment" in the flow of actuality. Berlin perhaps stands for popular music itself, his name invoking those extraordinary powers that Noel Coward ascribes to such "cheap music."[15] This, on a more practical level, may be imagined as Berlin's special resonance for the drama's estranged couple, as their composer of "our song." If so, citation of his anniversary reads as an ease-making opening gambit for a difficult conversation. It may be Berlin's longevity, the extraordinary achievement of one hundred years, that matters, as exemplum of endurance in midst of transience all around. The singer asks of Berlin, hopefully, "Are you glad just to be alive?"

Berlin, as a master of popular music, may also serve as emulative model. He, though certainly never a cowboy, may be another analogue, like Will James and Charlie Russell. Tyson composes the very song his cowboy wonders about, one that Berlin did not write but Tyson can. But the song "Irving Berlin" is not a pastiche of an Irving Berlin song. Requisite timbres for an "imitation" Tin Pan Alley piece are not in Tyson's musical lexicon, nor would they be to his audience's taste. He puts on no "ritz," no "Easter bonnet." The song is pleading for rain, not dreaming of a white Christmas.[16]

There may be, however, one way in which Berlin and his career's achievement do aptly parallel Will James, Charlie Russell and Ian Tyson. All four are outsiders who as artists so successfully engaged a chosen culture that they have become exemplars of that culture. It is the immigrant, born Israel Baline in Siberia, who wrote quintessentially

American popular songs, ones that, once written, seem always to have been around, like "Blues Skies," songs mythic enough to relay God's blessings on the nation. It is the *p'tit gars* from 1890s Québec, born Ernest Dufault, who invents a new self as "Will James" and writes the fictional west of Tyson's father's thrall and, indelibly, of Tyson's own formative imagination. It is the kid from St. Louis who paints Montana sunsets better than God can.

And it is Tyson, reborn without need for a name change, a Victoria native, a long-time Toronto resident, an ex-1960s urban folksinger, who writes, as one of the chores on his Albertan ranch, as an authoritative insider, authentic "cowboy culture classics"; whose cowboyography documents a remote, marginal but still-extant life, work and world; who, out of closely observed particulars, makes truly alternative contemporary popular songs for the "northern range." He extends the western musical tradition into our time and rides a cutting-horse of metaphor into imaginative reaches of the eastern slope, beyond clichéd timbres and unhip connotations, to high mythic realms where he shares in creation with God.[17] And then goes out and has a few.

NOTES

1   The recordings are *Old Corrals and Sagebrush* (1983) (a subsequent 1988 release on CD of this recording, augmented by early 1984 recordings that had been released as *Ian Tyson*, gains the subtitle *& Other Cowboy Culture Classics); Cowboyography* (1986); *I Outgrew The Wagon* (1989); *And Stood There Amazed* (1991); and *Eighteen Inches of Rain* (1994). These discs are released on the Stony Plain label, an independent recording company in Edmonton, with an eclectic list of music by artists, most of them Canadian, in blues, rock, singer-songwriter and country and western genres.

   A thorough discography of Tyson's work, including those recordings from his early career as half of the Ian and Sylvia duo, can be found in Colin Escott, *I Never Sold My Saddle* (Vancouver: Greystone Books, 1993), 111-12.

2   "One of his albums, *Cowboyography*, went gold in Canada, and is closing in on platinum. Astonishing for a song cycle that can only truly be understood by no more than a few thousand people in the whole of North America" (Escott, *I Never Sold My Saddle* 8). Tyson has received several Canadian music industry awards including Juno Awards for Album of the Year, Male Vocalist of the Year, and Canadian Country Artist of the Year in 1987; the Canadian Country Music Awards Male Vocalist of the Year in both 1987 and 1992; and the RPM Big Country's Artist, Album and Male Vocalist awards in 1988.

3 Many songs, in folk, popular and elite modes, use the structural device of a "burden line": a recurring musical and lyrical phrase, often including the words of the title, that "carries" the song in several senses. By sheer repetition, it takes up more of the song than any other element. Usually set to the main musical theme (or "burden," in one sense of that word) of either verse or chorus, the words of a burden line contain a succinct statement of the song's concerns, often metaphorically. They bear the "burden" (in another sense) of meaning, which may accrue and change through repetition, appearance in different contexts, and also, perhaps, by slight alteration in the wording.

4 A core of recurring musicians, some of them also members of his touring band, the Chinook Arch Riders, appears on most of Tyson's recordings. Among them are Adrian Chornowol, on keyboards, arrangements and production; Louis Sedmak, guitars; Tom McKillop, guitars; Stan Stewart, pedal steel; Myron Szott, fiddle; George Koller, bass; Thom Moon, drums; and Cindy Church, among several others, background vocals. As wanted, the band is augmented by additional fiddles, mandolin, and accordion.

The prominence of a capella singing in Tyson's arrangements is a notable exception to its "country and western" conventionality; this trait may reflect and extend the campfire vocal harmonizing traditions of the "cowboy song" (heard, for example, in the works of the Sons of the Pioneers). Likewise, highlighted use of acoustic and "archaic" instruments such as the mandolin often seems intended to evoke folkloric associations (as in Tyson's song "Alberta's Child").

5 All but one of the CD covers (and/or booklet photos) depict Tyson on horseback or leading a horse; that one has him posed with guitar. Content analysis shows a reference made, if not prominence given, to "the horse" in approximately three-quarters of Tyson's songs. Other animals that have their own song include "The Coyote" (from *Cowboyography*) and "Magpie" (from *And Stood There Amazed*).

6 "Tyson and I both made our separate runs at riding bareback broncs. A half-dozen donated entry fees and their accompanying bone-jarring, yet benign, buck-offs were sufficient to exorcise my delusions of forkedness. But Tyson really cowboyed-up and kept a-hookin' it on down the road until a shattered ankle landed him in Calgary General Hospital. There he took up the infinitely saner art of guitar pickin'." Jay Dusard, in liner notes to *Old Corrals and Sagebrush*.

7 From which comes the title phrase for the 1991 CD *And Stood There Amazed*. A performance of this clichéd cowboy song, so hopelessly encumbered by unhipness, concludes the recording, a performance of such absolute sincerity and conviction that one hears the song's virtues for the first time and stands there amazed.

8 "Ernest Nephtali Dufault, a Francophone Canadian, could travel to Montana to pass himself off as an orphan from Texas raised by a kindly French-Canadian trapper (thus that accent) and thereby become Will James, one of the major American western writers." Arnold E. Davidson, *Coyote Country: Fictions of the Canadian West* (Durham and London: Duke UP, 1994), 2. More details about "Will James" are found in Blake

Allmendinger, *The Cowboy: Representations of Labor in an American Work Culture* (New York: Oxford UP, 1992). He is the subject of the 1988 NFB documentary *Alias Will James*, directed by Jacques Godbout.

9   The printed lyrics read "twenty years," but Tyson sings "thirty." In this, as in a few other cases where printed and sung versions do not accord, I take the recorded performance as authoritative text.

10 The choruses are commentary on this geographic and psychic "Great Divide" that "[o]ld cowboys cross." The singer asks Jesus' help to "pull this heavy load," insists "You answer all our questions further down this muddy road." It is a curious shift in rhetoric and perspective, from secular differences to religious salvation, although both realms are rendered through cowboy metaphors.

In juxtaposition with the American-Canadian contrasts of the verses, the "Great Divide" also becomes a metaphor for the international border. Tyson here seems to echo the figurative use of this geographic feature in the song "Across the Great Divide" by the four-fifths Canadian rock group The Band. That same phrase is put to similar purpose by the critics Barry K. Grant (in "'Across the Great Divide': Imitation and Inflection in Canadian Rock Music." *Journal of Canadian Studies* 21.1 (Spring 1986): 116-27) and Barney Hoskyns (in *Across the Great Divide: The Band and America*. London: Viking, 1993).

11 In the first version, the band emulates a generic Nashville arrangement behind these names; in the second, Tyson does vocal evocations of both Jones and Harris.

12 One lyrical change in the latter version replaces the opening line "Don't you stick a fork in me cause I ain't done" with the more thematically pertinent "Open wide the gate boys / Let my ponies run."

13 The singer notes as well that he has a bet "on the Oilers in five." Tyson has taken some licence here to have his protagonist win his bet. Edmonton did indeed defeat the Bruins for the Stanley Cup that spring, but the final series did not begin until a week later, on May 18. The Oilers actually won in four straight, but took five games to do so; the fourth game was suspended because of a power failure in Boston Gardens, with the teams tied at 3 goals.

14 The title song of 1994's *Eighteen Inches of Rain* may be heard as a sequel to "Irving Berlin." The drought of both sorts is still on, wind "from the east;" with calf prices "gone to hell again"; there's "[n]ot a broke horse on the place" and "the tractor lost a wheel 'bout a week ago." The singer "make[s] do with what I got" in the dissatisfied present of the verses, while, in the chorus, wishes for better, including "broke horse," "one good woman," "[c]lear blue skies and eighteen inches of rain." If wishes were horses…

15 "Extraordinary how potent cheap music is." *Private Lives*, Act 1 (1930).

16 The allusions are to the Berlin compositions "Puttin' On the Ritz" (1930), "Easter Parade" (1933) and "White Christmas" (1942). Berlin also wrote the lyrics and music for such standards as "Alexander's Ragtime Band" (1911), "Always" (1925), "Cheek to Cheek" (1935), "How Deep Is the Ocean" (1932), "Top Hat" (1935) and the anthemic "God Bless America" (1939).

17　Since his declared completion of the Cowboyography sequence of recordings, Tyson has released two further CDs: *All The Good'uns (The Best of
Ian Tyson)*, a compilation that features songs from six Stony Plain albums,
plus two new ones—"The Wonder of It All" and "Barrel Racing Angel"—
released in 1997, and *The Lost Herd* (1999).

　　The latter features new Tyson compositions that would not be out of
place thematically on earlier discs. Titles such as "Brahmas and
Mustangs" and "Legends of Cutting" pursue the working cowboy theme.
"Smugglers Cove" explores the personal past; "Blue Mountains of
Mexico" extends the range geographically and "La Primera" imagines as
far back as the coming of horses with Cortes. Sonically, *Lost Herd* adds
to Tyson's tonal colours those of Spanish guitar and, for several songs
recorded in Toronto, features a band of jazz musicians. The CD's only
cover is a departure: a version of Arlen and Harburg's "Somewhere Over
the Rainbow."

WORK CITED

Hutcheon, Linda. *The Canadian Postmodern: A Study in Contemporary
Canadian Fiction*. Don Mills, ON: Oxford UP, 1988.

SPORTS

CANADA, THE OLYMPICS
AND THE RAY-BAN MAN

Andrew Wernick

In the time since George Grant wrote *Lament for a Nation*, the sense of Canadian cultural difference, especially from the United States, has continued to erode in the face of commercial and technological pressures to assimilate Canada, like everywhere else, into McWorld. For nationalists of Grant's generation, the issue was Americanization, the threat to Canadian independence posed by a branch-plant economy, TV and coca-colonization. In the age of Microsoft, Benetton and karaoke, attention is turning to the post-Cold War globalization of the market. The issue for those concerned to sustain Canada as a collective project—whether for its own sake, or to legitimate the pan-Canadian state—is no longer just the place of Canada on the continent. It is the meaningfulness of imagining collective identity in any such terms, given the move to a free trade in capital, goods and communications that has made all borders, and the national particularity of what they enclose, increasingly fuzzy.

Against that background, I would like to offer an analysis of a recent commercial advertisement that explicitly addresses its audience as Canadians. I do so not in order to make a cheap point about the self-interested exploitation of national sentiment, nor even to make a subtler one about how using the flag to merchandise products weakens nationhood as a symbolic force—and thus, in the end, its use-value

Notes on pages 318-19.

even as promotion. My aim, rather, is to explore a specific instance of national imaging as it arises in a global marketing context. While this is not the only context for such imaging, it is a highly important one, and essential to grasp if we are to understand the wider situation within which representations of nationality, and appeals to them, have come to present themselves. In a mediascape pervaded by advertising and consumer culture, political symbols like those surrounding "Canada" are commercially transcoded, externally to promote tourism, internally to add lustre to branded goods and services. These latter have become increasingly transnational, which should make us wonder not only about the authenticity of their patriotic appeals, but about the significance of their making such appeals at all.

The ad I want to examine is for Ray-Ban "Xray" sunglasses, and it appeared on the inside cover of *Maclean's* magazine on August 5, 1996. Under the headline "Triumph and Tragedy," the issue was dominated by the Centenary Olympic Games in Atlanta. The "tragedy" was the pipe bomb explosion at a rock concert in Olympic Centennial Park (first assumed to be the work of anonymous "terrorists"). The "triumph" was that of Canadian athletes, most notably Donovan Bailey in the 100 metres. Erasing the shame of Ben Johnson's disqualification at Seoul, Bailey brought Canada the glory of fielding "the fastest man in the world." The title was later challenged by the American Michael Johnson, winner of the 200 metres, building great commercial interest in a runoff between them over 150 metres. (The runoff was held on June 1, 1997, at the Skydome in Toronto. Bailey won after Johnson pulled up short with an injury.) Just as the Canadian dollar is measured against the American, so with the Olympics. The fact that the Games had been awarded to Atlanta rather than Toronto had been taken hard in some quarters, and there was a hint of envious glee in the well-publicized logistical problems—from failing computer systems to transport chaos—which marred what (American) media hype called "America's Games."

Maclean's bills itself as "Canada's national magazine." The Ray-Ban ad addresses itself to Canadians just by virtue of being placed there. But what gives the ad its special interest is that it does so in a manner which seamlessly integrates its message into the nationally framed Olympic coverage that dominates the surrounding text. The model for the glasses is Curt Harnett, whose smiling face beams out at us from atop the bicycle on which he is leaning. His T-shirt is embla-zoned with maple leaves. The explanatory note says it all: "Curt Harnett...He covers 200 metres in 9.865 seconds and will pursue Olympic Gold at Atlanta with Xray vision."

The Ray-Ban Man. Permission of Bausch & Lomb.

The product is endorsed, then, by a Canadian Olympic athlete. At first sight this is all that is going on. The glasses must be of excellent quality, because Curt Harnett, presumably an excellent judge of sports equipment, is publicly prepared to say so. But this would be a superfi-cial understanding. Imagistic ads work through the manipulation of signs and meanings.[1] Through the semiotic magic of the Ray-Ban ad, the glasses acquire all the qualities with which the posed figure of Curt Harnett is himself identified. In riding the sunglasses into competition on "our" behalf, he not only attests to their excellent technical qualities, but transforms them, like Curt in his shirt, into a proud bit of Canada. At the same time, a certain way of being "Canadian" is projected through the presentation of this Olympic cyclist as "Ray-Ban Man," i.e., as the composite figure Harnett makes up when shown modelling the glasses.

The question I want to address, through disentangling the chains of significance through which this image is built up, is the cloud of meaning it comes to associate, via the Team Canada shirt, with "Canadaness" itself. If the analysis seems to draw too much from too little, it should be stressed that I do not attribute any particular power to this or any other particular ad. Such ads come and go in the flicker of an eye. The subjective effects of advertising (which no amount of empirical research can rigorously assess) are cumulative, and McLuhan's amended dictum (1989) that "the medium is the massage" provides an apt metaphor.[2] The thought is just that the world may be seen in a grain of sand, and the promotional effluvia of the market, if we reflect on the complexities of even a single image, can teach us a great deal about the culture it uses and refracts.

THE FORM OF THE AD

The Ray-Ban ad is organized around two geometrical shapes. The first is a triangle whose base is the strip beneath Harnett's feet and whose two sides follow a line from the front and back wheels of his bike through his arms and up to his head. At the apex are the dark sunglasses Harnett wears as a black slash across his tanned, smiling face, a face that is jut-jawed, white-teethed, fringed by a well-groomed shock of wavy blond hair, and illuminated from the front. Overall, it is as if the glasses of this athletic sun-god physically absorb the power of legs and machine, together with the entire personality of the Canadian competitor to whom they belong. The triangular structure makes the glasses into a metonymic sign (the part standing for the whole) for all that is signified by their wearer. But who, and what, is he? An answer is given by the second geometrical figure. This is an X that comes into focus when the eye moves between the graphics in the lower left and the top right, and then traces the line from the front strut and handlebars of Harnett's bike to the writing in the top left.

Each diagonal in the X implies an association between the terms it connects. Consider the line that runs from bottom left to top right. At one end is a white rectangle that contains the official logo for the Atlanta Games and, beneath that, the motto "Bausch & Lomb: Official Sponsor of the Olympic Games." At the other end, against a red background, is the registered product logo and, in smaller print below, the caption "serious sports sunglasses." The same link, of brand to Games, but with the athlete standing in for the event, is made by the second diagonal. This one, from top left to bottom right, connects the copy about Curt Harnett (in gold) with the particular model of "Xrays" he is wearing, and which is also displayed, beneath the wheel of his bike, as the right-most item in the product line below.

The X frames the triangle. Thus we read the picture of Harnett leaning against his bike as embodying the equations that are made, crosswise, through him. In his very person he brings together Ray-Bans and the Olympics, testifying to their inseparability through the sunshaded gaze he directs our way. The X also reminds us of the x in "Xray," so that the very movement of the reader's eye traces out a name for the product. As a further feature of the design we may note that the lines of the X intersect through his shorts. This becomes an alternate focal point to the primary one presented by the glasses on his face. The mutual echoing of crotch and eyes eroticizes the product, though only obliquely and in a way that can be easily (and heterosexually) ignored. The black of the shorts reveals no contours and conceals, just as effectively as the dark glasses, what lies beneath.

The colour scheme, indeed, is a coding device in itself. The black of the shorts picks up the colour of the bike, and is relayed through the black in the shirt to the black glasses above. The red maple leaf—Canada itself—on the front of the shirt similarly continues into the red behind the top-right product logo, and is echoed in the dark orange Olympic flame in the bottom left. Red plus white (in the second diagonal of the X) are the colours of the Canadian flag. The sun-yellow strip at the foot of the ad, finally, refers us both to the (supposed) light source that shines on Harnett's face and to the (Olympic) gold that glisters from the letters that spell out his name. In fact, all three colours of medal are used. Besides the gold Harnett is pursuing, the silver of his shoes and of the bike metal, and the bronze wash against which he has been photographed, allude to the consolation prizes he might win instead.

At every level of its formal composition, then, the ad identifies the branded sunglasses with the Olympics, and more especially with all the qualities that are leading this Canadian, we hope, to competitive glory. However, the values transferred onto the product are not just "there" to be invoked. The Olympic complex, with its multiple historical resonance, is selectively appropriated. Through the image of Harnett and his Ray-Ban's, moreover, this complex is further modified, and, if we think about it, in a most paradoxical way. What presents itself as an Olympic icon turns, before our very eyes, into a lifestyle fashion statement. The ad's mythicization of the product involves, in fact, a two-step process. The first assembles signs of "Olympicness" around and through the picture of Harnett. The second reconfigures this totality so as to align the product and its consumer with another set of meanings that blend with the first. The result is a figure that is simultaneously projected as a Canadian Olympic athlete and as "Ray-Ban Man." The modification, which leads naturally (it seems) from the first cluster of meanings to the second, is crucial to the working of the ad. But to understand how, and with what import, we must look more closely, first, at the Olympic element itself.

The Olympics as Promotion

The fact that a promotion for sunglasses is using Olympic symbolism at all is worth pondering, especially when we consider the emphatically non-commercial principles on which the Modern Olympic Movement (as it still calls itself) was launched, and on which the power of its symbolism still to some extent rests. That the Games have become an intensively commercial event is evident. What is striking is that they have done so while in some measure retaining the "amateur" form that de Coubertin and his associates originally imparted at their founding congress in Paris in 1894.[3]

The Games are owned by the International Olympic Committee, which sets the rules, awards the Games to host cities, and presides over a pyramid of national Olympic committees and international sports federations that select teams and govern standards. The notoriously regal style in which the self-appointing and non-accountable members of the IOC—dubbed "Lords of the Rings" by one critical commentator (Jennings and Simpson)—came to conduct their business during the 1980s and 1990s suggests private gain, as in any corporation. However, the IOC is a non-profit organization, has no shareholders, and does not, in the ordinary sense, accumulate capital. Funds raised by the IOC support the infrastructure of Olympic sport that its charter commits it to establish.[4] The Games themselves are supposed to be self-supporting.

However, gate receipts and sales of memorabilia, plus private and government patronage, have never kept pace with their cost, still less with the IOC's ambition to promote the infrastructure needed to make the Movement truly global in scope. Olympic organizers have been increasingly driven, then, to worry about revenue. The issue became critical from the 1960s onwards when the IOC sought to expand its reach into de-colonized and poor countries in Africa, Asia and Latin America. Financial salvation was at hand, though, from two related sources. The first was television, with the first sale of TV rights occurring at the Melbourne Games in 1956. The second was corporate sponsorship, with Adidas leading the way via deals that gave sports equipment companies the right to display logos (tastefully) on footwear, clothes and gear. Under the presidency of Juan Antonio Samaranch both sources were carefully cultivated, and the gross take now exceeds 2 billion dollars per year.

The basis of this revenue should be carefully noted. At a first order level, what the IOC has to sell is a global spectacle. But, beyond the stadium itself, that spectacle is not sold directly to the spectators. What makes TV networks compete furiously for the broadcast rights is the advertising revenue that high viewing figures are able to attract on the basis of the guaranteed mass audience such programming is able to deliver. That indeed is the primary form of profit making that has come to prevail in all forms of spectator sport, whether commodified at the point of spectatorship or not. It is the same audience power, we may add, that provides the economic value of sponsorships as well. Despite the high-minded intentions of its founders, then, the modern Olympics have become completely integrated into the commercial sports industry. They have done so by the way that "amateur" sport, just like "professional" sport, has become entertainment fodder for ad-supported media.[5] To be sure, this is commerce at the second degree. The non-profit form of organization (however tainted at the top), and the prescriptions and proscriptions of the Olympic charter, still preserves for the Games an aura of ideal motives. By the same token, however, the mystique this lends to the world's premier sports festival only enhances its promotional value.

The significance of the Olympics as, and for, advertising spreads in every direction. It extends to secondary (non-broadcast) media, which feed off the Games as news. The Olympics provided copy for *Maclean's*, helping the circulation figures on which the magazine's advertising rates depend. In turn, by providing coverage, *Maclean's* helped to promote the Games. The Ray-Ban ad itself highlighted the Olympics, thus advertising not only Ray-Bans but also an event that had publicity value both for the magazine and for advertisers using this and other media. The Ray-Ban example shows also, however, that the promotional value of the Olympics is not exhausted in its audience-drawing function. The promotional power of the Olympics may be enlisted for advertising directly. By paying to become sponsors, companies pay the IOC for the exclusive right to use the Olympic logo in ads for their products. Some, for national brands, are handled regionally through the National Olympic Committees. The most lucrative sponsorships, in which world-wide rights are sold to transnationals, are organized through The Olympic Program (TOP). In 1996, Bausch and Lomb, Ray-Ban's parent company, were members of TOP as were, amongst others, Coca-Cola, IBM, Kodak and Visa. For all these, the Olympics provided (as they say) a global marketing opportunity, as well as a globally recognized repertoire of symbols for global campaigns.

A related process has overtaken Olympic athletes themselves. The eligibility code of the Olympic charter [IOC 59] continues to state that "entry or participation of a competitor in the Olympic Games shall not be conditional on any financial consideration." However, with the ever-continuing rise of the advertising-entertainment industry, the star value of athletes *outside* the Games has soared, with accompanying pressures to relax the rules against such trade. By Atlanta, even the rule against an Olympic competitor letting their "person, name, picture or sports performances be used for advertising purposes *during* the Olympic Games" (my emphasis) had gone, as the Ray-Ban use of Harnett shows. Not that this was crucial, considering that athletes were already permitted to wear sportswear logos,[6] and that the biggest sponsorship deals are generally made *after* the medals are won. Be that as it may, the form of revenue available for Olympic athletes parallels closely that of the IOC. It comes from athletes renting themselves out as promotional signs, i.e., as names and icons that can be employed to market other products and services. The payoff—Olympic gold—depends on the degree of competitive success, convertible into cash through the advertising contracts to which it can lead.

Overall, in fact, the Olympics have become not merely enmeshed in promotion, but a veritable feeder industry for advertising itself. They have become so, moreover, at two levels: first, by becoming organized *in toto* as a spectacle and image-source with which advertisers would want to associate; second, by serving as an apparatus for converting the individual competitors into sponsorable material as well. Both types of promotional product are employed in the Ray-Ban ad, though so carefully do they intertwine that the reader is unlikely to separate them out. An Olympic cyclist endorses the sunglasses whose maufacturer brings us the Olympics themselves. At the same time, the athlete embodies the Games, whose sublime spirit might lead us to forget that the same sponsor is paying for both.

FASTER, HIGHER, STRONGER

At the core of Olympic symbolism is an archaic classicism that the founders of the modern Games tried to restylize as an internationalist humanism for the industrial age. The aim was not profane entertainment.[7] How Spartan ideals mixed with Roman in nineteenth-century upper-class education, how this revived neo-classical brew became associated with the rise of an amateur sports culture in England, the United States and the countries of Northern Europe, and how this connected with an upper-class humanist mission to unify the industrializing world, need not concern us here.[8] Today, in any case, the grandiose project launched by de Coubertin provides less of a motive for the Games than an alibi. The opening and closing ceremonies, the white doves, the Olympic flame, the five-ringed flag, the honorifics and protocols are still punctiliously observed. But the cultural matrix from which de Coubertin's project took rise has passed. If such trappings still succeed in elevating the spectacle today, it is at several removes from their originating impulse, conferring on spectators and participants only a vague sense of belonging to a timeless tradition of ecumenical intent.

From this echo chamber of associations, the Ray-Ban ad builds its own version of Olympic spirit around two axes. Both pertain to the figure of the competing athlete, but in different respects. The first concerns what the Olympic athlete *does*; the second concerns the *body* that is both the instrument and the end of activity.

With regard to the first, we are told, simply, that Harnett "covers 200 metres in 9.865 seconds and will pursue Atlanta Gold." The tone, we may note, is prospective. The cycling final in which Harnett will compete has not yet occurred. He stands before us as an *aspiring* champion. Note too that he is not shown actually in competing mode. He is dismounted (I will return to this). He is also alone, with no other competitor in sight. In so far as he *is* a competitor, then, the qualities he is presented as exemplifying have little to do with the relational aspects of competition. Of course, if he wins gold there will have been losers. But the struggle against others, with its noble mixture of rivalry and etiquette that so excited the Greeks, is of no account here. The pursuit of "Atlanta Gold" presents itself as a solitary mission.

How are we to interpret all this? Let us begin with the obvious. The striving of an Olympic athlete, whether for records or for gold, evokes an ideology of competitive individualism, which has shadowed the rise of market society from its beginnings. This complex still, perhaps more than ever, serves both to legitimate and motivate the socio-economic forms of life that arise on a liberal-capitalist basis. The sporting contest—with the Olympics at the summit—*mirrors*, but also *idealizes*, the competition that traverses every level of the market, whether for capital, goods and services, or for jobs, careers and status. It idealizes market competition by presenting the image of a "level playing field" in which ability and execution alone are the deciding factors, and which serves, metaphorically, as a regulative ideal for all such competition. In fair competition, the aims of justice, efficiency and individual freedom are combined and optimized: self-interest and the desire to win bring out the best in all. The ethos of competition may even lead to a fairness not initially written into its terms of play. In the Olympics, the grudging but irreversible rise of women's sports, and the growing participation, and success, of Afro-Asian countries, give the closing assembly of competing athletes an "inclusionary" character that has ethical value for Western liberalism and promotional value for global marketers.

The appeal of competitiveness as a socially sanctioned value also has a subjective side. Olympic champions are heroes of inner-directedness. The strenuous work and ascetic training of competing athletes incarnate the principle of reward for effort. The same principle, as Max Weber's classic 1930 study showed, linked the Protestant ethic to the spirit of capitalism. Moral worthiness is manifest in worldly achievement, and successful individuals—those who win gold—mark themselves out as members of the elect. Hence the power of sports heroes as "role models" and their highly sought after qualities as icons that will move the merchandise.

Through the figure of an Olympic athlete, then, Ray-Ban mobilizes for its glasses whatever positive values surround competitiveness and individual striving in general. This, though, is only a first approximation. The posing of Harnett alone with his bike de-emphasizes certain aspects of this complex and grafts onto it features that point in a somewhat different direction. The absence of other competitors softens the analogy between sports contests and the play of the market. What is foregrounded instead is the single athlete, grasped from the side of his sheer capacity to perform. Harnett has (already) clocked 9.865 seconds over 200 metres. The precise time, of course, has no particular significance for the ad's (largely non-expert) audience. What impresses is the precision itself, a precision that measures Harnett's best performance so far, to the thousandth part of a second. The race to be run, indeed, is less against other people, or even against himself: it is against the clock. It is an absolute race, whose point is simply the maximization of speed. The ego is drawn to surpass its own best performances, and in so doing to surpass those of all others, pressing against the limits not just of the singular athlete, but of human possibility itself.

All this is in line with the official Olympic motto, *"citius, altius, fortius"* (faster, higher, stronger). Yet the same slogan, which seemingly summarizes the classical ideal of sport, itself points to a further transformation that has overtaken the modern Games: their assimilation by the imperative of technological progress. By this I mean not just those changes in staging and recording races that stem from advances in chronometry, but also the increasing help given to athletic performance by all manner of special sciences like ergonomics, physiology, dietetics, aerodynamic design, pharmacology and motivational psychology. The Olympics, together with the whole system of international athletic competition, has come to assume something like the form of auto racing. In both cases the contest and its promotional stakes provide a stimulus for the engineering of better and better machines. Just as auto racing serves as a research and development laboratory for automakers, the Olympics serves in the same way for those who work on humans.

The analogy, to be sure, is not perfect. The (heavily regulated but spottily enforced) ban on performance-enhancing drugs restricts the technical aids that may be applied to the body of the human performer. Drawing a moral line, however, between medication and "doping," or between the latter and dietetics, does not lessen the technological imperative itself. The distinction between human-centred and machine-centred sports should not, in any case, be pressed too far. Cycling, like auto racing, is a hybrid of both. Harnett on his bike, like Villeneuve in his Formula One Williams, is a cyborg, a synthesis of human and machine, and the time he can clock relies on their combined and integrated technical power. This is important to the ad's composition. For one of its rhetorical points is to present the sunglasses as being just as integral a prosthesis for Harnett-the-athlete as the bicycle itself. From this angle, the ensemble of Harnett, bike and glasses presents itself as the incarnation not so much of competitive spirit—though this is present in the reference to the winning prize—as of technical excellence, that is, of the capacity for efficiency-in-action, particularly as this translates into a measurable performance. In *The Postmodern Condition*, Jean-François Lyotard (following Marcuse) terms this quality "performativity." He identifies it as a dominant norm in post-industrial capitalism, particularly at the level of public or quasi-public administrative and service systems. "Performativity" has nothing to do with any ends it might serve. It is a purely formal value, corresponding to that rational instrumentalism which German critical theorists take to have become ascendant in a socio-economic system that is driven by a purely systemic logic.

But what is the performativity of the glasses? In commonsensical terms it derives from their suitability to enable wearers—including the racing cyclist—to see clearly where they are going, despite having the sun, and perhaps also wind and dust, glaring and blowing in their eyes. But in the rhetoric of the ad the performative value of the glasses is higher still. It is "with Xray vision" that Harnett will go for gold. Here, *techne* crosses over into magic. X-ray glasses, if they existed, would enable their user to see into solid forms. Of course, we do not take the hype literally, and receive its exaggeration as a knowing witticism. Of dubious use in an actual race, this sci-fi quality nonetheless builds upon the idea of technically aided performative excellence that is thematic for the ad. X-rays make visible the invisible, and stand in for technological power. X-rays also travel at the speed of light, which associates the racing cyclist with a force much speedier still. The algebraic X complements the exact arithmetic of "9.865 seconds" and conjures up the *mythos* of science as such. "Xray vision," however, also suggests something else. It refers us to the difference between Clark Kent and Superman, and thus to the super-enhancing transformation that the glasses can bring about to *every* aspect of their wearer.

THE ATHLETIC BODY

I will return in a moment to the magical function of the glasses. But our consideration of how the ad mobilizes the Olympic complex is not yet complete. If the first axis around which the ad organizes its Olympic material is the event and activity of *competition*, the second is the *body* of the athlete. On this site, too, a modernized set of classical athletic values is selectively appropriated in a direction favourable to the pitch.

The highlighting of thighs and calves foregrounds the muscles that drive the bike. The well-tanned skin of legs, arms and face, and the golden halo of wavy hair, suggest the outdoor training that makes the cyclist's whole being an exemplar of perfectly honed athleticism. Harnett radiates health, or, as a newer jargon has it, "wellness." In every sense, his body is in superlatively good shape. It is so, moreover, not merely as a natural attribute but as the effect of an effort that gives the result a moral meaning. Now, on one level these qualities are no different from those that led the Greeks to idealize Olympic athletes as gifts from, and to, the gods. They connote the perfect integration of performative virtue with physical (male) beauty through the application of self-disciplined training (*paideia*) to the exuberant energies of youth in the formation of the athlete's total character. But there are details that shift the picture.

Some details to be sure, not very many. For example, it is a *male* athlete on display. Because of labour market and related cultural changes, achievement competition is no longer an exclusively male-identified value. It is, though, part of a "traditional" gender coding that is still culturally alive and clearly invoked here. This is unsurprising, not only because of the ad's fidelity to what was originally an exclusively male event and ideal, but because in the first instance it is targeting men. There is, then, a gender subtext. There is also a racial one. The male athlete depicted is a Nordic "blond beast," to use Nietzsche's unfortunate phrase. This unconsciously reflects, perhaps, the continuing "whiteness" of cycling as a sport. It may likewise suggest consumer targeting, though this could be risky (or worse) given the ethnic heterogeneity of the broadly national market that the ad also aims to reach.

The more immediate significance of Harnett's genotype, however, lies elsewhere. It lies in the connection drawn between it and the product via the sun. The connection is both physical and symbolic. The fair-skinned are sensitive to the sun's burning rays. By the same token, they manifest its effects, and so can signify, indexically, the sun itself. For the Greeks, "fair-skinned Apollo" was the solar god. The ambivalence of the solar, as life and danger, is made visible on the surface of a white body. The promotional use of such a body brings out the positive meaning for this duality, which sunglasses themselves have come to acquire. On a sunny day they enhance vision and cool the eyes; but they also serve culturally as a sign of that same pleasurable and life-giving power whose overwhelming effects they are designed to mitigate.

In Northern climes, sunshine means relief from winter. By extension it means vacation time, when ease replaces effort, and work is set aside for play. This further slide of meaning is reinforced by an additional feature of the athletic body we are shown. He is dismounted, as I have noted. But more: he is positively relaxed. Not only is Harnett smiling, he is resting, half-sitting, on the bike's frame, and his arms lean lightly on the seat and handlebars, his right one without any grip. The bike itself is being used as a chair, or prop, rather than as an instrument of transportation and speed.

The ambiguity of the bike's function deepens when we look at it more closely. What kind of machine is it? With its sleek black frame, slender spoked wheels and dropped handlebars it could be used to race. However, that kind of design has been superseded in competition, and is more often seen in leisure models out on the road. The craze for cycling as a healthy hobby has been with us since bicycles were mass-produced at the end of the last century. The modern Olympics themselves came into being partly as an outgrowth of such a hobbyist sports culture, of which cycling was certainly a part. But about this, the same observation might be made as is commonly made about the current North American vogue for fitness. Such practices exhibit not so much a high value placed on the all-sided development of the personality in the context of an autonomously integrated life, as the application to health of the ascetic morality of the work ethic. The body itself becomes the compulsive object of a kind of work. At the same time, in the narcissistic post-1960s concern for "working out," and in the multifarious leisure and equipment industries that have arisen to serve it, an additional factor has come into play. It is how the body *appears* and *appeals*, and not only the achievement of health (and longevity), that has become the focus of attention.

Viewed one way, in other words, the relaxed body before us is indeed athletic. It is between races, enjoying a moment of rest. Viewed another way, the exertions this moment of ease interrupts are them-selves only for the sake of the appearance that Ray-Ban Man here pres-ents. He works out well and it shows. As such, moreover, he is not only healthy and wholesome. With his hands resting back, and his pelvis pushed forward, he is both inviting and ready for action. In singles-bar terms, he is a hunk. The ascetic Spartans had their athletes unclothed. The prurient moderns cover theirs up, but turn them (tacitly) into sig-nifiers of erotic desire. In addition to what is veiled at the crossover point of the ad's organizing X, the eight s's in "serious sports sun-glasses" embed the model in a snake image that goes back to biblical tradition. These semiological tricks on the margin of attention faintly underline a counter-theme that undercuts, and even reverses, all the active, striving, work-oriented values that the ad is otherwise careful to preserve. The sunglasses, with their super powers, are not only a cru-cial ingredient of the technical equipment that turn Harnett into a (potential) winner. They are an accessory that accentuates and draws attention to his manly desirability. Among their magic powers is that they help turn him into the passive object of an admiring and desirous gaze—the gaze which, if we buy the glasses, might just as easily be directed towards ourselves.

LEISURE AND THE LOOK

The "serious sports sunglasses," then, are not only being sold as sports equipment, but as leisureware. As such, they are offered not just as something to *look through*, but as something to *look at*. When we scru-tinize the passage from one meaning to the other we can see that they are inextricably linked. All the associations with the Olympics—as high-performance athletics, competitive individualism, cyborg technol-ogy, wholesome living, going for gold, etc.—that the ad transfers onto the glasses are transferred as an aspect of that look. The same goes for the motif of speed. For all his laid-back manner, Ray-Ban Man is con-stantly on the move. But we do not have to be athletes, or cyclists, or even physically active to wear them. Just by being seen in them—for their design is continuous with how they are promotionally coded—all these strenuous and heroic associations will be drawn along.

The transformative force of the sunglasses as a fashion sign, though, does not end there. The fact that they are "Xrays," and confer "Xray vision," cues us to something that is again generic to sunglasses as used. The eyes that gaze out from the ad see directly into ours. They see right through us, through to our very core. But we cannot see that gaze itself. The eyes that see ours are invisible behind their black shades. Jacques Derrida has referred, in another context, to what he calls "the visor effect," the visor being that part of a suit of armour that covers the face, leaving only a narrow slit for the knight to see through. The obscuring of facial expression confers an advantage, since it gives no evidence of surprise or fear. More importantly, the eyes that can see without being seen, but yet which belong to a body that can be seen to be seeing, exercise a certain power. Jeremy Bentham's "panopticon,"[9] not to mention surveillance cameras in today's public places, relied on just such a principle, by whose means a prison or a factory could be controlled from one single vantage point.

Of course, the power in play with Ray-Bans is not that of the military, of property owners, or of the state. We are in the land of consumerdom and fashion. In that context, what the sunglasses provide is the compensatory power of visible invisibility for an ego that is vulnerable by virtue of putting itself, physically, on display. The glasses project strength by enabling their wearer to hide the self while being able to gaze, imperturbably, and with complete clarity on the brightest of days, on the gaze of the gazer. They also enable the wearer to enjoy that gaze, and to savour it all the more because there is no risk of that enjoyment being disrupted by locking eyes. The "gazee" can look back at the "gazer" without registering or triggering embarrassment at being caught out in such self-gratification. The circularity becomes evident when we realize that the sunglasses are worn for image, to "look cool." Like any mask, they fascinate for just that reason. As an adornment that draws attention to the eyes they hide, the black glasses serve precisely to attract the other's gaze.

The Ray-Ban Xrays promoted in the ad provide an intriguing and special case of what can be said of all fashion products. Not only is their use-value for the consumer heavily dependent on what they are promotionally made to mean. In their very use they are promotional.

They are designed, and sold, as symbolic props that will help consumers sell themselves. The result of the successful selling of self can be gains in the struggle for jobs and careers. But the markets in which individuals compete with one another are not all money mediated. In the sphere of leisure, informality and interpersonal life, the competition is for friends, influence and mates. The currency of exchange here is not money (at least not directly), but status, esteem and desirability.

To this there is an important corollary. We have already seen that the active, self-realizing ego presented through the figure of an Olympic cyclist is belied by its being harnessed to an appeal which pushes the sunglasses as an imaging accessory that might be worn in all manner of leisure contexts. But for that appeal to work, the ad's reader must identify with the self that would have such a want. This means, in the first place, that the consumer must be appealed to *as a consumer*. Ads for consumer goods, including this one, project a Paradise away from work where all needs can be satisfied, at least in a surrogate fashion, by buying something. The ego that sees things this way is itself organized around consumption. Like the infant at the breast, the *ego consumans* is centred on the desire for intake, and is active only in the appropriation of the requisite stuff. Like the suckling infant, too, the "I" of consumption derives psychic satisfaction from the primal unity thereby regained. But the self that the Ray-Ban kind of ad constructs for the reader to identify with is not just a consumerized one. Paralleling the promotional character of the product, the self appealed to is promotional also. It is the self that wants to look good—the self, indeed, that *needs* to look good, given the socio-sexual competition that, for (young) men as much as (young) women, is a fact of life in a pervasively liberalized culture. This self is consumerized, in fact, precisely *as* a promotional self. The commodities it is induced to desire are those that would promotionally enhance its own value on the markets on which it, too, circulates.

ABSTRACT NATIONALITY AND GLOBAL CONSUMPTION

But what of Canada? Try as we might, we will be hard pressed to find anything distinctively Canadian about the figure in the ad other than the maple leaves on his shirt. To be sure he is named as one of ours. For those who had been following the Olympic story, Harnett will already be identifiable as one of Canada's brightest hopes for a gold, and thus a potential contributor to the all-important medal count, which turns the Games as a whole into a popular index of national standing and collective esteem. However, with suitable substitutions, we can easily imagine the same ad being used in any number of countries. Change the emblem on the shirt and the particular cyclist used as a model—though not his general qualities—and the meanings of the ad, as we have traced them out, would hardly change at all. Within the frame of the ad, the national athlete displayed is only incidentally national. Ray-Ban Man is crafted to embody a set of ideological and lifestyle values, and a form of consumer self-identification, which have spread round the world.

According to a rule of the Olympic charter, all athletes compete as members of national teams (IOC 58-59). They are entered into competition through their own national Olympic organization, they wear national team colours, and in all the ceremonials of the Games, including the anthem that greets medal winners on the podium, they are identified as representatives of their country. The political premise of the modern Olympics was that by fielding national teams in an international competition—the whole billed as a festival for the world's youth—nationalism itself could be channelled into a common enthusiasm for the cause of co-operation and world peace. This is the famous "Olympic paradox," and it had a certain plausibility in the decades leading up to the First World War, when inter-imperialist rivalries were mounting, fuelled, at a popular level, by intense nationalist feelings. The Games never prevented the outbreak of war. But over the longer term the Olympic ritual has no doubt encouraged a countervailing "one world" sentiment, mass involvement in which would have been less intense if national team identification had not been used to draw people in. The Cold War rivalry between competing superpowers added another level to the passions being chanelled this way. In its troubled aftermath, with a fresh round of resurgent nationalisms upon us, the "Olympic paradox" still has some operational force.

With the rise of sponsorships and global marketing, however, the question of national vs. international identification in relation to the Games has come to present itself in very different terms. The Olympics and its imagery become shaped by its advertising function, with effects on both the national and international meanings put in play. Where identical products are being marketed worldwide, there are incentives to fashion ad campaigns centrally, so that they are everywhere and simultaneously the same. This economizes on design costs. There is also a sales advantage to be gained by imparting a brand identity that will be recognized wherever the product is sold. In some campaigns, for example, the Visa and IBM television ads that accompanied Atlanta, identical ads are run in many countries, with only the (spoken or written) language being changed. In others, like the Ray-Ban one, there are national variations on a common theme. This costs more but has the merit of deriving extra promotional force from a patriotic appeal while still building up an internationally consistent brand image. In the construction of such ads national difference is explicitly introduced, both to add meaning to the product and as a basis for addressing the reader/consumer. Yet variance with respect to this variable leaves unaffected what is common to the imaging of the product from one national setting to another. Nationality, in such advertising, incarnates a difference that makes no difference to the globally diffused meaning given to the product.

It may be said that nothing crucial is at stake here, since the notion that nationality is anything more than the ideological glue that holds together pseudo-unities in the face of their internal social contradictions is highly suspect (Anderson). In which case, we should not regard the cheering, face-painting and flag-waving for Team Canada as an unmixed good. Nor should we worry if marks of national difference are treated in advertising as artificial, interchangeable and completely secondary to ways of subjectively being in the social world that transcend territorial borders. On the other hand, borders can help define projects of community building in which the state and national institutions can play a positive role. There is also a world of difference between the spread of human solidarity in the active, help-my-neighbour sense, and common absorption into the cosmos of consumption. We might do well then to maintain a critical vigilance where forces that are dissolving borders pretend to address us as national citizens.

This need not mean taking refuge in a purely defensive, even lamenting, attitude—which is all too easy in a Canadian context. To be critical in relation to the Ray-Ban ad is to question ourselves as well as its cultural message. Considered in that light, the ad has an exemplary significance, as well as its own moment of truth. It illustrates a paradigm shift in which national identity becomes reconfigured as a market category in the context of a global consumer culture. In this new dispensation, the ad maps being "Canadian" onto the being of a promotionalized consumer.

The marginality of the ad's Canadian difference is emblematic not only of cultural homogenization at the level of shared symbols (here the Olympics), and of the reduction of flags to logos, but of a form of self-identification that, with the spread of the "high intensity" market, is itself becoming universal. Achieving the critical distance necessary to see the (self)promotional subjectivity presupposed in the ad as a *false* universal, i.e., as pervasive but dependent on historical and social conditions, is made difficult by cultural continuities between the reader/consumer, even a critical one, and itself. But reflecting on these continuities can also help. The ad's transfiguration of a Canadian Olympic athlete (with the stress on all three terms) into Ray-Ban Man replicates the larger cultural and economic process that has brought such advertising into being. Meditating on this can be an antidote to its spell.

NOTES

1 Classic accounts of the semiological structure of advertising are "The Rhetoric of the Image" in Barthes, and Williamson. See also chapter 2 of Wernick.

2 The impossibility of isolating the effects of advertising led Schudson to cast doubt on any "manipulation" thesis, though he joins other critical commentators in assuming an overall cultural impact of some kind. The latter is even less susceptible to empirical investigation, of course, than the purely sales effect.

3 The organizers of the (inaugurating) Athens Games in 1896, wedded to the Hellenic ideal of "leisure as the basis of culture" (Pieper), attempted to disqualify an employee of the British Embassy solely on the grounds that he worked for a wage. For an account of the early history of the modern Olympic Games see MacAloon.

4 "The Olympic Games are the exclusive property of the IOC which owns all rights relating thereto, in particular, and without, limitation, the rights relating to their organisation, exploitation, broadcasting and reproduction by any means whatsoever. All profits derived from the celebration of the Olympic Games shall be applied to the development of the Olympic movement and of sport" (IOC 18).

5 For the rise of mass media advertising in the context of Fordism see Ewen. McKendrick traces the wedding of production, promotion and design back to the industrial revolution. The harnessing of the "culture industry" to advertising in the inter-war period was first critically examined in Horkheimer and Adorno's essay "The Culture Industry:

Enlightenment as Mass Deception," which is one of the excursuses in *Dialectic of Enlightenment.*

6 The rules on the use of logos by athletes in the Games are specified in section 61 of the Olympic charter (IOC 82-85).

7 Historians have pointed out that the original Olympics went through their own form of commercialization—victorious athletes could expect high material awards from their *polis*—so we should be wary about identifying the ancient Games with their own founding myth, particularly as revived by de Coubertin. See Young.

8 De Coubertin gave his own account in *Olympic Memoirs.* See also Boulongne.

9 Foucault's *Discipline and Punish* treats Bentham's projected "reform" of the prison system in early nineteenth-century England as heralding a shift not only in punishment regimes, from exemplary punishment to confinement, socialization and control, but in the whole operation of social power. Bentham's own writings on the subject have recently been republished.

WORKS CITED

Anderson, B. *Imagined Communities: Reflections on the Origins and Spread of Nationalism.* London: Verso, 1983.

Barthes, Roland. *Music, Image, Text.* New York: Hill and Wang. 1977.

Bentham, Jeremy. *The Panopticon and Other Prison Writings.* London: Verso, 1975.

Boulongne, Y. *La vie et l'oeuvre de Pierre de Coubertin, 1863-1937.* Montreal: Leméac, 1975.

de Coubertin, P. *Olympic Memoirs.* Lausanne: IOC, 1979.

Derrida, Jacques. *Specters of Marx: The State of the Debt, the Work of Mourning, and the New International.* New York: Routledge, 1994.

Ewen, S. *Captains of Consciousness: Advertising and the Social Roots of the Consumer Culture.* New York: McGraw-Hill, 1976.

Foucault, Michel. *Discipline and Punish: The Birth of the Prison.* New York: Pantheon, 1977.

Grant, George. *Lament for a Nation: The Defeat of Canadian Nationalism.* Toronto: McClelland and Stewart, 1965.

Horkheimer, Max, and Theodor Adorno. *The Dialectic of Enlightenment.* New York: Herder and Herder, 1972.

International Olympic Committee. *The Olympic Charter.* Lausanne: IOC, 1992.

Jennings, Andrew, and Vyv Simpson. *Lords of the Rings: Power, Money and Drugs in the Modern Olympics.* Toronto: Stoddart, 1992.

Lyotard, Jean-François. *The Postmodern Condition: A Report on Knowledge.* Minneapolis: Minnesota UP, 1984.

MacAloon, J. *This Great Symbol: Pierre de Coubertin and the Origin of the Modern Olympics.* Chicago: Chicago UP, 1981.

Marcuse, Herbert. *Eros and Civilization: A Philosophical Enquiry into Freud.* New York: Vintage, 1955.

McKendrick, N., ed. *The Birth of a Consumer Society: The Commercialisation of Eighteenth Century England.* London: Europa 1982.

McLuhan, Marshall. *The Medium Is the Massage.* New York: Simon and Schuster, 1989.

Pieper, J. *Leisure: The Basis of Culture.* New York: Pantheon, 1952.

Schudson, M. *Advertising, the Uneasy Persuasion: Its Dubious Impact on American Society.* New York: Basic 1984.

Weber, Max. *The Protestant Ethic and the Spirit of Capitalism.* London: George Allen and Unwin, 1930.

Wernick, Andrew. *Promotional Culture: Advertising, Ideology and Symbolic Expression.* London: Sage, 1992.

Williamson, J. *Decoding Advertisements: Ideology and Meaning in Advertising.* London: Boyars, 1978.

Young, D. *The Olympic Myth of Greek Amateur Athletics.* Chicago: Ares, 1984.

HOCKEY AS CANADIAN POPULAR CULTURE: TEAM CANADA 1972, TELEVISION AND THE CANADIAN IDENTITY

Neil Earle

I t is a commonplace to assert that ice hockey signifies something about Canadian popular culture, indeed, Canadian culture as a whole. Yet what it does signify has not been a question that scholarship has settled or even studied exhaustively. The 1972 Canada-Soviet series is a useful model to probe these and other questions. How does electronic technology impact upon a mass audience? Is there a bardic function for television? How does it work?

In *Canada Learns to Play*, Alan Metcalf relates that G. M. Trevelyan wrote the social history of nineteenth-century Great Britain without once mentioning the most famous Englishman of his time, the cricket champion W. G. Grace (James qtd. in Metcalf 9). If Canada were substituted for England, perhaps Donald Creighton for Trevelyan, and Foster Hewitt and Wayne Gretzky for W. G. Grace, we would be going far toward framing the theme of this study. The subject is ice hockey in Canadian culture as perceived through the codes and aesthetics of electronic technology.

Hockey and television still seem inseparably linked in the popular imagination. On October 7, 1992, the Canadian Broadcasting Corpor-

Notes on pages 340-42.

ation (CBC) presented a televised documentary of the 1972 international hockey series between Team Canada and the former Union of Soviet Socialist Republics (USSR), a program that explored the lyricism and the menace that suffuses hockey at most levels. Later that winter the hockey announcer Danny Gallivan, for years the eloquent and elegant voice of the Montreal Canadiens, died. On February 28, 1993, hockey's dark side was further probed by another CBC "hybrid drama" involving the career of former Toronto Maple Leaf Brian "Spinner" Spencer. The theme was a "life cursed by violence" both on and off the ice (Righton 2).

Popular culture theory provides the methodological tools to more systematically study the game that—either for good or for ill—has helped define Canadians (MacIntosh and Greenhorn).[1] Though no irrefutable thesis has yet come to light as to why hockey looms so large in the Canadian popular imagination: "Canadians value hockey so highly," wrote the authors of *The Social Significance of Sport*, "it has been called Canada's culture" (McPherson, Curtis and Loy 21).[2]

The Canada-Soviet Series of September 1972 is a useful paradigm for a study of "our game" on two levels: first, the occasion the series provides for a reflection on the cultural nexus of the great national signifier; second, for the fact that electronic technology was sufficiently developed by 1972 to allow a fairly sustained probe into some of its codes and structures. Especially interesting is mass technology's capacity to transform play into a form of collective drama.

Hockey broadcasts and telecasts have long been a recognizable staple of Canadian popular culture. This article blends the insights of such theorists as Horace Newcomb, John Fiske and Paul Rutherford with the observations of players and keen followers of the game such as Ken Dryden, Michael Novak, Jack Ludwig and Doug Beardsley. "Technology," taught Martin Heidegger, "is a way of revealing" (12). Remarkably, in September 1972, at least twelve million Canadians gathered around their television sets and radios to hear the animated voice of hockey broadcaster Foster Hewitt exclaim: "Henderson has scored for Canada!" (Morrison 14).[3] The question is: what did this electronic national drama signify?

For twenty-seven days in September 1972, Canadian television was the matrix for a sports event that has become an enduring folk memory, a cultural text. Disparate notions of class, ethnicity and gender were welded into a rare Canadian moment. Millions of adult Canadians reserve hallowed psychic space not just for Pearl Harbor or the assassination of President John Kennedy but also for the memory of Paul Henderson's winning goal in Game Eight of the 1972 Canada-Soviet series. Hockey as mythos; the ice arena as locus for a technologically driven actuality drama? Perhaps.

If hockey is just a game in Canada, then the Rockies are just hills on the prairies. The game, like the mischievous puck itself, has the ability to ricochet and career unexpectedly in and out of the Canadian experience. Rick Salutin, in preparing his 1977 play *Les Canadiens,* was astonished to hear a sportswriter for the Montreal *Star* relate how the enduring success of the city's celebrated franchise had been seen by many as a ritualistic act of revenge for the Plains of Abraham. Wayne Gretzky's move to the United States in 1988 during the prime ministership of Brian Mulroney was a cultural signpost to an era, as was the refusal of Eric Lindros of Ontario to play for the Quebec City *Nordiques* in the aftermath of the Meech Lake constitutional crisis. The cultural significance attached to the 1972 series is further attested to by the fact that both President Nikolai Podgorny and Premier Alexei Kosygin were in the audience that September night in the Luzhniki Arena in Moscow when the Soviet team won their home-town opener over Team Canada, 5 to 4 (Morrison 135).

There were even those who claim that the series helped to pave the way for *glasnost,* long before Gorbachev. Students of sport, especially sport as a staple of popular culture, have elaborated upon it's myth-making potential (Novak xii). Michael Novak's provocative probe of hockey helps mollify such fair concerns as gender and physicality: "What is the basic underlying myth dramatized in hockey? One can't help noticing hockey's speed, its teamwork, its formal plays, its violent contact and exceptionally hot temper tantrums…and finally the exhilaration of slapping a tiny rubber puck into a narrow, low net" (94). Novak is one of the few analysts willing to penetrate through to hockey's mystical core:

> The game is played on ice. Its symbolic matrix lies in the lands of snow, blizzards and dark, freezing nights….One gets suggestions of an Ice Age once again smothering the planet. One senses the sheer celebration of hot blood holding out against the cold, the vitality of the warm human body, of exuberant speed rejoicing in its own heat, of violence and even the sight of red blood on white ice as a sign of animal endurance. (95)

Novak's study of our gender-biased and yet pervasive national pastime applies to Canada, even though we are not his prime focus: "Hockey celebrates the heat and passion of survival. Take the worst, accept and conquer. Give as well as get. Take it to them. If hockey is, with chess, the national sport of Russia, let the world recognize the fierce resolve of people toughened by their climate; let them remember Stalingrad" (96).

Doug Beardsley's personalized account of the game, *Country on Ice*, argues that in Canada hockey is played for its own sake, for the fact that almost every Canadian has been touched by its mystery and mystique. It is noteworthy, too, that hockey is a sport played with equal relish on both sides of the Ottawa River. Ice hockey has been called the "common coin" of Canada. Roch Carrier's tender and moving short story *The Hockey Sweater*, for example, touched both solitudes. It is hard to forget the impact of Maurice "the Rocket" Richard on French *and* English Canadians of the period just after World War II.

Hockey as our authentic "national anthem" (Beardsley 26) may indeed form one of the few imaginative knits for a huge country with a diverse population.[4] Jack Ludwig offers anecdotal evidence for the significance of hockey as a Canadian badge of identity on the international scene. At Munich, where over three hundred expatriates gathered to watch Canada lose 7-3 in the series opener, an Australian flung out this challenge to a disappointed Canadian: "Aye, mate, isn't this your game....What's going on losing to the Ruskies?" (Ludwig 46).[5]

Yet at home it was televised hockey that had elevated the game into a national preoccupation. Canadian content is alive and well on prime time each April to June, as the Stanley Cup playoff series skate its seemingly interminable way across the nation's television screens. Even today, with the "global game" in place, 60 percent of the NHL's players are Canadian. Broadcast historian Paul Rutherford offers this perspective:

> Hockey on television was an actuality broadcast. The broadcasters adjusted to the rhythms and routines of the game itself....The experience wasn't all that different from being in the arena....The camera's role was always to focus on the puck, providing close-ups around the nets or when the action got heavy and personal, say, on the boards or in the corners....The first producer of hockey was Sydney Newman who hadn't any real experience with the sport. After watching a game he told two old pros that it would be easy to cover—it was really like ballet.[6] (242-43)

Rutherford argues that television and hockey seemed to be made for each other: "The audience for hockey grew to about 3.5 million English Canadians and around 2 million French Canadians....The success of hockey, first on CBC and later on CTV, had no counterpart in the United States, until the birth of ABC's 'Monday Night Football' in 1970....Many people experienced hockey only via the television set or the radio" (245).

Television played well to the game's strengths. Hockey is a transition game—everyone gets a chance to jump "over the boards" and into the fray, and it is one of the few games where players can change "on the fly." Crucially, the spectators are very much part of the action in the confined, enclosed arena; they are close to the ice surface. This serves to heighten the intensity of crowd reactions, reactions which the cameras and microphones—in that relatively small space—can easily amplify. It is not extravagant to assert a parallel between televised hockey's participatory dynamic and the presentational and affective aspects of Greek and Shakespearean drama, the Odeon and the "wooden O." As noted, the audience is very much involved. Add to this the distinctive pacing and "rhythm" of a hockey game, the changing mood and psychological tempo created by the switches in focus from the team to the individual player and back again. This makes for a superb aesthetic spectacle. An abstract from a game narrated by the accomplished Danny Gallivan in the early 1960s is illustrative:

> The Hawks regrouping behind their own line coming out over centre. Beliveau STEALS the puck, takes a shot right on the short side and Hall was there to stymie him with a scintillating save...Cournoyer now CUTTING IN on goal, trying to get right IN FRONT...ANOTHER SHOT...the Canadiens really firing the puck around with authority...Lemaire WINDS UP, Beliveau takes a poke at it...COURNOYER A REAL SPINNERAMA...THEY BANG AWAY AT IT, THEY BANG IT IN! and the Montreal Forum crowd goes crazy.[7] (Gallivan qtd. by Beardsley 24-25)

Hockey's speed and intensity played well to the myth of a rough, tough game demanding skill, effort, commitment, endurance. "It was the Canadian game because we had created it....It suited a land in which the winter always loomed so large," explains Rutherford. "Even more the game fitted an image of Canadian manhood" (Rutherford

248). If there is no Canadian Stalingrad or Marathon, might not the Stanley Cup playoffs (at least historically) and the international Canada Cup competitions form an imaginative substitute? Ward Cornell, a broadcaster from the 1960s, expressed one aspect of hockey's overweening maleness: "We're tough, rugged guys from the north," he expostulated half-jokingly to Rutherford (Rutherford 248).[8] The element of catharsis encouraged the "juvenile" facets of the game ("Stand your ground, don't back down from a fight!"), the ugly primitivism that led inevitably to the outcries and protests against hockey violence. Ludwig's comments are still apt: "Canadian seamen of long professional foulmouth careers would sound like Little Lord Fauntleroy at any NHL practice session....To be a man in Canada is to *fight*. The sweetest hero this side of heaven is someone like Derek Sanderson, who isn't really very good at fighting, but fights nevertheless, because getting beaten shows much more macho than skating away" (41-42).[9]

Yet hockey reflects another part of the male sensibility that televised hockey enlarges, magnifies and transmits. This aspect is its most redeeming cultural feature and lies close to the core of the hockey mystique. This was and *is* the game's evocation of a peculiarly Canadian paradisaical myth, the appeal to "the boy inside the man," a myth that intelligent students and players of the game have captured. Ken Dryden is a former goaltender in the National Hockey League. One of the photographs in Dryden's *Home Game* is simply and tellingly entitled "Icons." It features a small square photograph of the Montreal Forum scoreboard imposed upon a two-page spread of boys in toques and sweaters playing shinny (the unstructured form of hockey) on a slough in St. Denis, Saskatchewan (Dryden and MacGregor 4-5).

The picture brilliantly enframes hockey's imaginative hold over millions of Canadian males.[10] The image of the boy with his hockey stick on the outdoor pond evokes something distinctive: "the true north strong and free," a myth that, as we shall see, can be strengthened by technology. What Dryden elsewhere characterized as "the voice in my head" was an electronic imprint. The alchemy of electronic technology thus made possible in televised hockey a synchronization of the mythopoeic and the mechanical. A flooded driveway became a locus of myth:

It was Maple Leaf Gardens filled to wildly cheering capacity, a tie game, seconds remaining. I was Frank Mahovlich or Gordie Howe. I was anyone I wanted to be, and the voice in my head was that of Leafs broadcaster Foster Hewitt: "...there's ten seconds left, Mahovlich, winding up at his own line, at centre, eight seconds, seven, over the blueline, six—he winds up, he shoots, he scores!"

It was a glorious fantasy, and I always heard that voice. It was what made my fantasy seem almost real. For to us, who attended hockey games mostly on TV or radio, an NHL game, a Leafs game, was played with a voice. If I wanted to be Mahovlich or Howe, if I moved my body the way I had seen them move theirs and did nothing else, it would never quite work. But if I heard the voice that said their names while I was playing out the fantasy, I could believe it. Foster Hewitt could make me them. (Dryden 67-68)

This is the romance of hockey: play as idyll. The mysterious bonding of millions of Canadian males to "the game" traces back to the pond, the slough, the indoor rink, to the iced driveway, to the time when they, in their youthful fantasies, were Gordie Howe or Bobby Orr or Wayne Gretzky. Here is hockey's spiritual core, the central explanation for its mystical attraction for prime ministers and pipefitters, for Nobel Prize winners and new immigrants. This beguiling innocence mitigates and helps neutralize the often embarrassing sexism and violence.

On September 28, 1972, both Ken Dryden and Foster Hewitt were on hand when twelve million Canadians—not all of them male—heard the most memorable lines in Canadian sports history: "Cournoyer has it on that wing. Here's a shot. Henderson makes a wild stab for it and falls. Here's another shot. Right in front. They score! Henderson has scored for Canada" (Morrison 15).

Televised hockey is superb participatory drama. Drama needs heroic, antiheroic or otherwise transcendently significant leading characters. Keith Cunningham believes that sport resembles sacred time:

There is a festival time in the soul. We dress ourselves up and jump from profane time, time as linear continuation, 9 to 5, week in week out, into sacred time. In sacred time, as Mircea Eliade has called it, we enter the flight of mythic fantasy. We enter again the old tales, we live again the high adventure of the soul. Everything becomes fluid in a shifting landscape; we are Hercules as much—or as little—as our existential selves. We are here and we are there.[11] (Cunningham 30)

Sacred time is re-emphasized in the ritual aspects of sport. The lighting of the Olympic torch is one example. Cunningham links the mythos of sport to drama:

> Always at issue is man's relation to Being. Is he going to remain a dreamer in the cavern, repeating the round of illusions and pleasure-principle fantasies forever, or is he going to recognize the dynamic patterns behind the scenes which govern his own life....The drama is itself a symbol, unfolding in time....The dramatic hero, like the dream ego, acts as our magic double, inhabiting the compressed underworld of the drama, subjected to trials and experiencing incredible delights for our sake. [Drama] immerses us in the emotional experience of growth through crisis. (33, 35)

Drama, argues Cunningham, is an acting out, a symbolic participation in ritual. As such, ice hockey's values of actuality and involvement provide an experience with the potential to "wound us with knowledge." In September 1972 technology created an electronically centred national drama, a conclusion attested to by popular culture theory.

Many theorists of popular culture refuse to ascribe a mere passive or negative role to the television audience. John Fiske, for example, sees culture making as a social process. Fiske differentiates popular culture from mass culture. In the popular, he asserts, the people themselves actively engage in shaping social meanings from the products offered by the consumer society. A hockey stick is a product of mass culture, but a hockey stick advertised by Mario Lemieux becomes an artifact of popular culture. People, in effect, invest mass commodities with socio-cultural meanings. In Fiske's term, "meanings meet" (*Reading* 2, 84). The public, the consumers of mass culture, give mass-produced items a meaning that they "decode" from the product.

Semioticians speak about "the phenomenon of duplicity" (Hawkes 68), a larger possibility of meanings than is connoted by the obvious, intended meaning (Marchand 154-55, 235-38, 270). Thus, for a mass-culture item—a three-piece suit, a pair of blue jeans or a Canadiens sweater—to become a significant item of the popular culture, a process of mediation must take place. In the Fiskean analysis, the consumer is engaged in cultural production, in giving an artifact of mass culture—a record, a T-shirt, a television program—a meaning that will assure it a place in the public imagination (*Television* 14). Just as millions of teens had their "favourite

Beatle" in the 1960s, so millions of Canadians have been able to identify with Maurice "the Rocket" Richard, Ted "Teeder" Kennedy, Gordie Howe, Bobby Hull, Bobby Orr, Wayne Gretzky, Doug Gilmour and Brendan Shanahan.

In theory, it is at least probable that Canadians are involved in a form of collective myth-making when watching hockey telecasts. The mass audience "decodes" the game polyvalently. On one level, there is a fairly straightforward hero-worship dynamic at work. Yet there are hidden duplicities as well. Some enjoy the "We're rough, tough guys from the North" message; hence hockey's violence and juvenility has never hurt its ratings. Others perhaps enjoy the social segmentation that Rutherford noticed. ("Where are all the women?" said one woman to her husband during her first game at Maple Leaf Gardens.) Then as the wrestling phenomenon illustrates, excess is appealing. The striking uniforms, the crowd noises, the bodychecks—these aspects of excess throw into bold relief conventional notions of decorum, propriety and law and order. Hockey's very physicality is part of its appeal. For good or ill, the violence has rarely hurt its ratings in Canada.

Ice hockey thus represents a multifaceted, rich and duplicitous text, rooted in rural signifiers, the symbolic recall of simpler, more innocent days on the pond or slough when life was fresh and bright and bracing and friendship seemed forever. Here are aspects of a northern pastoral myth that, in Canada, at least until fairly recently, was not all myth. Is this hockey's *sanctum sanctorum*, a locus of that elusive, intangible, "true north strong and free"?

In 1972 "meanings met." The series with the USSR stirred potent cultural signifiers. Ken Dryden felt it. He wrote at the time: "[A]s far as the vast majority of Canadians are concerned, this series was not conceived in a spirit of brotherhood and understanding but as a means of putting down the Russians and asserting our claim to hockey supremacy" (Dryden and Mulvoy 65). The mass audience across Canada functioned as an imaginative sensorium capable of being "wounded with knowledge," of experiencing Aristotelian tragic pity and fear as well as moments of transcendence. In September 1972 the codes and aesthetics of television gave a heightened dramatic spin to a moment of high nationalist tension: an imaginative echoing of the Greek-Persian wars, at least metaphorically.[12] In September 1972 Canadian television tapped the latent myth-making inherent in all sport:

> Sports [offers] cohesion and identity, the mythic model. Because of the powerful visibility of such a model, it has always been used as far more than either entertainment or cultural unifier. It is quickly transformed into a vehicle for cultural values, and we translate the playing field into an image for "real life." The virtues of practice, hard work, dedication, desire, competitive spirit, fair play, "good sportsmanship," and a host of other commodities are pointed out to generation after generation of young people. The language of the games, the initiations into rituals, the formalities of winning, are transformed into mystical moments. Sport is hallowed as holy text. (Newcomb 193)

Some twelve million Canadians came to share in the vicarious climax when Henderson scored for Canada. Many were to watch the last game at home, at work or at school as—in some cases—television sets were brought into classrooms by excited teachers aware that a moment of Canadian history was being made.

Sports writer Scott Young remembered the excitement the series generated in the country:

> Nothing to match the excitement of this series had ever happened in Canada; rarely anywhere in any sport. The last time Canada had beaten the Soviets at hockey was in the world championships of 1961....Nine years of regular beatings later Canada said to hell with it and withdrew from world competition.
>
> The ultimate...then and now, is for world championships to be decided by the best against the best; the best, in Canada's terms, meaning professionals. (Young 172)

Ken Dryden caught the embedded nationalist agenda:

> The talk all through the summer of 1972 was about the series. And because Canada was the best and sure to win, Canadians couldn't wait for the series to begin. It would be a glorious "coming out" party, a celebration of us. This gave to it a more fundamental dimension. For though much may be special about Canada, surrounded as it is historically and geographically by countries that are bigger, richer, more powerful, whose specialness seems more obvious, we cling to every symbol. A game is a game. But a symbol is not. We had to win this series.[13] (Dryden and MacGregor 202)

Dryden is right; symbols are important. The name of the team, "Team Canada," was studded with meaning. It was put in a form that would be easily translatable into both French and English, thus fitting the bilingual ethos of the times. Little wonder that opening night, September 2, 1972, at the prestigious Forum in Montreal resembled, in retrospect, Act One in a true national drama. Phil Esposito, the rugged goal-scorer from the Boston Bruins, was nearly manic over the need to win the opening event: "It was only a ceremonial face-off, but I had to win that draw.... I mean, I had to win that draw!! This guy didn't even try and it really aggravated me....I remember I drew the puck back and put up my hand like, wow, we won the first face-off!" (Dryden and MacGregor 204-205). The tension was contagious: "At that same moment, sounding a little surprised himself, Foster Hewitt, who had in his lifetime described thousands of games, was telling his nation-wide audience, 'I can't recall any game that I've ever been at where you can just feel the tension. And it keeps building up'" (Dryden and MacGregor 205).

The opening moments exploded with emotional energy and harbingers. Esposito scored for Canada after the first thirty seconds, Paul Henderson six minutes later. But in the next fifty-three minutes, recalled Dryden, "Team Canada's players, its fans, Canadians, could feel everything slipping away" (Dryden and MacGregor 205). After such an explosive start the Soviets efficiently fought back to win 7-3. It was the worst of all possible scenarios: Team Canada humbled in one of the holy of holies of Canadian hockey, the Montreal Forum. The exhilarating spectacle that was to engage the entire nation for the next few days was launched.

As the continued fascination with "horror" movies reveals, popular culture is pleasurable even if it resembles the nail-biting intensity of pseudo-masochism or humiliation. After the first game Canadian coach Harry Sinden chronicled: "A little piece of all of us died today" (Sinden 8). Scott Morrison captures perfectly that mingled feeling of exhilaration and apprehension as the second game opened two nights later in Toronto: "The best players the NHL were allowed to assemble playing under the name Team Canada had been soundly beaten, and their pride had been deeply wounded. So, when they stepped on the ice that night for a second game in Toronto, they weren't playing for a doubting nation, but mostly for themselves. As a team" (Morrison 65-66).

The nation-wide audience knew that by the tried and true rhythm of playoff hockey this second game would be crucial. The feeling in Maple Leaf Gardens was palpable. The cameras framed a bright red maple leaf on the television screens of the millions who watched:

> There existed in historic Maple Leaf Gardens that night more stifling
> pressure than excitement…though the support of the fans was stagger-
> ing. In conservative Toronto, where the fans are generally quite
> reserved…on this night they stood as one and chilled the air singing the
> national anthem. But there also remained a sharp sense of trepidation, of
> apprehension. This sense no longer pertained to what the opposition
> would bring, but the home team. (Morrison 64-65)

The cameras and commentary were relaying bardic television, func-
tioning as an electronic Aeschylus or the airwaves encompassing the
Atlantic and Pacific coasts.[14] It superbly transmitted tragic pity and
fear. Once again the chorus-like presence of Foster Hewitt accentuated
the strained emotion. A hapless Team Canada felt the sting of tragic
reversal: after Game One a solid majority of their countrymen condemned them for refusing to shake hands with the Soviets, a convention of international hockey, and an echo of the Greek ethos of sacred
play. This was a harbinger. That night, however, Maple Leaf Gardens
was the venue for the spectacle of redemption: Team Canada won 4-1.
It was to be their most decisive victory of the series.

Television's superb "theatre of the ether" synergized ice hockey,
Team Canada and the electronic aesthetic in a transcendent moment.
Peter Mahovlich's shorthanded goal at 6:47 of the third period incar-
nated the ideals according to Novak:

> One imagines that in every human life is cocooned an ideal form, the
> ideal beauty of which the human race is capable….Imagine that we walk
> through our days on hidden tracks, in cycles round and round, and at
> foreordained moments we are lifted out of the ordinary sphere and
> allowed momentarily in the eternal "time of the heroes."…In the sacred
> time of sports, the time of the heroes occasionally breaks through. No
> one dictates the moment. It comes when it comes….One experiences a
> complete immersion in the present, absorption in an instantaneous and
> abundant now…life in a different mode from that of the life we normally
> lead in time. (130, 131)

Mahovlich scored as the Soviets, with a one-man advantage, were
pressing hard. Paul Henderson would never forget it: "I can still see
that goal….He was one-on-one with the defenceman [Evgeny
Poladyev], and when he got to the blue line he faked the slapshot,
pulled in the puck and froze the defenceman. Then he just barged

through and reached around Tretiak to tuck the puck behind him. It was an absolutely incredible goal. That one put the icing on the cake for us. It was short-handed and put us ahead 3-1 (Morrison 69).

Yet, the Drama of Redemption that unfolded in Game Two was only a prelude to the Theatre of the Absurd that would unfold in Games Three and Four. Professional hockey's crude commercialism emerged in full force. The public squabble about the exclusion of superstar Bobby Hull began it. Hull had signed with the Winnipeg Jets of the rival World Hockey Association. The rival National Hockey League, which supplied most of the roster for Team Canada, refused to let him play despite urgent pleas from Prime Minister Trudeau. Like fractious Greeks bickering while a hostile force remained unsubdued, the internal team squabbles went public. A few of the highly touted stars found that relative newcomers like Bobby Clarke and J. P. Parise were outplaying them and getting more ice time as a result.[15]

Thus a fractious Team Canada was forced to endure the irony of superstar Bobby Hull watching from Winnipeg as his brother Dennis played. Game Three was a heartbreaking encounter. The Canadians gave up two leads on brilliant shorthanded goals by the Soviets (i.e., scoring while Team Canada had the one-man advantage)—the cruellest cut in ice hockey. Team Canada was thankful just to skate away with a 4-4 tie. An "eerie feeling of impending doom" was intensifying as Game Four loomed in Vancouver.

The ambivalence about Team Canada that was building up across the country is best expressed in theatrical terms: the footlights were definitely down; the spectators were very much part of the action; and they were angry. One of the pleasures of popular culture is the opportunity sometimes presented to vent feelings of rage or frustration at an object of disapproval. The sneering at politicians or at inane commercial advertisements on television are classic examples. Oppositionality—having it both ways—is an earmark of the popular. The mass audience treasures its freedom to pick and choose, to mediate between alternatives, to have it both ways.

On September 8, 1972, the Vancouver fans chose revenge. The feverish Fourth Game in British Columbia saw Team Canada crushed 5-2. Worse, it was a loss Team Canada perhaps made inevitable by drawing two rather silly minor penalties in the first ten minutes. The "home" part of the series had ended with the Soviets holding a commanding 2-1-1 lead. The final four games were to be played in Moscow. Ken Dryden related later: "It seemed as though it had all slipped beyond us" (Dryden and Mulvoy 94).

Then came an unusual chain reaction of events. First, the players, seared by the reaction of the Vancouver fans, steeled their determination and decided to "win it for themselves" (Dryden and Mulvoy 97, 102). Second, what Horace Newcomb has called "the aesthetics of television" began to emerge as a factor in its own right. According to Newcomb: "The central symbol of television is the family...a tightly knit circle" (Newcomb 261). The perennially popular situation-comedy format is television's stock in trade: "The smallness of the television screen has always been its most noticeable physical feature. It means something that the art created for television appears on an object that can be part of one's living room, exist as furniture. It is significant that one can walk around the entire apparatus. Such smallness suits television for intimacy; its presence brings people into the viewer's home to act out drama" (Newcomb 245).

Television, claims Newcomb, has a bias for intimacy: "Television is at its best when it offers us faces, reactions, explorations of emotions registered by human beings. The importance is not placed on the action, though that is certainly vital as stimulus. Rather, it is on the reaction to the action, to the human response" (Newcomb 245-56).

Not action but reaction—an interesting thesis. That wild night in Vancouver did not end with Team Canada's loss. Something else happened. Television beamed the spectacle of a totally believable Phil Esposito—his "sad-eyed, washed-out face, bathed with the sweat of the world," in Dryden's words—speaking "heart to heart" with the Canadian public. Esposito, who had emerged as the unofficial leader of Team Canada, had his moment of personal angst captured by the camera in extreme close-up as waves of frustration convulsed his countrymen. Yet Esposito treated the television audience to what television does effectively, some would say too effectively: the personalizing and humanizing of a complex, mass spectacle:

> To the people of Canada, we're trying our best....The people boo us. We're all disappointed, disenchanted. I can't believe people are booing us. If the Russians boo their players like some of our Canadian fans— not all, just some—then I'll come back and apologize. We're completely disappointed. I can't believe it. We're trying hard. Let's face facts.

They've got a good team. We're all here because we love Canada. It's our home and that's the only reason we came. (Morrison 95)

The "intimate" medium was about to transform the thirty or so players of Team Canada into "our guys," an embattled little family up against life's bewildering complexities and letdowns. This was what television had been transmitting and celebrating for decades: the embattled little surrogate families of *Star Trek* and *The Beachcombers*, of *A Gift to Last* and *Upstairs, Downstairs*. Audiences identified with the tight little worlds of the Plouffes and the Bunkers, the Kings of Kensington and the Waltons.

If there was intimacy there was also *continuity*, the second of Newcomb's televisual aesthetics. Prime time's dynamics helped make Team Canada as familiar as extended family: Clarke and Cournoyer, Henderson and Ratelle, Esposito and the Mahovlich brothers. Heroes are often found in defeat, as the reputations of Winston Churchill, Charles de Gaulle and John Diefenbaker can attest. The shrill voice of Foster Hewitt crackling across the ether from the grim and dour Soviet capital for the last four games thus deepened the element of participatory drama. In Ken Dryden's words, those scratchy transmissions over the pole came embedded with their own dramatic intensity, "momentous with distance…never certain of getting through" (Dryden and MacGregor, 194).

The Canadians seated at their sets that night of September 22, 1972, for the first telecast from Moscow, were involved by now in something deeper than sport. There was an element of heroic daring in the fact of a middle power contending with the largest country in land mass in the world, a nuclear-armed superpower at the time, for hockey primacy. The denouement would be played in a capital that had refused to yield before Napoleon and Hitler. Who were the Canadians to think they could redeem themselves in such a place?[16] The very audacity of the attempt seemed heroic. The fight had to be played out to the final seconds according to the prescribed codes of sport. If this was not Newcomb's "mythic model," then what was?

Team Canada lost their first game in Moscow 5-4. Yet the Canadians "were adjusting, adapting, experimenting…now able to break up the Soviets' intricate passing plays" (Morrison 151). Thus Game Six was do-or-die for Team Canada, a spiritual *ne plus ultra*. They chose to "do." Game Six produced the first Canadian victory since that seemingly long-ago night in Toronto. It was noted for something else as well, a particular piece of infamy that starkly reflects hockey's dark side. Canada's Bobby Clarke purposely set out to "tap" the speedy Russian Kharlamov's ankle. Years later Clarke was only mildly repentant: "It's not something I would've done in an NHL game, at least I hope I wouldn't. But that situation…at that stage in the series, with everything that was happening, it was necessary" (Morrison 167).

"With everything that was happening"—if there was little grace in Clarke's confession there was admittedly some in his candour. For by now these were obviously more than just hockey games; the whole experience had been lifted beyond sport.[17] The series was pointing to something beyond itself, something primal, something of hockey's own elemental origins in the ice aspic of snow and frost. The juvenility and sexism, the Odysseus-like cunning and calculated cruelty—hockey's eternal dark side was always present though somehow counterbalanced by a sense of transcendence. The three thousand-plus fans who flew to Moscow to shout "Da, da Canada; nyet, nyet, Soviet" testified to that. So did Bobby Orr's desire to sit behind the bench as a supporter, his bad knees making it impossible for Sinden to play him. Another quiet piece of heroism was the way players of the calibre of Stan Mikita and Rod Seiling waited patiently for ice time that hardly ever came.

All added to the drama, a drama that wounded with knowledge. Technology's bias for revealing transmitted more and more of the pride as well as the insecurity welling up from deep inside the psyche of an awkward, still insecure nation at a "coming out party" with the whole world watching. "They were Russia. We were Canada," Harry Sinden recalled. The attitude was: "I'm playing for…every Canadian in the world who ever put on skates and thought about being the best in the world, if only in his dreams" (Sinden 15). The emotional intensity of this electronic actuality drama stunned all the participants. "Some of them [the players] after that series were never the same," Tony Esposito related years later.

After Team Canada pulled together for a 4-3 victory in a wild stick-swinging Game Seven to tie the series, the stage was set for the final resolution:

> "Hello Canada! I'm Foster Hewitt and I'll be doing the play-by-play for tonight's eighth and final game of the series…" The game was broadcast on both CBC and CTV. All other programming came to a stop. Canada's

population in 1972 was 21.8 million. On this Thursday afternoon, a
work day, 7.5 million watched. (Dryden and MacGregor 212)

"Hello Canada!" He'd been saying that for decades but it never seemed
to resonate with such meaning before. For, in an amazing moment of
postmodern reflexivity, it was Foster Hewitt "playing" Foster Hewitt
that added to that sense of other-worldliness that last night in Moscow.
The aura lingers even today. The eighteen year old at the checkout
counter said, "Oh, you mean the Big One!" when asked to locate the
video cassette of the 1972 series. As a sporting phenomenon that ended
in a memorable display of the power of the television aesthetic and of
the mythos of sport, the Canada-Soviet series is unique. It carried the
freight of multiple, embedded meanings.

The last four games evoked another shared folk memory. There was
the weighted sociological meaning of over four decades of families
huddled around the radio as Foster Hewitt's voice came crackling from
far away, from one of the few big cities in Canada at the time. From the
1930s to the 1960s it was Foster Hewitt who had set up, for millions of
Canadian boys, the electronic voice in their heads:

> How old were we when we first heard the nasal, rasping voice of Foster
> Hewitt's "He shoots! He scores!" coming at us over the airwaves? [Foster
> Hewitt]...convinced me that the world of the imagination was where I
> wanted to be....Sitting by the fire having supper or doing the dishes. On
> the farm. In a tiny fishing village. No other game has been such a force
> in bringing our country together. A Canadian boy's dreams were nurtured
> by Foster Hewitt....To steal a famous baseball announcer's axiom:
> Nothing happened until he said so. (Beardsley 19-20)

On the night of September 28, 1972, twelve million Canadians heard
that voice say that they were the best in the world at the game of
hockey. It was a unique Canadian epiphany. A Soviet coach commented
years later: "We do not have the spirit to draw on that these Canadians
do." To him, the Canadian players had "a light that cannot be put
out....You defeat them sometimes, but you discourage them never"
(Beardsley 36). What was the source of that light? Was it money and
commercialism? Was it male physicality and exclusiveness? It was
something much deeper. It was being caught up in the rapture of a collective myth as enhanced by electronic technology.

The national fervour unleashed across the country was unprecedented in modern, peace-time Canada, but not just there. "Muscovites saw them everywhere," the Toronto *Sun* reported on the three thousand Canadians who had travelled to Moscow. "Walking hand in hand through the Gum department store. Singing Da, Da, Canada—Nyet, Nyet, Soviet; waving their little Canadian flags in the lineup which occasionally stretched for a mile outside Lenin's tomb" (Creighton 19). Back home, Ontario Education Minister Tom Wells intervened to allow half a million elementary and secondary school students in the province to watch or listen to the final game in school auditoriums or cafeterias. A *Toronto Star* survey "failed to find a single school where students would not get the chance to follow the game" ("500,000" 2). On September 29, the day after the final victory, the *Globe and Mail* led with "From Russia With Glory." Colin McCullough's report from the USSR interestingly profiled "the fans who discovered their own nationality in Moscow":

> The games have been splendid of course...[b]ut the series produced more than hockey scores. For one thing, a lot of Canadians discovered their nationality. Had any of them ever before stood up and loudly sung O Canada, even the high notes, with tears running down their cheeks? They did it at the Palace of Sports at Lenin Central Stadium, and it was because of Canada, not hockey....In the hotels and in the streets, the factory worker from Hamilton felt quite comfortable discussing hockey on the Moscow subway with Seagram's president Edward Bronfman of Montreal or any other available Canadian. (McCullough 1)

The Halifax *Chronicle-Herald* reported that the federal election campaign of 1972 had "ground to a standstill" for the last act of the drama ("Feared"). Frank Moores, then premier of Newfoundland, invited all members of victorious Team Canada to spend a week's holiday hunting and fishing at government expense while, on the other end of the country, British Columbia leader Dave Barrett exulted: "The French couldn't do it [i.e., conquer Moscow], the Germans couldn't do it; now Canada has done it and they had better get out of town before it starts snowing" ("Giant"). The *Calgary Herald*, whose front page on September 28 pictured a crowd of Calgarians watching the game in a downtown department store, a scene "undoubtedly repeated in stores, offices and living rooms across the country," recorded how actor

William Hutt, declaiming King Lear at Stratford, Ontario, paused dramatically during the storm scene, to announce the score to the two thousand students in his audience ("Canadians").[18]

Hockey, with all its regrettable "male-only" encodements, its violence and occasional juvenility, ice hockey—warts and all—serves as a primal source of identity reinforcement for Canadians. It is rooted in a paradisiacal locus in the imagination drawing upon the game's rural, northern signifiers. To play that game on the rivers, ponds and frozen rinks that dot the icy landscape appears to be nothing less than a Canadian rite of passage, a vital part of the acculturation process. It begins in the backyards and on the rivers and even now, in the arenas and indoor stadiums, it has become ingested into the growing-up process as something Canadians do that is distinctive in a way that no one else does with quite the same intensity and devotion: "firewagon hockey."[19]

If the 1972 series was a Canadianized form of the Greek-Persian Wars, and Foster Hewitt—to stretch the metaphor—was our electronically transmitted Homer with a microphone, then television served in 1972 as a national theatre, a theatre of the ether. The tiny screen became the locus for moments of transcendence, "the time of heroes." Television's bias for intimacy helped enshrine one of those rare moments of collective national myth-sharing, an electronically catalyzed national drama.

In 1972 television superbly transmitted the poetry of hockey, its lyricism and its menace. Paul Henderson's game-winning goal in Game Eight is illustrative. With four Soviet players close around him at the centre line, he somehow scooped up the bouncing puck and pulled away with the Russians in hot pursuit. Moving in over the Soviet line he had one defenceman draped around him as he began to fall. Incredibly, he somehow squeezed away a shot at Tretiak, to beat the Russian goalie from an almost impossible angle. Finally, he and the Soviet defender slid gracefully out of camera range together, a freeze-framed tribute to the poetry of hockey and to the poetry of television.

To watch that goal is to see incarnated Novak's sense of northern hardiness wresting narrow victory against the primitive elements of ice and snow, not a Canadian epiphany set against the inhospitability and bleakness of the landscape. Something vital, something spiritual had broken into the mundane world of profane time: "the time of heroes." A game nurtured amid the eternal mountains, lakes and prairies that make up Canada—scenes of both lyricism and menace—does indeed fulfil Novak's celebration of "hot blood holding out against the cold." Through hockey, Canadians most characteristically celebrate a delight in speed and skill and gracefulness of form in the face of a bleak and often unforgiving environment.

The 1972 series lives in the popular imagination. It demonstrated as never before or since that televised hockey, perhaps the most characteristic artifact of Canada's popular culture, points to something essential about Canadians as a northern people. Thus winter, with its abstract black and white patterns, its long shadows and desolation, has nurtured—perhaps to their surprise—a nation of myth-makers after all.[20]

NOTES

1   The authors construct the thesis that it was concern for Canada's prestige on the international level that was a prime springboard for the 1972 series.
2   Unfortunately the authors do not expand on that statement.
3   Morrison, a sports reporter for the Toronto *Sun*, is president of the Professional Hockey Writers' Association. His book is a valuable resource for the series not the least because of the fairly thorough interviews conducted with the help of his colleague Pat Grier. The interviews amount to as thorough a personal retrospective as we presently have from the principals involved with Team Canada 1972.
4   A key organizer of the series, Allan Eagleson, shared his reflections on his reception in Montreal upon arrival from Moscow. He was overwhelmed by excited spectators crowding the train station, "everyone talking about the series, and all of it in French" (Morrison 220).
5   Ludwig's engaging and frank account is a valuable reference for anyone studying the 1972 series as a cultural signifier. His string of colourful recollections still resonates more than twenty years later.
6   Rutherford is an indispensable source for anyone analyzing television's impact upon Canadians in its early years. He is generally fair and objective, both on the issue of "Canadian content" and on the subject of the medium itself.
7   Perhaps more attention needs to be paid to the aesthetics of hockey announcing as a cultural form. Hewitt's and Gallivan's styles are the best places to start.
8   The loquacious Howie Meeker, another of the game's intense analysts and a television commentator of note, opened up all kinds of possibilities for postmodern students of ideology in a personal interview at Maple Leaf Gardens in November 1991. "Boy, it's rough," Meeker told the writer. "We play it hard. I tell you it's free enterprise….[It] reflects the countries it's played in…it's a reflection of the free market system."
9   Of course Ludwig happily provides evidence of this Canadian equation of manliness and hockey in his gripping series of vignettes sprinkled through

his account of the 1972 series: Wayne Cashman playing with a serious gash in his tongue; Serge Savard likewise afflicted with a hairline fracture; the six-foot, eight-inch (on skates) Peter Mahovlich charging over the boards, stick at the ready, to rescue a beleaguered Alan Eagleson in the final game.

10 This seems to apply to many women as well. One thing that surprised me at a University of Toronto graduate seminar on hockey was how the co-eds accepted hockey's "boy inside the man" mythos as more than compensating for its physicality. "Well, it's a rough game played by rough people," was a common response.

11 The linkage between film and television, though not absolute, is clear enough for our purposes.

12 CBC-Television production, "Summit on Ice" (October 7, 1992). Earnest testimonials to this deduction were not lacking on this telecast: "It wasn't a game, it wasn't a series," Phil Esposito declaimed to an interviewer, "it was our society against their society." Allan Eagleson, a key organizer, stated: "In those days, the Soviet Union was the...home of communism, the enemy of democracy." Serge Savard speculated on what a Canadian defeat would mean: "It was like the...communist country sending the world a message that the our system was better than yours."

13 Dryden's summation of the series in chapter 5 has a fine postmodern ring in its title, "No Final Victories," perhaps an illustration of the crossover between hockey and the realities of Canadian life in the past two decades.

14 "He not only invented the drama," says Hamilton, "he raised it to a height which has only once been equalled" (182).

15 Interestingly, the debate Plutarch related between Themistocles and the Spartan leader Eurybiades included a reference to sports: "You know, Themistocles, at the games they thrash anybody who starts before a signal," Eurybiades chided his rival. Meanwhile Xerxes was on the march (Scott-Kilvert 88-89).

16 The military analogy was also seized upon by Jack Ludwig, as noted in his comments after the game opener: "Not only had the headlines in the Montreal papers been of a size and blackness one associated with a World War but the metaphors used in the days that followed were frequently derived from World War I and World War II. Ypres was invoked. Dieppe. Dunkirk" (45).

17 By now Team Canada was, in Cunningham's phrase, "out of the body and flying." Yvan Cournoyer considered the experience: "Better than ten Stanley Cups." Paul Henderson testified: "Almost every day of my life a Canadian will come up to me and shake my hand and say, 'Thank you for one of the greatest thrills of my life.'" Ron Ellis ruminated: "Folks alive at the time can remember where they were and what they were doing," while Ken Dryden speculated darkly before the last game on the chances of being "the most hated man in Canada" if his team had lost. The Soviet participants were equally enthralled: "It will never again be the same as it was in '72. The series with Canada was an historic affair," said Boris Mikhailov (CBC, "Summit on Ice").

18 The article also mentioned how Quebec premier Robert Bourassa telegrammed to Team Canada that "[y]our teamwork and your determination to win has earned you the admiration of Quebeckers and all Canadians."

19 Trevor Brown, a Jamaican-born mathematics professor at York University, attests to hockey's significance for today's youth, and immigrant youth in particular. Brown's son, Daniel, enjoys informal league hockey Saturday nights at Chesswood Arena in northern Toronto. The team includes Vietnamese and Trinidadian immigrants and has at times involved both Jewish and Arab Canadians. "Hockey is far more than a puck and a stick to a youngster living in Canada," says Brown. "It is a ceremony, a ritual, an almost mystical rite....The playing of the game credentials a boy and makes him an authentic Canadian" (Personal communication, November 16, 1993).

20 The closing of such venerable hockey shrines as the Montreal Forum (1996) and Maple Leaf Gardens (1999) and the national outpouring on the death of former Montreal Canadiens great, Maurice "the Rocket" Richard, in May 2000 showed the game still stood high in the popular imagination.

Works Cited

Beardsley, Doug. *Country on Ice*. Winlaw: Polestar, 1987.

"Canadians flip as Russians slip—WE'RE THE CHAMPS," *Calgary Herald* September 29, 1972: 1.

Creighton, Douglas. "Canadian Unity at Peak in Moscow." *Sun* (Toronto) September 30, 1972: 2.

Cunningham, Keith. "Myths, Dreams and Movies: Exploring the Archetypal Roots of Cinema." *Quest: A Quarterly Journal of Philosophy, Science, Religion and the Arts* 5.1 (Spring 1992): 30-40.

Dryden, Ken. *The Game: A Thoughtful and Provocative Look at a Life in Hockey*. Toronto: Harper and Collins, 1983.

Dryden, Ken, and Roy MacGregor. *Home Game: Hockey and Life in Canada*. Toronto: McClelland and Stewart, 1989.

Dryden, Ken, with Mark Mulvoy. *Face-Off at the Summit*. Boston: Little Brown, 1973.

"Feared Winter of Discontent: Hockey Win Helped Campaign—Trudeau," *Halifax Chronicle-Herald* September 29, 1972: 3.

Fiske, John. *Televison Culture*. London: Routledge, 1987.

_____. *Reading the Popular*. London: Unwin Hyman, 1990.

"500,000 in Metro Schools May Be Watching Hockey," *Toronto Star* September 28, 1972: 2.

"Giant Welcome for Team Canada: They'll Return as Conquering Heroes," *Sun* (Vancouver) September 29: 1972: 1-2.

Hamilton, Edith. *The Greek Way*. New York: Norton, 1930.

Hawkes, Terence. *Structuralism and Semiotics*. Berkeley: U of California P, 1977.

Heidegger, Martin. *The Question Concerning Technology*. New York: Harper and Row, 1977.

Ludwig, Jack. *Hockey Night in Moscow*. Toronto: McClelland and Stewart, 1972.

MacIntosh, Donald, and Donna Greenhorn. "Hockey Diplomacy and Canadian Foreign Policy." *Journal of Canadian Studies* 28.2 (Summer 1993): 96-112.

Marchand, Roland. *Advertising the American Dream: Making Way for Modernity, 1920-1940*. Berkeley: U of California P, 1985.

McCullough, Colin. "The Fans Who Discovered Their Own Nationality in Moscow," *Globe and Mail* (Toronto) September 29, 1972: 1

McPherson, Barry D., and James E. Curtis and John W. Loy. *The Social Significance of Sport: Introduction to the Sociology of Sport*. Champaign: Human Kinetics Books, 1989.

Metcalf, Alan. *Canada Learns to Play: The Emergence of Organized Sport, 1870-1914*. Toronto: McClelland and Stewart, 1987.

Morrison, Scott. *The Days Canada Stood Still: Canada vs USSR*. Toronto: McGraw-Hill, 1989.

Newcomb, Horace. *TV: The Most Popular Art*. New York: Anchor, 1974.

Novak, Michael. *The Joy of Sports: End Zones, Bases, Baskets, Balls and Consecration of the American Spirit*. New York: Basic, 1976.

Righton, Barbara. "Waking Up 'The Spin.'" *TV Times: Sun* (Vancouver) February 26, 1993: 2.

Rutherford, Paul. *When Television Was Young: Prime-Time Canada, 1952-1967*. Toronto: U of Toronto P, 1990.

Scott-Kilvert, Ian. *The Rise and Fall of Athens: Nine Greek Lives by Plutarch*. Middlesex: Penguin, 1960.

Sinden, Harry. *Hockey Showdown: The Canada-Russia Hockey Series*. Toronto: Doubleday Canada, 1972.

Young, Scott. *Hello Canada: The Life and Times of Foster Hewitt*. Toronto: Seal, 1985.

CONTRIBUTORS

Nick Baxter-Moore is an associate professor in the Departments of Political Science and Communications, Popular Culture and Film at Brock University. His current research interests include popular music and politics; media and cultural policy; and the evolution of Canadian popular music.

Christine Boyko-Head is an adjunct professor for the Creative Arts in Learning, Masters of Education Program, Lesley University, Cambridge, Massachusetts. She has contributed essays to *Theatre Research in Canada* and the *Journal of Canadian Studies,* and has published over fifty theatre reviews. She resides in Dunnville, Ontario.

Valda Blundell is a professor of anthropology at Carleton University. She is a co-editor of *Relocating Cultural Studies: Developments in Theory and Research* (1993), and the author of *Changing Perspectives in the Anthropology of Art* (2000) as well as numerous articles on Indigenous culture and art in Canada and Australia.

Terrance Cox writes poems and non-fiction in St. Catharines, Ontario, where he also teaches popular music, film and drama at Brock University. His published collections include a "spoken word with music" CD, *Local Scores* (Cyclops Press, 2000) and *Radio & Other Miracles* (Signature Editions, 2001).

Loretta Czernis is a professor of sociology in the Department of Sociology and Anthropology, Bishop's University. Her publications include *Weaving a Canadian Allegory* (1994). She is the director of Bishop's Communication and Cultural Studies Programme, and is currently an executive member of the Canadian Association of University Teachers.

Karen Dubinsky teaches history at Queen's University. She is the author of *The Second Greatest Disappointment: Honeymooning and Tourism at Niagara Falls* (1999) and *Improper Advances: Rape and Heterosexual Conflict in Ontario, 1880-1929* (1993).

Neil Earle is an ordained minister who serves as adjunct professor of American history at Citrus College, Glendora, California. He is the author of *The Wonderful Wizard of Oz in American Popular Culture: Uneasy in Eden* (1994). His articles have appeared in the *Social Science Journal* and the *Los Angeles Business Journal*.

William Echard is an assistant professor of music at Carleton University. His teaching and research concern the social and textual dimensions of popular music as a signifying practice. His work has appeared in various publications, including the *Indiana Theory Review*, *Popular Music*, *Semiotic Review of Books*, and *Topia*.

Jim Leach is a professor in the Department of Communications, Popular Culture and Film, Brock University. His research and teaching interests include Canadian, British and popular cinemas, and film and cultural theory. He has published the first study of Claude Jutra's films, and adapted a Canadian edition of a film studies textbook.

Joan Nicks is an associate professor in the Department of Communications, Popular Culture and Film, Brock University. Her writing on Canadian cinema and popular culture has appeared in the anthologies *Gendering the Nation: Canadian Women's Cinema* and *Documenting the Documentary*, and in various journals and encyclopaedia.

Sheila Petty is a professor of film and video at the University of Regina. She has written extensively on issues of cultural representation, identity and nation in African and African diasporic cinema. She is completing a book on African diasporic film and has a forthcoming monograph on the TV series, *Law and Order*.

Jim Shedden is the studio producer at Bruce Mau Design in Toronto. Previously he worked as a film and video curator at the Art Gallery of Ontario, where he also programmed music and performance. He has directed two documentaries: *Michael Snow Up Close* (1994) and *Brakhage* (1998).

Jeannette Sloniowski is an associate professor in the Department of Communications, Popular Culture and Film, Brock University. She has published articles in the *Journal of Popular Film and Television*,

Canadian Communications and the *Canadian Journal of Film Studies*. She is co-editor of *Documenting the Documentary* and *Canadian Communications: Issues in Canadian Media and Culture.*

Will Straw teaches communications in the Department of Art History and Communications Studies at McGill University. He is the author of numerous books on music, film and culture, and is a co-editor of the *Cambridge Companion to Pop and Rock* (2001).

Bart Testa teaches film studies and semiotics at the University of Toronto. His research interests include avant-garde, Canadian and European cinemas. He is the author of *Back and Forth: Early Cinema and the Avant-garde* (1992), *Richard Kerr: Overlapping Entries* (1994), *Spirit in the Landscape* (1989), and numerous essays in anthologies and journals.

Rinaldo Walcott is an associate professor in the Division of Humanities, York University. He is the author of *Black Like Who: Writing Black Canada* (1997) and editor of *Rude: Contemporary Black Canadian Cultural Criticism* (2000). He is currently completing *Disturbing the Peace: The Impossible Dream of Black Canadian Studies.*

Andrew Wernick teaches cultural studies at Trent University. He is the author of *Promotional Culture: Advertising, Ideology and Symbolic Expressions* (1991) and many other writings on social theory and contemporary culture. His most recent book is *Auguste Comte and the Religion of Humanity.*